THE
FLOWER
ARRANGER'S
HANDBOOK

This book is dedicated to the memory of
Kenneth James Pedder, a skilful
plantsman and man of high principle,
formerly Parks Superintendent of the
Royal Borough of Kensington and
Chelsea, London

THE
FLOWER
ARRANGER'S
HANDBOOK

JOHN DALE & KEVIN GUNNELL

Macdonald

A Macdonald BOOK

Conceived and produced by
Breslich & Foss
28-31 Great Pulteney Street
London W1R 3DD

Designer: Edward Kinsey
Editors: Judy Martin
Julia Warner
Illustrators: Janos Marffey
Elly King
Simon Roulstone
Indexer: Christine Bernstein

Text © John Dale and Kevin Gunnell 1986
Design © Breslich & Foss
First published in Great Britain in 1986
by Macdonald & Co (Publishers) Ltd
London and Sydney

A member of BPCC plc

British Library Cataloguing in Publication
Data
Dale, John C.
  The Flower Arranger's Handbook
  1. Flower Arrangement — Dictionaries
  I. Title II. Gunnell, Kevin
  745.92'03'21   SB449

ISBN 0-356-10953-4

Photoset by Lineage Ltd, Watford
Printed and Bound in Hong Kong by
Mandarin Offset Ltd.

Macdonald & Co (Publishers) Ltd
Maxwell House
74 Worship Street
London EC2A 2EN

CONTENTS

Introduction

A flower arranger has a desire to be creative, to gather colour and form, painting a picture with living materials. This may not be as lasting as a true picture, but its fleeting beauty is the more precious because of its transient nature.

There is something richly satisfying about choosing, growing and arranging flowers. Growing your own plant material allows you to plan ahead, to grow certain flowers for a special occasion, to have sufficient foliage for the occasional grand display, to decorate your home with an inexpensive and continuous supply of plant material all year round.

Growing and arranging should have no boundaries. Thanks to the skill of the dedicated plant breeder, some plants that were considered too rare or too tender to grow in certain parts of the world are now commonplace. We can see flowers that were once restricted to the botanical hot-house growing in the most unexpected places. A progressive interest in flower arranging and plant display has helped to awaken and develop our ideas about gardening, challenging the basic pattern of a broad lawn with privet hedge surround, making us more aware of the beauty of individual plants. Television, with its increasing range of broadcasts for the gardening enthusiast, has been responsible for showing us unusual plants and encouraging us to grow them. Winter evenings spent poring over plant and seed catalogues are also part of the flower arranger's life, selecting flowers for their colour, form, growing habit, or simply because they appeal. When your garden is later ablaze with colour, the time spent as an armchair gardener is justly rewarded.

Unfortunately not all the plants that you are able to grow in particular conditions will be suitable for cutting. Some flowers, and many more foliages, just refuse to take up water and wilt rapidly in an indoor environment. Certain flowers have a dislike for water-retaining foam. Not only the plant material, but also the container you wish to use can present certain problems in arranging – a favourite vase may have a slim neck or insufficient water space, for example.

Success in flower arranging consists of getting to know the mechanics of the craft, that is, the methods of creating your display, and the best ways to condition and maintain particular materials to keep them fresh and long-lasting. These techniques are clearly described in the opening chapters of the book, as are the various means of drying and preserving plant material. Preservation does occur by natural means, but modern aids such as drying agents can actually improve on nature in this case, rapidly removing the moisture from a flower while leaving its colour and shape intact. This fascinating subject is fully described in the appropriate chapter.

Colour has the strongest influence on gardening and flower arranging. The colour of a flower is usually what attracts us first, tempting us to find complementary materials and to create the perfect shape of arrangement to show off the flower at its best. Advice on design and simple colour theory in arranging explains the principles of a number of traditional and modern styles of flower arranging, both taking full advantage of the more sophisticated mechanics now available.

The delight in colour is also the theme for organization of the Encyclopedia of Plants. Hundreds of different species and cultivars listed under their generic names are divided into colour sections according to the dominant colours, so that you can readily find the availability of pink, blue and even green flowers, according to your preference. The colour sections – yellow, orange, red, pink, purple, blue, green and white – are cross-referenced to provide the widest possible choice. There are separate sections on plants which yield a glorious range of mixed flower colours, and on shrubs and small trees which offer spectacular foliage and additional blooms in due season.

To enable you to get the best out of growing and arranging plant material according to your own preferences, every plant is fully described with notes on cultivation and propagation, as well as its uses in flower arranging and individual tips on conditioning and preserving. The Encylopedia of Plants is followed by a valuable guide to propagation. The techniques are simply described and fully illustrated, so that even the most inexperienced gardener can rapidly increase a basic stock of plants. Not only can you enjoy a greater range of plant material for use in your own decorative schemes, you can pass on coveted items to your friends and exchange new plants for other treasures.

Sharing your increased knowledge and expertise can be part of the pleasure of cultivating and displaying flowers. Joining a local flower arranging society or garden club is a useful and enjoyable step, especially if you are new to flower arranging. A club will provide the opportunity to see the work of visiting demonstrators, undertake practical classes and participate in large-scale decorative displays and flower arranging competitions. This offers a new and challenging approach to designing with plant materials and in addition, the stalls and sales tables organized by a club or society offer an Aladdin's cave of practical equipment and decorative items which can spark off new ideas.

Take care to choose the best seed, grow it correctly, harvest the flower when it is ready and arrange it sensitively – the result is surely worth the effort. Remember that a cut flower is a precious life. It may have taken a long time to grow and its beauty is too breathtaking to be wasted. There are no short cuts to growing and arranging. This book has been written to smooth the path towards an expert flower display, and above all to increase your enjoyment of the art of flower arranging.

Equipment, Mechanics and Containers

The equipment for flower arranging can be extensive, like any artist's 'tool box': a key for every lock, a brush for every stroke. It is in the nature of a flower arranger to collect and hoard things that will be useful. However, when you start flower arranging, it isn't necessary to acquire all the equipment at once. A wise arranger will learn what equipment and mechanics are about. Some of the items may be expensive and not very useful. Equipment and mechanics have long been favourite words of the flower arranger. In this context, they mean the apparatus needed to cut, arrange and maintain plant material. They are not precise words; equipment generally covers such items as scissors, tape or wire, and mechanics refer to the method of stem support. Containers come in the widest possible variety, from vases and baskets to bottles and cans. Using the appropriate mechanics, all kinds of objects can become suitable and versatile containers. Driftwood, too, is a valuable flower arranging accessory, and this chapter explains how to adapt and convert such items.

CUTTERS Flower-arranging scissors come in a variety of shapes and sizes. They must have a good cutting edge and one blade will probably be serrated; this will be useful for stripping the outer covering from certain stems. Handle the scissors before you buy them, making sure they are well balanced and that they fit your hand. Check the pivot screw – often the cutting arms are simply screwed together and will work loose with constant movement. Choose a pair that has the end of the screw knocked back in the manner of a rivet. They will slacken slightly with use but not fall apart.

Secateurs have become a popular alternative. Longer handles give greater leverage to cut through thick stems more efficiently. The spring-loaded action, common to nearly all brands, allows the blades to re-open automatically. Further refinements, like pivoting handles, reduce the physical effort needed in a cutting action.

A small sharp knife is useful for scraping the bark from woody stems prior to conditioning. Choose one that will close up – open blades become dull and can be dangerous. I favour the multi-blade type: the screwdriver blade is sometimes useful; the corkscrew indispensable.

TAPE AND FIXATIVES There are two basic types of tape available. One is an adhesive tape, the other is made from latex and has a self-sealing quality. The chief use of adhesive tape is for securing water-retaining foam. It is sufficiently narrow to be concealed by plant material. False stems, to extend the length of dried plant material, can be permanently fixed using adhesive tape.

Gutta Percha was originally made from latex. Modern technology now provides the same qualities in plastic and waxed crêpe paper. Lacking any strong adhesive, Gutta Percha is a temporary tape. Under pressure, it will unwind and should never be used to secure the mechanics of an arrangement.

Oasis Fix is a semi-permanent fixative, often found in over-copious quantities anchoring a pinholder to a shallow dish. Deposits of fixative remain on the separated surfaces and can be removed using a cloth soaked in nail polish remover or a similar spirit thinner.

Plasticine or similar modelling material, once the property of the toy box, is now used extensively in flower arranging. It lacks the holding strength of Oasis Fix but it will remove cleanly. A small pellet discreetly placed under an apple, for instance, will prevent it from rolling on to a surface that it favours.

WIRE Wire, in reel form or straight lengths, should be free from rust and almost black in colour. The colour indicates that it has been treated to make it malleable. Some wires have a plastic coating, protecting them from oxidation – a quality to be appreciated – but you

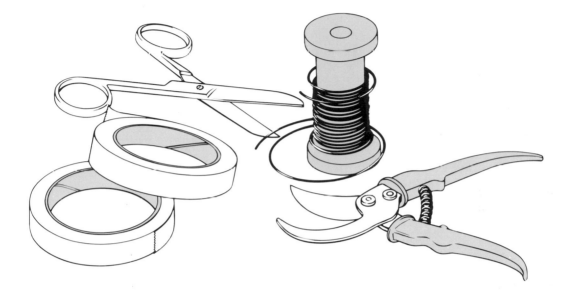

may find them slippery and difficult to use. The gauge, or thickness, affects the use of the wire. Thinner gauges are easier to bend and are less damaging if they are used as a tie for delicate stems. Reel wire has the advantage of length. It is ideal for encircling the lip of a container to secure wire netting. Reel wire in the hands of a dextrous florist is almost an art form, combining the individual pieces for a bouquet with a speed that is blurring to the unskilled. Single wires vary in length from about 6in (15cm) to approximately 18in (45cm). Their uses are numerous. Thick-gauge wire acts as a perfect splint, secured with tape, for damaged stems of dried plant material. The lighter gauges will bind flower stems together, secure mechanics or, inserted into a soft wayward stem, straighten it. For drying, flower heads that need an artificial stem can be given one by inserting a medium gauge wire through the head or into the back of the calyx. This should be done when the flower is fresh; the wire will be easier to push through and any residual moisture will slightly rust the wire in contact, producing a stronger bond.

Chicken wire was used extensively as a form of stem support before the introduction of water-retaining foam. Flowers were pushed through the crumpled mesh into the water in the dish. This severely restricted the direction of the plant material; foliage and flowers with a natural bend were jealously guarded, to be used as 'downward' flowing material. Chicken wire is still very useful as mechanics for arrangements of very heavy materials, branches of spring blossom or thick trails of ivy. The mesh size must be 2in (5cm), for anything smaller will prevent the flower stem from passing through. Crumple sufficient chicken wire into a loose ball and place it in the container, extending it to the bottom of the dish. Pull the wire ball slightly to raise it above the lip. To secure the mesh, thread reel or stub wire through the mesh and tie it around the lip of the container. You may find a cap of chicken wire over moist foam reassuring, particularly when some of the stems need a little extra support.

PINHOLDERS A pinholder is the simplest method of supporting a flower stem. Usually made from lead, it is flat and circular in shape, with a concentric pattern of inset steel pins. Like all good ideas, it has been improved upon, both in size and shape. Oblong, half-moon, semi-circular and square are some of the alternative shapes. Well pinholders are containers in themselves. Circular with sloping sides, the pins are set in the centre of the base. Most flower clubs carry this indispensable item, in a range of sizes and weights.

As your pinholder collection increases, like me you will find other uses for them. They make marvellous counter-balance weights at the back of an arrangement that is slightly unstable, when time doesn't permit its rearranging. The weight of the pinholder must be considered. The heavier it is, the more stable it will be.

The principle of a pinholder is simple: flower stems are impaled on, or wedged between, the pins. Choose the pinholder carefully, as not all the pins are spaced to a standard. Pins that are close together readily support fine stems but will bend and close up should you attempt to force on a hard woody stem.

Flat pinholders are used in shallow dishes where a minimum amount of water is required. To prevent them sliding around the dish, fix four pellets of Plasticine to the base of the pinholder, and with a slight twisting movement, attach it to the bottom of the dish. This must be done when both surfaces are perfectly dry.

If the pinholder is to be used with water-retaining foam, avoid closely set pins, as the pins get blocked with particles of foam. The only successful method of cleaning that I have discovered, is to allow the particles to dry and remove them with a wire brush. Holders specially designed for use with foam are better.

Because the holders are made from lead, they are expensive to replace. After-care will make them last indefinitely. Always clean the pins after using the holder, removing any foam and stem debris and straightening pins that have become bent. The back of a table knife slipped between the pins will do this.

Keep the pinholders dry when they are not being used. The pins are made from steel and will rust very quickly if moisture is allowed to collect between them. Store them on a piece of cloth, pins downward. This will prevent the sharpness becoming dulled should anything be accidentally placed on top of them.

WATER-RETAINING FOAM Water-retaining foam is a substance made from minute compressed plastic granules. It has the quality to absorb and retain large quantities of water without losing its rigidity. The foam is yielding and can be cut to any shape with a sharp knife.

Water-retaining foam is something of a verbal handful. Much as I dislike umbrella words, I am grateful that we refer to all makes and brands as 'oasis'. It is a word that has been generally adopted by the flower arranger, although it is in fact a brand name. It is available in oblong blocks and small tubular 'rounds'.

To soak the foam, submerge it in water. When the foam sinks just below the water level and no air bubbles are being released, it is then fully charged.

Once wet foam has dried out, it will not readily reabsorb moisture. Resoaking in water with a few drops of washing-up liquid added is recommended as a rejuvenator. Any excess moist oasis should be stored in a polythene bag, to prevent it from drying out.

Oasis has replaced many of the traditional methods of flower support, as it allows greater flexibility for positioning plant material. Stems can be inserted at any angle and will remain in position. Generally it is used in conjunction with containers that have no capacity for holding water. Wrapped in thin polythene, oasis will act as mechanics for swags and plaques. It must be thoroughly saturated before it is wrapped.
Water-retaining foam, being a substitute for a free well of water within the container, usually fits the neck or interior of the container quite tightly. It must be supplied with moisture each day, so to facilitate pouring in fresh water, cut a small wedge-shaped passage down the back of the foam block.

Try to get as much use as possible from the foam. When one side has too many holes it can be reversed and used again. When the foam is of no further use for flower arranging, don't throw it away. Instead, allow it to dry and crumble it over the garden. It works into and lightens the soil and helps to retain moisture, which can be useful for areas that drain quickly.

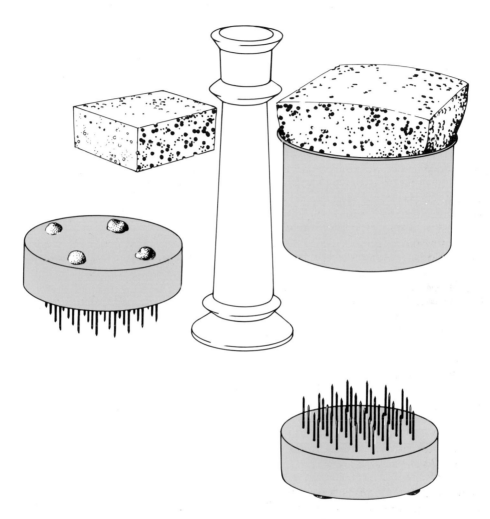

DRY FOAM Dry foam is used in the same way as water-retaining foam, though, as its name suggests, it is a support for dried plant material. It will not absorb water and should never be used as a substitute for water-retaining foam.

CANDLE CUPS As the name suggests, these were originally made to adapt candlesticks as containers. They are bowl shaped, made from plastic or metal, with a base projection that fits into the candlestick. If the fit is not exact, a collar of Plasticine or fixative will act as packing. Enterprising manufacturers have now given us a very useful refinement, candle cups with screw-threaded bases. They are obtainable with internal and external threads. The thread is usually very short, not suitable for using with candlesticks, as their chief purpose is to convert table lamp bases into containers. There are a large number of variations on the market to suit every mechanical contingency.

BASES AND DRAPES In the home a base should always be used to prevent furniture being marked by the rough under-surface of some containers. A cake board covered with soft cloth is the cheapest and easiest to make. Bases of different textural finish add to the atmosphere of an arrangement. Wood, slate and stone relate well with naturalistic designs, velvet harmonizes with flowers of a soft delicate colour and texture. Hessian has become very popular as a base covering with plant material that is rough in texture. It can be purchased in a range of colours, which gives a stronger colour link between base and plant material. Where flower colour needs emphasizing, a base of contrasting or toning colour will achieve this.

A base will often make an arrangement portable, particularly when a secondary grouping of plant material has been included.

The visual balance of an arrangement may be affected by the base. To please the eye, the height of an arrangement must be balanced by the proportional width of its base. A base that is too large will accentuate the width of the arrangement and one that is too small will over-emphasize the height. Either will destroy the proportions. A base the same width as the widest dimension of the arrangement usually provides a happy medium.

A selection of bases need not mean a large collection, since one lightweight wood board with interchangeable 'mob caps' of material will give you flexibility of colour and finish without taking up a lot of storage space. There will be occasions when a base is used to support components in a more permanent way. Lichened branches to represent a tree in a landscape design aren prime example. A base made from wood is the obvious choice. Hold the branch on the wood base to establish the correct angle before you fix it permanently into position. Screw a small angle bracket onto either side of the base of the branch. You will be able to select a pair of suitable size from your local DIY shop. To establish the position of the holes in the wood base, hold the branch against the base and mark with a pencil through the holes in the bracket. The branch may be screwed on to the base but this will make the fixing permanent. Drilling holes through the base to accommodate a bolt and wing nut, will make the positioning stable, at the same time allowing you to dismantle the base and branch should you want to use them separately.

As the kitchen has always been a treasure chest for providing containers, the same applies to bases. One of the most useful bases that I own is the breadboard. The advantage of a culinary base is that it won't require extra storage space; once used, it can be returned to its original, albeit mundane, purpose. Quite a number of bases used for aesthetic reasons will have a rough under-surface, so again, to protect furniture surfaces, glue pads of felt on to the bases.

Drapes made from cloth are usually confined to the flower arrangement show bench. They were a forerunner to the now over-used back boards and are at present considered out of fashion. They helped to present the flowers in much the same way as wallpaper in the home. I cannot, therefore, see any need for them in the home. However, should you decide to use one, avoid bringing it into contact with the mechanics of the arrangement. Most cloth is absorbent and will act as a syphon.

FLOWER BUCKETS I am not being flippant, by including a section on such a humble object. Flower buckets are a neglected subject in most flower arranging and gardening books, yet we use them constantly. Arrangers should keep them specifically for holding plant material, as multiple use inside the home increases the risk of water pollution. Buckets made from plastic, with handles at the side, are light and easy to carry. The depth of the bucket must be sufficient to support the length of the flower stem. Various sizes will be needed for different lengths of stem. It is important to keep the foliage and flower head dry, while at the same time ensuring that the stem end is in contact with the water. Rinse the flower buckets each time they are used and scrub them periodically with a mild detergent, to remove any algae that have built up. If space allows, a plastic dustbin is very useful for holding large quantities of long-stemmed plant material.

Store plastic buckets in a shed or garage. Plastic is affected by extreme temperatures and will crack when exposed to excessive heat or cold. The bath, something of a joke among flower arrangers, is often used as a large bucket. Ideally it should be used to float plant material that requires conditioning through both stem and leaf.

The association of water and vessel allows me to mention briefly the flower arranger's watering can. Choose one that has a small-bored spout, so that the water is introduced at a steady pace. The same reason for including the watering can also applies to a water mister. The water mister is generally sold as a hand-held spray for liquid pesticides. Because of this, keep it clearly labelled to avoid any misuse. The spraying action is mechanical, operated by hand. Choose one of good quality – bargain-price kinds, in my experience, fail to work efficiently.

CONES Cones are generally used to achieve a secondary area of mechanics. Their name accurately describes their shape – conical, with an internal reservoir for water or oasis. Unfortunately, the amount of plant material that they will hold is limited, by virtue of their shape. The sloping sides of the cone will cause unsupported flowers to lean. This can be corrected by wedging short stems of waste material between the cone side and the flowers. Flowers that have an aversion to oasis should be arranged in a cone filled with water. This can then be included in the design, using the surrounding material to disguise the cone. When the cone is used to extend the height of an arrangement, this can be accomplished by taping the cone to a garden cane. Always position the mounted cane before you start to arrange the flowers, as any attempt to do it after the arrangement has been completed will cause undue disturbance. Orchid tubes are handy for single stems that dislike oasis. The plastic cap should be left in place to reduce evaporation. The end of the tube is usually rounded; a cocktail stick taped to it makes it easier to push into the oasis.

CONTAINERS There was a time, before flowers were 'arranged', when the glass vase was king. Sadly it is now scorned by today's arranger for being old-fashioned and restricting. This may be so. In a world of oasis, wire and pinholders, who wants a container that will not allow downward movement and exposes to the admirer an expanse of crossing stems? That said, do not be too eager to dispose of this forgotten king; some flowers and settings demand its continued use. Not all flowers need arranging – indeed, some benefit from not being arranged. Poppies and forget-me-nots, picked from a morning garden, maintain their natural beauty when they are simply placed in a vase. Spring blossom does not have to be forced into a jungle of wire netting and oasis. One or two sprays will look just as elegant in a cut-glass vase as they would in a more contrived design. If you find the exposed stems offensive, colour the water with a non-toxic vegetable dye to disguise them.

Having rescued the vase from oblivion, there are occasions when plant material has to be arranged and a vase will not be suitable. These occasions have given birth to one of the new umbrella words . . . containers, which sweepingly describes anything that will physically hold water and plant material.

There are a considerable number of custom-built containers sold in florists shops and at flower or garden clubs. They generally follow a pattern, being of pedestal type, featuring two suitably clad cherubs, with odd looking faces, clambering up a corinthian column. Low containers tend to be less ornate but still have the attached cup on the top, for oasis.

Adapted containers are legion, and their charm often lies in their individuality. Heavy containers are best, as they are less likely to over-balance. They provide that feeling of security, essential when you are arranging flowers for the first time. An adapted container should be sympathetic to the plant material. Unglazed pottery blends with preserved foliages and flowers that are in the lighter colour range, yellow, orange and green. A surface with a high glaze can be very distracting; its reflective quality quarrels with plant material and is best avoided. Hand-thrown pots with a geometric direction lend themselves to flowers that are sculptured, almost moulded, in form. Baskets have an unsophisticated air about them, so flowers and foliage should be allowed to flow naturally in this medium. The earthy colour of basketwork is not intrusive, and will accept virtually any flower colour. Kitchenware, with a vegetation motif, can be very amusing in association with a design of fruit or garden vegetables. Silver or glass cakestands, with a well pinholder secured to the top, will raise the height of an arrangement. The sophisticated finish of this type of stand usually calls for a formal, elegant style of arrangement. Dishes that will eventually be concealed by the plant material may be of any sort. Pie tins, cake tins, loaf tins, even the humble sardine tin, are possibilities.

Containers are both easy and interesting to make. Packaging is an established part of our throw-away society – jars are emptied and discarded, boxes burned, plastic bottles tossed in the bin when they are empty. What to some people is waste is a prospective container for others, so consider these rejects for potential use.

Empty detergent or similar plastic bottles can be turned into basic containers. Cut away the top with a sharp knife and cover the outside with two coats of matt finish paint. To make the container more interesting, roll the bottle in a tray of bird sand, while the paint is still wet. Your rough-textured container is almost complete. A generous measure of sand poured inside will give stability, and a small tin to fit the top will site the mechanics. This basic adaptation of the washing-up liquid bottle is quite well known. I am sure that we have all attempted it at least once, then pushed it aside as being too ordinary. The secret of a container, in part, is its uniqueness. To give this type of container an identity, try physically altering its shape. Heating it in the oven or plunging it into boiling water will distend the plastic. While it is warm and still malleable, and using protected fingers, pull and press the surface into shape. To prevent any fire hazard switch off the heat supply before you start the process.

Empty soup tins can be soldered together – the completed shape will be unique, governed only by the amount of soup consumed. A local plumber or electrician could be persuaded to do the soldering if you felt unable to attempt it yourself. It need not be dismantled when you have tired of it as a container for cut flowers. Use the tins as holders for 'potted up' seedlings; they will look attractive on the window sill. Sheet lead is sufficiently pliable to be moulded into a shallow dish without heat. A wooden mallet should be used to turn up the edges. A pinholder fixed off-centre will support branches of catkins and spring flowers, while the area of exposed water adds to the landscape mood.

Empty coffee jars have always been useful as temporary piggy banks for those small copper coins or as somewhere to soak a paint brush. Try instead, swirling different coloured paints around the inside of the jar. Stand it upside down to drain and dry – the paint will run back over itself creating further patterns. A well pinholder taped to the opening will form the mechanics. Alternatively the flowers may be placed directly into jar, for the opaque finish will conceal the stems.

Don't restrict yourself to the kitchen for inspiration – arrangers are well known for their seeing and discovering eye. Most objects, precious or simple, can be adapted; few things are left unconsidered by the resourceful arranger.

We may be seduced by a fascinating ornament, and not be satisfied until it is adorned with flowers, only to find that it has no capacity for supporting flowers at all. It can't be instantly or easily adapted but somehow it must be converted. Sensations of this nature are common to all of us, to change its purpose will often mean creating ingenious mechanics. According to the circumstances these need not be complicated, but will, no doubt, be unusual. Figurines very rarely present an obvious position for taping or wiring mechanics. An extended arm is sometimes offered, but it may be too delicate or too short to accommodate mechanics of any reasonable size. A figurine that I remember, a lady with heavy feet and slender arms, posed such a problem. Finally it was decided that the mechanics would have to be slung across her back, papoose style. Two frames were made from joined stub wire; one holding a small wooden platform that would site a bowl and oasis, the other encasing a parcel of dry foam to use with dried and preserved material. To prevent the frame slipping from the figurine, wires were crossed over the front and twisted together at the back. Small dried flower heads glued to the wire made a perfect disguise.

In my opinion conversion should not be permanent. Too often we appropriate items that are in constant use within the home and they should be allowed to revert now and again. There is something undignified about a graceful shepherdess with a candle cup or meat tin nailed permanently to her feet. Free-standing lamps are one of the most usual conversions. The universal candle cup has made it almost obligatory. Remove the power supply plug from the flex, unscrew the light bulb adaptor and pull the wire through the stand. Disconnecting the adaptor exposes a section of hollow screw-thread, to which the candle cup can be fixed. Explanations are always over-simplified, and the candle cup may not fit. To make a substitute candle cup isn't difficult. This homely alternative has more

than one use – providing that the hole is not too small, it will fit inside the narrow neck that some bottle-type containers have.

With driftwood, it will be necessary to drill a suitable hole in the wood to accept the device. To make this alternative cup, you will need a plastic dish with a flat under-surface, one 1in (2.5cm) wood-screw, strong glue and a piece of wood dowel that will fit inside the hollow screw-thread of the lamp base. The length of dowel will be dictated by the height of the stand. A minimum length of 4in (10cm) will reduce any movement when the cup is in position. A certain amount of movement will be unavoidable with unsecured mechanics. Melt a hole in the base of the plastic dish, to accept the tapered end of the wood-screw. Screw the dish on to the end of the pre-cut dowel. To make this operation less arduous, ask the local wood supply merchant to drill the end of the dowel into a hole smaller in diameter than the wood-screw.

Dismantle the dish and coat the thread of the screw with a strong bonding agent. Araldite produce a glue that will bind wood and metal together. Immediately assemble the dish and dowel and allow the glue to dry. Coat the inside of the dish and the screw head with a thin coat of glue. By assembling and dismantling the components first without the bonding agent, the coated screw will be accepted more easily, with less frustration to you. The glue strengthens the join and provides a film of waterproofing inside the dish. Eventually the join around the screw may not remain totally waterproof, but you can use a small polythene liner to prevent any leakage.

DRIFTWOOD Wood has a natural beauty, so it should not be altered to any great extent. Driftwood describes a wide range of wood used in association with flowers and foliage, such as bark, roots, branches. Its name suggests the seashore; indeed, the beach is a favourite source for gnarled and weather-worn pieces. If the wood has been in seawater for any length of time, its natural colour will become bleached, adding to its appeal. Strangely, wood from this environment is rarely waterlogged. Usually cleaning with a wire brush is all the preparation it requires. Woodlands are the more obvious places to find driftwood, bits of bark, fallen branches. It is important, however, that you have permission to take away any wood and never cut any from a living tree. Some pieces you may have to unearth, and the section below ground is often more interesting. If it fails to live up to any expectation, leave it in position, to provide a home to a good number of insects. Anyone without access to the woodlands or the beach need not despair, for driftwood can now be bought. Agricultural shows and national flower shows have lately become venues for enterprising people with an eye for what the flower arranger wants. The fact that the wood has been prepared and sometimes mounted, offsets what seems a rather high price for a piece of wood. Wood that you have unearthed will also require a certain amount of preparation. This job is best done out of doors. Begin by brushing the wood with a strong wire brush, to remove any dirt and loose wood fibre. Sections of rotten wood that will not dry should be cut away with a sharp knife. When the wood is clean, treat it with a woodworm eradicator – a wise precaution even if the wood does not show signs of infestation. Leave the wood outside for a few weeks, turning it each day. Any stubborn insects that would like to remain soon leave as they dislike strong light and constant movement.

In an arrangement, small pieces can be wired on to the mechanics before the flowers are added, the tape or wire being concealed by the surrounding plant material or covered with moss. Heavier wood that displays awkward balance and is not suitable for wiring in can be made to fit. Establish the angle that you want the wood to take by placing it on the mechanics. Mark the point of contact and screw or nail a piece of wood dowel to this. This will act as a positioning leg in oasis; if the dowel is sharpened to a point, it can be used with a pinholder. Very large pieces of wood are on occasions almost arrangements in themselves, needing only a limited amount of plant material to emphasize their beauty. With free-standing pieces, the plant material will be in a separate dish, so a base will help to unify the design and make it portable. Driftwood that is free standing may have required a little carpentry beforehand to give it this ability. Study the shape carefully. It might be easier to add a wedge to a certain place than to cut off an offending piece. Before you decide to attach mechanics to the wood permanently, try to visualize the completed design. This mental check will tell you if the arrangement will have good visual balance or whether the completed design will be stable. Attaching mechanics to wood can appear quite daunting. The finished job need not be attractive, but it must be secure. A neighbour or local DIY shop can often be persuaded to assist.

The prime concern is the size of the mechanics. The dish must be large enough to supply sufficient moisture to the fresh plant material. If the dish can be rested and taped on to the wood, consider yourself lucky. A natural depression can be enlarged, using a rasp or wood chisel. The wood may be generous enough to have a projecting ledge, where a platform of thin wood can be fixed, on which the dish can be rested. A further, but not so convenient, place is at the tip of the wood. Smooth it down to form a small plateau with a wood rasp. It isn't necessary to achieve a professional finish – plant material will cover any imperfection. Plastic plant-pot saucers make excellent oasis dishes for this situation, either nailed or screwed into position. It must be remembered that dishes that have been punctured in their fixing will no longer hold water. The inside of the dish should be lined with polythene to counter any seepage.

Exciting pieces of wood, that always belong to someone else, are more often than not several pieces joined together. Small sections of a manageable size can be wired together. You may need someone to hold them together while you wire. Anything large demands assistance; the fixing must be rigid and, if at all possible, temporary. Wood permanently fixed is bulky to store and you may want to use the pieces individually on other occasions. Hold the sections together and mark the point of contact with a felt pen. If the position allows, drill a hole through both pieces. Fasten them together using a bolt and wing nut. Where one piece is too thick to drill completely through, penetrate to a minimum depth of 1in (2.5cm). The bolt will have to be permanently fixed in this instance. Measure the thickness of the wood to be attached; add 1in (2.5cm) for the fixing and a further inch (2.5cm) to include the nut. This is the length of screw thread that you will require. Most hardware shops carry these and will cut a specified length. Glue one end of the screw thread into the wood to act as a permanent bolt. Allow it to dry before you assemble the two pieces.

You may consider this section on driftwood conversion a little over-simplified. No two pieces of wood are alike and it is not possible to say how the wood should be used, adapted or converted. It is only possible to suggest – often the wood will do that for you.

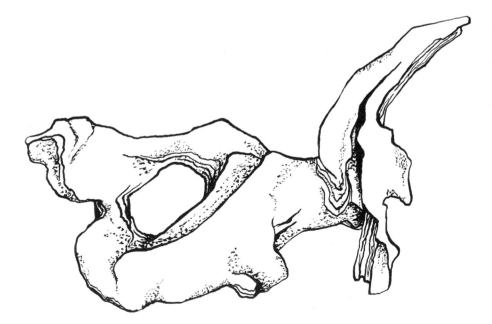

Conditioning and Maintaining

Without careful conditioning, cut flowers and foliage will soon wilt and die. The flower arranger works with living material and it must be sustained in all its stages. The gardener will provide water and fertilizer for the growing plant and protect it from pests and diseases. Once the plant material has been cut, this standard of care for its specific needs must continue.

The process we call conditioning allows the flower time to recover after separation from the parent plant and to charge itself fully with water. Maintaining is, as the word suggests, any method of prolonging the cut life of flowers and foliage once they have been arranged.

The time of day when plant material is cut is an important part of the preparation. Avoid cutting during the day when the sun has been shining on the plant for any length of time. Direct sunlight quickly dissipates moisture in the petal and leaf. This is often recognizable as a temporary wilting on very hot days, particularly with hydrangeas. Experience has shown that flowers cut at this time continue to wilt and rarely recover. Morning and evening have proved to be the best times. The plant has then had sufficient time to absorb moisture from the soil and the atmosphere. The stage of development of a flower at which to cut will be your choice – some flowers just showing colour will continue to develop once they have been arranged; others will keep their cut size and form. Flowers that are almost mature are usually the best choice. Those that have passed their obvious best are not suitable, for they don't survive much longer once they have been cut.

Carry a suitable container of water with you as you collect the material and place each flower in the bucket as it is cut. With any that exude a glutinous fluid, for example daffodils or *Euphorbia*, dip the cut stem in the soil to staunch the flow and then put them in water.

Prepare the flowers for conditioning in a draught-free room and handle the cut stems as little as possible. Bruised petals and stems quickly go brown and decay, often affecting the surrounding plant material. Have ready sufficient buckets of fresh water to receive the prepared flowers and foliage. There are a number of chemicals sold to mix with water and prolong the cut life of flowers. Should you decide to use them, follow the instructions carefully, as some react to containers that are made of metal. Sugar and bleach are sometimes recommended as life-giving additives, in various quantities. I am wary of these and use only plain water with garden plant material.

Remove any foliage that will be below the water level, as this will decay and pollute the water. Thorns and blemishes are best removed at this point – it saves time when you come to arrange the flowers. If the stem has a bark, remove this for a length of about 2in (5cm). Woody stems benefit from a slight crushing, as this opens the stem fibre and allows the water to be absorbed.

Delphiniums and flowers with hollow stems need to be filled with water. Use a small, lipped jug to trickle water into the stem and seal it with cotton wool or a plug of old oasis. This can be cut off when the flowers are arranged. Some flower stems, mainly the *Euphorbia* family, exude a latex-like sap, which is caustic. Great care should be taken to avoid it coming into contact with your skin or eyes. Sap of this nature generally continues to flow after the plant has been cut. To seal it, hold the stem end over a naked flame for up to 10 seconds. Burning the stem forces any moisture present upwards to the flower and breaks down any airlock that might be present in the stem. The burnt stem end becomes charcoal through which water will still be able to penetrate. Cut away this section when arranging. It is not necessary to prepare all materials in this way. In fact I restrict this method to *Euphorbia* and poppies.

Immature foliage is very prone to wilting. To avoid this the stem ends should be dipped in boiling water. Heat ½in (1.2cm) of water in an old pan, wrap the foliage in a cloth to protect it and your hand from the steam and stand the ends in the boiling water for about 10 seconds. You will notice a colour change in the end of the stem; use this as a time guide. Next float the immature foliage in water for no more than 2 hours, then stand it upright in cold water to complete its conditioning. Foliage with a felted or hairy surface shouldn't be submerged, since the leaves will become waterlogged and discoloured. Individual leaves, such as *Hosta*, *Bergenia*, vines and *Hydrangea*, are easier to condition if they are given a short period completely submerged. The majority of flowers and foliage do not require any special preparation. Recut the end of the stem at an angle to maximize the area of water intake. As plant material also absorbs water through the side of the stem, stand the cut material in water covering at least one-third of the stem.

The length of time for conditioning should be about 6 hours, or where possible overnight. There is no short cut to conditioning. Using the flowers before they have been fully conditioned will only result in a tired and wilted arrangement. Do not worry if the material has to stand for a long period in water – plant material will not over-condition. Stand the buckets of flowers in a cool, draught-free room. A darkened room will retard the development of the blooms. Any that you want to open should be moved close to an indirect source of light. The enemies of plant material at this stage are heat and direct sunlight.

During the conditioning period, check the flowers for any that are not taking up water, recognized by drooping foliage and limp flower heads. These wilted stems can be revived by boiling the stem ends, as described above. Florist's roses are particularly susceptible in this way. Return the revived stem to the conditioning bucket. The cause of this fault is usually an airlock in the stem.

Arranged plant material requires a constant supply of water to maintain life. For most stylized arrangements it will be impossible to change the water completely. If the container has a large reservoir, top it up each day, possibly twice if the house temperature is high. Water-retaining foam should be checked daily, topping up when necessary. If the container is not affected by water the arrangement can be removed to the draining board and water poured in liberal quantities over the foam.

Both flowers and leaves respond favourably to a daily spray of water. Adjust the mister to fine spray and direct it at the back of the arrangement as well as the front. Where it is not possible to move the arrangement, position a sheet of polythene in such a way as to protect the surrounding furniture. Central heating has caused a general increase in house temperatures, something that cut flowers are not fond of, so a frequent check is essential. Avoid putting the arrangement close to any source of heat – fire, radiator or direct sunlight.

Having discussed conditioning and maintaining in a general way, there are a number of specific materials that have peculiar conditioning habits.

Tulips tend to grow after they have been cut. The stems will bend without wilting while they are conditioning. To prevent this, wrap the stems together in a sheet of newspaper and tie it loosely. Condition them in the ordinary way.

Lilac foliage is very demanding, reducing the amount of moisture getting to the flower. As it is not terribly attractive it should be completely removed from each stem before conditioning.

Dianthus (pinks and carnations) condition more and are less likely to wilt if they are allowed to stand in lemonade. In thundery weather, carnations are liable to go sleepy and rapidly fade, I find that lemonade helps to counteract this. Ethylene gas, given off by ripening fruit also adversely affects carnations, so do not place them near fruit.

Anemones can sometimes be difficult to condition. A method often tried is to run a pin from the end of the stem to the flower head, scoring the surface. I am lucky that I find anemones easy and don't need to resort to mutilation – doubly lucky, as I am unable to explain why it works.

These guidelines explain the basic techniques which allow you to make the most of the plant materials you choose for an arrangement and prolong their cut life. Further comments relating to specific types of flowers and foliage are included under each entry in the Encyclopedia of Plants.

Drying and Preserving

There is something quite satisfying about selecting, preserving and eventually hoarding the best from your garden for use in the bleak winter months. How the first skeletonized leaf was used we do not know, but we do know that methods of preserving have changed since those far off days when only Nature provided such material. Though the garden and hedgerow still offers a selection of naturally dried plant material, this supply is often limited and lacking in colour. The desire for an elegant spray of beech leaves in midwinter has caused the flower arranger to challenge the seasons and prolong the beauty of a summer garden. Autumn and winter are the seasons usually associated with preserved materials, but they have their uses at other times of the year. The arranger with limited time to spend will find it helpful to create a permanent arrangement and add fresh flowers when they are available. Now that central heating is a feature in most homes, dried foliage and flowers are a good substitute for fresh material that needs replacing all too often. The reasons that you have for drying and preserving will change as your enthusiasm increases, but the care must always be taken over selecting the correct method of preserving particular materials. If you attempt to press a 4ft (120cm) spray of holly under the carpet, apart from the unsightly bulge, the drying leaves will disintegrate with the passing of time and feet. Deciding which method of preserving to use will be a matter of experience, though a list of suitable plant material is suggested under the separate headings.

Generally, drying and preserving is done when the flower or leaf is fully mature, usually during the summer and early autumn. However, don't overlook the blossom and flowers of spring which mature early, or certain foliages of late autumn.

Select your material when it is fully charged with moisture and the flower is open and dry – early morning and late afternoon are usually ideal. Carry a bucket of fresh water for cut stems and a small box for individual flowers, to prevent them drying out. The material must be processed immediately it is harvested, so allow plenty of time to carry out the job from start to finish.

Desiccant, glycerine, pressing and air drying are the most common methods of preserving flowers and foliage. As you become more proficient other ideas may develop, but they must not be used as a short-cut. Instant preserving, like instant gardening, could give an effect which does not last.

DESICCANT This drying method of preserving is used for individual flowers, leaves and small sprays of delicate foliage. Flower petals can be removed and dried separately and reassembled on to a false centre. Cut off long stems – they contain more moisture than the flower and invariably collapse before the drying process is completed. The flower heads can be taped or wired on to false stems when they are required.

Desiccant comes in three forms, sand, borax and silica gel. They all absorb moisture from the flower, leaving the structure and colour intact. Sand is more readily available and probably the cheapest. One major disadvantage is its tendency to harden against the flower petal, often damaging the flower when you attempt to brush it away. Borax is a fine white compound available at most chemist shops. Because of its fine granular structure, it is easier to use than sand. Drying agents must be in contact with all surfaces of the flower. As borax is a fine powder, it does not flow evenly and you may experience some difficulty in getting it between the petals of multi-petalled flowers. Silica gel is the most free-flowing of the three compounds. It remains granular and is easy to remove from the dried flower. You can often buy it from your local garden or flower club. Other equipment needed for using desiccant is a rigid plastic container – ice-cream cartons from a freezer shop are ideal – and a tablespoon. Cover the bottom of the container with desiccant to a depth of ½in (1.25cm). Carefully lay the flowers in, with a space between each one, using the tablespoon to sift the compound gently into and around each flower. Continue the operation in layers until the carton is full. A slight tap on the edge of the box will settle the preservative around the plant material. Finally, top up with desiccant and replace the lid. If it is possible, store the box in a mildly warm room to prevent any moisture from the atmosphere affecting the drying process.

The drying time will vary depending on what flowers have been used, but don't be surprised if some take up to a fortnight to complete the cycle. To get an even drying result, it is a good idea to use flowers of an even size or similar form in each box. Leave the flowers for about a week, then check on your success. Carefully empty the contents on to a large sheet of newspaper. Put aside any flowers that appear crisp and dry, for storing, and return the rest to the box. No harm will be done if they are then checked on a daily basis. It is important that the dried flowers do not reabsorb moisture, so particular care should be taken over where and how you store them. The storage box can be of the same ice-cream type but it must have an airtight lid. Sprinkle a fine layer of the drying agent in the bottom of the box and cover it with a sheet of absorbent paper (kitchen roll). Lay the flowers on the paper, the heavier flowers at the bottom, with the lighter flowers laid on top of them. Don't overfill the box, for considerable damage can be done if you are constantly searching for a certain flower. Space to store dried material is often at a premium. 'Under the spare bed' has now become something of a flower-arranging joke, but providing the atmosphere is dry, it is an excellent place.

Periodically, dry out the preserving compound in a warm oven, to evaporate absorbed moisture. You will find that it can be used indefinitely. The advantage of flowers preserved in desiccant is that they are not crushed flat. This makes them suitable for picture designs that will not be glazed. I am sure the ingenious flower arranger will find many uses for them.

Flowers and foliage to dry in desiccant

Anemone japonica
Astrantia
Delphinium (individual florets)
Garrya elliptica (catkins)
Helleborus
Myosotis

Narcissus (small varieties)
Rosa
Zinnia
Individual petals
Small lengths of foliage
Tendrils

GLYCERINE In dilute form glycerine preserves by replacing the moisture present in plant material, through stem and leaf absorption. Flowers do not readily absorb glycerine, so foliage is the medium commonly chosen. Unlike the drying process of desiccant, glycerine does affect the colour of the plant material. In most cases, this is a chemical change, and in others it is caused by the amount of light present during the preserving process. The colour change is not drastic, in some instances it can be desirable. *Choisya ternata* will change from glossy, almost dull green to a light biscuit colour. This foliage goes well with pink Zinnias. It is, of course, necessary to protect the stem ends of dried material if they are to be used with wet foam. This can be done very easily by dipping them in a polyurethane varnish and allowing them to dry.

There are two schools of thought as to when plant material should be put into the preserving solution – immediately it is cut, or after a brief conditioning. I favour doing it straight away, so this means that the solution should be prepared before the plant material is cut. Glycerine is available at most chemists shops, and they will usually make up any quantity that you want. If possible use a glass jar for standing the material in – you will then be able to check the level of the liquid and top up if it is required. The solution is two parts of warm water to one part of glycerine. Use the chemist's bottle as a measure.

Pick the mature plant material in the morning or late afternoon, carrying a bucket with you to put the material in directly it is cut. Trim away any leaves from the bottom of the stem in case they prevent other stems from reaching the glycerine solution. Place the stems in the solution to a depth of 2 to 3in (5 to 7.5cm) in a cool but light room. Included in this chapter is a table indicating the length of time it takes for certain plants to be preserved. It is a good idea to check them every day, as some preserve more quickly than others. Over-preserved material tends to sweat the glycerine and is most susceptible to mildew. When the leaf has changed colour, which is the usual visual indication that it is ready, check it by touch. It should be pliable with a slight oily feel. Remove the stem and lay it in a box to dry the stem end. To store glycerine-preserved material, either stand it in a container in a moisture-free atmosphere or keep it in a box lined with newspaper.

Some plant material reacts mysteriously to this method of preserving. *Molucella laevis* is one such, and is one of the most exciting plants to preserve. The pale green, shell-like calyx turns to a soft cream colour. When the *Molucella* is in the glycerine solution, it has the annoying habit of slowly bending over, preventing the solution from reaching the top. The tip quickly starts to wilt, the stem weakens and gives the appearance that it is not going to preserve. To counteract this, tie a piece of string loosely around the top of the *Molucella* and prop the jar against a corner to keep them straight. After three days, though they may still be green, take them out of the solution and hang them in a bunch, upside down, in direct light. The glycerine present in the stem will continue to preserve and the direct light will highlight the colour. When the stems are dry and the calyx is crisp to the touch, they can be taken down and stored. There isn't a satisfactory explanation why *Molucella* adopts this awkward attitude. Some people prefer to grow the plants in pots and at the end of summer water them with the glycerine solution until they have changed colour and are pliable to touch.

Single leaves with a smooth tough surface may be preserved by floating them in a shallow tray of glycerine solution. The solution is absorbed through the surface of the leaf, so they should be moved around frequently to ensure maximum coverage. *Camellia*, *Aucuba*, and *Fatsia japonica* do very well in this way. The leaves can then be wired together to form a spray for later use.

An alternative to glycerine is motor car anti-freeze, which is used undiluted but in exactly the same way. The disadvantage is that the dye present seriously affects the colour of the dried material, leaving it a dull browny green.

Material preserved in glycerine or anti-freeze is quite tough. Should it get squashed in any way, holding it over steam will revive it or it can be ironed with a cool iron. Leaves covered in dust are best wiped with soapy water, rinsed thoroughly and allowed to dry.

You will find that the leaves are most accommodating in accepting paint, both oil-bound and water-based. Apart from the obvious permanent colour change, there is no other effect. If you have any glycerine solution left over, it can be used again if it is not too dilute. Should the liquid become discoloured, pass it through a sieve to remove any debris and boil it to kill any bacteria.

TABLE OF PRESERVING TIMES
Herbaceous plants that preserve well in glycerine
(M) Medium, up to three weeks
(F) Fast, up to five days
(S) Slow, six weeks possibly more

Amaranthus caudatus (M)
remove leaves
Astilbe (F to M)
Ballota pseudodictamnus (M)
Bergenia (M)
Briza maxima (F to M)

Eryngium (M)
Escallonia (M)
Lunaria (F)
Molucella (F)
Physalis (F) when pods are
green, remove leaves

Polygonatum (F) may react
like Mollucella (see text)
Sisyrinchium (M) when
seed has set
Verbascum (M) when seed
has set

AIR DRYING Air drying is probably the oldest method of preserving plant material. Quite a number of the plants will in fact dry naturally on the parent plant, but harvesting them and home drying prevents any weather damage. There is a considerable amount of colour loss and shape distortion with air-dried flowers. The material must be cut when it is perfectly dry. Remove any marked or superfluous foliage and wrap the stems in small bundles. Hang them up, heads down, in a cool, dark but airy atmosphere. Sufficient air must be allowed to circulate around the flower heads to dry them properly. The drying process will shrink and possibly distort the stems so they must be checked and retied if it is necessary.

Select only mature flowers for drying. The range is restricted – *Eryngium*, grasses, *Limonium*, *Achillea*, *Echinops* and *Helichrysum* are some plants that will dry successfully.

Dried flowers are very brittle and should be stored carefully in a rigid box with a sheet of newspaper laid over them to protect them from dust and moisture.

PRESSING Pressing flowers has become a hobby in its own right. The pressed flower loses its moisture to the medium used for pressing, but it still retains its colour. The subject should be almost flat to begin with, as the pressure exerted during the process will distort any three-dimensional effect. The range of material for pressing is quite wide – individual leaves, flowers, separated petals, tendrils or florets. Flower presses from a hobby shop will press small quantities of flowers. The flowers are laid between sheets of cardboard with a wooden cover secured by corner wing nuts. I find the process of checking the flowers irritating and the corrugations in the cardboard often mark the flowers. Large books are more convenient, particularly telephone directories. Lay the material for pressing between sheets of blotting paper and slip them into the directory. If you don't use blotting paper, you might find that the flowers stick to the page and tear when removed. A large elastic band around the book will keep them in place and exert sufficient pressure. Pressed flowers can be left in the book or press until you need them; the alternative store is an air-tight box. A thin layer of desiccant on the bottom of the box will prevent any re-absorption of moisture. Pressed flowers are extremely delicate, so all handling, checking and arranging should be done with a pair of fine tweezers.

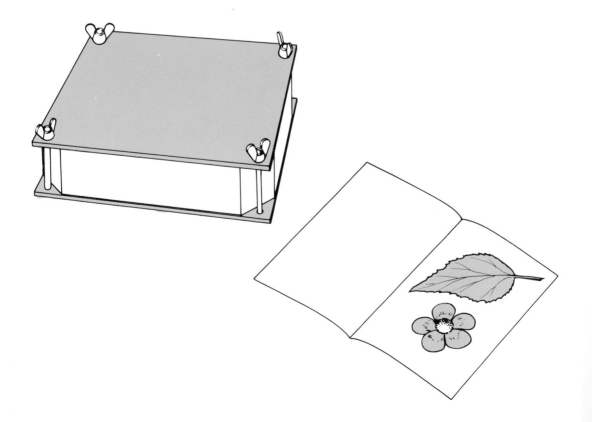

TABLE OF PRESERVING TIMES

Shrubs and trees
(F) Fast, up to five days
(M) Medium, up to three weeks
(S) Slow, six weeks possibly more
(G) Glycerine
(P) Pressing
(D) Desiccant

Acer (P) (M)
Aucuba (G) (M to S)
Ballota (G) (M)
Berberis (D) (F) Use very young leaves for best colour
Buddleia (D) (M)
Buxus (G) (S)
Chamaecyparis (P) (M)
Cupressus (G) (P) (M)
Camellia (G) (M to S)
Carpinus (G) (M)
Choisya (G) (M)
Corylus (G) (M) Catkins only
Cotinus (P) (M) Leaves only
Cytisus (G) (M) Will dry naturally
Deutzia (D) (F)

Eleagnus (G) (M)
Enkianthus (G) (M)
Eucalyptus (G) (M)
Fagus (G) (M)
Fatsia (G) (S)
Forsythia (D) (F)
Garrya (G) (M) Tassels and leaves
Griselinia (G) (M to S)
Hamamelis (P) (M) Autumn foliage only
Hedera (G) (M)
Hydrangea. See p.187 for special instruction
Ilex (G) (M to S)
Ligustrum (G) (M to S) Not always successful
Mahonia (G) (M)

Purrotia (P) (M) Autumn foliage
Pernettya (G) (M) Summer foliage only
Philadelphus (P) (D) (F)
Pittosporum (W) (M)
Prunus (P) (D) (F to M) Flowers only
Pyracantha (G) (M)
Rhododendron (G) (S) Foliage; (D) (F) Flowers
Ribes (D) (F)
Rubus (D) (F) Flowers only
Salix (G) (M)
Skimmia (G) (M to S)
Spiraea (D) (F)
Stephanandra (P) (M) Leaves only
Thuja (P) (D) (M)

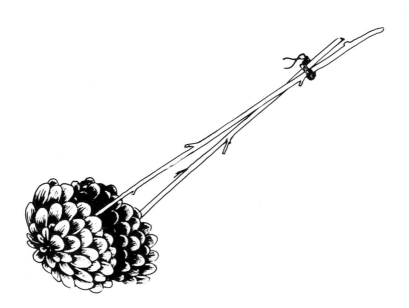

Shape and Design

Flower arranging is not a new art form, nor has it always been necessary to cut flowers in order to arrange them. Gardens were planned to a shape as long ago as the fifteenth century BC. Archaeological discoveries have allowed us a glimpse of this early garden arrangement. Like the gardeners of the past, gardeners today rarely plant flowers and shrubs in careless order. A plan is established, a design is considered, to encompass plants that are already growing, to accommodate plants that you want to grow, sometimes as an extension of the environment you have already created inside your home. Whatever the reason, a design emerges.

The order of line and shape in garden design and flower arranging is governed by several factors. We understand them as the elements and principles of design. No one invented them, they have been passed on to us by generations of artists, evolving quite naturally as a sense of what is right. In our world this is translated as something that 'looks right'.

The elements of design are present in plant material – colour, form, texture, line and space. Gardeners and arrangers use them in varying amounts to achieve an effect that is both satisfying and beautiful. Flowers and shrubs are often chosen for their colour, so colour is possibly considered the prime element. It is used to create harmony or contrast within associated groupings in the garden. In a flower arrangement it is often the strongest influence on the decision for a basic scheme, perhaps even relied upon to evoke a particular mood or association.

Form, whether expressed in the individual shape of a flower or the whole plant, is equally important. It breaks down visual monotony – a vista becomes more interesting when the horizon is relieved by the different shapes of trees. Plants with differing forms are used in the garden for the same reason. As an element in flower arranging we may use one or several forms together. The secret is in striking a happy balance. Excessive amounts of one form soon become uninteresting, because there is no interruption to make us appreciate the next flower. Overloading an arrangement with too many forms, on the other hand, has a most confusing effect. In the confined space of an arrangement, rapid changes in shape unsettle the viewing rhythm.

Texture is a fascinating quality in plant material, making us immediately want to experience it by touch, but we are able to recognize texture instantly without using our fingers. No doubt a lifetime of recognizing objects by their surface sensation has given us this ability. It can be a deceiving element – for instance the surface of a *Mahonia* leaf is smooth to the touch, but the indented shape and sharp pointed spines create a visually rough, almost menacing, textural impression. In the garden and as a component for arranging, texture may be used for emphasis. Like opposing colours, contrasting textures excite each other.

Space can be an ignored element in the garden as well as the arrangement. We must be able to see each flower and leaf as it is arranged. There would be very little point to an arrangement that is simply a block of colour. Space surrounding the material puts it in isolation, enabling us to see and appreciate it. A gardener friend of mine refers to space as areas of nothing. By this he means a gap that exists for as long as it takes him to raise a plant to fill it. But space should not just happen by accident; it has positive qualities and should be a deliberate part of the overall design. It acts as a momentary resting point for the eye before it moves on to the next area of interest. The space does not have to be barren – gravel, stone or a piece of statuary will at least diminish the weed problem. Small gaps between plantings will help to increase the dimension of the garden, by allowing you to look through to distant groupings. In the same way, an arrangement that is not overcrowded with flowers enables us to appreciate the way they have been selected and combined.

The shape of a garden or flower arrangement is based upon line. Most good garden designs start as lines on paper, erased and altered until the proportions are correct. The proportion and harmony of line is as important as direction. Getting the proportions of a series of lines correct does not need an accurate measure. Visual senses instinctively react to line, telling you when a particular grouping of lines is in harmony or that a series of lines are in proportion with each other. Straight lines of equal length may seem pleasing at first but very soon we find them monotonous and long to alter them. Now take the same straight lines but vary the lengths. They cease to be monotonous because your eye is forced to change its rhythm, so the desire to change the lines diminishes and they become more acceptable.

Though line is used generally as a physical element in gardens, for creating patterns, extending a viewing angle or emphasizing form, it can be used to create an illusion. Plantings based on curves and circles, that are small gardens in themselves where the viewer pauses and appreciates the area in isolation, give an impression of greater overall size. Straight lines of plants on either side of the garden, planted at a gradual angle so they appear closer together at the furthest point, create the illusion of increased length. This is accentuated when the tallest plants or trees are closest to the house.

Flower arrangements also require a planned line, though not quite as detailed as a garden plan. The completed shape is usually an image in the arranger's mind. A number of factors determine the line of an arrangement, such as the situation, material available, or container. These are combined in our thoughts, together with a sense of proportion and scale, to illustrate the shape of the arrangement.

In certain designs, line is a dominant feature. Vertical and horizontal arrangements have clearly defined linear direction. The first placements of plant material firmly establish the line. The length of the material is critical for accurate proportion. Measure the stem against the height or breadth of the container and increase by one half, and always cut the stem slightly longer when positioning the first placements. Any adjustments can be made at this point, stems that are cut too short are wasted.

Other linear designs use line to create shape. In these instances, line is at first an imaginary boundary, becoming real as the shape is built up. A symmetrical or asymmetrical triangular arrangement is defined by its three points, linked by the plant material radiating from the centre until the shape becomes clear.

Flower arrangements with a curved shape have a closer relationship between directional line and outline. Outlines that are straight disturb the balance of curving directional line. The curve may be established with one piece of plant material, a twist of driftwood anchored to the mechanics or several pieces of material positioned to create a curving line. The outline should echo the direction of movement, coming closer to the central line at the extreme points, widening slightly at the central or focal area.

The principles of design are intangible, and include proportion, scale, rhythm, balance, contrast, dominance and harmony. To some degree they should all be present in a flower arrangement. This sounds a more arduous task than it is. Some arrangers achieve the elements and principles of design naturally; others may find them a little difficult at first. It is a good idea to learn and understand them. A curving branch will introduce rhythm into a design by virtue of its flowing movement. Repetition of the curve using a recurring flower shape threaded through the arrangement will also do this. A container that looks right with its final surroundings and plant material will add to the harmony.

A visit to an art gallery can help to clarify design principles. The study of a landscape painting, in particular, will be a great help. Write the elements and principles on paper and look for them in the painting. A number of interesting points will emerge. Dominance, for instance, isn't necessarily overwhelming size – it can be very small areas of striking colour. Before you go to the gallery armed with pencil and paper, a brief explanation of the five elements and seven principles may be of some value.

The elements of **form**, **colour**, **texture**, **line** and **space** tend to be self-explanatory and are discussed at the start of this chapter. A simple illustration is to look at something that you are familiar with – a dining-room chair. Its dimensional quality of form, the line of the back, the colour and texture of the material and the spaces created by its shape all combine to give a pleasing effect. Each of these elements will be important when you come to assemble your plant material. Where nature provides the elements of design for flower arranging, you, the artist, bring the principles.

Balance is both a visual and physical principle. The physical aspect relies on sturdy mechanics used with plant material of a suitable weight. The visual effect is the symmetry of the design. In basic terms, this means plant material placed to one side of an imaginary central line in an arrangement, balancing with materials placed to the other side. This balancing of flowers and foliage may be achieved through length of stem – identical lengths for symmetrical balance, or proportional lengths for asymmetrical balance. Colour and size of flower will accentuate this, small amounts of vibrant darker colour used with greater quantities of contrasting lighter colour. Check the balance of the arrangement as you build it up, standing back to get an overall view, so that any imbalance can be corrected before it is too late.

Incorrect height and width often upset the **proportions** of an arrangement. The use of halves as a guide to establish dimensions is recommended. The height of the first placement should be one and a half times the height of the container. With a low container, for a horizontal design, use the same measurements for establishing width. The corresponding height or width can be gauged by holding the material in the required position to see if the proportion will be right. Then cut the stem and place it in the arrangement. Care taken over checking the height and width before you cut the material is never wasted.

Scale and **proportion** are allied principles. Generally, the word scale is used as a link for size of flowers and foliage, either with each other or with the container and surroundings. Bold forms of plant material need a large heavy container, not only for visual and physical balance but to stabilize good scale. Small flowers would be out of scale in such a container. Within the arrangement the range of flower sizes should not be jarring. I think of scale as graduated steps, each one slightly larger than the last. Use the smallest flowers at the extremities of the design and work towards the centre, grading the flowers upwards in size. You will find that as you appreciate scale more, the principle of visual balance becomes easier.

To understand **rhythm** as a design principle, look at something as basic as clothes on a washing line. On a still day they simply hang and are nothing more than clean laundry. On a breezy day they move, taking on different shapes as they whip to and fro. The curves and lines created catch your eye and hold your attention. It may only be for a moment, but you found the experience interesting. Interest is what you want to project in an arrangement. It isn't enough simply to assemble flowers and foliage in a design; it must be done in a way that will be admired, studied and appreciated at least by you and hopefully your friends. The interest will be lost if the eye has no means of crossing the design in a rewarding movement. Regular recurrence of rhythm will alter this, by taking the eye from one area through to the next. Repetition of one flower type or colour is a rhythmic factor. The distinct shape of flower stems on either side draws the eye across the arrangement without any disturbing interruptions. This is particularly relevant in designs that are based on a curve. The placement of each flower should be done in a way that creates gentle movement. Stagger each flower slightly, recessing darker colours and advancing the lighter ones so that your eye follows the line with increasing interest.

Contrast as a design principle works very much in the same way as texture does as an element. Plant material which contrasts with its neighbour makes us more aware of both. An arrangement has to be lived with. One with components of too-similar qualities soon becomes uninteresting, so this is why we include materials of contrast. Contrast is not directly affected by the other six principles and is often used carelessly, possibly because it is so obvious. Variety of form is an important effective contrast. Positioning different shaped flowers next to or opposite each other, though they may be similar in colour, increases the appeal of the grouping. It can be a difficult principle to appreciate in the context of flower arranging, until you see it in action. I was taught to remember it as a series of antonyms, broad and narrow, ornate and simple, light and dark, rough and smooth, bold and delicate. The list is endless, but it is a useful method for recalling the importance of contrast.

By now, you should be aware that flower arranging is not only an art of the hands, but one very much of the eye. An arrangement of flowers may satisfy many emotional needs, but to do this it must be looked at. The eye needs a focus, a reason why, or possibly a place to rest. This influence we generally call **dominance**, which is a strong word and if used literally may offend its fellow principles. Use it as you would punctuation in a sentence. It may be introduced into the central area of the design as a single feature by using a larger or more strikingly coloured flower. More than one area may be used to draw the attention of the viewer. Arrangements with two placements of plant material are designs that generally require this split usage. The dominant area need not be plant material – it may be a space created by a curving branch in a landscape design. In this style, flower colour is usually low down at the base of the branch or arranged at a distance to effect stronger balance. These two areas, by virtue of their separation, have inbuilt dominance. Without care, this is where dominance can so easily become too dominant and destroy the balance of the arrangement.

The final principle is **harmony**, which for me is the most satisfying. All the elements and principles are in accord with each other. Nothing is out of place; all is correct. The colour scheme in flowers has been chosen carefully, with an eye for unity. Flowers, foliage and container combine aesthetically, for a reason and not by chance. The surroundings accept the arrangement without the slightest sign of irritation. However, to throw a very small spanner in the works, I must say that harmony is not attained instantly. It is a measure of your skill and artistry as a flower arranger. Understanding and accepting the elements and principles of design is certainly the road to harmony. The individuality and creativity that you introduce in combining them is the destination.

It is very easy to register design principles as points of 'interest' or for 'pleasing effect', but this is what we are trying to achieve by arranging flowers. We have within us, to a varying degree, a desire to create something of quality and beauty. It may be an extension of a natural ability – people who are good cooks or talented painters often transfer to flower arranging with amazing success. Those of us who didn't quite know where to start needed a framework for our enthusiasm. If you are tempted to recreate an arrangement from one seen in a book, to my mind a good start, try not to copy it too accurately. Introduce an idea of your own to give it a personal feel and provide a salve to your conscience.

The greatest framework is to use design principles as guidelines, never as rules. They evolved long ago to give us a sense of what is right in art, so use this innate sense as a starting point in flower arrangement. Some people will urge you to forget accepted design and aim for personal expression, in an endeavour to create something new. Be wary of this – just because something is new does not mean that it is acceptable or pleasing. Artists of the past developed new styles as new materials were discovered or invented. Plant material, the medium that we work with, isn't new. Over the years, flower arrangers have used it to its maximum. You can, of course, associate flowers with objects of a personal nature, which will give the design a look that is unique to you. But the plant material will invariably be arranged to a traditional line. Flowers and leaves have a distinct growth pattern, and this natural line has underpinned the shape of most traditional styles. Look at the silhouette of a tree, the growing habit of delphiniums or a clump of daffodils and recognize the influence of these on triangular, vertical and landscape arrangements. It would not be a rewarding exercise to humiliate and distort the plant material.

If tradition has provided us with styles that are appreciated, based upon accepted design principles, why do we need new and original concepts in flower arranging? It cannot simply be that our arranging must be modern because we live in a modern world. Possibly it is the need to be artistically individual. The introduction of plant material from abroad has given us the opportunity to arrange in a totally different way. You may find that so-called modern/abstract flower arrangements are questionable in their originality. A comparison between prints of ancient Chinese flower arrangements and modern work reveals a strong similarity. The urge to create lies dormant within all of us, but creativity may not always be channelled into modern arranging; it may act as a catalyst for other areas of arranging.

Arranging in what is termed the modern way is totally unique; the essence is so very personal. Design principles are exaggerated, not to a point of distortion but to please and satisfy you. Don't be guilty of ignoring this type of arranging, which is an amalgam of principles, without an instantly recognizable definite shape. At the same time, don't be confused by the enthusiasts who decry traditional arrangers as non-progressive. There is nothing wrong with saying 'I am going no further, I am satisfied with my limits'. Satisfied limits are not restricting, they can become points of concentration – a plateau, where you work at perfecting what you have learned and styles that you simply prefer.

GUIDE TO DESIGN Before you cut the plant material for a flower arrangement, assemble the necessary equipment first. Decide where it is to go and what style of container is suitable for that position. Prepare the mechanics, making doubly sure that they are secure. Stand the container in its situation and try to visualize the completed arrangement. This will give you some idea about the line to follow, the colour and lengths of material needed.

When all the decisions have been made, cut the flowers and foliage, and give them adequate time to condition. It is best to arrange the flowers *in situ*. The proportions of the arrangement will be more accurate and there is less likelihood of spilt water if the arrangement does not have to be repositioned. Protect the surrounding area with sheets of polythene, which can also be used to lay your flowers upon. They will not suffer any harm if they are out of water for a short period. Laying them out separately allows you to see each piece clearly and much less damage will occur if you don't have to pull each piece from a tangle of stems in a bucket.

SYMMETRICAL DESIGN Symmetry refers to the balance and uniformity of an arrangement, rather than the distinct line or shape. Regular triangles, buffet table arrangements, pedestals and low informal arrangements are some of the shapes best suited to symmetrical designs. Choose a suitable container for the situation and the shape of the design. Arrangements that are triangular may be done on a pedestal-style container, or in a dish if the design is placed on a piece of furniture.

Balancing the shape is critical. When you begin the arrangement, locate an imaginary vertical central line and arrange the flowers and foliage on either side so that they appear equal. The lengths of the side material stems do not have to be accurately identical. If they are, there is a strong possibility that the finished arrangement will be static. Aim for a relaxed movement in the plant material, without destroying the shape. Without attempting to influence your decision on what shape to achieve using this sort of balance, I have a suspicion that you will find the ubiquitous triangle the easiest.

Use water-retaining foam as the mechanics, as this will allow the flowers to be positioned at a downward angle. Locate the first piece of foliage towards the back of the oasis. This should be a continuation of the imaginary central line of the container. Place the first side pieces next. These should be about the same length and visual weight, but avoid very stiff pieces. Bring them over the lip of the container to flow downwards, creating the three points of the triangle.

Complete the outline of the shape with graded lengths of foliage, again placed towards the back of the oasis. Positioning the framework of the design towards the back will leave plenty of room to get the bulk of the flowers in without them appearing flat. At this point use two or three large leaves, low down, at the centre, to cover the mechanics and to act as a foil for the focal area flowers. Work from the outer edges of the shape in towards the centre with smaller flowers, increasing their size until you get to the central area. During this period of filling in, arrange some of the material to flow over the front edge of the container. This will increase the rhythm of the design and prevent a hard line from forming.

The imaginary central line now has substance, so keep checking that the balance is uniform. This does not mean having exactly the same flowers on each side, but balancing the size and form of flowers and foliage. Colour should be harmonious throughout the arrangement.

The focal area flowers are generally positioned last, although this is something that the flowers themselves, or your method of working, will dictate. For this, choose perfect flowers that link with the rest of the material. Because of their position, they will be the hinge of the design and the most commented upon. Odd numbers seem to be appropriate, as the triangular shape has three lines of direction. Position the flowers with this in mind. Bring at least one flower over the lip of the container to increase the transition from the front of the arrangement to the back.

The size of the arrangement does not affect symmetrical balance. The same principles are used in large pedestal arrangements, or low informal shapes, where breadth exceeds height. Remember that you are trying to create a proportionate balance on each side of the arrangement, not an unnaturally fixed mirror image.

Symmetrical design
A triangular shape of arrangement demonstrates the principles of symmetrical design. The mass, tone and texture are evenly balanced on either side of a central vertical axis.

ASYMMETRICAL This also is a style of balance, but opposite to symmetrical balance. It can be described as off-set or lopsided. The popular shapes are triangular and curving designs, such as the Hogarth curve. Asymmetrical arrangements require a greater knowledge of the principles of design. The shape will be created with materials that are unequal in length and visual weight. These varying lengths mainly affect the width of the arrangement at any given level. As in a symmetrical design you should place the flowers around an imaginary axis. This time, one side is longer than its opposite, so proportion in the length of the first placements is important. It is always a good idea to establish the height of any arrangement first, using the guideline of one and one half times the height of the container.

Position this first placement slightly off-centre towards the shortest side of the design. To gauge the length of the longest side-piece, use the height material as a guide, as they are often equal. The opposite side should be shorter. The points of the triangle created should have acceptable visual balance. You will find that a heavier piece of foliage on the shorter side will do this. Complete the outline of the shape using fine material. Again, work towards the centre with graded flowers, keeping in mind that the focal area is slightly off-set. As good balance is achieved through position, check constantly to ensure that one side is not overpowering the other.

A greater number of flowers of a lighter shade placed on the longer side will balance a smaller quantity of a darker shade. Size of flower is another balancing method – increase the number of smaller flowers to balance fewer larger ones. Where the focal area is not regular, study the situation before you arrange the flowers. An emphasis to the right or left can rectify any slight imbalance.

To understand asymmetrical balance further, look at kitchen utensils that are irregular in shape. A coffee pot is a good example. Its fine curving handle, large enough to accommodate your hand, balances perfectly the small, bulbous pouring spout.

HOGARTH CURVE This design is often called the lazy 'S', because of its shape. It follows a loose 'S' shape, using a distinct rhythmic line, that flows from the upper point of the arrangement, through the central area to the lower point. There will be little evidence of natural growth pattern. The plant material should radiate from a central point without being obvious. William Hogarth, the painter, referred to flowing curves as 'lines of beauty' and this is where the name probably derives.

For this shape the container needs to be of the stem type, to prevent the plant material interfering with its surroundings. At first glance this design looks difficult to recreate. It is in fact, surprisingly easy and does not require as much plant material as massed designs of a similar size. The balance of the arrangement is asymmetrical, with a strong emphasis on line. Water-retaining foam will be the most convenient form of mechanics. The curving shape calls for a careful selection of outline material. The first placements of flowers and foliage should establish the outline and shape. The difficult task will be in finding suitable pieces that curve in opposite directions.

The curves need not be exaggerated – a gentle movement will be sufficient. Again, an imaginary axis will help you to position the first pieces. The upper material may be placed at a backward-leaning angle, though a more upright position will give you a stronger effect. Fix the lower sweep of plant material so that it follows the line of the upper placement, in one rhythmic movement. The flowers should be arranged in graded sizes, the smallest at the extreme points, to the larger sizes at the centre. The Hogarth curve is quite a delicate design and care must be taken in disguising the mechanics without losing the shape of the arrangement.

Some plant material may be artificially curved to suit this shape. *Cytisus* will allow itself to be gently moulded into a curving shape, with your fingers. An alternative method is wrapping the *Cytisus* around a bottle, securing it in position with tape and immersing it in water for several hours. Never contort plant material that is not flexible. At certain times of the year material with natural curves will not be available in the garden. This can be overcome by using preserved foliage for the line of the arrangement. Sprays of preserved beech foliage can be trimmed into shape. Use the discarded pieces as material for concealing the water-retaining foam. The Hogarth curve is a classical shape, lending itself to flowers of one variety as easily as it does to a mixture of varieties.

Asymmetrical design
A deliberate off-setting of line and form is the mark of asymmetry. In this style balance is achieved through unequal distribution of the materials.

Hogarth curve
This graceful, S-shaped curve requires free directional movement of the plant stems from a raised, stem-type container.

VERTICAL This is a useful shape when ground space is at a premium. Its statuesque shape looks most effective against a wall echoing any strong upward line in its surroundings. The container should also follow this upward movement, an excellent opportunity for using converted washing-up liquid bottles. The weight of the arrangement will be distributed over the centre and high above base level, so the container must contain adequate ballast. One fault with this shape is that it can look severe, almost sword-like. There is little opportunity for rhythmical movement, without losing the direction of the shape. The proportions of plant material and container should be correct, the tallest material at least one and one half times the height of the container. *Phormium tenax* and *Iris* leaves make excellent background foliage to determine the shape. Plain leaves that are round or pointed, angled downwards over the lip of the container, are not only useful as cover for the mechanics but give added direction. The focal-area flowers should be included low down in the design, close to the container lip so that the balance is proportionally correct. You may find it convenient to position the focal area flowers first and add the transitional flowers and foliage around them. The transitional material should be used to emphasize the shape and create interesting upward movement. Avoid any flowers and foliage that are of a spreading habit, as they will destroy the effect. Vertical designs are suited to bold forms of plant material when arranged in a modern way, a very useful exercise when economy of plant material is called for or if the arrangement has to be done in a hurry. Try three graded strap-like leaves as height material with two or three large leaves at the base and a couple of striking flowers. If you think of this category of design as upright instead of vertical the resulting arrangement will lose its formality, which is needed on the showbench but is not particularly appropriate in the home.

HORIZONTAL The horizontal arrangement is commonly used as a table decoration. By implication it has length as its greatest dimension, supposedly allowing dinner guests to talk across the table without the flowers creating a barrier (though on occasions I have longed for an obscuring arrangement!). It is, of course, not restricted to the dining-room table. Horizontal shapes are very sympathetic to positions that are low, coffee or occasional tables, for instance. The container may be slightly raised or concealed, the latter being the most usual. As this design is invariably viewed below 'eye level' it should be arranged *in situ*. This will allow you to check the design from varying levels, to ensure that it looks attractive from any viewing angle. The balance is usually symmetrical. As very little container is exposed, the proportions of the arrangement will be to suit the situation. Position the horizontal line first. Choose flowers or foliage that are not stiff, so that a soft flowing line will eventually develop across the arrangement. The material for fixing the height of the arrangement can be gauged for length using the width material as a guide. Work in towards the centre of the arrangement with graded flowers and foliage. Alter the angle of some flowers so the eye gets drawn across the design. More flowers will be required for the focal area if the design is viewed from both sides. Be mindful of the scale – they must look right with the width of the arrangement and the height. A harmonious effect is to use buds of the focal flowers as the height plant material. Once you have mastered the horizontal shape, you will realize that it is not necessary to have a distinct focal area of flowers. Distributing the flowers through the arrangement with a slight emphasis of size at the centre will result in a less formal arrangement.

CRESCENT Flower arrangements should follow the growing patterns of nature, radiating from a central point with the stems following a natural line. The crescent is one shape that uses curving lines. To use straight stems defeats the object of this design. The completed shape is quite unique – it should look like a new moon. The position of the crescent may be tipped slightly, but the shape should not alter. Changes in position will alter the balance from symmetrical to asymmetrical. An alternative is the inverted crescent where the shape remains the same, but the side sweeps of plant material hang downwards. With both the regular and inverted crescent, a stemmed container is appropriate. Because the material at the outer edges flows in a downward direction, oasis will be the easiest form of mechanics to use.

Set the outline of the shape so that it appears to be one unbroken line, flowing from one

Vertical design
Bold shapes and tall, pointed stems of flowers and foliage are suited to formal styles in vertical arrangements.

Crescent design
Naturally curving flower stems are essential to create the elegant sweep of a regular or inverted crescent.

Horizontal design
The emphasis on width in this style often dictates a symmetrically balanced arrangement. The horizontal massing of flowers and foliage may partially or wholly conceal the container.

side of the container to the other side. Position the side pieces first, close to the lip of the container, flowing over the side in a curving movement. The length will vary according to the height of the container. Using fine flowers or foliage, continue across the arrangement until the outline resembles a crescent moon. If you intend to use one or more candles in the design leave a slight hole at the top of the oasis to accept them. The flowers may be arranged close to the candle but allow for sufficient length of candle so that the flame does not come into contact with the flowers.

Continue to fill in the design with graded material until you reach the central area. At the focal area introduce some larger leaves to soften the edge of the container. The flowers at the centre should be positioned so that they complete the curving line. Turn two of the flowers to point towards the ends of the arrangement, then arrange the remainder as the design demands.

I mentioned briefly using candles with this shape of flower arrangement. They may be used in conjunction with the regular crescent, but are more often used in the inverted crescent. The candle should be fixed centrally, following the upward line of the container. The thickness of some candles may damage the oasis, so it is better if they can be fixed firmly into position without actually piercing the oasis. One simple method is to tape three cocktail sticks on to the lower end of the candle. Leave at least 1in (2.5cm) projecting over the end of the candle for positioning in the oasis.

Annual and biennial flowers are ideal material for this charming shape. Their slender stems adopt the curving shapes that are necessary for the crescent shape.

FRONT FACING Changes in personal life style have brought about change to the art of flower arranging. The greatest change has taken place in where we live, as houses have become smaller. Room size has decreased, the way furniture is arranged around the room has altered. It is no longer possible in the average house to have free-standing furniture in the middle of the room, on which to arrange flowers. Because furniture is now generally placed around the edges of a room, flower arrangements placed on these are only seen from a frontal angle. Obvious exceptions are arrangements for the dining table and those arranged specifically to be seen 'all round'.

Flowers that are arranged for frontal effect have no restrictions on their shape, but the principles of design still apply to get the desired effect. The major stumbling block that I encounter is in avoiding a flat look in the completed arrangement. The written word does not convey exactly what is meant by 'flat'. It is when the flowers are arranged so that the heads are in one vertical plane. If you place the palm of your hand on the flowers, you are able to feel that they are all at the same level. The solution is in the placing of the flowers and foliage, particularly the first four or five pieces. It is essential that the whole area of stem support, whether oasis or pinholder, is used.

Position the first stem, usually height material, towards the back of the mechanics. This fixes the dimension of depth and leaves sufficient room for the remaining plant material. The side stems should be on or behind the central horizontal axis. Flowers and foliage used to strengthen the first placements may be positioned to the back and front of it. There will now be a physical and visual thickness to the outline. Once the framework has been completed, arrange shorter pieces over the front lip of the container so that you have a workable depth from the tip of this to the rear of the arrangement. Place a number of leaves at the centre, some flowing over the front to break the line of the mechanics. Position one or two leaves pointing backwards, so they direct the eye to rear of the arrangement. Fill in the shape with transitional flowers, staggering them across the horizontal axis so that some are close to the front of the arrangement while others stand further back.

Colour is a factor in establishing depth. Darker colours recede, placed deeper into the design, while lighter colours are advancing and give the appearance of being closer to you. If the plant material being used will allow, angle the stem slightly so that the flower head relieves any strong frontal direction.

Flowers for the focal area should not be arranged in a way that makes them too eye-catching. It is easy to assume that because they are special their purpose is solely to attract attention. Bring at least one flower over the rim of the container and use the rest as an accent to the line of the arrangement. One piece of advice that I was given about attracting the eye from front to back in flower arranging was the inclusion of the colour yellow, in small quantities, low in the design towards the back of the focal area. I have done this many times and am pleased to say that it works successfully.

LANDSCAPE This is a design to convey an impression of nature – a landscape arrangement should indicate natural growth. With traditional styles of arranging we try to effect a natural growth pattern, but the sophisticated shapes of the completed arrangement often deny this.

Inspiration for this type of arrangement surrounds us. Woodlands will conjure up pictures of stately trees casting shadows over carpets of bluebells and primroses, while wild moorland will make us think of stunted trees, contorted by eternal winds, balancing precariously on lichen-covered rocks. Landscape extends to the water's edge, lake pond

Front facing design
Many different shapes of arrangement may be styled for a frontal rather than all-round viewpoint. Stems should be positioned to enhance the depth of the design from front to back.

Landscape design
This broad category allows highly imaginative use of material, which may incorporate stone or driftwood and special features such as statuary or other appropriate objects.

or sea. The inclusion of water in an arrangement has a most calming and tranquil effect.

Landscape arrangements that depict the countryside should be composed of wild plant material. Permission to pick the material is essential and then only pick flowers that you know are common. It is almost a duty of those who are concerned with plant material to know which wild flowers are endangered, particularly in your own county. Protect these by not cutting them and ensure that fellow enthusiasts are also aware of them.

Manageable branches with interesting shapes that resemble trees are useful in creating an atmosphere of the countryside. The branch can be fixed on a pinholder, inside a dish that will hold sufficient water. Bases of natural material – slate, wood and stone – are more in keeping than cloth-bound bases. Natural groupings of plant material may be placed at the base of the branch, or positioned at a distance. A secondary placement away from the main stem introduces a sense of perspective. The plant material for a landscape arrangement is endless and quite a lot can be grown in your own garden. To protect the flowers of the countryside, you may find it useful to turn a small section of your garden into a wild patch. An increasing number of seed merchants now carry a stock of wild flower and grass seeds. These can be grown with other flowers and foliages, ferns, moss, funghi, sedges, thistles – even the humble dandelion.

Driftwood is a logical piece of landscape influence. Its natural origins make it a common denominator for the various styles of landscape.

As wild flowers look better in a country landscape, cultivated flowers are an obvious choice for the garden-style landscape. The principles are still the same, to convey an impression of the garden. Garden flowers are more sophisticated than their country cousins and the setting for them should convey this. Popular features in garden landscapes are pieces of statuary. If it is possible to enclose the statue with a pergola in miniature, the effect is much stronger. Be careful not to include too much garden atmosphere. The flowers should be allowed to convey their message, without being hidden under a pile of gardening gloves and broken plant pots.

Seascapes in flower show competitions always attract a great deal of attention. The design is often a combination of unusual plant material, of colours, that, in any other situation would scream at each other. Soft pinks with orange, lime green and sludgy purple are some of the combinations that I have seen. Flower arrangers who favour this type of arranging have a knack for searching out unusual things and combining them with restraint. The framework for a seascape is often driftwood, sometimes lightly coloured with an aerosol paint. Small sections of fishing net draped across, used with seaweed and shells, heighten the effect. Very little plant material is required, as seashores tend to be hostile to luxuriant growth.

Suitable flowers and foliages are *Acanthus, Achillea ptarmica* 'The Pearl', *Agrostemma, Armeria,* preserved or fresh *Ballota,* Grasses (especially *Briza maxima*), *Centaurea, Senecio, Salvia, Echinops* and *Eryngium.* When you are walking along the seashore gathering bits and pieces to arrange, take time to stand and study the landscape and the water's edge. The authenticity of a landscape is part of its appeal.

DESIGNS FOR PRESERVED PLANT MATERIAL Without due care, dried and preserved plant material can become a collection, rather like stamps torn from old envelopes. There is a great temptation to preserve everything in sight, just because it might come in useful one day. The 'one day' very rarely comes and the collection grows until you no longer have space to store it. This is a waste of your time and effort, not to mention the preserving agent. Preserve with a purpose – always have an idea when and where it is going to be used. It is a good idea to have a box of spare preserved flowers and foliage to use when fresh material is not available.

Preserved flowers and foliage may be used in the same way as fresh plant material. Care should be exercised to avoid them coming into contact with moisture. The containers for dry flower arrangements should be of a natural colour that will harmonize with the flower colour. Basketry and pots that are made of clay have a greater sympathy with the texture of preserved plant material. Once it could be said that dried flowers were dull, but with today's methods of instantly preserving colour this should not be so. If an arrangement lacks a colour that is missing from your preserved cache, fresh flowers can be easily included. Assuming that you are using dry foam for mechanics, put the fresh flowers in tubes. The type used for transporting fresh orchids will do, and a small length of cane taped to the tube will make the positioning easier.

Other preserved materials require a background to support them. Garlands, plaques, swags, collage and dried flower pictures are such arrangements. The backgrounds should be flexible for garlands and on occasions swags, and rigid for plaques, collage and pictures. The method of stem support is different for each type of background.

A garland is a collection of plant material assembled rope fashion on a flexible background. Its name suggests its use, for example decorating the edge of a buffet table or twisted around columns for church decoration. Two easy methods of constructing the mechanics use sphagnum moss or discarded water-retaining foam. To make a garland base, measure the length of the garland by pinning a piece of thin string into the position the garland will finally be. This template will enable you to gauge the balance of the loops that the completed garland will assume. Cut a piece of thick cord to the same length – a washing line, but not the plastic type, is ideal for this.

Sphagnum moss is a naturally occurring plant, growing in water-logged areas of the countryside. In its fresh state it is a bright green colour and looks strangely like compressed parsley. Closer inspection will reveal an intricate ball of fine fibres reminiscent of deep sea sponges. Once it has been harvested, it quickly dries out and becomes firm, changing its colour from green to a silvery grey. The outstanding quality of this moss is its ability to reabsorb moisture and to regain its original soft, springy texture. Large quantities of this moss may be difficult to locate naturally, but it is available commercially. Your local flower club will probably carry a supply or be able to tell you where to buy it. Any left over will not be wasted, as it can be used as a foundation mechanic for other forms of flower arranging.

Swag
A looped or garlanded swag is a delightful variation of the flower arranger's art. It is a suitable subject for preserved materials which form a permanent decoration, but can also be made up with fresh foliage and flowers for a special occasion.

Large quantities of this moss may be difficult to locate naturally, but it is available commercially. Your local flower club will probably carry a supply or be able to tell you where to buy it. Any left over will not be wasted, as it can be used as a foundation mechanic for other forms of flower arrnging.

The tricky job is fixing the moss on to the rope. For this you will need a reel of florist's wire – a thin gauge is easier to handle. Tie the free end of the reel wire to one end of the cord, and place a suitable amount of moss around a short section of the cord. Pass the wire around, working in a spiralling movement along the section, spacing the wire to a width of your thumb. This distance may be altered depending on the amount of moss being used. The tension of the wire should be enough to secure the moss without compressing it. Remember that flower stems have got to pass through it. Progress along the cord until it is covered with moss and tie off the wire at the completed end.

Once the moss has dried out it becomes slightly brittle and then very fine stems are difficult to position. To overcome this, before you begin to arrange the material, spray the moss with water and allow it to dry. Arrange the plant material at the point when the moss has almost dried, but is still flexible. The method of arranging a garland is similar to arranging in the conventional way. The garland will have a central focus if it is for edging a table. The plant material should radiate from this point, and a repeated pattern is appropriate. Larger pieces of plant material will be required at certain points where the garland reaches the top of the table. If it is twisted around a column, these will be where the garland comes into line of view. Before the garland is arranged, mark these areas with a spot of paint, so that you know when to change the size of the plant material.

Dried garlands are permanent, and with careful handling they require the minimum of maintenance. Dust will be the only problem, which can be removed with a hair dryer.

Sphagnum moss does not hold water for long periods. If fresh flowers are to be included, saturate the assembled moss and wrap it with very fine polythene.

A similar base can be devised using old water-retaining foam. Used oasis does not successfully reabsorb moisture, so where fresh flowers are being used replace the old oasis with new. Allow the discarded foam to dry completely and carve it into sections with a knife. Assemble the sections against the cord and wrap them with plastic. The plastic must be thin enough for the stems to penetrate – kitchen film or the protective bags from the dry cleaning shops are suitable. A wooden cocktail stick will pierce the plastic to accept stems that would otherwise break. Arrange the plant material in the same way as suggested for the sphagnum moss garland.

Fixing the completed swag or garland often presents a problem. For a covered table, use nylon fishing line and a darning needle to catch the top of the garland loop. Pass the thread under the cloth and secure it to the table leg. Fishing line will act as a strong support where garlands are suspended, but it should not be used to tie around large pillars. Special methods will be required for this, peculiar to the situation.

Plaques, collage and flower pictures are collections of plant material attached to a rigid background. The plant material is linked together to form a pattern or create a picture. Plaques must have no visible background for competitive work, but for domestic purposes it need not be so. Collage generally has a visible background, and requires less plant material, which need not be linked. This type of picture work is an ideal medium for studies in texture and colour. Flower pictures always look more attractive on a framed background; the addition of glass or similar protection is optional.

The above descriptions are basic and are suggested for use in the home. Should you consider entering a flower competition that calls for any of these designs, always consult the official definition handbook of the society which is staging the show. It will tell you exactly what is required.

Common to the four categories of design is the rigid background. It is usual to make them of thin wood, though transparent or coloured plastics are interesting alternatives. Where the design is to be permanent, thin plywood is recommended. The local do-it-yourself shop will probably cut it to the size you require. Peg board may be more suitable if you want to dismantle the plant material or if the material is too heavy to be fixed into position with glue. Large, heavy pieces of material can be wired to the board, passing the wire through the holes and securing it at the back. Smaller pieces, too delicate to be wired, may be glued on to complete the design and conceal any exposed holes.

Whether the background is covered or not, the finish should always be of a high standard. The dimensions are important – if the board is oblong, the length and breadth should be in proportion. Ovals and circles can be formed by tracing around plates. This might mean taking the plate to the DIY shop, but I'm sure they won't mind.

Smooth the edges of the wood using a sheet of glass paper and blow away any wood dust. The hanging device should be fixed to background before any other work is done. Rings or picture hooks are obtainable from hardware shops and picture-framing shops. Any advice from the picture framer about how to fix them will be useful. My method is that great boon to the flower arranger – 'super glue'. In many instances it has superseded the nail and screw. Always read the instructions carefully, as such glue dries very quickly and from my experience it is permanent.

The background can now be painted or covered with cloth. If you paint the background, choose a matt finish paint in a shade of colour that will enhance the design. Dark colours, viewed from a distance, tend to dominate the scene, almost obscuring the plant material. Gloss paint is reflective and, like a strong colour, will detract from the plant material. If the background is covered with cloth, select the texture carefully, choosing one that suits the plant material. Cloth with a broad weave such as hessian, is more in keeping with plant material that has a rough texture or a very strong colour. Linens and velvet will be suitable for delicate forms and colours.

Cut the fabric to the size of the background, allowing at least a ½in (1.2cm) overlap all round for glueing on the back. Where the board is oblong or square, mitre the corners of the cloth to prevent it distorting. Oval and round shapes should have the overlap cut at intervals, for the same reason. Before you fix the fabric into position, test a small piece to check if the glue seeps through and marks the surface. Raise the background from the working surface on to a cake tin or something similar. This makes turning the board over to work on the reverse easier. Spread the adhesive over one surface of the background. Fold the cloth in half, front to front and lay it on one half of the glued surface. Turn back the folded section and smooth out the trapped air bubbles, working from the centre outwards. Allow the adhesive to dry completely before you attempt the next stage. Place the background on the working surface face down and apply adhesive around the edges. Fold the overlap material on to the adhesive, doing each cut section separately. Press the cloth towards the centre to prevent any bumps appearing on the edge of the background. Any faults that appear at the edges can be camouflaged with braid, and in any case a border will give a much neater finish. To do this, run the braid around the background to determine the length required. Use a pair of very sharp scissors to cut the braid, for it frays easily and the ends will be difficult to conceal neatly. Run a fine line of adhesive on to the braid. Let it soak in, and do not apply the adhesive to the background, for any error means a lot of hard work to be done again. Place one end of the braid to the edge and pin it into position. Continue round the background pinning the braid at intervals.

Now that the background is completed, decide how you are going to fix the plant material. Dry foam is one method, which can be glued to the board or wired on through previously drilled holes. Slow-drying clays, specially designed for holding dried plant material, are available commercially from art and craft shops. The clay will need to be secured to the background. Determine the size that you will need and bore four equidistant holes into the board. Using a cross-over pattern, thread wire through the holes over the clay and secure them at the back of the background. The most popular method is adhesive. Buy a good-quality brand – one that does not set instantly – as you may need to reposition some of the material. The glue should be non-stringing with a fine dispenser for accurate positioning, without a puddle forming. You may apply the adhesive directly to the plant material or spread a small amount on an old dish to dip the plant material in. Very delicate flowers and fine stems should be held by a pair of tweezers. Fingers and thumbs, no matter how light the pressure, always get in the way.

Assemble everything that you need on a protected surface. Work under a strong light so that you can see clearly where each piece is to be fixed. Consider where the completed picture is going and choose your colour scheme and design accordingly. Lay the dried materials in position, trying out combinations of line and form until you are satisfied. I rarely decide on the first layout; other ideas often occur as you introduce new materials. Part of the fascination of dried flower picture work is the dry-run arranging and rearranging. When you have decided on a design, remove each piece in reverse order and place them on the working surface in an orderly line. Clean the surface of the background, use a dry paint brush or dab the surface with a piece of cellophane tape. Starting with the last piece of plant material removed, re-create the design permanently.

The art of arranging dried plant material on a background is a subject in itself. It is worthwhile investing in a book about this subject to discover the many ideas that exist about flower pictures.

MODERN ARRANGEMENTS Modern flower arrangements by definition are arrangements of today. They are a break from traditional styles of arranging, where the emphasis was on massed line using quantities of flowers. This has resulted in arrangements that are imaginative in their use of colour, form and line. The appeal should be instant – like modern art or sculpture, it should attract your attention immediately. To gain this attention, modern flower arrangements should not be composed of excessive, distracting plant material. The line should be positive and the flowers bold and well defined. Modern arrangements have a place in the home whether the decor is traditional or modern.

Containers for modern work are often custom-built on lines that are smooth without any traditional embellishment. The surface finish should not be sophisticated – unglazed or a matt glaze are suitable. Generally the mechanics are built in, with holes and recesses that will accept oasis or a pinholder. The overall atmosphere of the container should be one of restraint coupled with a feeling of solidity and permanence. The plant material should echo this restraint. Very often the mechanics will not allow a large quantity of material to be used. For this reason, use flowers that are unusual and interesting. These will create the impact that you need. The method of arranging the flowers and foliage is similar to that for traditional work, but a greater emphasis is placed upon the elements and principles of design. Space is a very important element in modern design as a balancing element or as an area of design interest.

Leaves of the *Iris* and *Phormium tenax* can be rolled at the tip to form a circle, and fixed with a staple. These may be used high in the design, as a complement to round-form flowers positioned lower down. Fixed low down in the container, at an angle, they balance a tall piece of driftwood arranged at an opposing angle. The balance of the arrangement should be strong, possibly exaggerated, but at the same time visually acceptable. By using limited numbers of flowers and associated plant material, the variations in scale will be slight, so good balance should be secured first. It can rarely be corrected by adding additional plant material. In most cases you will find asymmetrical balance easier. The arrangement should follow natural growth patterns, with a focal area. The movement or rhythm of a modern arrangement is distinctly linear, and by altering the focal area flowers to form new shapes, the interest of the design will be enhanced. Flowers used in this area should be bold and arresting to look at. Numerous small flowers are fussy and generally detract from the line of the arrangement.

Depth and transition of plant material are often lacking in modern arrangements. Grading the size of the flowers and turning them at slight angles is one way of introducing them. If it is possible to use foliage with a pointed leaf, arrange some with the point aimed towards the back of the arrangement. This will carry your eye from the front to the back. Contrast and proportion are essential principles. With limited amounts of plant material you will have to work harder at achieving these principles. Consider colour, texture and the container for this. One of the easiest principles to introduce is rhythm, simply through repetition of colour and form.

A number of outside influences can affect modern arrangements. The increased use of space as a design element alters the amount of light surrounding the flowers. Where there are no adjacent flowers to cast shadows or influence the flower colour, the colours will be clearer. The shape of the arrangement can be transformed by the surroundings. A well-balanced arrangement, for instance, with the balance from top left through to bottom right, can appear unbalanced if something distracting is placed close to the left of the arrangement. There may be occasions when painted plant material is used. Dried and preserved plant material accepts artificial colour, but use it sparingly and with taste. There are aerosol paints available to change the colour of fresh flowers, though to me this defeats the object of gardening and flower arranging. Nature has provided a limitless list of colours so why change them? The instructions on the aerosol can will state that it does not affect the cut life of the flower, but I am sure that it must.

There is a certain curiosity value attached to modern flower arrangements. Other arrangers and friends will want to know about the mechanics or what inspired the design. Because of this interest, the components of the arrangement must be immaculate. Where space permits, use oasis as the mechanics. The greater the volume of water, the longer the flowers will last. Though oasis is easy to use, it requires more material to conceal it, and this may confuse the impact of the arrangement. Try an alternative covering medium that is not so distracting. Sphagnum moss, bound with short wires, allowed to dry, is unusual, and its neutral colour will not be eye-catching. Pinholder mechanics may be covered with a handful of pebbles or glass marbles.

This category of design is useful for displaying some of the more fascinating preserved materials. A semi-permanent display can be arranged using dried foliage within dry foam. Fresh flowers can then be included to suit the occasion. They will have to be positioned in plastic tubes of water before being arranged. The *Allium* family provides an array of interesting seed heads, particularly *Allium siculum*. The stem can be anything up to 4ft (120cm) long and the bell-shaped green-white flowers have a spread of up to 4in (10cm). When fresh, the flowers hang downwards, but as the seed pod develops the flower stem straightens until it resembles the turrets of a Walt Disney castle. *Allium albopilosum* has an even larger seed head, reaching 6in (15cm) in diameter. Lightly gilded with gold, they are a fascinating inclusion for Christmas arrangements. The stem is somewhat smaller, about 18in (45cm). *Nigella* is a common favourite. The seed head is an inflated, pale brown pod. For me, its charm is in its generosity, as from a single packet of seeds, you have an eternal supply of fresh and self-dried material, due to its remarkable self-seeding property.

Artificial flowers can be constructed from dried plant material for use in modern flower arrangements. Their individuality will give the arrangement distinction, especially if the combinations of plant material are unusual.

No reference has been made to the shape of a modern flower arrangement in this chapter. There is no tradition on which to base a shape. In most cases the container will dictate the line of the flower arrangement. The modern arrangement is an amalgam of design principles arranged with freedom and personal expression. Once you have generated an interest in modern arranging, you will be absorbed, constantly looking for new materials and accessories to try out new ideas.

Modern style
Space is an important feature of modern design. Bold, well defined lines and unusual shapes are arranged to create a striking impact.

COLOUR

My first recollection of colour was as a child at school. To help us memorize the colours of a rainbow, a long-suffering teacher made the entire class repeat 'Richard Of York Gave Battle In Vain' (Red Orange Yellow Green Blue Indigo Violet). It wasn't until some years later, as a flower arranger with an awareness of colour, that I thanked Richard for losing that battle.

Contact with colour usually comes before we become interested in gardening and flower arranging – almost by tradition, but more often by fashion – blue for a boy, pink for a girl or the latest autumn fashion colour dictated by an unseen and sometimes unflattering designer.

Tradition and fashion have also influenced garden colour. The garden of a country cottage is often very colourful, created by the traditional plants associated with that style of garden. Blue and purple lupins, rose pink hollyhock, white daisies and large red roses were typical of the plants that had to be grown. In contrast, the large, landscaped garden of the stately home was a rolling expanse of green, the shape and form of plants, usually trees and large shrubs, being of prime importance. The more humble garden had a tendency towards vegetables, which, though colourful in themselves, often hid their beauty below ground.

The popularity of annual and biennial flowers has certainly changed the appearance of gardens today. Colour is now a mobile unit, which can be brought close to the house, extending the interior colour schemes to the garden, or shaded into the distance to indulge a prejudice for a favourite colour. Remember also that shrubs with seasonal colour changes or variegated foliage serve to widen the range of colours for co-ordination with flowering plants.

Allow your eye to influence your choice of material for growing and cutting. The colour guidelines explained in this chapter are intended to create a link between the flower colours listed in the Encyclopedia of Plants and the context and surroundings in which a completed arrangement will be seen. There is much to be gained from a clearer understanding of basic colour theory but flower arranging deals, after all, with a purely natural range of hues. There are no fixed rules; no 'right' scheme or combination. You have only to think of the glorious variety of a summer garden in full bloom to realize this principle. Sticking rigidly to a choice that is generally considered acceptable denies you the pleasure of colour and the excitement of experimentation.

The colour chart reproduced at the end of this chapter is not designed to overpower you with technical detail, but to explain the basic relationships of colours and their 'behaviour' in different combinations. It is not uncommon to find that the colours you would mix instinctively do correspond to one of the systematic schemes demonstrated by the colour wheel. The basic appreciation of harmonies and contrasts tends to come naturally. But colours have moods, associations and reactions which can be put to use. By identifying these elements, you may be able to extend your range of choice and select more deliberately towards a planned effect. The following paragraphs explain the basic principles of colour grouping and should be read with reference to the chart on page 49. Examples of selected flowers for the main types of colour arrangement are included, also taking account of the shape, line and direction of the material within the design.

MONOCHROMATIC A monochromatic colour scheme is one using hues, tints, tones and shades of one colour. This style of arrangement, for me, is an indulgence. It is an opportunity to use a favourite colour. This is perfectly acceptable if the situation is right. All too often an arrangement of one colour will lose its impact if not enough attention has been paid to its final position. Decide first where you are going to put the arrangement, then select flowers that will complement the surroundings. A monochromatic arrangement can be both subtle and elegant against a pale background, or quite arresting if one colour from a 'busy' background is chosen and accentuated.

Certain seasons, particularly high summer, provide a wide range of colour to use in this way. Pure colours are best kept to a minimum. If the arrangement is large, the eye soon gets tired of large areas of bright colour. A modern or free-form design is more acceptable. Traditional designs are easier to create using tints, tones and shades. As most garden flowers have this variation in colour, you will not be restricted to one type.

It can be an interesting exercise in colour blending. Using the palest tints at the edge of the arrangement, work towards the centre with tones and shades, completing the design with a focal area of pure colour.

Some colour ranges are not as prolific as others. Violet and blue do not have the range of colour deviation that red, yellow and orange have. This lack of colour shading can be compensated by using extra toning foliage. Self-coloured foliage of a darker shade is an excellent foil for pale coloured flowers. A variegated green, or soft grey leaf, used with flowers of a pure hue, can often lighten the effect. Foliage shouldn't be overlooked as a component for a monochromatic arrangement. The innumerable shades of green and variegated greens make it almost indispensable when flowers are not available.

An arrangement of one colour will not always be possible, as flower colour has an infuriating habit of not coming to order. When this happens, introduce plant material of an adjacent colour. Giving an illusion of colour, when you can't be accurate, is better than nothing.

COMPLEMENTARY At first glance, complementary colours can appear discordant, particularly when using pure colour. They are on opposite sides of the colour wheel and are not related by colour. They excite each other, so care must be taken over the amount of flower colour used. The traditionalists amongst us will find pure colour too strident for use in an arrangement with lots of flowers. Use the tints and tones of the lighter colour, on the outside of the arrangement and fill in the centre with shades of the darker complementary colour. The focal area can be pure colour of the darker complement, or a mixture of both. Introducing colour from the edge of an arrangement to the centre helps to increase the visual balance.

Pure colour is usually present in the larger flowers. These can be used to great advantage in a modern or free-form complementary design, used almost as blocks of colour. The flowers can be placed very close together, with an accent on line, or used to form a pattern. Like the traditional arrangements, lighter colours can be taller and more numerous, with the darker colours, creating the central balance of the design.

As complementary arrangements contain only two colours, they are best suited to a surrounding of limited colour. Complementary colours can be used to emphasize or play down a particular room colour. Selecting the weakest room colour and highlighting this, using flowers of the same colour with a strong chroma, will make the room colour more noticeable. Conversely, a very strong area of colour can be reduced, by using its complement in flower colour.

Flowers for a complementary scheme should be easy to find in the garden. Most growers have a passion for diversity in flower colour. It is this contrast in colour that often attracts us to them. We may not like the combination at first, since we always look for harmony between colours. It is only with constant use that you begin to appreciate the combination of opposite colours. The colours don't have to be of the same value, to complement. Red and green, in its pure form, is a dazzling combination, but change the green to a softer tint and the combination becomes more acceptable.

ADJACENT Adjacent colours generally cover four sections of the colour wheel and have one unifying primary colour.

Most homes feature adjacent colours, for they are easy to live with and are comfortable on the eye. For this reason you will find adjacent colours easy to use.

Nature also favours this easy blending of colour, particularly with foliage. A slight change of colour in a leaf or flower has always been of interest to the gardener and flower arranger. It acts as a physical link between plants of a plain colour in the garden and expands the range of colour for this type of arrangement.

Adjacent colours containing yellow are the most common. It is one of the brighter colour schemes and is most suited to highlighting a shaded area of the home. Against a background of a darker colour it has great definition. A dramatic effect can be created using adjacent colours with red as a primary, especially in surroundings that have complementary colours to act as a foil.

Adjacent colours that include blue should be used carefully. Blue is a receding colour and will dilute, if it comes into contact with certain strengths of artificial light. To correct this draining of colour will be a matter of trial and error. Repositioning the arrangement closer to natural light will help. Testing the flowers against the chosen situation before they are arranged is probably the best answer. Some people regard adjacent colours with blue as an intimate association, more suited to smaller, delicate arrangements, where each flower remains an individual. This regard is probably the saviour of blue, because the smaller the arrangement, the easier it is to relocate.

Certain adjacent colour schemes are more appealing than others. Greens/yellows are welcoming and cheerful, blues/greens create a cool, tranquil atmosphere, and in this lies their appeal. The area of reds/violets can be a vibrant combination and is often ignored. This is where the use of colour tone is important – adjacent colours blend more easily when tints, tones and shades are used in place of pure hue.

NEUTRAL COLOURS Black, white and grey are considered to be neutral colours, and their purpose is to alter the value of pure colour. Neutral colours are useful when used in association with flower colour, as container, base or background colour. Most basic containers are either black or white, and don't intrude on the flower arrangement. Grey is often used as a background colour in competitive flower arranging, as it has the ability to enhance all colours shown against it.

Though black, white and grey do not appear on the colour chart, they should not be overlooked as plant material colour. Nature somehow is at odds with the artist in this respect. Very little black is available in plant material; grey is reduced to a small area of foliage and the odd flower, but white is in abundance. The lack of black in plant material has led to a fashion for painting dried plant material. You must decide whether you find this acceptable. A limited number of plants have an almost black appearance – the *Ophiopogon planiscapus nigrescens*, usually described as a bedding plant in some catalogues, can be potted up and used in a pot-et-fleur. The grey foliage of *Senecio laxifolius* or the more interestingly shaped leaf of *Senecio monroi* blends perfectly with flowers in shades of pink and blue.

White as flower colour often changes from its pure form under certain conditions, and will often fade to cream or adopt streaks of colour as it ages. When arranged with flowers of a strong, pure colour, white will reflect a glow of the pure colour.

Moods can be conveyed in white flowers, something you will find yourself doing unconsciously. White combined with blue has a soothing, tranquil effect, the more so on a warm day. White is not a colour restricted to the artist's palette but has a part to play in flower arranging.

BACKGROUND COLOUR Colour cannot be isolated, so it is important to choose plant material in a colour that will suit the background. The flowers can complement, blend or even compete with it. Colour in the home is usually fixed; you may have lived with it for a long time and be unaware of its strength or weakness. Flowers that you thought would associate well suddenly do not. It is always a good idea to think of the position of the arrangement first, then what flowers to use.

Make background colour work for you – its colour should always be subservient to the flower arrangement. Even walls painted vivid red can be dulled with the skilful use of adjacent or monochromatic flower colour. It is often said that nowhere in the home is safe from a flower arranger, but this also holds the challenge of situation colour. Do not allow it to defeat you. There is a colour scheme for all conditions – your arranger's 'eye' for colour will make everything possible.

CONTAINER COLOUR Choose a colour that will at all times enhance the flower arrangement. An ill-matched container will reduce the harmony of the design, splitting the design into two separate sections, flower and container. Neutral colours – black, white and grey – have proved to be satisfactory, as their lack of colour makes them less intrusive. Certain styles of container demand a natural colour, earthenware pots in shades of brown, metal in silver or brass. These can be varied a little with the application of paint, though it should not be to a point of unrecognizability. Some containers have no recognizable colour, for example, glass. This special quality satisfies all colour schemes, providing the surface is not so highly polished and reflective that it will compete for attention. As a general guide to container colour, have at least one colour that is common to both the plant material and the container. If you are unsure about the choice of container, try one or two differing colours against the chosen background before you begin to arrange the flowers.

Flowers for a monochromatic arrangement

Tints, tones and shades of pink

Gladiolus **'Peach Blossom'**
Height material

Agrostemma **'Milas'**
Intermediate round flowers which may be placed to lead from the edge of the design to the centre.

Dicentra spectabilis
This is a unique flower of great distinction which may be used in limited numbers to hang gracefully over the front and sides of the container.

Erigeron speciosus **'Dimity'**
A useful filler in a clear light pink tint and having a good textural contrast to *Agrostemma*

Saxifraga **'Rosea'**
A very dainty flower which will lighten the focal area

Clarkia
The long stems and variety of colour will offset the taller, pointed flowers and foliage

Dianthus allwoodii, **or Border Carnations**
Delightful flowers for the focal area

Valuable foliages for an arrangement of pink flowers are *Senecio laxifolius* (grey), *Acer palmatum* 'Dissectum Garnet' (crimson) and *Bergenia cordifolia* 'Purpurea' (purple-bronze)

Flowers for an arrangement of complementary colours

Blue and orange – hues that are opposite and mutually enhancing

Aconitum napellus **'Newry Blue'**
Tall flowers to establish a strong upward line and side spikes bringing the colour down to the lip of the container

Kniphofia **'Fiery Fred'**
A flexible-stemmed flower that will accentuate the linear direction of the design and flow downwards from the central axis

Gaillardia **'Mandarin'**
The round, brilliant orange flowers will create a contrast of form adding special interest

A fine sculptural effect is gained from the addition of the broad, glossy foliage of *Fatsia japonica*

These striking materials should be used in limited amounts to create a free form design. The container colour may be chosen to enhance the focus or either of the flower colours

Flowers for an arrangement of adjacent colours

Green, yellow-green, yellow, yellow-orange – hues that are graded and harmonious

Sisyrinchium striatum
A small but tall-stemmed flower that establishes the outline of the design

Achillea filipendula **'Moonshine'**
Rounded forms with a good length of stem to strengthen the contours of the design

Solidago canadensis **'Golden Baby'**
Spray flowers introducing a softer texture

Euphorbia palustris
A flat shape and intriguing yellow-green tone to introduce contrast

Molucella laevis
Select material from this plant in different stages of development, an unusual addition introducing a distinctive green

Rudbeckia
Intermediate focal area material selected in colours to suit the range

Attractive foliages for this flower choice include ferns and grasses or material from *Aucuba*, *Choisya* or *Wiegela florida* 'Variegata'

COLOUR COMMENTS I have attempted to indicate the flexibility of flower colour in this chapter. No two people see the same colour and it would be unfair for me to influence your judgment about colour. There are, however, one or two facts that will help you to avoid any disastrous associations, without minimizing the enjoyment of using colour.

Colour weight Colour can appear to be light or heavy according to the amount of black or white present. More white creates a light effect, more black makes the colour look heavy. Pure colour is a fixed value; its colour weight is governed by its surrounds.

Pure colour Small areas of pure colour are easy to look at and less tiring to the eye. Large areas can be harsh and often adversely affect the visual balance of an arrangement.

Colour illusion Some colours appear closer to you than others. Orange, red and yellow are advancing colours and have the effect of being nearer to the viewer. Blue and violet are receding colours and give the illusion of being further from you. Green is considered to be neutral, though it can be influenced by yellow or blue.

Colour temperature Colour temperature illustrates the psychology of colour, how it affects our moods and associations. Orange and red remind us of fire and heat and are considered warm colours. When they are used in the autumn, they create an atmosphere of comfort and wellbeing. Blue and green are the illusive colours of water and are cooling colours. The cooling effect of a blue and green arrangement, particularly on a hot day, can be almost physical.

At certain times of the year it is difficult to meet set colour requirements accurately. Arrangements for the home generally follow a basic colour scheme, but attention to accurate detail is not necessary.

To complete this chapter, I will relate a comment, that I once heard at a flower show. It was about an arrangement in a class entitled 'Monochromatic Glory'. A small voice very close to me said 'I always thought red was red, until that judge told me it was purple.' It amused me at the time and I use it now as an answer if anyone asks me the question, 'What is colour?'

A GUIDE TO COLOUR The outer band indicates pure colour. Yellow, blue and red are primary colours, green, orange and purple are secondary colours. Secondary colours are made by mixing two primary colours. The remainder are tertiary colours, a mixture of primary and secondary, neighbour by neighbour.

Band two shows *tints* of pure colour, they are primary, secondary or tertiary mixed with white.

Band three *tones* of colour, pure colour mixed with grey. The inner band is pure colour mixed with black, known as *shades*. There are many tints, tones and shades of colour, depending upon the amount of black or white present in the pure colour. The amount of black or white modifying the lightness or darkness of a colour is referred to as the 'value' of colour.

The strength of a colour, that is, the degree of pure hue that is present and recognizable in the tone of a colour, is known as 'chroma'.

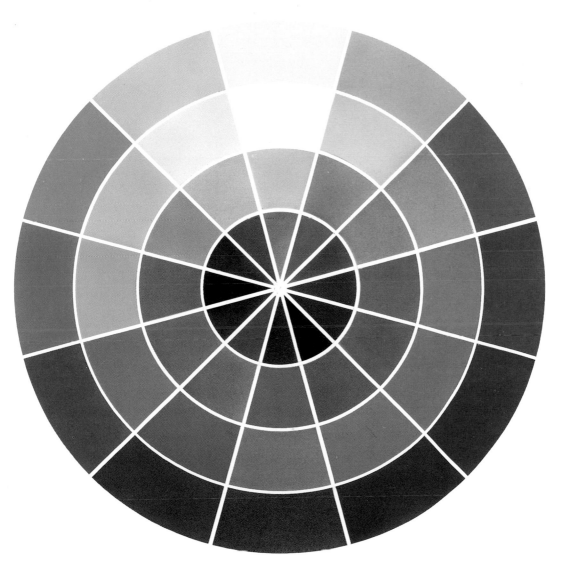

Monochromatic Using tints, tones and shades of one colour.
Adjacent Using up to four colours next to each other on the colour wheel.
Complementary Using colours that are opposite each other on the wheel.
Polychromatic Using many colours together.

Encyclopedia of Plants

The plant encyclopedia lists a wide range of plants producing flowers and foliage suitable for use in fresh and dried flower arrangements. Annual and biennial flowering plants and herbaceous perennials are organized in colour categories which enable you to plan co-ordination or contrast in an arrangement, whether you have a particular theme or occasion in mind or are searching out appropriate choices to decorate a favourite room. The plants are categorized according to dominant colour, or by the colour of particular species and cultivars which flower arrangers will find of constant value. To increase the range, a useful cross-referencing section is included at the end of the encyclopedia where you will find alternative possibilities for choice throughout the colour spectrum.

Many types of foliage deserve attention in their own right, as well as providing background and filler material for cut flower displays. The colours, textures and variegations are of immense variety and an arrangement of carefully selected foliages can match any flower display with its subtle beauty. The final section of the encyclopedia describes ornamental shrubs and trees offering beautiful and versatile foliage, with the added bonus that a number of the plants also bear attractive flowers and others provide decorative tassels or fruits to increase the arranger's stock of material.

Each entry in the plant encyclopedia describes the range of species and cultivars suitable for growing and arranging, followed by details of cultivation and propagation of the plants, the arranger's uses of the plant material and the specific techniques of conditioning or preserving the flowers or foliage. To assist in the selection of suitable material, a panel of symbols appears below the heading of each entry, enabling you to see at a glance the season in which the plants offer the best cut material, the length of stem and size of flower, the ability to preserve and the duration of cut life.

YELLOW

Achillea

Yarrow
Caucasus
Compositae

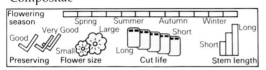

Flowering season	Spring	Summer	Autumn	Winter	
Good Very Good Small	Large Long	Short		Short	Long
Preserving	Flower size	Cut life			Stem length

Achillea filipendula

Achillea filipendula has stout stems which rise erectly from a basal tuft of grey-green feathery, richly pungent foliage and need no staking. The flowers, which are produced through the summer and autumn, are formed in the shape of densely packed heads, or corymbs, of yellow flowers. While these make splendid cut flowers during the flowering season, they are also a very useful dried flower subject. The most suitable hybrids to grow are:
'Gold Plate', bright yellow flowers, midsummer, height 4-5ft (120-150cm);
'Coronation Gold', lemon yellow flowers, midsummer to autumn, height 3ft (90cm);
'Moonshine', sulphur yellow flowers in midsummer, height 2ft (60cm).
A. millefolium 'Cerise Queen, bears cherry red flowers, midsummer to autumn, height 20in (50cm).

A. ptarmica 'The Pearl' has sprays of white button flowers, midsummer to early autumn, height 20in (50cm).
'W. B. Child', pure white, early summer, height 20in (50cm).
Cultivation and Propagation Achillea will grow successfully on a wide range of soils. It prefers a sunny situation. Propagation is by division of the roots in the late autumn or by seed in late spring. Germination will take some 14 to 21 days. When they are large enough to handle thin the resulting plants to 12in (30cm) apart in the row. Leave to grow on undisturbed until the late autumn when they are transplanted into their permanent position in an open sunny part of the garden. Leave plenty of space between the plants as their roots spread over a large area.
Uses As fresh material *A. filipendula* may be used as a focus for traditional arrangements in shades of yellow or as a highlight to a foliage design. *A. ptarmica* has white button flowers that are more suited to informal designs.
Conditioning Both varieties condition simply once they are mature. Crush the ends of the woody stems and stand them in deep water for at least 2 hours.
Preserving The flowers will dry on the plant but are susceptible to damage from rain. To keep the preserved flowers in good condition, collect them when all the flowers are fully developed and the stem has become woody. Tie them in very loose bunches and suspend them in a light airy atmosphere.

Anthemis

Ox-eye Chamomile
Europe
Compositae

Flowering season	Spring	Summer	Autumn	Winter	
Good Very Good Small	Large Long	Short		Short	Long
Preserving	Flower size	Cut life			Stem length

Anthemis tinctoria has lovely single daisy-like golden yellow flowers up to 3in (7.5cm) across, excellent for cutting, summer, height 2½ft (75cm). There are several hybrids available which have somewhat more upright habit.
A. t. 'Mrs E. C. Buxton', with light lemon yellow flowers.
A. t. 'Beauty of Grallagh', rich golden yellow flowers, height 2½ft (75cm).
A. t. 'Kelwayi', rich yellow flowers, height 2ft (60cm).
Cultivation and Propagation This is a very easy plant to grow on any ordinary garden soil which is reasonably well drained and enjoys full sun. It needs support if you want it to be of neat appearance and produce good straight flower-stems for cutting. Plant them 20in (50cm) apart

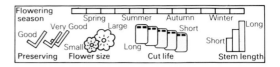

Flowering season	Spring	Summer	Autumn	Winter

Very Good — Good
Preserving · Flower size (Small · Large) · Cut life (Long · Short) · Stem length (Long · Short)

Anthemis tinctoria

in the row, with the rows 2½ft (75cm) apart. Regular weekly cutting of the flowers encourages flower production. Immediately flowering ceases in late summer cut the plants back to approximately 5in (12.5cm) above ground level to encourage fresh root development before activity ceases for the winter.

Propagation is usually by division of the roots in spring when fresh growth is commencing. New plants can also be produced from seed sown in the open ground in late spring. The resulting plants are thinned to stand 5in (12.5cm) apart in the row where they are left to develop. Transfer into their final flowering positions the following spring.

Uses Anthemis is not a flower that demands a dramatic or modern setting. Its unsophisticated appearance is best appreciated in a simple arrangement using an earthenware jug. Arrange them on their own or with a small amount of fern or grasses to extend the informal country atmosphere.

Conditioning They are undemanding to condition. Cut the open flowers at the coolest part of the day and remove any lower stem foliage. Stand them in cold water in a shaded area for 2 to 3 hours.

Preserving Desiccant and pressing are the only methods of preserving this flower. Its informality makes it a suitable subject for textural dried flower designs.

Coreopsis

North America
Compositae

Two species in particular are of importance to the flower arranger. One is the perennial species *C. grandiflora*, which is a native of the

Coreopsis grandiflora 'Mayfield Giant'

Southern United States of America. The other species is an annual, *C. tinctoria* syn. *C. bicolor* and *C. elegans*, which is a native of the Eastern United States.

C. grandiflora (Tickweed), height 3ft (90cm), produces yellow daisy-like flowers approximately 2½in (6.25cm) across at the top of good long stems which, as cut flowers, take up water very well thus giving them a long vase life. There are some good cultivars available.

C. g. 'Badengold', golden yellow flowers, 3in (7.5cm) across, will grow on very poor soil, height 3ft (90cm).

C. g. 'Mayfield Giant' deep yellow flowers, height 2½ft (75cm).

C. g. 'Perry's Variety' semi-double clear yellow flowers, height 2-2½ft (60-75cm). All flower during summer.

C. tinctoria has daisy-like flowers about 1½in (3.75cm) across. These are bright yellow in colour with a scarlet maroon central zone, height 2 to 2½ft (60 to 75cm).

C. t. 'Hybrida Double Mixed' has flowers which are fully double and semi-double in the colour range yellow, orange, crimson and maroon, height 3ft (90cm). These are carried on stiff wiry stems and ideal for cutting.

Among the dwarf cultivars there is *C. t.* 'Tiger Star', which is a real beauty, with its bronze striped and mottled yellow flowers, height 1ft (30cm). This succeeds everywhere even in the lead polluted area of road islands in the midst of our busy city streets traffic.

Cultivation and Propagation Coreopsis likes a sunny situation and seems to thrive in almost any type of soil providing it is well drained.

Propagation is by seed. Sow under cloches in

early spring or in open ground in late spring.
Seedlings of *C. tinctora* should be thinned to 9
to 12in (22.5 to 30cm) apart. They flower later
the same year. Thin plants of *C. grandiflora* to
6in (15cm) again in late summer and early
autumn. Watering may be necessary
throughout the summer. In the late autumn the
plants are transplanted into their permanent
position in either a flower border with other
perennials or in a special bed of their own. If
growing them in rows the plants should be set
out 2ft (60cm) apart in the row with the rows set
2½ft (75cm) apart.

Uses The simple form and clean colouring gives
this flower an unsophisticated charm. The
indented petals of the flower are an unusual
change when arranged with other rounded
forms. The intensity of colour associates well
with preserved foliage, particularly glycerined
beech with the addition of small amounts of the
lighter *Choisya ternata*. Cut the flowers in the
coolest part of the day, when they are charged
with moisture.

Conditioning To condition them, simply stand
them in deep water for up to 4 hours.

Preserving Individual flowers and petals may
be pressed or dried in desiccant. Once dried
they require careful handling as they become
very brittle.

Doronicum

Leopard's Bane
Europe, Asia Minor
Compositae

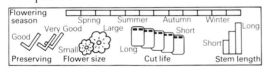

Doronicum is an important plant for the flower
arranger, as it is one of the first to flower in the
springtime. The earliest species to flower is
Doronicum cordatum, which has large golden
daisies in spring, on 6in (15cm) stems.
D. caucasicum has deep yellow flowers
approximately 2in (5cm) across in late spring,
height 16in (34cm) and *D. c.* 'Spring Beauty' has
fully double deep yellow flowers.
D. plantagineum is a native plant of Britain and
Western Europe and has a couple of very
attractive cultivars in the form of *D. p.*
'Excelsum', which produces a profusion of
bright yellow flowers, during early summer,
height 3ft (90cm), and *D. p.* 'Miss Mason', light
yellow flowers, in late spring, height 18in
(45cm).

Cultivation and Propagation *Doronicum* species
are very hardy and will flourish in any ordinary
garden soil providing that it is well cultivated
before their introduction and given a moderate
dressing of manure or garden compost. The

Doronicum caucasicum 'Spring Beauty'

roots benefit from being lifted and divided
every third year to keep the young and
vigorous plants. The best time to do this is just
after flowering. Earlier flowering can be
induced if some protection can be provided in
the form of a coldframe, or plants can be
carefully lifted and brought into a cool
greenhouse.

Uses *Doronicum* will produce an abundant
supply of flowers and if regularly dead headed
will crop again in the autumn. Once the plant
becomes established the flower stem length will
increase in height from that originally
advertised. The paler forms blend well with
pastel colours of early summer flowers, while
the brighter shades harmonize with light
orange flowers and variegated foliage.

Conditioning Cut the fully opened flower
when the central disc is young and fresh. It
rarely presents any conditioning problems if
stood in deep water for 2 to 3 hours.

Preserving To preserve the flower, select only
those that are uniform in shape. Press them so
that each petal is separated, for any that cross
can't be adjusted once the process is complete.
Though *Doronicum* is considered a spring
flower, the preserved flowers associate
perfectly with flowers and foliage in autumn
colours.

Helenium

Sneezeweed
*Canada and the eastern United States of
America*
Compositae

Helenium 'Butterpat'

Helenium autumnale is a free-flowering perennial plant with yellow daisy-like flowers about 1½in (3.75cm) across, height 4 to 6ft (120 to 180cm). Its flowering time is late summer to autumn. This is a very popular plant for cutting as it bears clusters of flowers on long stems. The following hybrids can be depended upon to provide lots of cut flowers on good sturdy stems:

'Bruno', dark red flowers, height 3½ft (105cm).
'Butterpat', large rich yellow flowers, height 3ft (90cm).
'Chipperfield Orange', orange-yellow flowers, height 4½ft (135cm).
'Coppelia', deep copper-orange flowers, height 3ft (90cm).
'Madame Canivet', golden yellow flowers, height 3½ft (105cm).
'Moerheim Beauty', rich crimson flowers, height 3½ft (105cm).
'Riverton Gem', red and gold flowers, height 4½ft (135cm).

Cultivation and propagation All the heleniums like a good rich moist soil and will grow equally well either in full sun or partial shade. Once clumps of plants are established they should be lifted and propagated by the division of the plants in winter every third year, so as to keep the stock young and vigorous. At this time dig in a generous dressing of manure, or well-rotted garden compost. Mulch annually in spring.

Uses The petals of this free-flowering plant reflex around a central disc rather like a shuttlecock. The colours are rich and bright which gives it a formal appearance. Plain green foliage would accentuate the brightness, so try using a variegated leaf to calm the vivid colour of the flower. The addition of a small amount of preserved foliage such as beech would also temper its luminosity.

Conditioning Cut the flowers before the central disc has changed colour, which means that the flower is still young. Remove any excess foliage and stand the stems in water for 3 hours. Once they are fully charged with water the flowers will last a long time.

Preserving The shape of the flower makes it impossible to press, but it can be dried in desiccant.

Heliopsis

North America
Compositae

Flowering season	Spring	Summer	Autumn	Winter
	Very Good	Large	Short	Long
Good				
	Small	Long		Short
Preserving	Flower size		Cut life	Stem length

Heliopsis 'Golden Plume'

The name Heliopsis literally means sun (Helios) like (opsis), and we are interested here in the perennial species, *Heliopsis scabra*, and in particular in its excellent garden cultivars. *Heliopsis scabra* has yellow, sunflower-like flowers, some 3in (7.5cm) in diameter, during the late summer, height 4ft (120cm).
H. s. 'Gigantea' produces rich yellow flowers throughout summer, height 4ft (120cm).
H. s. 'Golden Plume' has double yellow flowers, of outstanding quality for cutting, in late summer and autumn, height 4ft (120cm).
H. s. 'Incomparabilis', large double, orange-yellow flowers, in summer, height 3ft (90cm).
H. s. 'Patula', chrome yellow flowers, late summer, height 3ft (90cm).

Cultivation and Propagation Heliopsis will grow in a wide range of moderately fertile soils providing it is planted in a sunny position. It is naturally sturdy and erect, except on over-rich soil, when it becomes weak and floppy. Plants should be set out to 3ft (60 to 90cm) apart in each direction, when they are planted out either in the autumn or spring, with their fibrous roots placed barely beneath the soil's surface. Once planted they should remain undisturbed for a number of years at a time. Newly planted heliopsis generally prove rather disappointing during their first year of establishment, with their flowers being borne on shorter stems than was expected, but it is worth being patient with them until their second year.

Propagation is either by division of the plants or by basal cutting in the early spring.

Uses This is a very vigorous plant that produces a large terminal flower and smaller side flowers. The flowers are a dull yellow and make good companions for the brighter *Helenium*. As they are multi-petalled and can reach a diameter of 3in (75cm) they are flowers for large designs or pedestals. Their atmosphere is decidedly rustic and they need the companionship of other unsophisticated garden flowers to look their finest. The dull yellow compliments blue flowers, particularly delphiniums, when they are used in arrangements for church where large flowers are needed.

Conditioning The stems are fragile and need to be handled carefully. Always give them some support during conditioning which should never be less than 3 hours.

Preserving I have tried several times to dry this flower and I must confess with very little success. The multi-petals make it difficult to dry in desiccant and the result can be dull and disappointing.

Inula

Fleabane
Europe, Africa and Asia
Compositae

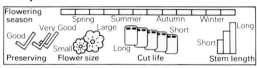

Several species have delightful daisy-like flowers suitable for cutting. The following selection provides cut flowers from early summer to autumn:

Inula ensifolia compacta, deep yellow rayed flowers on strong stems in summer, height 10in (25cm).

I. e. 'Golden Beauty' is similar to *I. e. compacta*, height 2ft (60cm).

I. hookeri, 3in (7.5cm) lemon yellow flowers in autumn, height 2ft (60cm).

I. orientalis, large finely rayed, orange yellow flowers, on stiff stems, in summer, height 2ft (60cm).

I. royleana, deep golden-yellow flowers, in autumn, height 2ft (60cm).

Inula hookeri

Cultivation and propagation Inulas are all easy to grow and often succeed where other plants fail, particularly in clay loams. Any ordinary garden soil will do, providing that it does not dry out too quickly during the warmer summer months. On sandy soils, introduce some old garden compost or peat to improve the moisture-holding capability. Planting is best undertaken in the early spring, setting the plants out 1ft to 1½ft (30 to 45cm) apart in each direction according to the height of the species. Once established *Inula* should be given the benefit of a spring mulch each year.

Propagation is by division of the plants in the spring, or by seed which is sown in a coldframe in early spring or in the open ground in late spring. The resulting plants are planted in the open, in a nursery bed, 6in (15cm) apart in each direction, as soon as they are large enough to handle, and transferred to their permanent positions either in the autumn or the following spring.

Uses *Inula* will provide masses of flowers on long stems that may be used in abundance in any style of arrangement. They are unsophisticated to look at and always seem to me to be out of place in arrangements where the colour scheme is pastel. They are an ideal flower to include in a design of preserved foliages, and you can replace any that fade from the constant supply in the garden.

Conditioning To condition remove any lower foliage and stand the long stems in deep water for up to 3 hours.

Preserving I have always considered the flower to be too coarse to preserve, though the rather fascinating shaggy appearance is interesting as a component when the flowers are pressed.

Narcissus

Europe, North Africa, China and Japan
Amaryllidaceae

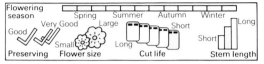

Narcissus jonquilla 'Bobbysoxer'

Apart from the many different species of the hardy bulbous plant *Narcissus* there are also countless numbers of hybrids which have been produced in the wild plus thousands more cultivars of garden origin. There is often some confusion as to the difference between *Narcissus* and the Daffodil! The fact of the matter is that there is no difference. Narcissus is the name of the genus and the name Daffodil is merely used to indicate Narcissi with long trumpets. Obvious examples are 'Golden Harvest' with deep yellow very large trumpet and 'King Alfred' with its very large, yellow trumpet and 'Mount Hood' which is a white-flowered daffodil. All these grow some 16in (40cm) high and make very fine cut flowers during late spring. There are some species which are not only delightful to look at but are also of considerable fragrance, which makes them doubly valuable as cut flower subjects, and it is well worth introducing some of these into the garden. All flower in spring unless indicated:
Narcissus jonquilla, single yellow, sweet scented flowers, height 1ft (30cm).
N. j. 'Baby Moon', light yellow flowers, with 3 or 4 per stem, late, height 9in (22.5cm).
N. j. 'Bobbysoxer', bright yellow petals with an orange cup, with several flowers per stem, height 9in (22.5cm).
N. j. 'Sugar Bush', white petals and a yellow cup edged white, height 10in (25cm).

N. j. 'Suzy', primrose yellow with an orange cup, with several flowers per stem, height 16in (40cm).
N. j. 'Trevithian', large clear yellow flowers, with several per stem, height 16in (40cm). Using the protection of cloches all may be induced to flower several weeks earlier than those grown in the open ground.
Narcissus obvallaris is only slightly scented but, as it is the harbinger of spring, it is worthy of inclusion within this selection. It is commonly referred to as the Tenby daffodil and it displays its golden yellow flowers in early spring, height 12in (30cm). This species is particularly good for naturalizing in the lawn or side borders.
Narcissus poeticus (Pheasants Eye) bears white petals and a small deep red cup in early summer, height 14in (35cm).
N. p. 'Actaea', large white flowers with a yellow cup edged orange-red, height 16in (40cm). This cultivar can be induced to flower earlier if protected with cloches.

Narcissus jonquilla 'Suzy'

Narcissus 'Actaea'

Narcissus 'Dutch Master'

Narcissus 'Cheerfulness'

Narcissus tazetta is a bunch-flowered form of Narcissus and it has many splendid named cultivars. First and foremost there is
N. t. 'Cheerfulness', white fully double flowers, height 16in (40cm) and its sport N. t. 'Yellow Cheerfulness' with double primrose-yellow flowers.
N. t. 'Cragford' is white with an orange-scarlet cup, early, height 1ft (30cm) and may be induced to flower several weeks earlier, with protection.
N. t. 'Geranium' large white flowers with a deep orange cup, height 14in (35cm).
N. t. 'Sir Winston Churchill' is a sport of N. t. 'Geranium' and it has white double flowers, height 16in (40cm).
Cultivation and propagation *Narcissus* likes a heavy well drained loam of some depth but can be grown quite successfully on a wide range of soils providing that they are not too shallow. Good drainage is important so that the bulbs

will not rot during the cold winter months. However, they do appreciate a moisture-retentive soil and on gritty and sandy soils, where the drainage is excessive, well rotted garden compost or peat should be introduced to improve the water-holding potential. They may be grown either in full sun or partial shade with the exception of *N. jonquilla* which requires a sheltered sunny situation, if it is to flourish. Plant the bulbs 3 to 5in (7.5 to 12.5cm) deep and 6 to 9in (15 to 22.5cm) apart. Once established they call for very little attention. When flowering has ceased cut all the seed heads from the top of the flower stems, so that the bulbs do not waste their energies trying to produce seeds. Do not remove foliage until it has died down. Quite large colonies are produced over the years. In time the soil will become exhausted and unable to maintain the *Narcissus* in flowering condition. Instead lots of leaves are produced. To prevent this apply hoof and horn meal at the turn of the year. Simply dust it over the surface of the soil or lawn and leave the rains to wash it down into the soil.

Narcissus propagates itself by offsets and by seed. Offsets can be removed from the parent bulb and grown on to flower in 1 or 2 years. Seeds are not a reliable way of propagation as the resulting plants take several years to flower and are variable in quality.

Uses *Narcissus* is the true herald of spring for gardeners and arrangers, and is the most popular of the spring-time flowers. The colour and form of the narcissus has certainly changed dramatically over the years. The leaves are long and slender, strap like, green in colour. The flower bud is quick to develop, extending beyond the leaves when it is fully grown. Once the flower was simple to describe, a yellow trumpet at right angles to the stem surrounded by six petals. Today that is not always so, as some *Narcissi* have no recognisable trumpet, 'White Lion' for instance, has broad white petals with a fully double centre of cream and white petals. Narcissus makes a good subject for a spring landscape. All that is required is a suitable branch to represent a tree, and a well pinholder to arrange the flowers in. Incidental pieces of moss and stone may be added to carry the theme through. Don't attempt a complicated linear design; the flowers should be arranged in a natural manner. Vary the length of the flower stems and include some still in the bud stage. I generally use other foliage, preferring to leave as much *Narcissus* foliage on the bulb to help feed it for next year's flower. If your grouping will allow you cut a generous quantity, simply place them in a clear glass vase. Cut the stems to varying lengths to prevent the flowers from being packed tightly in the vase.

Narcissi show a dislike for water-retaining foam – the foam particles block the cut stem and reduce the intake of water. Whenever possible arrange them on pins or directly in water. To use them in a basket, place a deep dish inside the basket and cover it with a cap of wire netting, 2in (5cm) gauge, crumpled into a loose ball is ideal. Arrange the flowers through the mesh of the wire making sure that they all make contact with the water. A basket of mixed spring flowers is a delightful arrangement for the breakfast table.

Conditioning The cut stem of the *Narcissus* exudes a glutinous liquid, which continues to flow for a short while. As you cut them dip each stem in the surrounding soil to staunch the flow. To make full use of this generous flower cut them when they are still in bud; they will develop and open in the arrangement. When you are ready to condition them, cut off the staunched end and stand them in cool water until you need them. Flowers that are not to be arranged, may be placed directly into the chosen vase. To hasten the opening of flower buds stand them in a warm atmosphere or use warm water in the container.

Preserving The trumpet of the *Narcissus* prevents it from pressing successfully. Experiment with the small-cupped varieties, *poeticus*, 'Polar Ice', or 'La Riante' Snip the cup at three equidistant intervals with a pair of fine nail scissors. This will allow the cup to flatten during the pressing operation. Drying the flowers in desiccant is most rewarding. Remove the stem and fill the trumpet with desiccant. Lay the flower on to a bed of drying compound and sift the desiccant around the flower until it is covered. The petals are paper thin and will reabsorb moisture, so the dried flower should be arranged under glass to avoid any distortion.

Rudbeckia

Coneflower
North America
Compositae

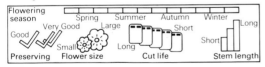

Several species of Rudbeckia are widely grown. They all have large daisy-like flowers, some of which are fully double, while single flowered forms all have a conspicuous central disc to their flowers. Their height varies from a mere 2ft (60cm) to 6ft (180cm) and their flowering season stretches from midsummer to late autumn.

R. fulgida syn. *R. deamii*, is a perennial with deep yellow flowers, with a dark centre, in autumn, height 2ft (60cm).

R. hirta (Black-eyed Susan) is an annual with

Rudbeckia hirta 'Double Gloriosa'

large daisy-like yellow flowers, with dark brown cone-shaped centres, height 1½ to 3ft (45 to 90cm).

The cultivar *R. h.* 'Irish Eyes' is without equal, its yellow flowers having an emerald-green cone-shaped centre, height 2½ft (75cm).

R. h. 'Marmalade' is highly floriferous with golden orange flowers, with a black cone-shaped centre, and these are fully 3in (7.5cm) in diameter, height 22in (55cm).

R. h. 'Rustic Dwarf' displays flowers of rich yellow, gold, bronze and mahogany shades, all bearing the characteristic black cone-shaped centre, height 20in (50cm). A strain which bears fully double flowers is *R. h.* 'Double Gloriosa', bearing rich golden-yellow flowers, some of which are so fully double that they resemble golden balls 5in (12.5cm) in diameter and these are borne in great profusion all the summer long, height 3ft (90cm).

R. lacinata is a perennial with golden yellow flowers with a greenish centre, during early autumn, height 5ft (150cm). Two excellent cultivars have been produced:

R. l. 'Golden Glow', double chrome yellow flowers, height 6ft (180cm) and *R. l.* 'Goldquelle', double, golden yellow flowers, height 2½ft (75cm).

R. purpuria is a very distinctive perennial with purplish-crimson flowers, through the summer, height 3ft (90cm). There are two desirable cultivars of this species which are well worth acquiring:

R. p. 'Robert Bloom', glowing, carmine-purple, flowers, and *R. p.* 'The King', glowing, rosy-red flowers. Both of these are 3½ft (105cm) tall.

R. sulivantii is a perennial which has provided us with *R. s.* 'Goldsturm', clear yellow flowers with a dark centre, throughout the autumn, height 2ft (60cm). All these various *Rudbeckia* are absolutely marvellous for cutting and may be had in flower from summer to the first frosts.

Cultivation and propagation *Rudbeckias* are easy plants to grow, in any well drained garden soil. Choose a sunny situation. Although the stems of *Rudbeckias* are naturally stiff and erect, the taller growing ones are best staked to prevent damage by the wind. Indeed, if they are to grow to their full height during the spring and summer months they must be watered in dry spells.

The earliest flowers of *R. hirta* and its cultivars are produced from sowings made under coldframes and cloches in early spring. Germination takes two to three weeks. When the seedlings are large enough to handle prick them out into other boxes and harden them off for planting out in late spring. When sowing in the open do so where flowering is to occur. Set the plants out 15in (37.5cm) apart in each direction.

Perennials should be lifted and divided every third year, with the opportunity being taken to incorporate a moderate dressing of manure or garden compost. Mulch annually.

Propagation of perennials is by division of the roots during the late autumn and early winter, as the plants become dormant. The setting out of new plants from the nursery may take place any time then. Planting distances will depend upon the height the plants are expected to grow and will be anything from 15in (37.5cm) apart for the smallest, up to 2½ft (75cm) apart for the tallest.

Uses These simple but bold flowers with their rich colouring of yellow to red bronzes are much used in their season. They are particularly suitable for harvest festivals in church where they blend well with vegetables and fruits. Some varieties grow very tall and can be useful in a pedestal arrangement. The round form of the flower may be used purely as a focal area or if the scale is correct they can be used throughout an informal design. By using soft variegated foliage you can tame some of the more brilliant lemon yellows.

Conditioning To condition them I prefer to stand them in deep water overnight. Cut them late in the evening when the flowers are open. Remove any stem foliage.

Preserving The flowers are large and are not sufficiently attractive to press or dry in desiccant. Allow a number to set seed in the garden. The petals fall to leave a conical-shaped seed head. Harvest them when the stem has started to dry. Suspend them from a line in a warm atmosphere to continue drying.

Sisyrinchium

Satin Flower
Asia and North and South America
Iridaceae

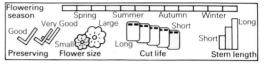

Sisyrinchium striatum

S. striatum comes from China, and bears iris-like foliage and slender spikes of primrose yellow flowers which are produced in abundance all summer, height 2ft (60cm).

Cultivation and propagation Can be grown equally well either in a sunny or partially shady spot in the garden in any well-drained soil containing some humus. Regular division is necessary to keep the plants floriferous.

Propagation is by division of the roots during the dormant season or by seed sown in autumn or spring. Grow on the seedlings before planting out in their flowering positions the following year.

Uses The flowers are arranged quite loosely along the long slender stem, and growth is strong and upright. The pale cream to primrose colour is both cool and tranquil when arranged in a low dish where an appreciable amount of water is exposed. In this style of arrangement they need no accompanying flowers, just a little of their own sword-like foliage.

Conditioning Pick early in the day as the flowers often close up during the hottest time. Condition them in deep water for at least 2 hours.

Preserving I very rarely attempt to preserve the flowers as they produce a very fine seedhead later in the season. After the flowers have faded and dropped from the stem the small round

seedpods are a bright green colour. At this
point collect them and stand them in a
glycerine solution. The process may take up to
two weeks to complete, and they change colour
to a rich mahogany brown. The stems can be
used to make an arrangement with other
preserved foliages.

Solidago

Golden Rod
North America
Compositae

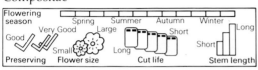

Solidago canadensis 'Crown of Rays'

Modern garden cultivars are of a much finer
quality than their parent *S. canadensis*. The ones
to grow for cutting are the dwarf forms of
Solidago. Their feathery plumes of flowers are a
delightful foil for the display of other cut
flowers.
Solidago canadensis 'Golden Baby', golden
yellow sprays of flowers on stiff erect stems,
later summer, height 1ft (30cm).
S. c. 'Crown of Rays', wide heads of bright
yellow flowers, late summer, height 1½ft
(45cm).
S. c. 'Goldenmosa', golden mimosa flowers of
neat habit, autumn, height 2½ft (75cm). Also
has attractive yellow foliage.
S. c. 'Mimosa', one of the taller cultivars but
with the same fine feathery plumes of flowers
as the dwarfer *Solidago* cultivars. It has mimosa-
like yellow flowers, late summer, height 3½ft
(105cm).
Cultivation and propagation These are easy to
grow in any ordinary garden soil in a sunny
place. To get the best from them lift and divide

the roots every second year, in the spring. This
is also the normal way of propagation. Flowers
are best cut when just showing colour.
Uses The tall elegant spires of *Solidago* are
bright yellow, with a warmth that is sometimes
missing from other yellow flowers. They are
quite stiff growing and are best used to
establish the height of an arrangement. The
smaller varieties such as 'Golden Baby' may be
used as transitional material. The foliage
generally is of little use with one brilliant
exception. *S. c.* 'Goldenmosa' leaves are a
bright yellow/green and should be left on the
stem to add colour and bulk to the design.
Conditioning The flower spike may be cut
when the flowers are in bud, though the colour
is brighter when the flowers are fully
developed. Remove any leaves that will be
below water and condition the flowers for up to
3 hours.
Preserving The small flowers are arranged
along separate stems springing from the main
stem. These can be removed from the growing
plant with a pair of small scissors and pressed
or dried in desiccant. The fine form of the
curving spray can be used to excellent effect as
outline material in a dried flower picture.
   There are two methods of air drying the
entire flowering stem. In both cases the stem
foliage should be removed, as it becomes brittle
and will disintegrate in time. The first way is to
stand the mature stem in a jar containing 1in
(2.5cm) of water. Let the stem absorb the water,
don't top it up, it will continue to dry. An
appreciable amount of colour loss will occur but
the pale creamy yellow it attains is not
unattractive. The second method is the
conventional air drying process. Pick the
flowers when they are fully developed, discard
the leaves, tie them into loose bundles and
hang them in a warm, airy atmosphere. Again a
certain amount of fading will take place but the
job will be considered worthwhile when you
arrange them with preserved *Choisya ternata*,
fresh trails of ivy and variegated holly in the
winter.

Tellima

North America
Saxifragaceae

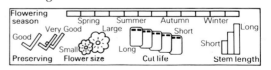

Tellima grandiflora is a good ground cover plant
which will smother weeds with clumps of
attractive bright green, round, hairy, leaves at
ground level. The spikes of bell-shaped flowers
are at first light green, but turn light yellow
with pink fringes as they mature, during late

Tellima grandiflora

spring, height 1½ft (45cm).

Cultivation and propagation *Tellima grandiflora* is a subject for the shadier parts of the garden. It will grow quite happily in any ordinary garden soil and being fully hardy will live for many years undisturbed. However, its mat of roots must have room to spread naturally. If you wish to keep it at its most floriferous it is best to lift and divide the roots every three or four years, selecting the younger clumps for replanting and discarding the remainder. This is the easiest method of propagation and it may be undertaken at any time during the dormant season. The new plants are then set out with their roots just beneath the surface 15in (37.5cm) apart in each direction. It is also possible to produce new plants from seed, which is sown in the open ground in spring. Sow the seeds very thinly and thin out the seedlings, when they are large enough to handle, to 8in (20cm) apart in the row. These plants are then transferred to their flowering places in the autumn or the following spring.

Uses As an evergreen plant this will prove useful in the winter when you need a change from preserved foliage. The leaves grow to a satisfying size, slightly rounded with a scalloped edge. Late in the season they change from green to a delightful marbled maroon colour. The flowers which grow above the foliage are very delicate in appearance. This delicacy is more visible when they are used in limited numbers for small pastel-coloured arrangements.

Conditioning Though they look fragile, they are amongst the easiest of flowers to condition. Simply stand them in water for 2 hours. The spring foliage should be floated in water before being stood in a glass of water to continue conditioning.

Preserving Choose the more striking leaves for pressing. It is possible to press the complete flower stem, but as the stem will dry at the same rate as the flower more benefit will be gained from drying them in desiccant.

Trollius

Globe Flower
Ranunculaceae

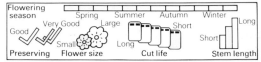

Trollius europaeus 'Superbus'

Trollius is a distant and much improved relative to the common buttercup. Two species are useful for cutting: *Trollius europaeus* is a European species and *Trollius ledebourii* from Eastern Siberia and China. The following selection will provide flowers from late spring throughout the summer:

T. e. 'Earliest of All', lemon yellow flowers, spring, height 1½ft (75cm).
T. e. 'Orange Princess', orange yellow flowers, early summer, height 1½ft (75cm).
T. e. 'Superbus', sulphur-yellow flowers, early summer, height 1½ft (75cm).
T. l. 'Golden Queen', deep orange flowers, summer, height 3ft (90cm).

Cultivation and propagation Both species will grow in any soil which is well supplied with organic matter and retentive of soil moisture. However, they will not survive for long under dry soil conditions. Choose a shady situation and ensure that the soil is supplied with lots of organic matter, e.g. compost, manure or peat, when preparing the ground. One should also water these plants during dry spells. Established plants should be lifted and divided every third year, in the autumn. They produce thick fibrous roots which can be easily propagated at this time, if further plants are required. This method is much quicker than propagating the plants from seed. Incorporate additional organic matter to maintain the soil's fertility and moisture-retention potential.

Plants should be set out 1ft (30cm) apart in each direction. In the spring following planting, it is advisable to provide a mulch of compost or peat. If starting from seeds, they should be sown, outdoors, in the autumn in a shady part of the garden. Growth is only slow at first and it will be two to three years before flowering may commence.

Uses This globe-shaped flower resembles a large buttercup, though the stem is much longer. It is often found in gardens growing along the edges of a pond. This sympathy with water can be extended by arranging them in a low dish, large enough to leave an area of water exposed. Use them on their own or with the addition of a little iris foliage.

Conditioning Cut the flowers when they are open or about to open, stand them in water for 2 hours to condition them.

Preserving The leaves, which are of little use in an arrangement, can be pressed. Once the leaf is mature the shape is quite intriguing, oval with deeply divided lobes. The central disc of stamens makes the flowers difficult to press. Ideally, they should be dried in desiccant.

Verbascum

Southern and Central Europe and the Mediterranean region
Scrophulariaceae

Verbascum 'Chaixii'

Good hybrids of garden origin include *Verbascum* 'Chaixii', mauve-centred yellow flowers, height 5ft (150cm) and 'C.L. Adams', spikes of yellow flowers, height 6ft (180cm).

Verbascum 'C.L. Adams'

'Cotswold Beauty' produces pale bronze flowers with lilac anthers.
'Cotswold Queen' has buff terracotta flowers with lilac anthers, height 50in (125cm).
'Gainsborough' has delightful primrose yellow flowers above grey leaves, height 4ft (120cm).
'Miss Wilmott' has fine spikes of white flowers, height 4½ft (130cm).
'Pink Domino' with deep rose pink flower spikes, height 40in (100cm).

Cultivation and propagation Any fertile garden soil containing a little lime will do for these plants, providing that it is reasonably well drained and not subject to winter wetness. Choose a sunny site for them and dig this deeply, incorporating sand or other gritty material to improve the drainage, if necessary, and introducing just a little manure or garden compost, if there is any doubt about the humus content of the soil. Planting may take place at any time during the dormant season. Plants will need setting out some 16 to 20in (40 to 60cm) apart in each direction, depending upon their vigour.

Verbascums are not long lived herbaceous perennials but they are readily propagated from root cuttings, secured during the late autumn and winter time, and this is the method used to maintain the stocks of the named hybrids. They may also be propagated from seed, sown in the open ground in the spring. Germination will take 14 to 21 days. When the seedlings are large enough to handle thin them out to 8in (20cm) apart in the row and transfer the resulting plants to their flowering places in the autumn.

Uses For a while it was widely held that *Verbascum* was too tall to be of any use to the flower arranger. Luckily arrangers are now aware of its arranging quality, particularly when it is dried. True, the main stem is of statuesque proportions but it flowers at a prolific time of the gardening year and is useful for pedestal arrangements. The side spikes are of a more manageable length, arching gracefully in a range of pastel colours for traditional style designs.

Verbascum bombyciferum is one species to search out for its foliage and seed head. The foliage forms a rosette of pointed ovate grey leaves, covered with downy silver hairs. This looks splendid grouped in limited numbers in silvered driftwood. The effect is luminous. Once the flowers have faded and the seeds start to form the stem colour changes from green/ grey to a silver grey. Like the leaf it has a fine covering of hairs which gives it a ghostly quality. I would always advocate waiting for the seed stem to develop, instead of using it in its fresh state. If you are fortunate it may adopt some of the interesting twists and fasciations that are peculiar to *V. bombyciferum*. It is an eyecatching stem for modern arranging **Conditioning** Cut the flower stem when the sun has gone from the plant. The flower head is most susceptible and wilts badly in excessive heat. Place the stem in cold water for 2 hours in a cool room. They are sometimes difficult to revive from a wilted condition, though treating them in boiling water should be successful. When conditioning foliage the leaves should be stood in shallow water. Any water touching the felted surface will discolour it. Check the water level often so that it can be topped up when necessary. Any of the leaves that start to wilt should be recut and the end treated in boiling water. Immature foliage responds to the boiling water treatment. Mature leaves may have the ends burned in a flame. The charred tip of the leaf can be left on for arranging, an advantage with this short stemmed leaf. A minimum of 2 hours should be allowed to fully condition the foliage.

Preserving Separate open flowers may be pressed or dried in desiccant. The real beauty of *Verbascum* is in its seed head, a slight contradiction as the seeds form the major part of the stem. When they set and begin to dry, the side stems straighten, moving closer to the main stem giving it a more attractive uniformity. Collect them when the seed pods have opened and the seeds have dispersed. The colour of the stem is dark oatmeal. A light spray of gold aerosol paint for a Christmas festival arrangement greatly enhances the colour. The alternative drying method is in glycerine. This must be accomplished as the flowers fade, while the seeds are still green. Stand the cut stem in glycerine solution, in a shady room. The process may take up to a fortnight to complete. When the stem is fully preserved, a change in colour will occur. The seed calyx and stem will darken and the seeds will become olive green with a slight oily sheen to them.

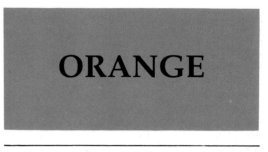

ORANGE

Calendula

Marigold
Southern Europe
Compositae

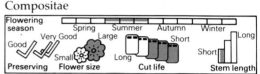

Calendula officinalis 'Art Shades'

Calendula officinalis, the well-loved Pot Marigold, is a hardy annual, an old cottage garden flower which is as popular today as ever. It has orange flowers which appear from summer onwards, height 2ft (60cm). A well liked cultivar is 'Art Shades', in delightful shades of apricot, orange and cream, with various coloured centres, height 1½ft (45cm). Here is a marigold which can be relied upon to give a good account of itself, even in the poorest of soils and most difficult of summers. 'Orange King Improved' has large fully double flowers, height 16in (40cm). 'Apricot Queen' is yet another excellent choice for vase work, height 2ft (60cm).
Cultivation and Propagation *Calendula* is very easy to grow. It does best on well-drained soils. The very earliest flowers are produced from seed sown in the open in early autumn. Except in mild districts plants should be given the

protection of cloches or coldframes through the winter. Choose a well-drained moderately fertile soil, not too rich, for this will lead to soft sappy growth which will be susceptible to frosts. Spring sowing should be as soon as soil conditions are suitable. Thin out the resulting seedlings to 12 to 15in (30 to 37.5cm) apart. A second sowing should be made in summer, as this crop will flower during the autumn and in the succeeding spring.

Uses With its simple form, rough texture and bright colour, this is not a flower to use with cut glass or silver against elegant velvet furnishings. Marigolds are immediately associated with informality and lend themselves to simple arrangements in unglazed pottery or terracotta containers. Following this rural direction of arrangings, *Calendula* could be used in conjunction with dried grasses, preserved foliage, berries, even fruit or vegetables possibly in a basket design.

Conditioning The usual conditioning process will keep them fresh for up to 5 or 6 days.

Preserving There is no satisfactory method of preserving, though some attempt can be made to press them.

Crocosmia

South Africa
Iridaceae

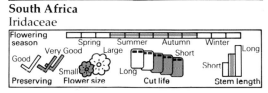

Crocosmia 'Lucifer'

There are two species of *Crocosmia*, *C. aurea* and *C. pottsii* and *Crocosmia* × *crocosmiiflora* (Montbretia Pottsii) is a result of a cross between these. Today there are several superb named cultivars which make fine cut flower

Crocosmia 'Vulcan'

subjects through the summer. Flowers are borne in arching panicles on stiff wiry stems and are yellow, orange or scarlet in colour. The foliage is sword-like in appearance and medium green in colour. Among the best cultivars to grow are:

C. 'Jackanapes' yellow and deep orange flowers, autumn, height 2ft (60cm).

C. 'Lucifer', brilliant flame red flowers, summer, height 3ft (90cm).

C. 'Vulcan', orange-red flowers, all summer, height 2½ft (75cm).

Cultivation and Propagation It grows best in light sandy soils which have been well enriched with a generous dressing of either manure or well rotted garden compost. Choose a sunny site. The corms are best planted some 3 to 4in (7.5 to 10cm) apart and 4in (10cm) deep. *Crocosmia* is not completely hardy and in more exposed areas is best lifted in the late autumn, when dormant. The corms are then kept in a cool dry frost free place until they are planted out again in the early spring. They multiply fairly rapidly and it is necessary to lift and divide the clumps of corms every third or fourth year. This is best done towards the end of the dormant season in early spring.

Propagation can also be by seed, sown in the autumn, as soon as it is ripe. Sow the seed in a seed pan containing a sandy soil, which is then placed in a coldframe or greenhouse. When the seedlings are large enough to handle they are pricked off singly into individual pots.

Uses The leaves of *Crocosmia* are as useful to the arranger as the flowers. They are sword-like, pleated like a partly closed fan, eminently suitable for modern and vertical arrangements. The flowers are carried on graceful arching stems, ideal for creating an outline for traditional arrangements. The colours range from yellow to flame/orange which contrast sharply with a background of plain green.

Conditioning The flowers open from the bottom of the spike upwards. Cut them when the lower flowers are open. The leaves can be left attached to the stem. Stand the stems in deep water for 2 to 3 hours.

Preserving The individual flowers can be preserved in desiccant, the luminous colour a striking item for a flower picture. During the autumn seed heads will develop, which should be collected when the seed has dispersed.

Gaillardia

Blanket Flower
Western North America
Compositae

Flowering season				
	Spring	Summer	Autumn	Winter
Good	Very Good	Large		Short Long
	Small	Long		Short
Preserving	Flower size		Cut life	Stem length

Gaillardia aristata 'Mandarin'

Gaillardia grandiflora

Gaillardia's gay daisy-like flowers only have a moderate lasting quality when cut. However, what they lack in longevity is more than compensated for by the constant availability of more fresh flowers throughout the summer and autumn. The following cultivars of *Gaillardia aristata* grow 2½ to 3ft (75 to 90cm) tall:
'Burgundy', rich wine red flowers.
'Dazzler', orange yellow flowers with maroon centres.
'Ipswich Beauty', bright yellow and crimson zoned flowers.
'Mandarin', orange-flame flowers.
'Wirral Flame', deep red flowers.
Cultivation and Propagation *Gaillardia* likes a sunny position and a moderately light, well-drained soil, which has been supplied with a dressing of bulky manure or well rotted garden compost before planting. Planting takes place during spring and it is wise to set the plants out at least 2½ft (75cm) apart in each direction, if good results are to be achieved. A surface mulch of peat or garden compost should be spread on the ground between the plants during late spring to help to conserve soil moisture during the summer. When cutting flowers do not remove any foliage from the plant as this continues to provide further material. Immediately flowering ceases in the autumn, all the remaining flower stems should be cut back and a top dressing of bonemeal applied. A similar dressing should be repeated the following spring.

In mild districts, propagation is by the division of the plants in spring, established plants being lifted and divided every third year. If plant material is in short supply, root cuttings can be taken during late spring. In the early summer the resulting plants may be planted out in a small nursery bed where they can remain until the following spring, when they are planted out into their flowering positions. In colder areas plants are propagated from seeds which are sown in a warm greenhouse in winter. The resulting seedlings are pricked off into seed boxes as soon as they are large enough to handle. Later they are put out in a coldframe to harden off before being planted out in their flowering positions in late spring.
Uses *Gaillardia* is a typical cutting flower, bright and showy on stems of a useful arranging length. The broad petals set round a central disc have a luminous quality which will highlight the focal area of any traditional design. The more intense colour varieties such as 'Wirral Flame' can be used to great effect in a modern arrangement.
Conditioning Cut them when the flower is fully opened, no preconditioning is needed, just stand them in cold water for about 2 hours.

Preserving Little loss of colour will occur if you dry them in desiccant. This happy situation is emphasized when they are used in a design of dried materials as a study in colour.

Gazania

South Africa
Compositae

Flowering season	Spring	Summer	Autumn	Winter	
Good Very Good		Large	Short		Long
Small	Long			Short	
Preserving	Flower size		Cut life		Stem length

Gazania × hybrida 'Sundance Mixed'

Gazania 'Golden Margarita'

The various Gazania hybrids all carry large daisy-like flowers on short stems and being tender perennials the general horticultural practice is to treat them as half-hardy annuals except in the very mildest districts where they might survive the winter as perennials. All the *Gazania* hybrids have brightly coloured exotic-looking flowers which look absolutely marvellous as part of the summer flower display in the garden and they make splendid cut flowers. If you wish to obtain them in straight colours then the following F1 hybrids are the best available.

G. × hybrida 'Golden Margarita', large Margarita-type flowers of brilliant golden yellow, with a dark contrasting central zone, almost 3in (7.5cm) across, height 8in (20cm).

G. × hybrida 'Sunshine Yellow Striped', brilliant yellow 3in (7.5cm) flowers with an attractive red stripe, height 8in (20cm).

G. × hybrida 'Sunshine Red Shades', is similar but with brilliant deep red flowers.

G. × hybrida 'Sundance Mixed', enormous flowers nearly 5in (12.5cm) across on strong stems 12in (30cm) high, in bright shades of copper, mahogany, red and yellow. Flowering

is about 10 days earlier than with the other named cultivars.

G. × hybrida 'Chansonette' has flowers in a fine array of colours and grows to a height of 10in (25cm). This hybrid will grow satisfactorily on poorer or drier soils than the others.

Cultivation and Propagation *Gazania* requires a sheltered sunny position in a well-drained fertile soil. Sow the seed in a greenhouse or on a windowsill in early spring. If the temperature can be maintained at 60°F (15°C) germination will be fairly even over the surface of the seed tray and take place within 2 to 3 weeks. If the temperature is lower than this then the germination will be erratic and take place over a longer period. When the seed lines are large enough to handle prick them out and, once they have had a few more days in the warmth to settle down, transfer them to a coldframe or cloches to be grown on without any heat. Protect the plants each night, for the first few days. The plants are hardened off in late spring and transferred to their flowering places in early summer setting them out 10in (25cm) apart. Cuttings can also be taken in late summer and overwintered in a warm greenhouse.

Uses Though the basic colour of *Gazania* is orange the garden hybrids have produced some very striking yellows and pink to ruby colours. The form of the flower is rounded with a distinct petal shape generally revealed through the marking at the base of the petal. As the stem is relatively short they are best used as a focal flower in a traditional design or as an individual flower in a modern container.

Conditioning This flower closes in the evening so it must be cut in the morning and immediately stood in water for 2 hours to condition.

Preserving The only method of preserving this brightly coloured treasure is by pressing.

Kniphofia

Red-hot Poker
South and East Africa and Madagascar
Lilaceae

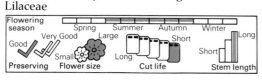

'Fiery Fred', fiery orange flower spikes early to late summer, height 3ft (90cm).
K. galpinii, spikes of beautiful clear orange yellow flowers, autumn, height 2ft (60cm).
'Maid of Orleans', exquisite slender ivory-white spikes of flowers, late summer, height 3½ft (105cm).
K. nelsonii Major, orange flame flowers, early autumn, height 2ft (60cm).
'Royal Standard', red and yellow flowers during late summer, height 3ft (90cm).
'Snow Maiden', creamy-white spikes of flowers, early autumn, height 2½ft (75cm).
K. uvaria 'Grandiflora', brilliant orange spikes of flowers, which turn yellow later, autumn, height 4ft (120cm).

Cultivation and Propagation *Kniphofia* prefers a light sandy loam containing a fair amount of humus, in a sunny part of the garden. Good deep cultivation is essential when preparing the site, as this plant likes to send its fleshy roots well down into the soil. Add sharp sand and other gritty material to heavy soils. Water during dry spells. Plants should be set out some 15 to 20in (37.5 to 50cm) apart in each direction. When once established they are best left undisturbed for a number of years. Plant in the dormant period.

Propagation is by the division of the roots in the early spring. These plants also produce suckers, which may be detached from the parent plants, which has the advantage that you don't lose a year's flowers from the parent. *K. uvaria* 'Mixed Hybrids', may also be propagated from seed. Sow in the late spring under glass. Germination will take about 4 to 6 weeks. When the seedlings are large enough to handle prick out into a coldframe. During warm weather the glass should be removed. Protect through the winter and plant out in permanent positions in the following spring.

Uses The stems of the *Kniphofia* curve slightly, and this will allow you to consider space as a design principle where two stems are used to create an oval void between them. The thicker-stemmed large-flowered varieties are particularly useful for creating this type of modern design. Smaller-flowered types that are not so strident in colour may be used in traditional arrangements. Arranged with lilies and light green foliage, they look most effective.

Conditioning Collect the stem when the lower flowers begin to open and the top buds are showing colour. Stand them in deep water for 2 hours; any flowers that die can be removed from the stem using a pair of scissors.

Preserving The flowers will not react to glycerine and are too fleshy to air dry. Single flowers can be removed from the stem and filled with desiccant to preserve them. The tubular shape of the flower is a contrast to round preserved flowers and leaves.

Kniphofia 'Bees Yellow'

Kniphofia 'Royal Standard'

There are several good cultivars available with stately poker-like inflorescences on sturdy erect stems, in a range of colours, and by careful selection flowers may be available for cutting through summer and autumn.
'Bees Yellow', bright yellow spikes, free-flowering, summer, height 3½ft (105cm).

Physalis

Chinese Lantern
Japan
Solanaceae.

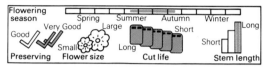

Physalis

Physalis franchetii is attractive for the orange-red lanterns which it displays in the autumn. The flowers are whitish and insignificant, hidden for the most part behind the leaves. It grows 2½ft (75cm) tall and roots are invasive. It can be grown in a tub or container to prevent this being a problem. The stems can be used freshly cut in the autumn, but its greatest value is as a dried plant.

Cultivation and Propagation This plant loves a deep fertile, moist soil containing plenty of decayed organic matter. If growing it in a tub or other receptacle, it is important to water it well in the warm summer months, as the plant is surface rooted and will soon begin to suffer. Stems have a habit of becoming too heavy, therefore some support with canes and string is needed, to provide long straight stems.

Propagation is commonly undertaken by division of the plant in the spring. Plants may also be propagated from seed sown in a coldframe in late spring. Germination takes up to 28 days. When the seedlings are large enough to handle prick them out into 4in (10cm) pots and transfer to permanent situation in the autumn 2ft (60cm) apart.

Uses Anyone already possessing this invasive plant will realize its worth as dried plant material. The leaves are of little use to the arranger as are the rather insignificant flowers. It is the striking lantern shaped calyx which develops in the autumn that appeals. The lanterns are green at first, then turn yellow and finally orange-red. Cutting should commence when the lowest lanterns have turned orange-red. Choose the straightest stems for cutting and make the cut just above ground level. Fresh stems, with their leaves removed, can be used in an arrangement with Dahlias and Chrysanthemums that flower at the same time. Once a stem has been arranged it will start to dry, so don't throw it away with the rest of the flowers. In its dried state, the lantern colour is so striking that few flowers need to be used with it. Arrange it with preserved foliages and dried grasses. If the arrangement is exposed to direct light the colour will begin to fade but in some cases a less vibrant note might be desirable.

Conditioning Remove all but the terminal rosette of leaves, as they rarely remain turgid once the stem has been cut. Stand the stems in cold water for at least 2 hours (this only applies to the fresh stems). Often *Physalis* will dry in the arrangement if the stem is mature.

Preserving Towards the end of autumn, the stem and lanterns will start to dry naturally. Collect them before any of the fruits are damaged by the weather. Remove all the remaining foliage and tie the stems into loose bundles. Hang them from a line to continue drying; one or two lanterns may fall but sufficient remain to make the harvest viable.

Naturally dried stems are brittle and the lanterns are crisp and unyielding, often getting crushed in store. Preserving Physalis in glycerine relieves this problem. The fruits remain pliable. Any that inadvertently become squashed can be reflated to their former shape, a form of floral kiss of life. Glycerine the stems when the calyx is still green. Remove the leaves and stand the cut stems in glycerine for 6 to 7 days. The lanterns will change colour to a light beige, a pleasant alternative to the usual orange. They can be preserved after the fresh calyx has started to turn orange. The success rate is not as high, but any that do preserve are worth it.

Tagetes

Marigold
Mexico
Compositae

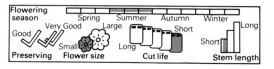

Tagetes erecta 'Orange Jubilee'

Tagetes erecta 'Gay Ladies'

Tagetes erecta (African Marigold) is widely grown as a source of cut flowers for indoor decoration. However, while some people like the strongly scented kinds others do not and it is wise to try a selection of these to see which prove most agreeable for indoor usage. There are some marvellous carnation-flowered and chrysanthemum-flowered cultivars available on good sturdy stems and these flower all summer long, making a very valuable contribution to the garden display as well as providing first-class cutting material. The Jubilee F1 Hybrids are very free flowering:
'Orange Jubilee', has light orange carnation-like flowers 4in (10cm) across, height 20in (50cm).
'Golden Jubilee', fine pure gold flowers some 3¼in (8cm) across, height 20in (50cm).
In the F1 Hybrid Climax Series the plants grow some 2½ to 3ft (75 to 90cm) tall and have huge almost globular flowers up to 5in (12.5cm)

across and about the same in depth, and are available in gold, orange, primrose, and yellow. These may be purchased in straight colours or as a mixed blend of all these colours. 'The Lady Series F1 Hybrid', produces fully double carnation-type flowers about 3¼in (8cm) across and is well noted for the large numbers. Plants are particularly fine for bedding, as they are compact, height 1½ft (45cm). Nevertheless, their flowers are just fine for cutting and they are certainly a dual-purpose summer flowering plant.
'First Lady', clear yellow flowers.
'Gay Ladies', yellow or gold flowers.
'Crackerjack', is an early flowering type which is an old favourite. It has giant fully double flowers and is available in a superb mixed blend covering the full range of marigold colours, height 2½ft (75cm).
Chrysanthemum flowered varieties are shorter.
'Spun Gold' masses of flowers, nearly 3in (7.5cm) across, of a bright golden yellow.
'Spun Yellow' equally bright canary-yellow flowers. Both of these grow to a height of 1ft (30cm) and will provide some very useful cut flowers for the smaller displays.
Cultivation and Propagation *Tagetes erecta* is a half-hardy annual which can be sown in a greenhouse or other warm place in spring. Germination takes 7 days. The resulting seedlings are then pricked out into other seed boxes, containing potting compost, and the boxes of seedlings are then placed within the protection of a coldframe or cloche until the frosts are passed, when the plants are transferred to their flowering position. In the open ground sow in late spring where they are to flower. Thin out the resulting plants to the appropriate distance apart. Choose a fairly fertile spot for these plants in a sunny part of the garden.
Uses The large bright solid coloured flowers are most useful and can be used with dramatic effect, creating blocks of colour in both traditional and modern arrangements. They are most accommodating in their growth pattern; partly open buds can be cut when small flowers of intense colour are needed. Fully developed blooms will last a considerable time once cut and can be used to vary the size of form where only one type of flower is being used.
Conditioning These flowers transpire heavily and need a lot of water, so it is necessary to give them an overnight drink to condition them. Remove all the lower leaves.
Preserving The smaller flowers should be dried in desiccant. They will add a note of vibrancy used in a picture or collage.

stems can be used to hang gracefully down the sides of a pedestal design, where the spectacular elegance can be seen without interruption. Smaller pieces, cut from the main plant during the growing season may be used throughout a traditional arrangement to introduce a different shape and texture. The foliage is of little use and should be removed from stems when used fresh or fry drying.

Conditioning Remove excess foliage and stand the mature stems in deep water for at least 2 hours.

Preserving To dry them, collect the mature stems when the flower colour is just starting to fade. Tie them into loose bunches and hang them in a light airy atmosphere. They will change from a deep scarlet or pale green to a pale beige.

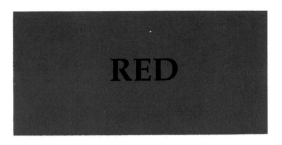

RED

Amaranthus

Love-Lies-Bleeding
Widely distributed
Amaranthaceae

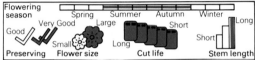

Amaranthus 'Molten Fire'

Amaranthus caudatus is native to the tropics and it is grown as a half-hardy annual. It produces long drooping racemes of crimson flowers from late summer to autumn and has large ovate green leaves, height 24 to 36in (60 to 90cm). There is also a form with very pale green flowers which is generally described in the seed catalogues as White 'Viridis'.

Cultivation and Propagation Choose an open sunny situation and any well drained soil. Sow the seed directly into the site where flowering is to occur, during late spring. Germination will take 2 to 3 weeks. Once the resulting seedlings are large enough to handle, thin them out to 18in (45cm) apart in each direction. The cut flowers have a long vase life.

Uses The long rope-like racemes of *Amaranthus* do not have a specific position in a flower arrangement. The longer, mature flowering

Astilbe

Japan and China
Saxifragaceae.

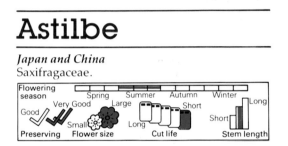

Astilbe × arendsii 'Fanal'

Astilbe comprises several hardy species of feathery plumed, ferny-foliaged plants. Many hybrids have been produced, particularly by Herr Arends of Rondorf in Germany, hence the name *Astilbe × arendsii*. Some of the best cultivars, which all flower in the summer, are: 'Amethyst', rosy-lilac plumes of flowers, on stiff erect stems, height 3ft (90cm). 'Bressingham Beauty', rich pink plumes of flowers, height 2½ft (75cm). 'Bressingham Charm', clear pink flowers, height 2½ft (75cm).

Astilbe 'Bressingham Beauty'

'Dusseldorf', compact growth, brilliant cherry red flowers, height 2ft (60cm).
'Fanal', intense deep red plumes of flowers, early, height 1½ft (45cm).
'Irrlicht', pure white plumes of flowers, very freely produced, height 2ft (60cm).
'Ostrich Plume', arching plumes of bright coral pink flowers, height 2ft (60cm).
'White Gloria', creamy-white plumes, height 2ft (60cm).
Other species from which useful cultivars have been produced include:
A. chinensis 'Pumila', small lilac-rose plumes of flowers, late summer, height 1ft (30cm).
A. simplicifolia 'Atrorosea', graceful plumes of pink flowers, late summer, height 15in (37.5cm).
A. simplicifolia 'Sprite', dense plumes of pearly-pink flowers, late summer and early autumn, height 10in (25cm).
A. taquetii 'Superba', superb plumes of erect, intense purple rose flowers, late summer, height 4ft (120cm).
Cultivation and Propagation *Astilbe* will succeed in any deep fertile, moist soil, either in full sun or partial shade and do particularly well on clay loams. Sandy soils will need a heavy application of bulky organic matter in the form of manure, well rotted garden compost, particularly well rotted grass mowings, if available, or peat. Astilbes may be planted at any time during the dormant season. Plants should be set out 1 to 2ft (30 to 60cm) apart in each direction, according to the height of the plants concerned. Once planted, Astilbes may be left undisturbed for some three to five years before they become too crowded and require lifting and dividing. Mulch annually in spring. On sandy soils they will need frequent watering in hot weather. The best solution if you have a pond or stream in the garden, is to plant them close to the water's edge, where they will feel most at home.

Propagation is by the division of the roots in spring, with a sharp knife, just as fresh growth is about to commence. Keep divided plants well watered. Alternatively, you can divide the roots late autumn and pot these up and keep them in a coldframe throughout the winter ready for planting out in spring.
Uses The shape of the flower spike restricts its use to being outline material in an arrangement, but this can be a very welcome change from foliage. Both the flower and the leaf are of considerable use to the arranger, not only for the range of colour but for longevity as cut material.
Conditioning Immature foliage should be floated in water before conditioning in deep water. Cut the flower spike when the panicle looks fluffy and bright. Remove any excess stem foliage and stand the stem in water for at least 2 hours. It prefers a cool atmosphere for conditioning.
Preserving Astilbe will dry naturally on the plant, so if the weather is kind they will grace the garden well into the winter with their brown feathery spikes. To reduce any weather damage they may be air dried. Collect them when the flower head looks crisp with a slight dullness of colour. Strip away any stem foliage and hang them to dry in a light airy room.

Geum

Avens
Chile
Rosaceae

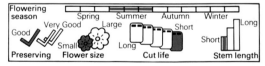

Geum chiloense 'Mrs Bradshaw'

Geum chiloense is a very easily grown and rewarding plant. It produces a dense clump of mid-green crinkled leaves which make good ground cover and help to conserve moisture about its roots. The panicles of flowers are born on long slender wiry erect stems some 1½ to 2ft (30 to 45cm) in height. This is truly a cut-and-come-again flowering herbaceous perennial, for the more the flowers are cut the more flowers it produces throughout the summer.

The following cultivars can all be depended upon to provide excellent results:
G. c. 'Mrs Bradshaw', crimson, semi-double flowers.
G. c. 'Fire Opal', glowing scarlet semi-double flowers.
G. c. 'Lady Stratheden', golden yellow semi-double flowers.
G. c. 'Prince of Orange', orange-yellow double flowers.

Cultivation and Propagation It seems to grow quite happily in any ordinary garden soil, preferring moist rather than dry conditions and flowers equally well in full sun or partial shade.

Propagation is generally by the division of the plants in the late autumn and this regular splitting-up of established clumbs of *Geum* keeps the plants so floriferous each year. New plants can also be produced from seed but these will not flower until the second year after sowing. The seed is best sown in a coldframe or cloche in spring. Once the seedlings are large enough to handle thin them out so that they are some 5in (12.5cm) apart in the row. Ventilate the plants whenever possible, so that by the end of spring the glass can be removed and the plants continue growing in the open ground. In the autumn these plants are transferred to their flowering positions and they should be spaced out some 15in (37.5cm) apart.

Uses The double, self-coloured flowers are extremely bright, carried at the top of slender stems. They are an eyecatching highlight when used in an arrangement of monochromatic colours. The soft ruffled petals lack sufficient dramatic impact to be of any use in a modern design, though the strength of colour may be desirable. It may be an advantage to reserve them as side pieces for inverted crescent shapes as the flower hangs in a most graceful manner.

Conditioning Select the flowers for cutting as they open and condition them in water for at least 2 hours.

Preserving Pressing would destroy the shape of the double hybrid flowers, drying them in desiccant will keep the shape and the colour.

Heuchera

Coral Flower
North America
Saxifragaceae

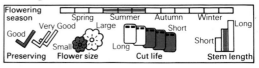

Heuchera 'Red Spangles'

Heuchera is a very hardy perennial plant which bears panicles of small flowers on slender wiry stems some 1 to 1½ft (30 to 45cm) long. The species *Heuchera sanguinea* has bright red flowers but subsequent crossing of *H. sanguinea* with *H. micrantha* and *H. americana* has resulted in the introduction of a number of very attractive hybrids which are far superior to their original parents. All retain their familiar evergreen clump of ground covering leaves but modern cultivars are more floriferous with flowers available in a range of colours and a height of 20 to 36in (50 to 90cm). The following cultivars flower throughout the summer:
H. 'Coral Cloud', coral pink flowers.
H. 'Greenfinch', greeny-white flowers.
H. 'Pearl Drops', pearly-white flowers.
H. 'Rhapsody', glowing pink flowers.
H. 'Red Spangles', crimson flowers.
H. 'Shere Variety', brilliant scarlet flowers.

Cultivation and Propagation *Heuchera* is extremely easy to grow, in any well-drained soil, in sun or partial shade. Heuchera are tough drought-resistant plants which cling tenaciously to the ground they have colonized over many, many years. However, they are inclined to lift themselves out of the ground after they have been there for some time. One solution here is to place well-rotted garden compost around the plants, which also stimulates the more vigorous production of flowers. The alternative is to replant more deeply every four or five years.

Propagation is by the division of established plants in the spring or by the rooting of offsets in a coldframe in the late summer ready for planting out the following spring. Plants should be set out 18in (45cm) apart in each direction.

Uses Heuchera is a long-lasting cut flower, particularly suited to water-retaining foam, as the stem is so fine. The small flowers extending down the stem make attractive material to use for establishing height in small arrangements. Though the stem is fine it can be coaxed between thumb and finger to form a gentle curve. The foliage is vaguely hairy, a bright green in the spring turning to greeny/bronze in the autumn. It is a very useful leaf to reflect focal area flowers in a massed design.

Conditioning Cut the stems with a pair of scissors as the plant is shallow rooted and will be disturbed by the slightest tug. Condition them in water for 2 hours. The leaves may be floated in water for an hour. Shake off any residual moisture and continue the conditioning in deeper water for a further hour.

Preserving The leaves are a fine medium for pressing. Be selective and search the plant for any leaf that displays an unusual colour or figuration. The fastest method of drying the flowers is in desiccant, the stem will not distort and the resultant flower can be arranged with other preserved material instead of being glued and crafted as with other pressed flowers.

Incarvillea

Western China and Tibet
Bignoniaceae

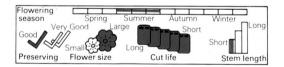

There are two exotic looking species of this herbacious perennial. The first is *Incarvillea delavayi* which bears five or six large deep pink trumpet-shaped flowers on each stem, during midsummer, height 1½ft (45cm). These flowers look particularly attractive against the dark ash-like leaves and equally so when used as part of a flower arrangement indoors.

The other species is *Incarvillea grandiflora*, which is a dwarfer growing subject at only 1ft (30cm). It too has the same large trumpet-shaped flowers in summer but these are deep rosy-red and the centre of the tube is suffused yellow. There is a cultivar *L. g.* 'Brevides' which bears carmine red flowers.

Incarvillea grandiflora

Cultivation and Propagation *Incarvillea* is easily grown in any rich, well-drained soil in a sunny position. Good site preparation requires deep cultivation and a generous incorporation of well-rotted organic matter, for once planted these plants resent any further disturbance, having fleshy fanged roots which penetrate deeply into the soil. Planting is best undertaken in the spring, setting the plants out some 6 to 10in (15 to 20cm) apart in each direction. Incarvilleas are particularly slow into growth in the spring, but when they do start development is very rapid indeed! Provide an annual mulch of well rotted organic matter about the roots of these plants in late spring or autumn.

It is possible to propagate established plants by division of their roots in the spring but the easier method is to propagate plants from seed sown in a coldframe in spring. Plant out in their flowering position the following spring. It takes two years to produce flowering plants by this means.

Uses This is a flower to challenge the arranger, as it is not the easiest subject to include in a mixed arrangement. The flowers are arranged at the top of a short stem, signpost fashion. They often interfere with or conceal adjacent flowers and leaves. However, the strong colour and unusual shape may be used in free form or modern arrangements. The flowers are produced before the stem has finished growing. Check the quality of the flower before you pick. Any that wither can be removed and this will encourage any buds to open.

Conditioning Cut them at the cool part of the day and condition them for at least 2 hours in a shaded area as the flower petals are paper thin and scorch easily.

Preserving Allow a number of flowers to set seed as the dried pod is extremely handsome.

Monarda

Bergamot
North America
Labiatae

Monarda didyma 'Cambridge Scarlet'

Monarda didyma has clusters of honeysuckle-shaped flowers, and it is the named cultivars of this species which give us such brightly coloured flowers for cutting as well as aromatic foliage! The following selection will provide cut flowers through summer and early autumn
M. d. 'Adam', immense cherry-red flowers, height 2½ft (75cm).
M. d. 'Blue Stockings', violet blue flowers, height 3ft (90cm).
M. d. 'Cambridge Scarlet', brilliant scarlet flowers, height 3ft (90cm).
M. d. 'Croftway Pink', delightful salmon-pink flowers, height 3ft (90cm).
M. d. 'Snow Maiden', pure white flowers, height 2½ft (75cm)..
Cultivation and Propagation All are very easy plants to grow on any ordinary fertile garden soil which retains summer moisture and is in a sunny situation. Sandy soils will require the addition of lots of manure or garden compost to improve their moisture-holding capacity.
Monarda forms a mat of fibrous roots, fairly quickly, and in order to keep the plant young and floriferous it will require lifting and dividing every second year, either in the late autumn or in the early spring. Plant out 15in (37.5cm) apart in each direction, with the tops of the crowns barely beneath the soil's surface. A mulch of peat or well rotted garden compost

should be placed around the roots of the plants each spring to help to retain soil moisture. Water in warm sunny weather.
The propagation of the named cultivars is by the division of their roots in the early spring or by seed. The older parts are discarded and the more recent roots are retained. If propagating from seed sow in a coldframe. When the seedlings are large enough to handle, they are pricked out 2in (5cm) apart in seed trays. The seedlings are then placed back into the coldframe and gadually hardened off. They are then planted outdoors in a nursery bed for the summer, with the young plants set out 9in (22.5cm) apart in each direction. In the autumn the plants are lifted from this nursery bed and transferred to their flowering positions.
Uses The loose, shaggy appearance is very informal and it is most useful as a transitional flower for relaxed designs of summer flowers. It associates well with *Physostegia, Penstemon* and garden pinks. In the wild, *Monarda* inhabits woodlands and water edges. Provided the cultivated flower colour is appropriate it can be included in landscape designs.
Conditioning Allow the main flower to open fully with the side buds showing colour. Stand them in water to condition for as long as possible.
Preserving The mature flowers will air dry, though the success rate is not high, so dry more than you will need. Hang them in a dry atmosphere as any moisture in the air will cause the square stem to twist.

Paeonia

Peony
Siberia, Mongolia, Caucasus
Ranunculaceae

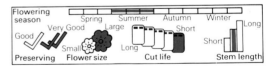

Peonies have grown in popularity, not only because of their flowers and fragrance, but more particularly because of their hardiness and reliability; once they have been given a suitable place in the garden they may remain undisturbed for many, many years. Planting a peony is rather like planting a tree, because once you have planted it the peony's life expectancy could easily be 50 to 70 years or even longer.
The Chinese peony (*P. lactiflora*, syn. *P. albiflora*) offers cultivars with large, fragrant, mainly double flowers which grow some 2½ to 3ft (75 to 90cm) tall and flower in midsummer.

Paeonia 'Chief Justice'

Paeonia 'Felix Crousse'

All the following are good for cut flower use:
'Bowl of Beauty', semi-double pale rose-pink flowers, yellow stamens.
'Couronne d'Or', double, creamy-white, scented flowers.
'Duchesse de Nemours', double, white, scented flowers.
'Edulis Superba', double, bright rose-pink flowers.
'Eve', semi-double, bright crimson flowers.
'Felix Crousse', double bright rose, scented flowers.
'Festiva Maxima', double, white laced crimson, scented flowers.
'Karl Rosenfield', double, dark crimson flowers.
'M. Jules Elie', double, light silver rose flowers.
'Sarah Bernhardt', double, apple blossom pink, flowers, without doubt the gardener's favourite peony.

'Torpileur', single, bright cherry to lighter rose pink flowers.

For earlier flowering one should grow *P. officinalis* as this flowers in early summer. Do not choose *P. o.* 'Rubra Plena' for cut flower purposes, as its dark crimson flowers are not satisfactory for this work. The more suitable ones to grow are *P. o.* 'Alba Plena', with double white flowers and *P. o.* 'Rosea Plena', with double pink flowers. Both of these grow to a height of 2ft (60cm). *Paeonia mlokosewitschii* produces single, lemon yellow flowers even earlier in spring, height 1½ft (45cm).

Cultivation and Propagation The peony is most at home in the heavier loams, providing that they are well drained, deep and fertile. The lighter loams can give good results also, if they are deep and have been well fortified with a generous dressing of organic matter prior to planting peonies. So be generous with the preparatory work, as once planted the plants resent being disturbed. Choose a site which enjoys partial shade, so that the flowers are not affected too much by strong sunlight, which curtails the flowering season. Dig the soil to a depth of 18in (45cm) and ensure that the manure, garden compost or peat is well dug in. Peonies need plenty of space, as they become quite bushy when fully established, so set them out 3ft (90cm) apart in each direction. The most suitable time to plant out is in autumn. When planting, place the crowns of the peonies 1in (2.5cm) beneath the finished surface of the soil. If one plants more deeply than this then flowering may be much delayed. In the spring when the young shoots appear, dust the soil about the plants with a dressing of finely ground bonemeal, and lightly rake this in. This dressing encourages the development of the peony roots. Water during dry warm weather, especially in late summer, as this is when the buds are being formed which will produce the

Paeonia lactiflora

flowers during the subsequent year. Provide a surface mulch about the plants each autumn and lightly fork this into the soil each spring, taking great care not to damage the roots.

Newly planted peonies take a year or two to settle down to flower. While the flowering season is short, it is possible, by making a judicious selection, to have a supply of peony flowers for cutting late spring to midsummer. Furthermore, they can be forced in the greenhouse. Dormant plants are lifted in the autumn and placed in a well ventilated garden frame until they are required. Maintain the greenhouse at a temperature of 62°F (17°C). Flowering will commence some eight weeks after the peonies are planted. Peony roots which have been forced need time to recover again in the garden.

Propagation is by division of the roots, with a sharp knife, while they are dormant in the autumn. Select only strong roots for this purpose.

Uses The peony provides a mixture of handsome flowers and attractive foliage. The leaves are composed of several leaflets irregular in size and shape growing on a single stem from the plant. A limited amount grows on the flowering stem. Be selective when you use peony leaves from a young plant, some must be left on to provide food for the plant. Autumn colour is another good reason for delaying the removal of foliage. The leaves develop streaks of bronze, red and brown as the season progresses.

The flowers are sumptuous in colour and form, rounded or bowl shaped, averaging 4in (10cm) in diameter. The bowl-shaped flowers have exposed stamens, and in some hybrids these have become ribbon-like filaments, increasing the novelty and beauty of the flower. Two superb examples are 'Bowl of Beauty' and 'Globe of Light'. As the flower is so large it requires an arrangement of suitable proprtion to accommodate it. Until your plant is able to produce lots of flowers use only a few in the focal area of the design. It has a soft, silky quality and should be used with flowers that harmonize with this. Surprisingly, it looks attractive when arranged lightly with driftwood, to create a design outline. Both the single and double flowers may be included in a modern arrangement. They should be positioned at the centre of the design or below centre, for placed any higher the size of the flower may upset the balance of the arrangement.

Conditioning Peony flowers and foliage suffer badly from high midday temperatures. They must be cut at the coolest time of the day, preferably in the morning. Cut the single flowers as they are about to open and the double flowers when they are about three-quarters mature. The flower will continue to unfurl after it has been cut. Stand them immediately in cold water in a cool room for 4 hours. Autumn foliage will not require such a long period to condition, but the spring leaves should have about the same as the flowers.

Preserving The leaves can be encouraged to absorb glycerine. I am not entirely satisfied with the result and prefer to use them in the autumn when they have changed colour. The seeds in the open mature pod are highly coloured and worth collecting. If you can resist the urge to pick *P. mlokosewitschii* flowers they will reward you with an array of scarlet/orange seeds spilling from five fat pods.

Penstemon

Bearded Tongue
Mexico
Scrophulariaceae

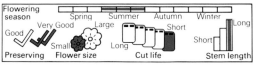

Penstemon hartwegii 'Garnet'

Penstemon barbatus has glossy green leaves and drooping, coral pink, tubular flowers, on long graceful stems, height 2 to 3ft (60 to 90cm), similar in appearance to the foxglove. There are several cultivars of *Penstemon hartwegii* including *P.h.* 'Firebird', graceful flower spikes, covered in lots of scarlet tubular flowers, all summer, height 2½ft (75cm). *P.h.* 'Garnet', deep garnet red tubular flowers, all summer, height 1½ft (45cm). A mixed seed 'Bouquet Mixture' is available giving a good variety of colours including light and dark blue, pink, red and violet..

Cultivation and Propagation It requires a sunny situation and a well-drained soil, containing just a little organic matter. Water during the warm summer months to prevent

Penstemon 'Early Bird' mixed

the roots from becoming too dry and encourage
the continued development of the flower
spikes. If the tubular flowers drop from the
flower spikes it is generally because the soil is
too rich in organic matter. If you transfer the
plant to a poorer soil this problem will
disappear.

Propagation is by seed or by basal cuttings
secured in the spring. Only the second method
is suitable for the named cultivars. These basal
cuttings are inserted in a sandy soil in a
coldframe during spring or early summer and
transferred to their flowering positions during
the autumn, with the plants spaced 1ft (30cm)
in each direction. When once planted they are
best left undisturbed for a number of years.
Add a little soil around the roots of the plants in
the late autumn to provide them with some
extra protection during the winter..
Uses *Penstemon* produce a continuous supply of
flowers during the summer for the arranger.
This and their splendid colour range is a good
reason for growing them. The flowers are
arranged loosely along a tall graceful stem. The
rich colours of wine and ruby red add a note of
distinction to an arrangement of pink flowers.
The tall stem is an elegant piece of outline
material arranged with grey foliage, roses,
Erigeron and the young flowers of *Eryngium*.
Conditioning Pick the stem when most of the
tubular flowers are open, strip any foliage away
that is likely to be under water and stand the
flowers in water for about 3 hours.
Preserving The complete flowering stem
cannot be preserved. Remove single flowers
from the growing stem and dry them in
desiccant or press them. When the flowers are
pressed arrange them in such a way that the
finest profile will result.

PINK

Agrostemma

Southern Europe
Caryophyllaceae

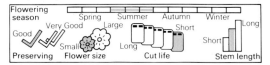

Agrostemma 'Milas'

Agrostemma coeli-rosa has rose-purple flowers
shading to white in the centre, height 1½ft
(45cm). Its foliage is grey-green, but
insignificant. The flowers form large sprays
with individual blooms on each stem. There are
two good cultivars:
A. 'Milas', large soft pink flowers which shade
to white in the centre, height 2½ft (75cm).
A. 'Purple Queen' rosy purple flowers shaded
white, height 1½ft (45cm). They all flower in
summer and are excellent for cutting.
Cultivation and Propagation *Agrostemma* grows
easily in a sunny situation in well-drained soil.
It is propagated by seed. Sow seeds in their
flowering positions in late spring. Germination
will occur in two to three weeks, and the
resulting plants should be thinned out to 9in
(22.5cm) apart. Seed may also be sown in the
open ground in autumn in sheltered areas, but

do not use over rich soil, as this will induce soft sappy growth which will not overwinter well. If young plants are given some protection in winter they will bloom earlier, thus prolonging the cutting season.

Uses This delicate flower has long, practically leafless stems which makes them highly desirable as outline material for both large and small arrangements. In very large designs the whole plant can be used. Remove the root system and place the stem directly in the oasis or into a water-filled cone. The soft pink colour is welcome as the flowering period coincides with peonies, stocks, dianthus and roses.

Conditioning The flower will continue to open after it has been cut, so do this when the flower is about to unfurl. Stand them in cold, deep water for 2 to 3 hours.

Preserving Fully developed flowers can be pressed or preserved in desiccant. The stem may be left attached when drying in desiccant as it is sufficiently fine to dry without distortion.

Armeria

Sea Pink
Europe including Britain
Plumbaginaceae

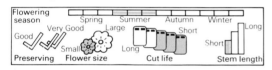

Armeria 'Bees Ruby'

A. *maritima* is a low growing, tufty, grass-like, perennial plant, found growing wild around coasts. It displays, pinkish lilac flower heads on thin wiry stems 6in (15cm) high, in early summer. It is a sun loving, drought resistant plant which can be depended upon to provide its attractive flowers, which are fine for small table decorations, regardless of the prevailing weather.

There are a number of delightful named cultivars:

A. *m.* 'Alba' neat white flowers, height 6in (15cm). This is a fine subject to grow along the edge of a path, as is A. *m.* 'Dusseldorf Pride', carmine red flowers.

A. *m.* 'Ruby Glow' has longer flower stems at 10in (25cm) and its red flowers are suitable for use in more general flower arrangements

A. *m.* 'Vindictive', rich rose crimson flowers on mere 4in (10cm) stems, but these are very useful for small flower arrangements. The more you cut the flowers of any of these plants the more readily they flower.

Another much taller growing cultivar is A. *pseudoarmeria* 'Bees Ruby', rose pink flower heads, height 16in (40cm).

Cultivation and Propagation *Armeria maritima* is one of the easiest plants one could possibly wish. It will grow on a wide range of soils, providing that they are not badly drained during the winter. Once established the plants can be left for years without being disturbed.

Propagation is by division of the plant roots in the spring. Seed can be sown in a coldframe, also in spring. Transplant to the flowering position in the autumn. Cuttings may also be taken in midsummer and rooted in a sandy soil in a shaded coldframe or cloche. Plant out rooted cuttings the following spring.

Uses The colours vary from soft pink to the rich ruby of *A.p.* 'Bees Ruby'. This range of colour makes them ideal companions for grey foliages. The association with the seashore makes A. *maritima* an obvious choice of flower for a seascape design. The pale pink colour blends well with wood that has been silvered by salt water.

Conditioning It is a greedy drinker and quickly becomes charged to capacity.

Preserving Its generosity of flower compensates for its disappointing preserving quality. Towards the end of the season the flowers will dry on the plant, but they tend to look a little dishevelled so collect them before they become weather damaged.

Bergenia

Elephant Ear
Siberia
Saxifragaceae

Bergenia 'Silver Light'

Bergenia cordifolia was formally known as *Saxifraga megasea*. It makes a very interesting evergreen ground cover plant with large glossy oval leaves which are green during the summer and flushed metallic purple-bronze during the cold winter months. This is a really tough plant which bears drooping racemes of deep pink, bell-like flowers on thick erect stems in spring, height 1ft (30cm). The flowers have a light fragrance which can only be fully appreciated when the cut flowers are taken into the warmth of a room.

B. c. 'Purpurea' has carmine purple flowers on longer stems, height 16in (40cm)

B. 'Silver Light' has the most delightful pure white tinged pink flowers, height 1ft (30cm).

Cultivation and Propagation *Bergenia* will accommodate itself to a wide range of soil conditions and is happy in either sun or shade. Once established it will survive for many years without being disturbed. However, it is better to lift and divide every several years, as younger plants bear more flowers. Division of the plants is best done immediately after they have finished flowering in the spring. Remove the old flower stems after flowering has ceased.

Uses Flower arrangers reached the decision a long time ago that the *Bergenia* is a useful foliage plant, though the flowers that grace the garden in spring are an elegant inclusion in an arrangement of spring flowers. The leaf is large and smooth often with a shiny texture, perfect material to act as a foil for special flowers used to create a focal area in a traditional or modern design. Look out for the varieties that change colour as the season progresses; some turn the most delicious mahogany red that links perfectly with Chrysanthemums and Dahlias..

Conditioning The leaf will condition perfectly well if floated on water. It is a temptation to use very young leaves that are a bright glossy green, but these wilt very quickly. Burning the end of the stem before the leaf is conditioned will help to counteract this, though it is better to allow the leaf to mature a little more.

Preserving The *Bergenia* leaf will preserve in glycerine. Use only perfectly fresh leaves and float them in a shallow dish of glycerine solution. The process is lengthy, but eventually the entire leaf changes colour to a dark brown almost black..

Clarkia

Western North America
Onagraceae

Clarkia pulchella

There are two species of this annual plant suitable for cut flowers: *C. elegans* and the smaller *C. pulchella*. Both come from California.

Clarkia has flowers which may be either single or double and the colour range covers pink, purple, scarlet, orange and white. The trend today is to sell mixed blends of colour rather than straight colours. *C. elegans* 'Royal

Bouquet Mixed' is a particularly good strain with double flowers 2in (5cm) across, height 2ft (60cm), in a superb blend of colours, which are good for cutting. There is also an excellent F1 hybrid with camellia-like flowers some 2in (5cm) across called *C. e.* 'Orange King' with bright orange scarlet flowers. *C. pulchella* is generally only available as a mixed blend of colours containing white, lavender and carmine and it has both semi-double and double flowers, height 1 to 1½ft (30 to 45cm).
Cultivation and Propagation Clarkia will grow quite happily in any ordinary garden soil which is well drained and is in an open sunny situation. Over-rich soils should be avoided otherwise foliage will be produced at the expense of the flowers. Seed is sown thinly where flowering is to occur, either in autumn or spring. It may also be sown under cloches, during early spring. Thin the resulting plants out to stand 10in (25cm) apart. The autumn sowing will produce plants which flower from the end of spring onwards. In cold districts the plants may need some protection against frosts. Spring sowings will flower about three months later.
Uses *Clarkia* is a flower with a rural feel. Arrange it in an informal way with other flowers that generate a similar feeling. It tends to dislike water-retaining foam, so if mechanics are necessary a pinholder or chicken wire is more suitable. I favour a container that will hold plenty of water where the flowers can be placed to arrange themselves.
Conditioning They have a long cut life. Condition them in deep water for about 6 hours if they are to be arranged in oasis. Where there is no artificial mechanics they may be placed directly in the vase. It is wise to keep them in a cool place for the first few hours.
Preserving Any side shoots or small flowering stems can be dried in desiccant.

Dianthus 'Doris'

Dianthus barbatus

Dianthus

Carnations, Pinks, Sweet Williams
Africa, Asia and Europe including Britain
Caryophyllaceae

The Greeks were very fond of this particularly fragrant flower and regarded it as being the 'Flower of Love', and used it in garlands and coronets for festivals. The common name carnation is said to be due to a corruption of the word coronation.

Dianthus 'Doris Majestic'

The *Dianthus* provides cut flowers from midsummer until late autumn, and the following selection of modern perpetual flowering *D. allwoodii* cultivars can be depended upon to flower continuously throughout that period:

'Cilla', pure glistening white flowers with red eye, height 10in (25cm).

'Doris', pale pink flowers with a distinct red eye, height 12in (30cm).

'Helen', bright salmon pink, scented flowers, bushy growth, height 14in (35cm).

'Ian', double, glowing crimson, very large, scented flowers, height 12in (30cm). This is very popular flower with the arranger, as it flowers well into the autumn.

'Susan', pale lilac flowers, with deeper eye and lacing on each petal, height 13in (32.5cm).

'Thomas', deep rose flowers, with a darker central zone, height 12in (30cm).

There are three new sports of the popular *D. allwoodii* 'Doris', all of which have flowers some 2¼in (5.6cm) across.

'Doris Majestic', fragrant salmon pink flowers with slightly serrated petals, produced in large sprays on strong stems.

'Doris Supreme', scented flowers, a delicate shade of pink married to carmine flakes and stripes.

'Doris Elite', similar to 'Doris' but has a deeper red eye and a longer flowering season. The flowers are fragrant and grow on strong stems.

Dianthus barbatus (Sweet William) is an old favourite. Not only does it possess attractive flowers it also has a tantalizing fragrance. *D. barbatus* is a perennial species which is a native of Southern Europe.

D. b. 'Scarlet Beauty' and *D. b.* 'Pink Beauty' are the most popular for cutting but there are others as good, such as *D. b.* 'Giant White, *D. b.* 'Auricula-Eyed Mixed', which has a white or pale centre to its flowers, and *D. b.* 'Messenger Early' which is 2 weeks earlier coming into flower and has a fine mixture of colours. All these plants grow to a height of 18in (45cm).

Old World Garden Pinks

The old-fashioned clove-scented pinks need little or no attention and thrive in any well drained soil in a sunny position, and can be left undisturbed for years. The following selection all flower in midsummer, grow about 12in (30cm) high and are readily available.

'Earl of Essex', double rose-pink flowers, in great profusion.

'Freda', bluish mauve flowers.

'Inchmery', exquisite shell-pink flowers.

'Mrs Sinkins', double white, heavily scented flowers, very popular.

'Pink Mrs Sinkins', a pink-flowered form of the above.

'Sam Barlow', large double white flowers with an almost black eye.

'White Ladies' pure white flowers which are produced in abundance and possess an intense fragrance.

While the pinks are related to *Dianthus plumaris*, another species, *D. caryophyllus*, is involved in the development of the hardy border carnations. They have longer stems than pinks and all are good for cutting.

Hardy Border Carnations

These are every bit as accommodating as pinks, as they will thrive in any sunny well drained spot in the garden. There are a large number of hardy border carnations and of necessity my list of recommended cultivars must be brief. The following all grow 1½ to 2ft (45 to 60cm) tall and flower during late summer:

'Alice Forbes', white flowers which are marked rosy-mauve.

'Beauty of Cambridge', large sulphur yellow flowers.

'Bookham Lad', exquisite white flowers which are striped scarlet.

'Eudoxia', superb pure white flowers.

'Fiery Cross', brilliant scarlet flowers.

'Leslie Rennison', beautiful purple flowers with a rose sheen.

'Lord Grey', heliotrope-grey flowers with a silver sheen.

'Sunstar', distinguished yellow flowers which are edged and marked scarlet.

Cultivation and Propagation Carnations, Pinks and Sweet Williams will grow in a wide range of garden soils, providing that they are well drained and not acid. If in doubt about the need to add lime, don't hesitate for one moment, as its presence may well do some good, and it will certainly not harm one's plants. Carbonate of lime can be raked into the soil immediately prior to planting. On established beds, apply a top dressing of carbonate of lime between the plants, in the spring. If the soil is heavy, it should also have a good dressing of sand worked into its surface, to further improve its drainage capability. Established plants will benefit from a dressing of general fertilizer in spring. Do not mulch as this leads to stem rot. When setting out the plants they should be spaced out 12in (30cm) apart in each direction. The soil into which they are to be planted needs to be fairly firm and it is desirable to 'tread' the soil prior to planting. Avoid over deep planting. Disbudding of the flowers on carnations is commercially practised but for flower arranging they look much more attractive if the side-buds are left to develop naturally. Pinks are not disbudded. The flowers are ready for cutting as soon as the terminal bud opens; the side buds will open as a matter of course.

While pinks do not require any form of support the taller growing carnations do. Wire hoops are the simple answer to this problem.

The named cultivars of both Carnations and

pinks are best propagated by means of cuttings or pipings. Pinks, with a naturally tufted habit of growth, may also be propagated by division of the plants best undertaken in the autumn or the spring. Propagation by cuttings or pipings takes place during midsummer. When propagating from cuttings, it is important to select healthy plants. Choose young non-flowering shoots around the base of the old plant and detach these with the aid of a sharp knife. Pipings are simply young shoots which are removed from the parent plant by pulling the top growth of a stem from out of its joint

When grown for cut flowers and for summer bedding purposes, D. barbatus is treated as a biennial plant. The seed is sown in the open ground in spring. Germination takes about two weeks. When the seedlings are large enough to handle, they are thinned out to stand 6in (15cm) apart and then left to continue growing there until autumn. The resulting plants are then transferred to their flowering places and planted out 10in (25cm) apart. Flowering occurs during midsummer of the following year. Alternatively, sow the seeds in a warm greenhouse in the early spring to produce plants which flower later the same year. It is quite hardy and will set seeds freely.

In the case of hardy border carnations, cuttings and pipings should have their lower pair of leaves removed and have their bases trimmed up just beneath a leaf joint (node). They are then inserted in either a coldframe or cloche in a well drained cutting bed composed of light sandy soil or a seed compost. Shade the cuttings to prevent wilting. Under the cool shady conditions rooting will take place in four to five weeks. Hardy border carnations may be planted out in their permanent positions during the autumn. Pinks may also be planted out at this time in the milder southern and western parts of the country, but elsewhere they should be given the protection of a covered coldframe during the colder wintry weather and be planted out in the following spring.

Uses These are well worth a place in an arrangement for their perfume alone. The range of colours extends their use into all areas of design. Paler shades are well suited to arrangements for informal parties, particularly as table arrangements where they highlight the colour of napkins and glassware. More sumptuous colours, crimson, scarlet and purple, are most effective in designs for formal occasions. The rounded, solid shape of D. barbatus makes it appropriate for the focal area of smaller arrangements. Allwoodii cultivars associate well with roses of a similar colour. Border carnations offer an interesting colour selection, on tall stems.

Conditioning Dianthus has the happy habit of quickly reviving in water whatever the time of day that you cut it. Cut the stem between the

nodes to facilitate easier water absorption and stand them in deep water for up to 4 hours.

Preserving The old-fashioned single pinks have been for a long time firm favourites for pressing. Those with a coloured edge to the petal look delightful as the focal point in a pressed flower picture.

Dicentra

Bleeding Heart
North America, China, Japan
Fumariaceae

Dicentra spectabilis

This is a genus of herbaceous plants, three of which are of some importance as cut flower subjects for garden cultivation.

D. eximia has flowers which are rose-purple in colour on drooping, branched racemes and fern-like, greyish-green foliage. Flowering lasts from spring to early summer, height 12in (30cm).

D. e. 'Alba', is a good white-flowered cultivar.

D. formosa is similar in appearance to D. eximia but with coarser ferny foliage, height 18in (45cm). Its flowers are pink and available for cutting from late spring to summer.

D. f. 'Bountiful', has carmine pink flowers and D. f. 'Luxuriant', bright red flowers.

D. spectabilis is an outstanding herbaceous plant and the best known species, with rose-pink, white tipped flowers in early summer and glaucous, finely divided, ferny foliage, height 1½ to 2ft (45 to 60cm).

Cultivation and Propagation *Dicentra* likes well drained, deeply cultivated soils which have been well supplied with organic matter, such as manure or well rotted garden compost, and prefers a slightly shady position in the garden.

Propagation of these species is by division of the roots or by root cuttings taken in early spring. Plants are set out 12 to 14in (30 to 35cm) apart in each direction. For some extra early flowers, *D. spectabilis* can be pot grown, in the cool greenhouse.

Uses It is easy to be carried away with enthusiasm and recommend every plant that grows, but this is one plant that all arrangers should have. The foliage is light and delicate, very much like a robust maidenhair fern. Its arching graceful manner is perfect in an all-foliage design. The heart-shaped flowers are also carried on arching stems. To see and appreciate the true beauty of the flower, place two stems in a tall glass vase with a little of foliage. Stood in front of a mirror they accurately reflect flower glory.

Conditioning Always cut these flowers during the cool part of the day and condition for at least 3 hours in a cool area. Arrange them away from direct heat as they are susceptible and will quickly wilt.

Preserving Cut the flowers from the plant with a pair of fine scissors. They may be dried in desiccant or pressed. The heart-shaped profile of the pressed flower can be added to dried vine tendrils to reproduce an arrangement for a flower picture. Selected pieces of foliage should be pressed. The stem is fleshy and does not dry satisfactorily in desiccant.

Erigeron

Fleabane
Western North America
Compositae

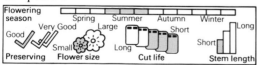

Erigeron speciosus resembles a Michaelmas Daisy in its appearance as it has the same daisy-like flowers, but this is a summer-flowering plant. There are a number of very good cultivars available, all flowering throughout the summer.

Erigeron 'Azurfree', lavender blue flowers, height 20in (50cm).
E. s. 'Charity', light pink flowers, height 2ft (60cm).
E. s. 'Darkest of All', deep violet blue flowers with yellow centres, height 2ft (60cm).
E. s. 'Dimity', large light pink flowers, height 1ft (30cm).

Erigeron 'Forester's Darling'

Erigeron 'Sincerity'

E. s. 'Forester's Darling', large, semi-double carmine-pink flowers, height 18in (45cm).
E. s. 'Prosperity', semi-double light blue flowers, height 18in (45cm).
E. s. 'Serenity', mauve blue flowers, late flowering, height 2ft (60cm).
E. s. 'Strahlenmeer', soft-blue flowers with yellow eye, height 2½ft (75cm).

Cultivation and Propagation This is a very easy subject to grow, in any ordinary well drained soil, preferably in a sunny situation, although it will tolerate light shade. Over-rich soils are not desirable as this stimulates over lush growth at the expense of the flowers. While this plant is a sun lover, its fibrous roots must be kept moist during the warm summer months. Every third year lift and divide the roots of the plants in the late autumn. Discarding the older parts of the roots, replant some of the young, more vigorous pieces, to stimulate flowering in the following year. In the intervening years, cut back the plants to within 4in (10cm) of the ground immediately flowering ceases in autumn, as this helps to strengthen the roots before the onset of the dormant season.

Propagation is either by division of the plants, as just described or by seed. When propagating from seed this is sown outdoors, during late spring. Germination will occur within 14 to 28 days. When the seedlings are large enough to handle, these should be pricked out in rows some 8in (20cm) apart with the seedlings 6in (15cm) apart in the row. The resulting plants should be moved to their permanent positions in the late autumn and planted out 1ft (30in) apart in each direction.
Uses *Erigeron* is very tolerant of salt-laden atmosphere; some cultivars can even withstand sea spray. The taller cultivars come in soft shades of lilac/mauve through to clear purple, while the shorter types are generally yellow to yellow/orange. This colour range adds a further dimension to a summer arrangement. The short cultivars are ideal for landscape designs as the stems are erect and easy to handle.
Conditioning Cut the stems when the flowers are open as any buds usually fail to develop. Any stem foliage that remains will not affect the cut life of the flower. Stand them in water for 2 to 3 hours.
Preserving Pressing and drying in desiccant are the two methods of preserving this flower. The lilac and mauve shades are suitable companions for pink and light red dried flowers and the pressed leaves of *Senecio* and *Eucalyptus*.

Helipterum

South Africa, Australia and Tasmania
Compositae

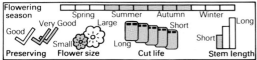

Flowering season	Spring	Summer	Autumn	Winter	
Very Good / Good	Large		Short		Long
Small	Long			Short	
Preserving	Flower size		Cut life		Stem length

The three species under discussion here are all annuals. *Helipterum humboldtianum* bears clusters of fragrant golden yellow flowers against silver foliage, height 1½ft (34cm). *Helipterum roseum*, syn. *Acroclinium roseum*, has large daisy-like flowers of pink, red or white, with yellow button centres, borne on stiff erect stems, height 1½ft (45cm). Seed may be obtained in straight colours or mixed. These flowers may be cut and used fresh, or dried for winter use. *Helipterum manglesii*, syn. *Rhodanthe manglesii*, is a species which lacks the character one

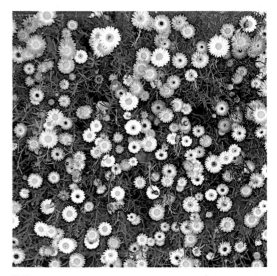

Helipterum roseum

normally associates with everlasting flowers, as it does not have stiff stems and it has clusters of drooping, daisy-like flowers about 1½in (3.75cm) in diameter. The flowers may be bright rose, carmine or silver-white in colour and have a yellow button centre. Seed is available in straight colours or as a mixture. *H. manglesii* attains a height of only 1ft (30cm), but what it lacks in size it more than makes up for in the abundance of flowers it produces.
Cultivation and Propagation All three species prefer dry poor soil in a sunny sheltered position. Sow the seed in the open ground where flowering is to take place, during late spring. Germination may take anything from 14 to 28 days, so be patient. When the seedlings are large enough to handle, thin them out to stand some 6in (15cm) apart. Flowering commences in late summer and continues to late autumn.
Uses Like the *Helichrysum*, this is also a flower for its preserving quality rather than for use as a fresh flower. Wait until the majority of the flowers are fully open and then cut the whole plant. Strip off all the foliage and tie the stems into small bundles. Suspend them in a warm, airy atmosphere for 2 to 3 weeks. Check them periodically to tighten any bundles that have become loose. The scale of the flowers somewhat restricts their use to smaller arrangements and collage or picture work. They make effective additions to Christmas decorations either in their natural colour or lightly gilded. Very inexpensive ornaments for a Christmas tree can be made by wiring the heads into a garland. Glass or plastic tree decorations can be given a face lift by glueing on a pattern of these flowers.

Lavatera

Mallow
Mediterranean
Malvaceae

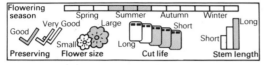

Lavatera trimestris 'Loveliness '

Lavatera trimestris is an annual species which
bears large trumpet-shaped, rose-coloured
flowers 4in (10cm) in diameter, height 3 to 6ft
(90 to 180cm). There are also a number of
named cultivars.
L. t. 'Loveliness', is a very popular summer
bedding plant with its glistening rich rose pink
flowers, and these are equally good for vase
work, height 3 to 4ft (90 to 120cm). This cultivar
may well need some discreet support with the
aid of twiggy branches.
L. t. 'Mont Blanc', glistening white flowers,
height 2ft (60cm).
L. t. 'Silver Cup', glowing salmon rose coloured
flowers, height 2ft (60cm).
L. t. 'Splendens Sunset' produces even deeper
rose pink flowers, height 2 to 2½ft (60 to 75cm).
All the above are very free flowering
throughout the summer.
Cultivation and Propagation Any reasonably
fertile soil will do for these plants, but they
must be planted in an open sunny situation.
   The seed should be sown where flowering is
to take place in late spring. Germination will be
sporadic over three to four weeks. When there
is a good stand of seedlings, and they are large
enough to handle easily, thin them out 18 to
24in (45 to 60cm) apart according to height. One
can also sow the seeds earlier in spring in boxes
in coldframes and cloches and prick these out

into boxes. Harden off before planting in the
open in early summer.
Uses This is a very popular flower for the
border and for cutting and arranging. The
flowers are on the large side and this restricts
them to arrangements of that scale. Although a
particular shape can be achieved through
artificial mechanics this flower lends itself to a
simple massed grouping in a glass or china
vase.
Conditioning The flowers are delicate and
should not be cut during the hottest part of the
day. Immediately after cutting place them in
deep water for at least 3 hours to condition. Do
this in a shaded room well away from direct
light.
Preserving The flowers may be pressed or dried
in desiccant, but the size of the individual
flowers may not make this a viable proposition.

Lychnis

Campion
Caryophyllaceae

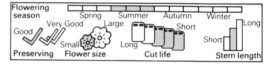

Lychnis chalcedonica 'Salomon'

Several of the perennial species are particularly
useful as cut flowers. *Lychnis chalcedonica* comes
from Eastern Russia and bears flat clusters of
brilliant scarlet flowers on leafy bright green
stems, during summer, height 3ft (90cm).
L. coronaria is native to Southern Europe and
has flowers which maybe red, pink, purple or
white. *L. coronaria* is readily available with
magenta flowers, height 2½ft (45cm). Other
good cultivars are:
L. c. 'Alba', white flowers, height 2ft (60cm).

L. c. 'Abbotswood Rose', bright pink flowers, height 1½ft (45cm).
All three flower during the late summer.
L. viscaria is another native European species with rosy-red flowers in midsummer, height 1½ft (45cm), but of much greater interest for cutting is *L. v.* 'Splendens Plena' with large double cerise flowers, height 15in (37.5cm).
L. × 'Arkwrightii' is the result of a cross between *L. chalcedonica* and *L. haageana* and the result is a cultivar with intense red flowers and purplish leaves which grows only 1ft (30cm) high, flowering in midsummer.

Cultivation and Propagation With the exception of *L. chalcedonica,* all Lychnis need a deep, well-drained soil. If necessary improve the drainage by the introduction of sharp sand or other gritty material. Very sandy soils will need some well rotted manure or garden compost to bind the soil and help moisture retention, otherwise the *Lychnis* will wilt during warm spells and the flowering be affected. *L. chalcedonica* prefers a moisture-retentive soil and will grow quite happily in clay loams and in boggy conditions.

All the Lychnis have sturdy stems and no support be will required. However, the soil must be kept moist during the summer months, if they are to flower vigorously. A surface mulch of peat or well rotted garden compost should be applied during late spring.

Planting is best undertaken in the early spring when new growth is about to commence. Actual planting distances will depend upon the height the plants grow and may be anything from 12 to 60in (30 to 50cm) apart. *Lychnis* will need lifting and dividing every third year and this should be done during the dormant season. Choose young vigorous pieces of root when replanting, as these will prove to be the most floriferous.

Propagation of named cultivars is by division of the roots as just described. New plants can also be propagated from seeds as *Lychnis* sets its seeds quite freely. Sow seeds in early summer. When seedlings are large enough to handle prick off into nursery beds. Plant out in autumn in flowering positions.

Uses *Lychnis chalcedonica* is one of the most brilliant scarlet herbaceous plants. The large multi-flowered head can measure up to 5in (12.5cm) in diameter. This shape and size easily satisfies the modern flower arranger. The bright colouration restricts its use in arrangements in mixed summer flowers but when possible it makes a fine focal area flower. *Coronaria* has a much smaller flower head in a wide colour range that is more suited to massed arrangements of an average size.
L. viscaria 'Splendens Plena' with double cerise flowers grows in an ovoid spike and blends perfectly with other blossom and roses in the pink range.

Conditioning Cut the flowers when they are open. Remove any stem foliage and stand the flowers in water for 2 to 3 minutes.

Preserving The petals of *L. coronaria* are a particularly fine shape and are worth pressing. To maintain the shape and strong colour preserve in desiccant.

Nerine

South Africa
Amaryllidaceae

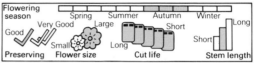

Nerine bowdenii

Nerine is a genus of bulbous plants. *Nerine bowdenii,* is the hardiest and grows in the open ground in most parts, producing its clusters of pink flowers, on 1½ft (45cm) stems, during autumn each year. The cultivar *N. b.* 'Pink Triumph' displays extra large pink flowers and attains a height of 2ft (60cm). Both are able to withstand slight frost. More importantly, when the flowers are cut they have a vase life of about 14 days.

Cultivation and Propagation The bulbs are globose at the bottom but taper to a thin neck at the top. These need planting in a well-drained light soil with their tops just beneath the surface and some 4in (10cm) apart. Choose a site with a southern aspect and, if possible flanked by a south-facing wall. If the soil conditions are heavy one can incorporate suitable gritty materials to improve drainage or, better still, excavate the unsuitable soil and replace this with a mixture of soil, peat and sand. Planting takes place in the late autumn to early winter. Once planted the bulbs are immediately covered with a mulch of peat, leafmould or straw to protect them from the worst of the winter frosts. This needs to be some 4in (10cm) deep and remains in position until new growth commences in the spring. At this time the leaves appear and do not die down again until late summer. When these leaves are seen to be dying one should give the bulbs a topdressing of bone meal, followed by a light mulch of garden compost. And when flowering has finished provide that protective mulch once more for the winter. Once planted these bulbs should be left undisturbed until such time that they become overcrowded and flowering begins to decline. They are then lifted and divided. They can also be propagated from seed but this is a slow process taking some five years before flowering can be expected.

Uses This is a flower of striking beauty. It extends all that is elegant in a summer garden through the months of autumn. Most of the hybrids are pink, some being deep, darkening to scarlet. The elegant lily form should be retricted to the choicest area of a massed design or used as a point of impact in a modern design. As it flowers late in the year it is an ideal companion to roses that are producing a last valiant flush of colour.

Conditioning Cut them when most of the flowers are open and stand them in deep water for 2 hours to condition. Any buds will develop in a warm room after they have been arranged.

Preserving The flowers are star-shaped with six slightly crimped petals, the most satisfactory method of preserving them is desiccant. The dried flowers can be fixed to false stems with adhesive and used in small arrangements or flower pictures.

Physostegia

False Dragon's Head
North America
Labiatae

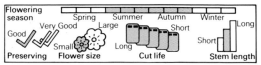

There are two species used for cutting. *Physostegia speciosa* has a cultivar, *P. s.* 'Rose Bouquet', with rose-purple flowers, which makes an important contribution among the cut-flowers, in autumn, height 2½ft (75cm). *P. virginiana* has stiff spikes of deep pink, tubular flowers, in summer and autumn, height 3ft (90cm). It also has two very desirable cultivars. *P. v.* 'Summer snow', spikes of pure white

Physostegia virginiana 'Vivid'

flowers, in summer, height 32in (80cm). *P. v.* 'Vivid', growing only 18in (45cm) high, spikes of bright pink tubular flowers in autumn.

Cultivation and Propagation *Physostegia* grows on any ordinary garden soil, providing it is reasonably fertile and well drained, either in a sunny or partially shady situation. *Physostegia* is best lifted and divided every year or two in early spring. Plants are set out in their flowering positions some 18 to 24in (45 to 60cm) apart, according to their height. A surface mulch of garden compost or peat between the plants will help to retain moisture around their roots, during the summer.

Propagation is by division of the fibrous, creeping roots, or by cuttings of the young shoots 3in (7.5cm) long, in the spring each year. When propagating from cuttings, these are inserted in a sandy compost and given the protection of a coldframe.

Uses *Physostegia*, known as the obedient plant, has hinged snapdragon-like flowers that will remain in an altered position if they are moved. The stem is upright, with the flowers on opposite sides, tapering up to a point. The spire effect puts them in the range of outline material. The flowers might be considered fussy and will benefit from an association with plain green foliages, *Griselinia* or *Hosta lancifolia*. The cut flowers are long lasting.

Conditioning Collect them when at least one-third of the flowers are open. Remove the lower stem foliage and condition the flowers for about 2 hours.

Preserving My only success in preserving the plant is to collect the seed head and this is mainly Nature's work, not mine. The result is not outstanding but it can be useful as a point element in a dried material design.

Pyrethrum

Poor Man's Chrysanthemum
Persia and Caucasus
Compositae

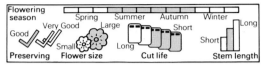

Pyrethrum 'Eileen May Robinson'

Pyrethrum roseum is an invaluable plant,
producing fine flowers with long stems which
last well when used as cut flowers. It forms a
clump of much divided, fern-like foliage at
ground level. Long fern-clad flower stems arise
from this clump, each bearing just one single or
double large daisy-like flower. Flowering takes
place during early summer, when the main
crop of flowers is produced. There is also a
second much lighter flush of flowers in
autumn. Several cultivars are available, height
2½ to 3ft (75 to 90cm):
'Bees Pink Delight', large semi-double flowers
of deep rich pink.
'Eileen May Robinson', single soft pink flowers.
'Jubilee Gem', large single bright cerise flowers.
'Kelway Glorious', single scarlet flowers and is
very early when grown under cloches.
'Vanessa', double rich pink flowers.
'White Madeleine', double white flowers..
Cultivation and Propagation *Pyrethrum* is very
easy to grow in any well-drained sandy or
loamy soil but heavy soils are not suitable
unless they can be lightened by the addition of
sandy or gritty material. Choose an open sunny
position but not an unduly exposed one.
Prepare the ground in the winter cultivating
deeply and incorporating well-rotted manure
or compost. Plants are set out 18in (45cm) apart
in each direction in spring. Mulch annually.

Established pyrethrums should be lifted and
divided every third year in spring in order to
keep them vigorous and floriferous. They will
flower very little that summer but more heavily
in autumn. This can help to spread the
flowering season, as can protecting the plants
with cloches in the spring.
Propagation is by division of the plants and is
usually done in spring. However, it can be
done several times during the summer if plants
are in short supply and one wishes to increase
one's stock rapidly. For this it is important that
the plants are kept growing vigorously and
prevented from producing any flowers.
Uses The flowers are daisy-like, with bright
pink or red petals surrounding a yellow disc.
The informal form is useful as a filling-in flower
in a massed arrangement. Some of the strident
colours can be used in a modern arrangement.
Bunch the flowers tightly together and use
them as elements of colour. My earliest
recollection of this flower was seeing them
massed in a redundant milk jug.
Conditioning An easy flower to condition.
Stand them in water for 3 hours, though they
will not suffer if they are left for much longer.
Preserving The flowers are large and they can
be bulky subjects for pressing or drying in
desiccant. Restrict yourself to the more
interesting colour forms.

Saxifraga

Saxifragaceae

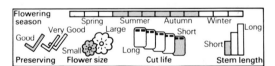

Saxifraga umbrosa primuloides 'Elliot's Variety'

Saxifraga umbrosa

The most familiar example is *Saxifraga umbrosa* (London Pride), deep pink sprays of tiny star-like flowers, in early summer, height 12 to 16in (30 to 40cm). These are very valuable to the flower arranger, as they can be mixed with other flowers to form a coloured background. Another dwarfer type is *S. u. primuloides* 'Elliot's Variety', deep pink sprays of flowers, height 10in (25cm). For *S. u.* 'Aurea Punctata', has sprays of pale pink flowers, and is good for any shady place in the garden, height 1ft (30cm). *Saxifraga umbrosa* can be seen growing wild in Britain and it is a variable plant with hybrid varieties as well as named cultivars. A good Bulgarian spring-flowering species is *S. aizoon,* and its cultivars *S. a.* 'Correvoniana', clusters of white flowers in early summer, height 10in (25cm). There is also a very dwarf cultivar, *S. a.* 'Lutea', with sprays of dainty yellow flowers in early summer, height 6in (15cm). These are very suitable for posy vases. *S. a.* 'Rosea', sprays of pale rose flowers, height 10in (25cm). *S. fortunei* is a native of China and Japan, flowers in the autumn and prefers a shady spot in the garden where the warm summer sunshine will not reach it for long each day. It bears clusters of drooping white flowers, height 1ft (30cm).

Cultivation and Propagation The above species are all hardy, easily grown perennials which will thrive in any semi-shady spot in the garden. They require a well-drained gritty soil to which has been added some peat and a little lime. Be careful not to choose a spot which lies wet during the winter time as *Saxifraga* will not survive long under such conditions.

Plants may be propagated by the division of their roots either in the autumn or the spring or they may be increased from seed. When producing plants from seed they must be sown in seed pans containing gritty soil, in spring. These are then placed in a coldframe or under a cloche where germination will occur in 3 to 5 weeks. When the seedlings are large enough to handle they are pricked out into pots or boxes and grown on in these until the autumn, when they are transferred to their permanent flowering places. The plants are then set out 9in (22.5cm) apart in each direction.

Uses Most of the species are associated with rock gardens, an area that is often overlooked by the arranger. Do consider creating a miniature rock garden in a suitable dish that can be left outdoors and brought inside when the flowers are blooming. *S. umbrosa* is, however, an arranger's plant eminently suitable for outlining a small arrangement. The leaves of the larger *Saxifraga* can be put to good use as a disguise for water-retaining foam.

Conditioning As the flower stems are fine, harvest them with a pair of scissors. No preconditioning is required; simply stand them in water for 2 hours.

Preserving The smaller alpine varieties have always been a subject for pressing. Those that grow in clusters can be dried in desiccant, the stems left attached. With their own stems they can be arranged in the same way as their fresh counterparts.

Senecio

Compositae

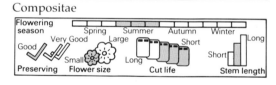

Senecio elegans

Senecio is a large variable genus distributed in most parts of the world. *Senecio elegans* is a half-hardy annual from South Africa. This is well worth growing for its pink, purple, mauve and white double flowers (similar to those of *Cineraria*) in late summer, height 1½ft (45cm). The seed is sold in mixed colours.

Cultivation and Propagation It is quite easy to grow. It requires a sunny sheltered situation and a well-drained soil. Some support with twiggy sticks may be necessary.

Sow the seed in the flowering position in spring. Germination takes 2 to 3 weeks. When the seedlings are large enough to handle thin them out to 9in (22.5cm) apart in the row.

Uses The form and colouring of this plant make it most suitable for filling in a design of high summer flowers. Used in profusion, it provides blocks of colour as a contrast to more dominant blooms such as lilies. The colour is sufficiently deep to recess them into the arrangement to create the necessary visual depth without the design looking too heavy.

Conditioning The flowers require about 3 hours conditioning. Strip away any foliage that will be submerged and stand them in deep water.

Preserving The flowers have a loose appearance that is quite informal. They can be successfully pressed to form rather striking components in a collage of textures.

Vaccaria

Siberia to Persia (Iran) and eastward to Southern Europe
Caryophyllaceae

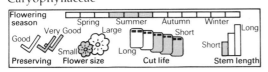

Vaccaria pyramidta

The species which is important as a cut flower

subject is the annual *Vaccaria pyramidta* syn. *Saponaria vaccaria*. It displays small dainty pink flowers in sprays on much-branched stems in summer, height 1 to 2ft (30 to 60cm).

V. p. 'Pink Beauty' is an improved strain both in colour and floriferousness, height 2ft (60cm).

V. p. 'Alba', bears star-like white flowers, height 1½ to 2ft (45 to 60cm). These flowers look splendid when massed in beds and are excellent for cutting. They are often used in association with *Gypsophilia* in floral arrangements.

Cultivation and Propagation Plant in a sunny situation in any ordinary garden soil. Propagation is by seed. Sow in spring where flowering is to take place. Thin the resulting seedlings to 8in (20cm) apart. Flowering is throughout the summer.

Uses These delicate flowers growing on a stem of a desirable length for arranging blend perfectly with the pastel shades of summer. Both the white and pink forms can be used, especially with roses and grey foliages.

Conditioning Cut the flowers when the majority are open, remove the lower stem foliage and stand them in deep water for 4 hours.

Preserving Small sprays of flowers preserve well in desiccant and they provide useful background material for miniature arrangements or dried flower pictures.

Xeranthemum

Southern Europe, the Mediterranean region and Persia (Iran)
Compositae

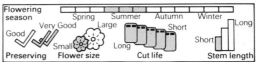

Xeranthemum annuum

Xeranthemum annuum is an annual which bears daisy-like flowers which keep their shape and colour well when dried. This is a particularly useful everlasting flower for use in dried flower arrangements, as its single or semi-double flowers can be obtained in white, rose, pink and purple. Straight colours are not readily available. *X. annuum* has stiff wiry stems and grows to a height of 2ft (60cm). For drying purposes the flowers must be picked immediately they open.

Cultivation and Propagation Choose a sunny place in which to cultivate this plant, as it is a true sun lover. Any well drained garden soil will do. The seed may be sown in coldframes and cloches in spring or in the open ground in early summer. If sowing in the flowering situation, sow the seeds very thinly as the resulting plants will need thinning out when they are large enough to handle. Germination usually takes about 2 weeks. Seed can be sown earlier either in the greenhouse or under cloches. Ventilate well on warm days and harden off prior to removing the protective covering. The plants are set out 1ft (30cm) apart. The flowering period is summer..

Uses The scale of these useful flowers is small. Though their value is as a dried flower, they do look most attractive as a fresh component in a posy of mixed coloured flowers.

Conditioning When used fresh, pick the flowers as they open and stand them in water for at least 2 hours. They have the ability to dry in the arrangement, so don't be in haste to discard them when the other flowers have faded.

Preserving They dry remarkably easily. Cut the thin, wiry stems as the flowers open and insert them in a block of dry water-retaining foam. This method prevents the stems being damaged. Keep them in a shaded place to prevent the colour from becoming bleached.

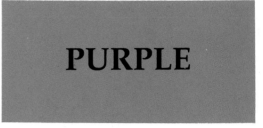

PURPLE

Hosta

Plantain Lily
Liliaceae

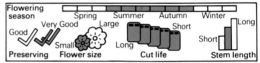

Hosta fortunei 'Albopicta'

Hostas have bold heart-shaped leaves on stout stalks and these may be green or variegated; flowers are spiked and generally taller than the leaves, carrying up to 15 to 20 flowers per spike, and may be lilac, violet or white, depending upon the species. Hostas are tough, long lived plants which are completely weedproof, once they become established. While the flowers are not long lived they are produced from summer to late autumn.
H. fortunei, bluish-green leaves and lilac blue flowers, summer, height 2½ft (75cm).
H. fortunei 'Albopicta', yellowish leaves with green margin, lilac flowers, late summer, height 2ft (60cm).
H. f. 'Aurea', leaves at first yellow later turning light green, purplish flowers, later summer, height 2ft (60cm).

Xeranthemum annuum mixed

H. f. 'Aureo Marginata', green leaves which are attractively edged golden yellow and mauve flowers, summer, height 2½ft (75cm).
H. 'Frances Williams', glaucous leaves with yellow margins which deepen in colour in late summer, mauve flowers, height 3ft (90cm).
H. 'Royal Standard', green leaves, sweet scented, ivory white flowers, autumn, height 18in (45cm).
H. sieboldiana 'Elegans', large, blue-grey leaves, lilac-white flowers, late summer, height 2ft 8in (80cm).
H. 'Thomas Hogg', fine emerald green leaves with a broad white edge and deep purple flowers, late summer, height 12in (30cm).
H. undulata 'Media Variegata', creamy variegated leaves, light-purple flowers, late summer, height 18in (45cm).
H. ventricosa, glossy green leaves, purple flowers, late summer, height 2ft 8in (80cm).
Cultivation and Propagation All species will grow quite happily in any ordinary garden soil, even relatively dry soils, though then they take some years to develop to any size. They prefer moist shady sites. Apply a generous dressing of manure or well rotted garden compost to such soils to improve their moisture retention prior to planting.

Propagation is by division of the crowns in the spring time when new growth begins. Once planted, hostas may remain undisturbed for a number of years. Lifting and dividing takes place in early spring. Plant 12 to 18in (30 to 45cm) apart in each direction depending on the height of the plants.

Uses Most *Hosta* flowers are in the white, white/lilac to rich purple range. They are informally arranged on strong straight stems hanging like bells, with just the tip of the anthers showing. When they are used in massed designs of pastel colours they are an ideal component for establishing height. In this type of colour scheme they may be used in generous quantities as the shape of the flower is not bold or likely to distract from the overall effect. In a scheme of darker shades use fewer numbers, sufficient to create an interesting change of colour. For those of you who prefer the sparse effect of driftwood and a few flowers, this one is perfect. The flowers last a long time, and any faded lower blooms can be carefully removed with little adverse effect. Though you will find the flowers of use, the leaf of the *Hosta* is what will give you the most pleasure. Once your affection for the *Hosta* family has been established you will soon be collecting more than have been named here. The leaf has its own qualities, colour, form and texture. These will instantly tell you where to use them. Fortunately the leaves come in a good range of sizes. Generally they are used to create the focal area. They are unsurpassed as a foil to the delicate tracery of fine ferns or the exquisite shape of a sweet pea.

Conditioning New growth should be cut cleanly from the plant and floated in a dish of water for at least 1 hour and then stood in deep water for a further 2 hours. Mature foliage may be stood in water immediately it has been cut. Flower stems should be cut when the lower flowers are open, as the flowers continue to develop in a limited way after they have been arranged.

Preserving I have not been successful at preserving the leaf of this noble plant. Many will change colour in the autumn, and these can be used in any design providing they have access to a limited amount of moisture. They generally last several weeks before the stem softens and flags permanently.

The flowers may be preserved individually in desiccant. The inside should be filled with desiccant before the flowers are completely covered. Pressing the flowers will give you a rather fine bell-shaped profile.

Hosta 'Thomas Hogg'

Liatris

Kansas Feather
East and South USA
Compositae

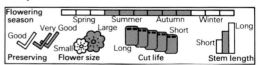

Liatris produces wand-like spikes of of flowers which open from the top downwards. When used as cut flowers, the stems are cut when the first few flowers have opened at the top. There are several species for cut flower use:
Liatris callilepis, lilac purple flowers, late summer, height 3ft (90cm).
L. pycnostachya, purplish-rose flowers, autumn,

Liatris pycnostachya

height 3 to 5ft (90 to 150cm) and being tall this species needs support either by staking or growing it through wire-netting.
L. spicata, stiff erect stems, reddish-purple flowers, late summer, height 2ft (60cm).
L. s. 'Alba', a white flowered form of the above.
L. s. 'Kobold', a lilac-mauve form of the above.
Cultivation and Propagation Choose a well drained soil in a sunny situation for the fleshy corm-like roots of *Liatris* and set them out 8in (20cm) apart in each direction, taking care that the tops of the corms are only just covered with soil. Planting may be undertaken any time in the dormant period. Plants are left undisturbed for several years before being lifted for division and subsequent replanting once more. Division merely calls for the pulling apart of the clumps of corm-like basal buds which have developed, best done in early spring. You can also treat this plant as a biennial, by growing it from seed sown in a coldframe in late spring, sowing the seeds as thinly as possible. When the seedlings are large enough to handle, set them in a nursery bed in the open 6in (15cm) apart. The resulting plants are transferred to their flowering positions in the autumn.
Uses *Liatris* is a feathery thistle-like flower that has the rare quality of opening from the top of the stem first. It is of an upright nature and can be used for establishing the outline of a formal arrangement. Its lilac-mauve colouration is good with silvered wood and grey foliage to recreate the feeling of the seashore.
Conditioning Wait until about the top inch (2.5cm) of flower has opened before you cut them. Remove any stem-borne foliage and condition the stem in water for about 2 hours.
Preserving To dry them select the flowers when the majority have developed, tie them into small bunches and hang them in a cool dry room away from direct light to preserve the original colour.

Lythrum

Northern temperate regions and Australia
Lythraceae

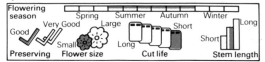

Lythrum salicaria 'Firecandle'

Lythrum salicaria 'The Beacon'

Lythrum has two herbaceous perennial species which have given rise to several cultivars of plants with spires of small flowers,
Lythrum salicaria (Purple Loosestrife) grows wild alongside rivers and besides ponds in Europe including Britain. It displays purplish-red flowers in spikes on erect stems, height 3ft (90cm) tall in summer and autumn.
L. s. 'Firecandle' intense rosy-red flowers on slender spikes, summer, height 3ft (90cm).

L. s. 'Lady Sackville', beautiful rose-pink flowers, early to late summer, height 5ft (150cm).
L. s. 'Robert', clear pink flowers, summer, height 2ft (60cm).
L. s. 'The Beacon', deep carmine-red flowers, summer, height 2½ft (75cm)
Lythrum virgatum is a native of the Taurus region of Turkey and forms a more slender and compact plant than *L. salicaria.*
L. v. 'Dropmore Purple', slender graceful spikes of rosy-purple flowers in early to late summer, height 2½ft (75cm).
L. v. 'Rose Queen', fine bright rose-red spikes of flowers, late summer and autumn, height 1½ to 2ft (45 to 60cm).
L. v. 'The Rocket', very stiff and erect, narrow graceful spikes of deep pink flowers, height 3ft (90cm).
Cultivation and Propagation All the *Lythrum* are very easy plants to grow in any ordinary garden soil especially in damp places. They are gross feeders and will require a good dressing of organic matter annually, during the dormant season. They also appreciate the application of a mulch of garden compost, leaf-mould or peat about their roots in spring. Given this kind of treatment they will thrive equally well either in full sun or partial shade and provide lots of cut flowers over many weeks.

Planting may take place at any time during the dormant season. Large growing cultivars of 3ft (90cm) or more should be set out 16 to 18in (40 to 45cm) apart in each direction, while the smaller growing cultivars may be set out 12 to 14in (30 to 35cm) apart in each direction. Keep the plants young and vigorous by lifting and dividing the roots every three to four years. No staking is required for these plants.

Propagation is generally by division of the roots either in the spring or the autumn. It is also possible to propagate by securing half-ripe cuttings in midsummer. These are inserted in a shaded coldframe and rooting will take place in three to four weeks. The resulting plants are then transferred to their flowering places in spring of the following year. *Lythrum* hybrids can also be propagated by seed sown in the open in spring and the resulting plants are thinned out when they are large enough to handle, so that they are left standing 6in (15cm) apart in the row. Transfer to their flowering places in following spring. When flowering commences discard the inferior plants.
Uses *Lythrum* grown in large clumps is a dazzling haze of pink to purple flowers. As the stem is erect and grows quite tall, its chief use in arranging is as outline material. The colour range will blend with most other garden flower colour though I would exclude it from a design that is predominantly yellow.
Conditioning Wait until the lower flowers have started to develop before you cut them. Remove any excess foliage and stand the

flowers in deep water for 3 hours.
Preserving Mature flowering stems can be air dried in the usual way. The small star-shaped flowers can be individually dried in desiccant. Whilst *Lythrum* is notorious for self-seeding the seed head is not very attractive.

Salvia

Perennial sage
Temperate regions
Labiatae

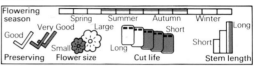

Salvia

Our concern here is with some of the herbaceous perennials.
S. haematodes is native to Greece and produces fine spikes of bluish-violet flowers in summer, height 3ft (90cm).
S. h. 'Indigo' has branching spikes of deep blue flowers, height 42in (105cm).
S. superba has the same branching spikes but of violet blue and with red bracts which persist after flowering has ceased. Flowering period late summer to autumn, height 32in (80cm).
S. turkestanica has spikes of bluish white flowers and pink bracts during late summer, height 4ft (120cm).
Cultivation and Propagation *Salvia* will grow in any well drained soil in either full sun or partial shade.

Propagation is by division of the roots during the dormant season.
Uses The value of growing *Salvia* for arranging is in the long life of the cut material. The colour is in the bracts, perhaps the most useful one is *S. turkestanica* where its size and the varying

blend of colour adds considerable interest to any design. The tall species are excellent for creating the outline of a shape and the smaller ones can be used throughout the arrangement.

Conditioning Once the bract has matured and the colour is at its most intense stems should be cut and conditioned in water for 2 hours.

Preserving At the peak of the growing season *Salvia* should be collected and air dried. It is essential to pick only those in perfect condition. Tie them in small loose bundles and hang them up in a dry room. Avoid strong light as this will drain the drying bracts of their colour.

Thalictrum

Meadow Rue
Ranunculaceae

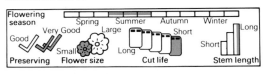

Thalictrum aquilegifolium

There are three species of this plant which are suitable for the provision of cut flowers.

T. aquilegifolium with loose fluffy heads of purple-mauve flowers in spreading panicles in summer, height 3ft (90cm). This species is a native of Europe and North America and it has a couple of very useful cultivars. These are:

T. a. 'Album', white flowers, height 2½ft (75cm).

T. a. 'Thundercloud', fluffy purple flowers, height 2½ft (75cm).

Thalictrum dipterocarpum has deep lavender flowers with yellow anthers in great panicles in summer, with stems ascending 6ft (180cm), and this species is a native of West China. There is also the cultivar *T. d.* 'Hewitt's Double', with its

cloud of fully double, deep lavender flowers in late summer, height 3ft (90cm).

Thalictrum flavum produces fluffy heads of lemon yellow flowers during midsummer, height 4ft (120cm). It comes from Europe.

Cultivation and Propagation *Thalictrum* requires a fertile, well-drained soil. *T. flavum* prefers a sunny position whle *T. aquilegifolium* and *T. dipterocarpum* are better suited to partial shade. They all need some support from pea stakes and require shelter from strong winds. Plants are set out 1½ to 2ft (45 to 60cm) apart according to the height of the species being planted. If some greenhouse space is available *T. dipterocarpum* can be greatly forced. Roots are potted up in the autumn and brought into the greenhouse. They flower a month earlier than plants outside.

Uses A most useful combination of flower and leaf for the arranger. The foliage is fine and delicate rather like maidenhair fern, a perfect foil for the large plain leaves of the *Hosta* or *Bergenia*. It is a splendid inclusion to an all-foliage design, though it loses impact when too closely associated with variegated leaves. The small flowers are arranged in a loose pyramid shape on the main stem. I prefer to include them around the focal area of a massed arrangement to lighten the effect.

Conditioning Condition them in a cool position. Any stems that show signs of wilting should be removed and the lower section held in boiling water for about 10 seconds. Return it to the water immediately.

Preserving The fern-like leaves are an excellent medium for pressing, the more so when they are young as they are a delightful bright green. Panicles of flowers can be pressed or dried in desiccant.

Thalictrum dipterocarpum

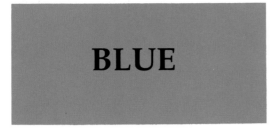

BLUE

Aconitum

Monkshood
Europe, Asia
Ranunculaceae

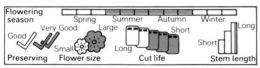

Aconitum napellus 'Spark's variety'

Although a useful garden plant which provides fine spikes of flowers, *Aconitum* is a poisonous plant to both man and beast so plant it well out of reach of grazing animals, and wash your hands when you have been handling it.
Aconitum napellus has dark blue flowers on erect spikes in summer, height 4ft (120cm). It is parent of a number of named cultivars:
A. n. 'Blue Sceptre', exquisitely shaped, erect tapering blue and white flowers, late summer, height 2ft (60cm).
A. n. 'Bressingham Spire', violet blue flowers, late summer, height 3ft (90cm).
A. n. 'Newry Blue', deep blue flowers, midsummer, height 4ft (120cm).
A. n. 'Spark's Variety', deep violet blue flowers, summer, height 40in (100cm).
Aconitum carmichaelii syn. *A. fischeri*, amethyst

blue flowers, autumn, height 5ft (150cm). This is a very reliable species for late cut flowers.
Aconitum orientale, exquisite ivory white flowers, tinged lemon, summer, height 5ft (150cm).
A. autumnnale 'Kelmscott Variety', fine lavender-violet flowers, autumn, height 4ft (120cm).
By selecting from those listed, it is possible to be cutting flowers from early summer to late autumn. Flowering is most prolonged if plants are kept moist.
Cultivation and propagation *Aconitum* grows most satisfactorily in damp shade, although it will also grow in sun, providing its roots can be kept moist in summer. Any ordinary garden soil will do, if it is well supplied with humus. Incorporate a generous dressing of manure or well rotted garden compost before planting. Established plants should be provided with a mulch of compost or peat early in the sring.
Propagation is by seed sown in the spring either in a coldframe or cold greenhouse. Established plants can be divided either in the autumn or the early spring. Planting may take place at any time during the dormant season. Plants should be set out 2ft (60cm) apart in each direction with their crowns barely beneath the soil's surface. Tall growing cultivars will need some form of support, unless they are growing in a sheltered place.
Uses An exquisite flower for those that favour blue. Used as fresh material it is most useful for creating an outline to a traditional design. The intense colour contrasts well with orange *Kniphofia* or *Alstroemeria* and harmonizes with the steel blue of *Echinops* and *Eryngium*. *A. orientale* is a stunning ivory form, ideal for arranging with pastel shades.
Conditioning To condition the flowers, remove the lower stem foliage and stand them in water for at least 4 hours.
Preserving The flowering stem will air dry. Remove all the stem foliage and hang them upside down in a dry atmosphere. Most of the flowers will be brittle so will need careful handling once the process is complete. Individual blooms can be dried in desiccant.

Agapanthus

African Lily
South Africa
Liliaceae

Flowers are borne in large numbers in shapely umbels at the top of sturdy erect stems, and

Agapanthus 'Headbourne hybrid'

may be of various shades of blue or white, while the foliage is light green and strap-like in appearance. These beautiful flowers are always much sought after by the flower arranger as their rounded form contrasts delightfully with spiky cut flowers.

Agapanthus campanulatus 'Albus' is a very hardy form and can be relied upon in cold districts. It produces dense heads of white flowers, late summer, height 2½ft (75cm).

A. c. 'Isis' grows to a similar height and produces its intense blue flowers during early autumn. There is also the exceptionally hardy race of *Agapanthus* hybrids introduced by the late Lewis Palmer, the 'Headbourne Hybrids' and their flowers are pale to deep blue in colour, a little larger than *Agapanthus campanulatus*, and appear from late summer to early autumn, height 2½ to 3ft (75 to 90cm).

A. praecox 'Blue Triumphator' has clear blue flowers in late summer, height 2½ft (75cm). It is not fully hardy but makes an ideal subject for growing in a large pot or flower tub and given the protection of a cold greenhouse or a coldframe during the winter.

Cultivation and propagation *Agapanthus* flourishes best on light, rich, well-drained soil and requires a sunny situation. Heavy soils will require the introduction of plenty of sand or other gritty material to improve their drainage, and all types of soils will benefit from a good dressing of manure or garden compost. The brittle roots are best planted in the early spring just before growth begins and should be set out 20in (50cm) apart in each direction. Growth will be quite disappointing during the first couple of years, but once the roots penetrate deeply into the soil flowers will be produced quite freely, so be patient. The less hardy species should be protected in winter with a covering of bracken or straw.

Propagation is by root division in early spring.

Uses The larger flowers of the *Agapanthus* are of sufficient scale for use in pedestal or large designs. The smaller varieties make an interesting central feature in traditional arrangements for the home. The colour and sea urchin quality of the flower makes it easy to associate with bleached driftwood and coral in a seascape arrangement.

Conditioning To condition the strap-like leaves, cut them with a pair of sharp scissors, as secateurs would tear and bruise the broad leaves, shortening their cut life. The flowers should be cut when they display a proportion of open bloom. Stand them in deep water for about 3 hours.

Preserving Individual flowers will dry quickly in desiccant. Allow a number of stems to set seed. Collect them after the pod has burst open and the seed dispersed.

Camassia

Quamash
North America
Liliaceae

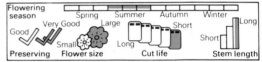

Camassia esculenta

Camassia is a hardy bulbous plant. The following species all make excellent cut flowers: *C. cusickii*, spikes of star-like wisteria-blue flowers, midsummer, height 2½ft (75cm) *C. esculenta* syn. *C. fraseri*, spikes of dark blue star-like flowers, midsummer, height 10in (25cm).
C. leichtlinii is perhaps the best species and

strains are available which have white, cream, blue or purple flowers. It is of vigorous growth and produces good sturdy spikes of star-like flowers on 3ft (90cm) stems in midsummer. *C. l. semi-plema* is a double form, spikes of star-like white flowers, midsummer, height 2½ft (75cm).

Cultivation and propagation The bulbs are fairly large and should be planted 4in (10cm) deep and 9in (22.5cm) apart in a deep moist fertile soil, in a sunny or slightly shaded position, in the autumn. Once planted they may be left undisturbed for three or four years, before being lifted and divided. It sets seed quite freely. The seeds are sown as soon as they are ripe ½in (1.25cm) deep and the resulting plants commence flowering 4 years later. Established bulbs should be given a mulch of leaf-mould or peat each spring, and watered during the growing period.

Uses This exquisite flower is still rarely grown by the British flower arranger. The spikes of starry flowers are always noticed first in any arrangement where they are used. The colour is clear and distinct. Its tall growing habit places it in the range of outline material. The statuesque shape lends itself perfectly to formal, symmetrical arrangements.

Conditioning Cut the stem when most of the flowers are open and stand it in deep water for about 2 hours in a cool place. Any tip buds will open within a short period.

Preserving The *Camassia* flower almost demands to be preserved. Remove individual flowers and dry them in desiccant. The seed head, though not as striking as the fresh flower, will develop on the plant and dry naturally. Collect this before it is damaged by wind and rain.

Campanula

Bellflower
Northern hemisphere
Campanulaceae

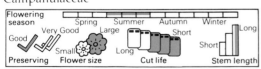

The two species of *Campanula* that are suitable for cutting both have spikes of bell-shaped flowers. The biennial species suitable for cutting is *Campanula medium* (Canterbury Bell, also lovingly referred to as the Cup and Saucer flower), a biennial species native to Southern Europe. It bears spikes of bell-shaped flowers of white, pink, blue or mauve, on sturdy erect stems, midsummer, height 1 to 3ft (30 to 90cm). *C. m.* 'Calycanthema (Cup and Saucer) Mixed' is a truly splendid blend of all the available

Campanula medium

colours, and the flowers are large, height 2½ft (75cm). It is also possible to buy the seeds in single colours.

C. m. 'Bells of Holland' is a dwarfer type which is very good for bedding-out purposes but it is equally good for cutting. The plants are compact and develop a conical shape with flowers of blue, mauve, rose, pink and white, obtainable either in straight colours or as mixed seed, height 1½ft (45cm).

C. persicifolia is a native British and European species which is perennial and produces flower spikes of blue, bell-shaped flowers, about 1in (2.5cm) across, throughout the summer, height 3ft (90cm). There are several excellent cultivars of this species, some with double flowers, which are superior to *C. persicifolia*.

C. p. 'Alba', white flowers, height 3ft (90cm).
C. p. 'Fleur de Neige', double white flowers, height 3ft (90cm).
C. p. 'Pride of Exmouth', semi-double, powder blue flowers, on slender stems, height 2ft (60cm).
C. p. 'Telham Beauty', single, large, china blue flowers, height 3ft (90cm).
C. p. 'Wirral Belle', double violet blue flowers, height 3ft (90cm).

Cultivation and propagation *Campanula* needs a fertile, well drained soil. It grows well on chalky soils, so if you have any doubt about the lime status of your soil apply a dressing of lime prior to introducing these plants. Choose a sheltered yet sunny situation.

Sow the seed of *C. medium* where flowering is to take place. If you have a few cloches to protect and encourage early growth sow in early spring, otherwise wait till late spring. Early sowings will give bigger and better plants. Germination takes about three weeks. Thin the seedlings out to stand 9 to 18in (22.5 to 45cm) apart. The resulting plants will flower in midsummer the following year.

Campanula persicifolia 'Telham Beauty'

C. persicifolia and its cultivars are propagated by division of the roots in the spring. Established plants should be lifted and divided every third year, otherwise the plants will deteriorate. When preparing the ground incorporate some manure or well-rotted garden compost. The plants should be spaced out in their flowering positions 15in (37.5cm) apart in each direction. For earlier flowering, plants can be carefully lifted when they are dormant and be placed in large plant pots in a cool greenhouse for gentle forcing. Flowering should be about a month earlier than normal.

Uses The pastel shades blend well with other summer flowers especially in massed arrangements for weddings and garden parties. The annual species can be used as a complete plant, giving conical sprays up to 3ft (90cm) long for outline material.

Conditioning Cut the stems when the lower flowers are beginning to open. Remove any excess stem foliage and condition them in deep water for 3 to 4 hours. Avoid strong sunlight. If the whole plant is to be used, supply water liberally for several days before cutting.

Preserving The blooms are very delicate, but can be pressed with a certain amount of patience. The dimensional shape is lost, but the profile is most interesting.

Catananche

Cupid's Dart
Southern Europe
Compositae

Catananche coerulea

Catananche coerulea is much desired for its long-lasting, semi-double, cornflower-like, blue or white flowers, which are borne on slender, wiry stems, all summer, height 2ft (60cm). Apart from being used as fresh cut flowers, flowers may also be hung up and dried for winter decoration. The flowers are not cut until they are fully open. The cultivar *C. c.* 'Major' is the most frequently grown and it has lavender-blue flowers with a dark eye.

C. c. 'Bicolor' has blue and white flowers.

Cultivation and Propagation This herbaceous plant is not fussy about its soil. It likes good drainage for its roots and a sunny position. Plant in spring.

Propagation of the species is from seed sown in spring in a coldframe. Germination takes 14 to 21 days. Once the seedlings are large enough to handle prick them out into seedtrays and set out the resulting plants into their permanent places during June. Allow 1ft (30cm) between the plants in each direction. Named cultivars are best propagated by root cuttings taken in winter and placed in a coldframe. Set out resulting plants in late spring.

Uses Although this is a short-lived plant the flower has an extremely long cut life. The grass-like foliage is of little use to the arranger, but the lavender blue flowers are a very useful addition to an arrangement of pastel colours.

Preserving Its major use is as a dried component. The flower resembles a cornflower with short florets and papery bracts. Collect them when they are fully developed, tie them in loose bundles and hang them in a darkened room to prevent excessive loss of colour. To retain the distinct colouration preserve a number in desiccant. Pierce the flower with a wire before the process begins, this will allow you to attach a false wire stem easily when the flower is dry.

Delphinium

Larkspur
Europe
Ranunculaceae

Delphinium 'Blue Bees'

Delphinium 'Blue Jade'

Delphinium 'Blue Tit'

Delphinium is a popular annual and perennial with showy spikes of spurred flowers. The annual species include *D. ajacis*, which is a native of Southern Europe and *D. consolida*, which is a native of Britain and Europe. They are generally found in seed catalogues listed under their common name Larkspur. Those suitable for cutting include:
'Giant Imperial Mixed' double flowers on strong stems in a wide range of colours, height 5ft (150cm). This is best treated as a biennial, with direct sowing in the open ground where flowering is to take place. Sow in late summer for early summer flowering in the following year.
'Rosamonda' is also suitable for late summer sowing. It has fine bright rose-coloured flowers in the early summer, height 3ft (90cm).

Delphinium 'Blue Nile'

'Giant Hyacinth Flowered Mixed', another double flowered type suitable for cutting, is best sown in spring. Flowers are white, violet, pink and carmine, height 2½ft (75cm). 'Dwarf Hyacinth Flowered Mixed', flowers in bright colours, height 1½ft (45cm). In addition to mixed colours, you can find specific colours with a bit of searching.

Lots of perennial delphinium cultivars have been produced from *D. elaturn*, many of which are suitable for use by the flower arranger. Some delphiniums grow too tall to be much use for vase work in the normal home, never-the-less, the smaller forms and in particular the Belladonna Hybrids are ideal for cutting. Their period of availability is midsummer.

Dwarf Delphiniums

'Baby Doll', pale mauve flowers with a white eye, height 4ft (120cm).
'Blue Tit', indigo blue flowers with a black eye, height 3½ft (105cm)
'Blue Jade', pastel blue flowers with a nigger-brown eye, height 4ft 120cm).
'Cinderella', heliotrope-mauve flowers, height 3½ft (105cm).
'Cupid', pale sky blue flowers with a white eye, height 3ft (90cm).
'Pageboy', brilliant mid-blue flowers with a white eye, height 3ft (90cm).
'Blue Fountain', blue, purple and white, height 2ft (60cm), is a useful seed mixture for the beginner,

Delphinium Belladonna Hybrids

'Blue Bees', clear pale blue flowers with white eye, freely produced, height 3½ft (105cm).
'Cliveden Beauty', sky-blue flowers, height 3ft (90cm).
'Lamartine', deep violet-blue flowers, height 4ft (120cm).
'Moerheimii', pure white flowers, height 4ft (120cm).
'Peace', intense blue flowers, height 3½ft (105cm).
'Pink Sensation', light rose-pink flowers, height 4ft (120cm).
'Wendy', deep gentian blue flowers flecked purple, height 4ft (120cm).

Delphinium Pacific Hybrids

'Astolat', shades of pink flowers, height 4 to 5ft (120 to 150cm).
'Black Knight', rich purple-blue flowers with a dark eye, height 4 to 5ft (120 to 150cm).
'Blue Jay', mid-blue flowers with a white eye, height 4 to 5ft (120 to 150cm).
'Cameliard', lavender-blue flowers with a white eye, height 4 to 5ft (120 to 150cm).
'Galahad', snow-white flowers, height 5 to 6ft (150 to 180cm).
'King Arthur', royal purple flowers with white eye, height 5 to 6ft (150 to 180cm).
'Silver Moon', exquisite silver-mauve flowers with a white eye, height 5½ft (165cm).
'Summer Skies', pale light blue flowers, height 5ft (150cm).

When grown in the open in the normal way, there are in fact two crops of flowers produced each year. There is the main flush of top quality flowers produced during midsummer and then there is a second somewhat inferior and lighter crop produced in autumn.

Cultivation and Propagation These plants like a moist, deep, reasonably fertile soil in an open sunny position. They need shelter against strong winds. Taller varieties need staking. Established perennial plants are usually divided every other year to keep the plants vigorous. It is the usual practice to sow the seeds where flowering is to take place as these plants do not like being transplanted. If a frame or cloches are available sowing may commence in early spring, otherwise a few weeks later. Thin the resulting plants to 10in (25cm) apart in a row.

For perennial delphiniums the propagation of named cultivars is generally either by division of the plants or by basal cuttings taken in spring. Cuttings must be secured from the parent plant before the shoots become hollow at the base (about 4in (10cm) long). They are then placed in a sandy soil in a coldframe to root. Delphinium Pacific Giants can also be grown from seed sown early in the year, either in a greenhouse or in a coldframe. When the seedlings are large enough to handle they are pricked out into 4in (10cm) pots. They are then planted in the open ground that summer, and some flowering will take place in the autumn. Alternatively, sowing may take place in midsummer and the resulting plants are transferred to their flowering positions in the autumn. It is possible to obtain a good selection of delphiniums from a single packet of mixed hybrid seeds if one is willing to undertake some roguing of inferior plants when they show colour.

Uses The form of this flower makes it an ideal outline material for very large arrangements. The flower spikes are less solid than those of the *Antirrhinum* and can be used in a similar way to create a lighter effect. Happily their flowering period coincides with that of the *Campanula* which with their similar colour but contrasting form can be combined to make an harmonious design. After the main spike has flowered, shorter side spikes develop for using in smaller arrangements. The feathery foliage adds considerably to the charm of these flowers.

Conditioning Give them a good drink in deep water for at least 6 hours.

Preserving This is one of the best flowers for air drying. The stem should be cut when it is about two-thirds developed. Remove most of the foliage and tie the stems into loose bundles with sufficient space between each stem to allow the air to circulate. Hang them upside down in a light, warm atmosphere. The process will take between 3 and 4 weeks, then they can be stored in a box until needed. The flowers may look a little crushed after a while, but they can be restored to their original form by applying a jet of steam from a boiling kettle. Don't attempt to dry the flowers when they are damp, as they will invariably start to rot during the drying process.

Echinops

Globe Thistle
S. Europe, Asia
Compositae

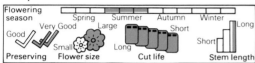

Echinops ritro

Echinops produces blue globule heads of flowers which are spiny before opening, upon stiff, erect, branching stems bearing much divided prickly grey-green, thistly foliage. Both the flowers and the foliage are of importance. The species best suited for cut flower production are *Echinops humilis* and *E. ritro*.
E. h. 'Taplow Blue', has blue flowers, height 5ft (150cm). *E. ritro* has steel blue flowers, height 3ft (90cm). Both these species flower in late summer.
Cultivation and Propagation Both species are equally easy to grow, as they are not fussy about soil and may be situated in full sun or partial shade. However, they do like to be able to thrust their fleshy tap-roots well down beneath the soil's surface, so some deep cultivation is desirable, with some bulky organic matter worked in.
Propagation is usually by the division of the existing roots in spring. Root cuttings can be taken when the plants become dormant in the

autumn. *Echinops ritro* can be propagated by seed sown in the open ground in spring. Germination will take some three to four weeks. When the seedlings are large enough to handle one can either thin out or prick out the seedlings, so that they stand some 9in (22.5cm) apart in the row. The resulting plants are transferred to their flowering location in the late autumn and set out 2ft (60cm) apart in each direction. Once established these plants should be divided every third year.
Uses The mature flowers of the *Echinops* are metallic blue, arranged in a tight ball at the top of the stem. If you remove any side flowers, the central flower will develop considerably. It is coarse in apearance and generally looks at odds arranged with flowers of a delicate form and colour. Its most popular use is in seascape arrangements, the unusual formation of the flower resembles that of a sea urchin.
The flower has an unyielding, permanent quality, which harmonizes well with driftwood. Both foliage and flowers may be used at any stage of development. The leaves have a silvery reverse resembling the foliage of the common thistle.
Conditioning Remove any leaves that will be submerged during conditioning and stand the stems in deep water for about 3 hours.
Preserving The seed heads will mature and dry on the plant, though the calyx will fall in adverse weather. To prevent this happening, collect the stems as the flowers fade and preserve them in glycerine solution. The stem foliage should be removed as this will wither as the stem absorbs the preservative. The seeds are an unusual shape resembling a torpedo. Collect them after the flower has faded, to add textural interest to a seed collage.

Eryngium

Sea Holly
Europe
Umbelliferae

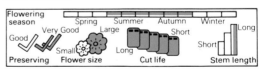

Eryngium is grown for its beautiful foliage and bracts, which are stiff and spiky. Its flower heads look quite similar to those of *Echinops* but more dome shaped in appearance.
There are a number of species from which one may make one's selection and it is an easy matter to have fresh *Eryngium* available from the garden from early summer to late autumn plus a further supply dried for winter use:
E. alpinum, light blue flowers, early, height 3ft (90cm).

Eryngium alpinum

Eryngium oliverianum

E. *bourgatii,* steely blue flowers, early, height 2ft (60cm).

E. *oliverianum,* extremely deeply cut leaves, feathery bracts, deep blue flowers, mid season, height 2½ft (75cm).

E. *planum* 'Blue Gnome' deep blue flowers, mid season, height 2ft (60cm)

E. *tripartitum* much-branched stems with lots of small, spiny, blue-grey flowers, late, height 2ft 4in (70cm).

E. *verifolium,* evergreen, deeply cut marbled silver leaves, silver-blue flowers, mid season. This makes a delightful subject for winter decoration, when dried, height 2ft (60cm).

Cultivation and Propagation It prefers a deep, well-drained sandy soil and a sunny situation. Heavy soils can be adapted by the incorporation of sharp sand or other gritty material to improve the drainage. Providing the soil is reasonably fertile there is no need to

introduce any manure, as this plant seems to manage quite well without this.

The common method of propagation is by root cuttings taken in the winter. It may also be grown from seed sown in a coldframe in spring. Germination takes 4 to 6 weeks. Prick out seedlings into 3in (7.5cm) pots, when large enough to handle, and set out the resulting plants in their permanent flowering position in the autumn, allowing a space of 18in (45cm) between plants.

Uses *Eryngium* is a very long lasting cut flower. The head is domed with a frill of feathery but sharp bracts behind it. The visual texture is coarse and when used in traditional designs it should be used with restraint. Generally it is best displayed in free form or modern designs where its dramatic beauty can be seen without distraction. As the common name sea holly indicates, it is very much a part of the seascape arrangement. Flowers that are on the point of drying naturally can be pinned to the back of driftwood to heighten the effect of the seashore.

Conditioning It is an easy flower to condition. The more mature the stems, the less they seem to need to drink.

Preserving The flower bract can be successfully air dried. Collect them once the flower has faded and hang them in bunches in a dry atmosphere. To achieve a bleached effect suspend them close to a source of bright light.

Myosotis

Forget-me-not
Europe including Britain
Boraginaceae

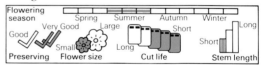

This plant, is frequently grown as a carpeting plant in spring bedding displays, as its tiny blue flowers make such a fine background against which the various types of tulips may be seen to best advantage. The two species in which we are interested here are both perennials but are usually grown as biennials. The first of these is M. *alpestris,* which is a short-lived perennial. The cultivar M. *a.* 'Blue Spire' has vivid blue flowers on erect stems, while M. *a.* 'Royal Blue' produces pretty deep blue flowers. Both these cultivars grow to a height of 1ft (30cm) and flower in early summer.

M. *oblongata* syn. M. *sylvatica* has an excellent cultivar, M. *o.* 'Blue Bird', with beautiful dark blue flowers, height 1ft (30cm). In mild districts this cultivar will flower in the open.

Myosotis alpestris 'Royal Blue'

Nepeta

Cultivation and Propagation *Myosotis* will grow in any ordinary garden soil either in light or partial shade. The seeds of both species are sown in the open in early summer. Germination takes two to three weeks. When the seedlings are large enough to handle they are pricked out 6in (15cm) apart in each direction. The resulting plants are transferred to their flowering places in the autumn and planted out 9in (22.5cm) apart in each direction.

Uses Because of their small size these flowers have a somewhat limited use in fresh arrangements, except perhaps as a small posy of welcome on a dressing table. Whole plants may be used in landscape designs by lifting them from the garden and wrapping the root ball in polythene. They do provide the blue colour that is sometimes difficult to obtain and look very natural providing the polythene is well concealed.

Conditioning They only need a short drink of water to condition them. I find that generally they do not appreciate water-retaining foam, so when possible arrange them in water.

Preserving Individual flowers and short sections of stem can be dried in desiccant for using in small arrangements of grasses and blossom or flower pictures.

Nepeta

Catmint
Northern Hemisphere
Labiatae

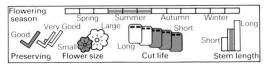

Nepeta × faassenii is a hybrid which is very useful for ground cover, for its fragrant grey foliage and its lavender-blue flowers which it produces all the summer long, height 12in (30cm). However, of much greater use in floral arrangements is *Nepeta faassenii* 'Six Hills Giant' which has the same lavender-blue flowers and the same fragrant foliage but it grows to a height of 2ft (60cm). There is also an intermediate form *Nepeta* 'Blue Beauty', with lots of erect lavender blue spikes of flowers, but has a more greeny longer, narrower, foliage, height 1½ft (45cm).

Cultivation and Propagation *Nepeta* likes an open sunny place and will grow on a wide range of soils providing they are well drained. Cut back the stems in the late autumn and fork a small amount of old garden compost into the soil's surface. The roots normally need lifting and dividing every third year, and this provides an opportunity to cultivate the soil and provide a more generous application of manure, prior to replanting.

Propagation is by division of the roots in spring, just as new growth is about to commence, by half-ripe cuttings taken in summer and rooted in a shaded coldframe, or by seed sown in the open ground during late spring. When the seedlings are large enough to handle they should be thinned out to stand 6in (15cm) apart in the row. They are then left to develop until the autumn, when they are transferred to their flowering places and set out 12in (30cm) apart.

Uses *Nepeta* has a soft colouration that will blend with most pastel colours. The flowers are small and tubular, growing in profusion along the stem. The tall spiky stem is often used as outline material for massed traditional arrangements. The fussy effect can be toned down by including flowers and leaves that are plain and bold. It is not a flower for modern

designs but as the plant is very generous with its flowers it can be used in profuse quantities in terracotta jugs to decorate the kitchen.
Conditioning Select the stems when the flowers are open. Pick them over to remove any dead flowers. No preparatory work is needed to condition them; just stand them in water for 2 hours.
Preserving As the flowers are so small they are best preserved by air drying. Do more than you will need as the flowers tend to become very crisp and fall from the stem.

Nigella

Love-in-a-Mist
Mediterranean
Ranunculaceae

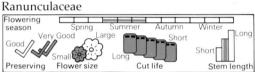

Nigella damascena 'Miss Jekyll'

The hardy annual *N. damascena* is the species for bedding out purposes in the summer, and this is excellent for cutting, both when it is fresh and also when dried for winter use. The winter attraction is the balloon-like seed heads and the finely cut leaves, and these can be sprayed with either silver or gilt paint.
N. d. 'Miss Jekyll' has semi-double bright blue flowers which look most attractive amongst fern-like foliage. There is also a dark blue strain which is very popular among flower arrangers. And for those who like a mixture of colours there is *N. d.* 'Persian Jewels' with flowers in mauve, lavender, purple, rose and pink. All these plants grow to 18in (45cm). *N. hispanica* is deep blue, height 1 to 2ft (30 to 60cm).
Cultivation and Propagation This is a plant

which will flourish in any ordinary garden soil. It is very easily grown. Sow where it is to flower, taking care to sow as thinly as possible. When the seedlings are large enough to handle thin them out to stand 8in (20cm) apart. Seed may be sown in the autumn or the early spring. The earliest flowers are produced by the autumn-sown seeds, when flowering will commence in early summer. The spring sowing will flower later.
Uses A light airy effect is easily achieved with these flowers. The whole colour range blends well with other material that is in the garden at the same time. The cut life is not long but the plant is so prolific that further supplies are always at hand. The fine, fern-like foliage is an added bonus in enhancing the delicate appearance of the flower in a traditional design.
Conditioning They are very easy to condition. Cut them when they are fully open and stand them in deep water for about 2 hours. Do not cut all the flowers, but allow a certain number to develop their characteristic balloon-shaped seedhead.
Preserving The naturally dried heads can be brittle. To obviate this, collect them when they have reached maturity but are still green and preserve them in glycerine solution. The process is rapid; a complete colour change will tell you when it is complete.

Platycodon

Chinese Bellflower
China, Manchuria and Japan
Campanulaceae

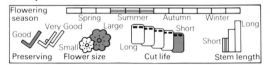

Platycodon grandiflora is a herbaceous perennial with wide bell-shaped, blue or white flowers which may be 2 to 2½in (5 to 6.25cm) across, borne several to each erect stem, in summer, height 1ft (30cm). *P. grandiflorum* 'Album' is a fine cultivar with white flowers tinged blue in midsummer, height 2ft (60cm).
P. g. 'Mariesii', fine large deep purplish-blue flowers, in late summer, height 1½ft (45cm).
Cultivation and Propagation These plants grow in any well drained soil, either in light or shade, providing that it is of some depth to enable their brittle roots to penetrate deeply beneath the surface. What they will not tolerate is badly drained wet soil during the cold winter months. Good soil conditions are essential before planting, as once planted they resent any disturbance. On sites which are poorly drained in the winter time, it would be advisable, not only to incorporate sharp sand

Platycodon grandiflora 'Mariesii'

and other gritty material, but also to plant on a raised bed, in order to solve the drainage problem. Planting takes place in the spring, setting the plants 14in (35cm) apart each way.

Platycodon is a bit late coming into growth in the spring and they die down completely in the autumn, so if one does not mark their exact position with a stake, it will be impossible to locate their position during the dormant season. Top dress with bonemeal in spring and mulch with peat or well-rotted garden compost.

Propagation is by division of the plants·roots in spring or from seeds sown at that time in a coldframe. The resulting plants are transferred to flowering positions the following spring.
Uses This is a plant whose fascination lies in its flower bud. The flower is cup shaped, with five pointed false petals. In the bud stage the points remain closed over each other and it resembles an inflated balloon. The open flower reflexes to reveal some remarkable colour shading. They can be used as a transitional flower or as a focal point in smaller massed designs.
Conditioning Pick the flowers as they are about to open and stand them in water for about 2 hours.
Preserving Only the opened flowers can be preserved either by pressing or drying in desiccant.

Scabiosa

Sweet Scabious or Pincushion Flower
Asia, Africa and Europe
Compositae

The annual species which is frequently grown as a cut flower subject is *S. atropurpurea* which flowers during the summer and is excellent for cutting. The flowers are fragrant, fully double

Scabiosa atropurpurea 'Blue Moon'

and may be purple, blue, red, deep crimson, pink or white in colour, 3ft (90cm). Most seed catalogues usually offer *Scabiosa atropurpurea* in blends of mixed colours only. However, you may find some offering straight colours such as *S. a.* 'Blue Moon' with lavender blue flowers, and *S. a.* 'Rosette' with fine deep rose coloured flowers. There are dwarfer strains which only grow to a height of 1½ft (45cm). These are of a more bushy habit but they are available in the same range of colours and are equally suitable for cutting. The perennial species grown is *Scabiosa caucasica* it grows to a height of 2ft (60cm) and has flowers of various shades of blue and purple, in addition to white cultivars. The most popular of these cultivars are *S. c.* 'Clive Greaves' with violet blue flowers and *S. c.* 'Miss Wilmot' with white flowers. Both of these cultivars are readily obtainable. There are several other cultivars worth seeking out if you can find them and these include *S. c.* 'Bressingham White', with creamy white flowers, *S. c.* 'Edith' with silvery-lavender flowers and *S. c.* 'Moonstone' with light blue flowers. All these cultivars flower throughout the summer.
Cultivation and Propagation *Scabiosa* prefers a well-drained light soil containing some lime, and an open sunny position. An annual dressing of lime may be beneficial. Taller growing *Scabiosa* may need some support with canes and string. Dead head regularly to stimulate new flowers and extend the period of flowering. Established plants of *S. caucasia* need lifting and dividing up in spring every second year, if first class cut flowers are to be assured. Choose young parts of the older plant which

have lots of fibrous roots, not ones of a woody nature. If possible, select a fresh site for the plants to occupy. Take the opportunity of fortifying the soil with organic matter well dug in. In mild areas seeds of *S. atropurpurea* may be sown in the autumn and the plants generally survive the winter quite happily, but elsewhere sowing is delayed until the spring, after the frost unless some protection is available in the form of coldframes or cloches. The seed is sown where flowering is to take place. Germination will take 2 to 3 weeks. When the plants are large enough to handle they are thinned out to stand 10in (25cm) apart. Where autumn sowing is possible flowering will commence in early summer. Spring sowings will flower later in the summer.

Propagate *S. caucasica* by division or by seed sown in spring. The seed is sown thinly in seed-boxes containing a sandy compost and then placed in a coldframe to germinate. When the resulting seedlings are large enough to handle, they are pricked out individually into 3½in (8.75cm) pots containing the same compost. They are then placed in the open during the summer months and given the protection of a very well ventilated coldframe through the subsequent winter months.

Uses The shades of blue are beyond compare. Under strong artificial light each flower has a silvery sparkle. The long stems make these suitable for large arrangements, where the somewhat quieter colour shading will not clash with other more dominant materials. They give a natural feel to both landscape and seascape designs. The dwarf strains are excellent for interpretative designs where they can be used to introduce bold areas of colour and form without appearing too sophisticated.

Conditioning They are remarkably easy to condition. All they require is 3 hours in water away from direct sunlight.

Preserving Some of the smaller blooms are ideal for preserving in desiccant. Do this when they have reached their peak of maturity. A small length of stem can be left on.

Veronica

Speedwell
Europe, N. Asia
Scrophulariaceae

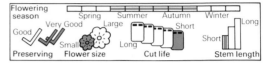

Veronica incana

The herbaceous *Veronicas* make a valuable contribution to the provision of spiky cut flower material from spring to autumn.

V. gentianoides produces dainty light blue spikes of flowers during late spring, height 2ft (60cm).

V. incana is particularly noteworthy, not only for its short spikes of deep blue flowers, but also for its silvery grey lance-shaped foliage. This is a dwarf plant 1ft (30cm) high which flowers during summer.

V. longifolia has graceful spikes of lilac blue flowers during summer, height 2½ft (75cm). Its cultivar *V. l.* 'Forester's Blue' is a little shorter at 2ft (60cm) and has deep blue flowers which are freely produced during the same period.

V. spicata has bright blue flowers in dense spikes in summer, height 1½ to 2ft (45 to 60cm). There are also good cultivars worthy of growing for cutting.

V. s. 'Barcarolle', spikes of rose pink flowers in late summer and autumn, height 2ft (60cm).

V. s. 'Heidekind', wine-red flower spikes in summer, height 20in (50cm).

V. s. 'Kapitan', which is an earlier flowering form, producing a profusion of bright blue flowers on its spikes in early summer, height 1ft (30cm).

V. teucrium has lavender blue flowers in slender spikes in summer. It also has desirable cultivars such as *V. t.* 'Crater Lake' with exquisite vivid deep blue flower spikes, height 1ft (30cm). None of these plants are difficult to grow and they all last well as cut flowers. No staking or tying is required.

Cultivation and Propagation These plants will grow in any reasonably fertile garden soil which is well drained. The presence of sand or other gritty material in the soil is very much to their liking. While they like a sunny situation they will also tolerate light shade. Once planted they may remain undisturbed for three or four years, before it becomes necessary to lift and divide their fibrous roots. Planting may take place at any time during the dormant season but, is best in the early spring. The roots of the plants should be set out some 12 to 16in (30 to 40cm) apart in each direction. When dividing old roots select some of the younger crowns and discard with the remainder. Established

plants should be provided with a light mulch of well rotted garden compost about their roots each spring and this should be forked in each autumn.

Propagation can be accomplished in one of three ways. First, by the division of the plants during the dormant season. Second, by cuttings secured in the spring or early summer. These are inserted in a coldframe or cloche to encourage rapid rooting and the glass is shaded to protect the cuttings. New plants can also be propagated from seeds. The seed is sown in the open, during the early summer. Germination will take 14 to 21 days. When the seedlings are large enough to handle they are thinned out to stand 8in (20cm) apart in the row. The resulting plants may then be transferred to their flowering positions either in the autumn or early the following spring.

Uses *Veronica* provides some of the deeper shades of blue that arrangers are fond of. The flower spike is erect with a luxuriant growth of glossy stem foliage. As outline material the darker shades such as 'Crater Lake' and 'Heidekind' link perfectly with *Penstemon*, *Scabiosa* and *Erigeron*. The pale colouration of 'Kapitan' is an attractive adjunct to a traditional design of pastel tones.

Conditioning The only conditioning problem that is likely to be encountered is with the stem foliage. Excessive amounts left on the stem tend to prevent an adequate supply of moisture reaching the flowers. Remove at least two-thirds of the leaves and stand the flower stem in water for 3 hours.

Preserving The very small flowers can be dried in desiccant, though it will be a tedious job. Allowing the seed spike to develop will give you suitable pieces of tall material for arrangements of preserved foliages.

Veronica longifolia 'Forester's Blue'

Veronica spicata

Veronica teucrium 'Crater Lake'

GREEN

Euphorbia

Euphorbiaceae

Euphorbia robbiae

Euphorbia wulfenii

Euphorbia is a very large genus of about one thousand species of widely differing habits, for it embraces annual and perennial plants, shrubs and trees which are distributed world wide. Several herbaceous species are suitable for cutting. *Euphorbia epithymoides* syn. *E. polychroma* is early flowering, its sulphur-yellow flower bracts appearing during spring; these later fade to green and remain green all summer. This is a trouble-free European plant of neat growth, height 1½ft (45cm).

E. griffithii 'Fireglow' has orange-red flower bracts during early summer, after which they fade green and remain neat throughout the season, height 2½ft (75cm). This plant is a native of the Himalaya region.

E. palustris has flattish heads of greeny-yellow flowers and lush green foliage, growing best where the soil contains plenty of moisture. Flowering period early summer, height 3ft (90cm). Native of Europe.

E. robbiae has pale yellow/green heads of flower during late spring and dark green foliage, height 2 to 2½ft (60 to 75cm). Native to Asia Minor.

Another species of particular interest to the flower arranger is *Euphorbia wulfenii*, with bluish-green oblong evergreen leaves, which are topped by sulphur-yellow flower bracts during the spring. This too is a European plant, height 3ft (90cm).

Cultivation and propagation All species grow quite satisfactorily in poor soil either in direct sun or partial shade. *E. robbiae* is inclined to run in good soil. Plants should be set some 1½ to 2ft (45 to 60cm) apart in each direction, during the dormant season. Propagation is either by seed, which is sown immediately it is harvested, or by division of the plants once the flowers have faded.

E. wulfenii is quite good at sowing its own seeds when they are ripe, in the immediate vicinity of where it is growing, and the resulting plants flower in their second year.

Uses The charm of this popular arranging plant lies in its acid green flower bracts. They are an excellent highlight when used as focal material in an all-foliage design. Some of the larger varieties make an ideal alternative flower for modern arrangements. As they have a long cut life one or two heads arranged on pins with a branch of foliage make a suitable design, and they can be quickly replaced as they fade.

Conditioning The cut stem exudes a caustic sap. This must be staunched immediately over a naked flame for 10 to 20 seconds and the stem then placed in water for 3 hours.

Preserving The fresh flowering stem will not preserve with any degree of success. Let a number of stems dry naturally in the garden and collect them before they are damaged by any adverse weather.

Hardy Ferns

No book of this nature would be complete without some mention of hardy ferns, as they make a very worthy contribution to floral artistry. There are usually shady moist places in the garden where other plants are difficult to grow but where ferns will thrive.

The following selection of ferns will supply lots of useful fronds for elegant arrangements from late spring until the autumn:

Asplenium
Polypodiaceae
Asplenium scolpendrium (The Harts Tongue Fern) is a most adaptable fern which has bright green fronds. It can even be grown quite successfully on chalky soils and once it has been planted it calls for the minimum of attention, height 1½ft (45cm).

Flowering season		Spring	Summer	Autumn	Winter	
Good	Very Good	Large		Short		Long
Preserving	Small	Flower size	Long	Cut life	Short	Stem length

Athyrium
Polypodiaceae
Athyrium filix-femina (Lady Fern), native to Europe including Britain, is a temperate species with lovely large lacy, pale-green fronds, height 2 to 3ft (60 to 90cm).

Dryopteris
Polypodiaceae
Dryopteris filix-mas (Male Fern) is indigenous to Britain, Europe and many other temperature regions of the world. It has pale-green, shuttlecock-like fronds, height 2 to 3ft (60 to 90cm). This is of robust growth and makes a fine ground cover subject where little else will grow.

Osmunda
Osmundaceae
Osmunda regalis (Royal Fern) is a widespread

species which requires a moist situation near a stream or pond if it is to be grown successfully and it does not flourish on chalky soils. It has large graceful pale-green fronds in the spring but with the approach of the autumn these become reddish-brown in colour, height 4ft (120cm) or more.

Polystichum
Polypodiaceae
Polystichum setiferum (Shield Fern) is a widespread species with elegant deep-green lance-shaped fronds, which in mild districts retain their colour during the winter, if they are in a sheltered place. This species is equally at home either in a sunny or a shady situation providing it is planted in a moist soil, height 3ft (90cm).
Cultivation and propagation Choose a site which gives some protection from the cold winds in the spring so as to protect the newly developing fronds. If there is any doubt about the soil's ability to retain moisture apply a generous application of well-rotted leaf mould, well-rotted garden compost or peat, before planting. Drought is the main enemy of hardy ferns. Planting is undertaken during the dormant season. In the spring mulch to retain soil moisture. This may be with rotted garden compost or peat. The mulching must be undertaken annually, so as to recreate the natural growing conditions to which ferns are accustomed.
    Propagation is by division in spring.
Uses If you have the space to grow the five types mentioned, you will have a supply of interesting foliage that will be of use from the spring through to mid-autumn. They are foliages for use in traditional designs, landscapes and informal arrangements. The solid form is a useful outline material in bold designs. The finer form (Lady Fern) looks more

attractive in an arrangement that is at close quarters, as in a dinner table arrangement. Fronds that are in the process of unfurling may be arranged in a modern way, using a limited number with a piece of driftwood or other sculptured leaves.
Conditioning Immature foliage may be a little difficult to condition. Burn the end of the stem over a naked flame and stand it in deep water for about 4 hours. Mature stems will condition without reducing the stem end to charcoal, though I always play safe and burn them before conditioning.
Preserving Ferns can be preserved by pressing them between sheets of newspaper and laying them under a carpet. The fronds tend to be brittle and will disintegrate with careless handling. The pressing must be done when the fronds are fully mature.

Molucella

Syria and the Eastern Mediterranean
Labiatae

Molucella laevis

Molucella laevis (Bells of Ireland) is the species of importance to the flower arranger, both when freshly cut and when dried. The small white flowers which are produced by this plant are of no real significance for floral displays. The attraction of this plant is the large, pale green, bell-shaped calyces which adorn the tall spikes and persist after the flowers have faded, height 1½ft (45cm).

Cultivation and propagation *Molucella* thrives best in light sandy soils of only moderate fertility and prefers an open sunny situation. If the weather is warm and dry during the early establishment of this plant watering will be necessary.

Although *M. laevis* is a perennial, it is treated as hardy annual and it can either be grown entirely in the open or an earlier start can be made with the aid of coldframes or cloches. The earliest sowing, with some protection, takes place in spring. Sowings in the open can take place in early summer. Germination is likely to be a gradual process over some 14 to 21 days, or even longer. The resulting plants are thinned out to stand 8in (22cm) apart. Early sowing will produce spikes ready for cutting during midsummer, while sowings made later in the open ground will be available for cutting in autumn. It is also possible to sow seeds in midsummer and give the plants some protection with coldframes and cloches to provide spikes for cutting in late autumn. The actual time of cutting is a matter of personal judgment for as the flowers develop it will be seen that the stems continue to lengthen with the calyces becoming further apart.

Uses Very few plants are as versatile as this. It is much prized by arrangers as fresh plant material, providing spikes of light green calyces up to 2ft (60cm) long as outline material for the largest arrangements. The smaller, side spikes are equally useful when working on a more modest scale. When the stem is growing in the garden it has a rather confused appearance, due to the presence of the leaf which obscures the calyces.

Conditioning Cut the fresh stems when they have reached their maximum development. Take off all the foliage and the lower calyces. Stand them in water for at least 4 hours in a cool room away from direct sunlight.

Preserving To preserve them again remove the stem foliage and lower calyces and stand them in a solution of glycerine and water. They are prone to wilting during the first few hours of preserving so it is essential to give them a certain amount of support. The process is quite rapid. After 3 days remove them from the solution. They will probably retain a certain amount of green colouring. Hang them upside down from a convenient line to continue the preserving, for any residual preservative in the stem will continue to act. If the position is against a window the colour will lighten even more. The tip of the stem often refuses to accept the solution, but this can be removed without damaging the stem. Store them in a box in a damp-free atmosphere. Should they get crushed they can be revived by a jet of steam from boiling water.

Ornamental Grasses

Gramineae

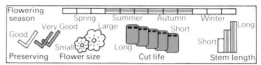

While ornamental grasses can be grown purely for garden decoration they do also have an important role to play in the provision of materials for use in the composition of dried floral arrangements. By acquiring a good selection of these it is possible to add the perfect artistic touch to any floral arrangement, whether it is to provide the impression of

Coix Lacryma-Jobi

Stipa pennata

Briza maxima

Panicum virgatum

Lagurus ovatus

height or width, either in their natural colour or suitably dyed.

The following selection of hardy annual grasses are all desirable subjects for growing and drying:

Agrostis nebulosa (Cloud Grass) is a tufted form of grass with panicles of what look like lots of dainty flowers, during late summer, height 1½ft (45cm). This species is a native of Spain.

Briza maxima (Pearl Grass) is another tufted form of grass with panicles of nodding spikelets and is particularly valuable for use in dried flower arrangements where it will add a touch of grace to an otherwise rather stiff floral composition. This species, which grows to a height of 1½ft (45cm), flowers in midsummer and is native to the Mediterranean region and the Canary Islands.

Briza minor (Little Quaking Grass) is a tufted grass which produces panicles of erect spikelets during late summer, height 1ft (30cm). This is a native of Western Europe and the Mediterranean region.

Coix Lacryma-Jobi (Job's Tears) This species is of vigorous growth. It produces thick maize-like leaves and decorative racemes of pearly-grey seeds in autumn, height 2 to 3ft (60 to 90cm). This is a native of the tropical regions of the world such as India and China. This is somewhat more tender than the other species and needs sowing in a warm greenhouse or frame during spring.

Hordeum jubatum (Squirrel Tail Grass) is a tufted grass with feathery silvery-grey flower heads during midsummer, height 1½ft (45cm). This is native to both North and South America and Siberia.

Lagurus ovatus (Hare's-tail Grass) is a European and British native species which produces panicles of soft, furry, creamy heads during midsummer, height 16in (40cm). This is best treated as a biennial. Sow the seeds in pots in the early autumn and provide the plants with the protection of a coldframe or cloches during the winter months. Give ventilation during mild spells of weather. Harden the plants off and plant in the open in late spring, 9in (22.5cm) apart.

Panicum is a large genus of annual and perennial grasses which are mostly native to the warmer parts of the world. *Panicum virgatum* 'Rubrum' is a hardy perennial which is native to North America. It has crimson-tinged foliage and panicles of much-branched flower sprays, on sturdy stems, in autumn, height 3ft (90cm). It may be cut and used in its fresh state or it may be dried. It may also be dyed to give it added brilliance. It is propagated by division in spring.

Phalaris canariensis is a tufted grass which is much grown for its attractive ovate spikes. This is the source of canary-seed which is fed to caged birds. Flowering is in midsummer, height 1½ft (45cm). This species is a native of

the Mediterranean Region.
Stipa (Feather Grass) is a native of Europe and
Siberia. *Stipa pennata* is of an erect habit of
growth and has bright green leaves. During
summer it produces feathery creamy-buff
plumes of silky flowers which make very useful
material for floral arrangements, height 3ft
(90cm). Seed should be sown in a greenhouse
in spring and later planted in open ground.
Cultivation and propagation Any ordinary,
reasonably well drained soil will do for growing
the grasses. They do not need to be on full
view, so a corner of the kitchen garden will do
just fine, providing that it is in a sunny
position. All one then has to do, is to wait for
the grasses to flower. Immediately they are
seen to be doing this, cut the flowering grasses
with as long stems as possible and hang them
up to dry in a cool dark place. Do not wait till
the whole of the flowers are at their maturest,
as by this time they will be past their best for
drying for use in winter decorations.

With the exception of *Coix Lacryma-Jobi,
Lagurus ovatus, Panicum* and *Stipa* the seed is
sown in the open ground in spring where the
grasses are to flower. Germination may take
some two to three weeks. When the grasses are
large enough to see quite clearly, one can take a
hoe and leave small clumps of the young
grasses at 9in (22.5cm) intervals.

At harvest time it is well worthwhile making
a trip out into the countryside to collect a few
heads of barley, oats, millet and wheat, as these
also make an important contribution to the
dried floral arrangements either in their natural
colours or dyed.
Uses With enterprising seedsmen introducing
new kinds for us to try there is really no excuse
for not devoting a corner of your garden to
grasses and wild flowers. Grasses will blend
with any style of arrangement, though they are
more at home in the natural landscape designs.
The tall nodding heads of grass seed blend
perfectly with preserved material. As the
harvest will be most prolific, you will be able to
create arrangements composed of grasses only.

The containers for this type of design should
be unsophisticated and if possible unglazed to
enhance the natural atmosphere.
Conditioning Grasses need almost no
conditioning. *Stipa* benefits from 2 hours in
deep water. They seem to suffer no ill effect if
kept dry after cutting.
Preserving Some grasses are best left until they
have dried naturally. Others, once they have
ripened, tend to shed seed which reduces their
value. Preserving them in glycerine when the
heads are mature and still green will lengthen
their effective life as dried plant material.

Considerable amounts of dried and dyed
grasses are available today, but the colours are
often harsh and strident. Experimenting with
cold water dye, I am sure that you can produce
a more tasteful effect at a fraction of the cost.

WHITE

Acanthus

Bears' Breeches
Southern Europe
Acanthaceae

Acanthus spinosus

This plant bears 'Foxglove' like spikes of
flowers, on sturdy erect stems and has
attractive large glossy foliage.
The earliest to flower is *A. mollis lactifolius*,
pale pink flowers flushed purple, during
midsummer, height 3½ft (105cm).
A. longifolius is more compact, height 2½ft
(75cm) and flowers freely during late summer.
A. spinosus has white and purple flowers in
late summer, height 4ft (120cm).
Cultivation and propagation These are deep
rooted plants, requiring a soil rich in humus
and well drained. They prefer a sunny
situation but will tolerate partial shade. Once
planted, Acanthus may be left undisturbed for
several years so it is important that the soil is
well prepared. Deep cultivation, to a depth of
18in (45cm), is a prerequisite. Heavy soils

should have coarse sand and other gritty material incorporated at this time, and all types of soil should be given a good dressing of manure or well rotted garden compost. Planting may take place at any time during the dormant season. Set the plants 2ft (60cm) apart in each direction. Established plants should be mulched with peat or leaf-mould each spring.

Propagation can be by division, in the autumn or winter. Acanthus can also be propagated by root cuttings. The easiest way of all to propagate this plant is from seed. As soon as the seeds are ripe in the autumn, soak them in water for 12 hours and then sow them directly into the soil in a coldframe. Cover the frame with glass throughout the winter. Pot up the plants when they are large enough to handle and place them back in the coldframe. Remove the glass during the late spring and set the new plants out in the permanent positions early the following spring.

Uses The tall flowering stems are best suited to bold vertical designs. Their rough textural appearance associates well with driftwood and the large smooth leaves of *Hosta* or *Fatsia japonica*. They may be cut at any stage of growth, though those stems that you wish to preserve should be left to reach their maximum height.

Conditioning The flowers condition very easily. All they require is a deep drink of water for about 3 hours.

Preserving The stems will preserve automatically if left on the plant until the autumn. To prevent any damage by harsh weather they may be collected when the seed pods have developed and hung up in an airy atmosphere to dry. Preserving the stem in glycerine solution will extend the life of the preserved material considerably. Cut the stems when the seed pods have developed, remove any faded flower petals, and stand them in the solution. The stem will change colour to dark brown, while the calyx varies from pale biscuit to brown, and preserving may take up to a fortnight.

Astrantia

Masterwort
Asia and Europe
Umbelliferae

Astrantia involucrata

flower as it produces its near-white star-like flowers continuously all summer and into autumn, height 2ft (60cm).

A. 'Margery Fish' also produces whitish flowers over a similarly long period, height 32in (80cm).

A. maxima produces shell pink flowers in summer, height 1½ft (45cm).

A. rubra has dark crimson flowers during the summer, height 16in (40cm).

Cultivation and propagation *Astrantia* likes a moist soil, and will grow equally well in sun or shade. Propagation is either from seed which is sown under glass during the spring or by division of the roots of established clumps in winter.

Uses The flower of the *Astrantia* is small but exquisite and for this reason should be confined to small delicate designs where the full beauty can be seen. The shell pink and wine crimson blend with most colours and look particularly fascinating arranged in a seashell. The flower resembles a pin cushion with numerous filaments growing in a dome on a frill of false petals.

Conditioning Cut the flower stem when the top flower is fully developed. Stand them in a container of water for about 2 hours to condition.

Preserving The flower is too intriguing not to preserve. The ideal method is desiccant. Providing the stem is reasonably thin it can be left attached to the flower for drying. If the stem appears fleshy it will not preserve at the same rate as the flower and is best removed.

Astrantia is a herbaceous perennial with broadly ovate glossy green leaves.
A. involucrata is one of the best for use as cut

Convallaria

Lily of the Valley
Europe
Liliaceae

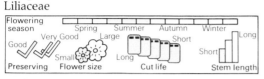

Convallaria majalis

Convallaria majalis is a hardy British native plant which thrives in any shady moist place. It has fragrant, white, bell-shaped flowers which dangle from the flower-stems, during early summer. It grows to a height of 6in (15cm).

Cultivation and propagation This is one of those perennial plants which can be depended upon to flower regularly each year in the garden and requires the minimum of attention. Ideally, it prefers a heavy loam. If the soil is light you will need to incorporate a copious dressing of manure or well-rotted garden compost, prior to planting. The site cultivation should be deep and thorough. The crowns of the plants should be set out 1ft (30cm) apart in each direction, with the tops of the crowns scarcely beneath the soil's surface. Planting is best undertaken during the late autumn. Every few years, take the opportunity of lifting and dividing the roots during the dormant season and at the same time fortify the soil with a fresh dressing of manure or garden compost. Alternatively, one can supply top dressing and mulch annually.

Where a warm greenhouse is available, established roots of *Convallaria* may be lifted and gently forced to produce fragrant flowers in the early spring time. When flowering has finished they may be planted outside in the garden once more to recover their strength.

Uses This small but elegant flower is a delight to cut and bring indoors. Place them in a simple glass vase or dish without artificial support. In deep water they will last for at least a week. The leaves of *Convallaria* are glossy green and extremely tough, of considerable use for concealing mechanics in mixed flower arrangements.

Conditioning Where the flowers are to be simply placed in deep water there is no need to condition them. If water-retaining foam is used, stand the cut flowers in a tumbler of water for 2 hours.

Preserving To preserve them cut the stems when the flowers are fully developed and bury them in desiccant. The stem is quite thin and will dry with very little distortion.

Cortaderia

Pampas Grass
Temperate South America
Gramineae

Cortaderia selloana 'Sunningdale Silver'

This is a very small genus of tall growing perennial grasses; their importance here is their silky plumes which are much sought after by flower arrangers for use in dried flower arrangements. The species most frequently grown is *Cortaderia argentea* syn. *C. selloana* which displays silvery plumes on stiff stems above a dense tuft of long, narrow, arching leaves, in the early autumn, height 9½ t (285cm).

C. a. 'Gold Band' is very similar, height 6ft (180cm).
C. pumila is a dwarf form, height 4ft (120cm), but nevertheless producing some very attractive shapely plumes on stiff stems.
C. a. 'Sunningdale' is just a little taller at 5ft (150cm) and its plumes are silky white in colour. The plumes are best picked as soon as they emerge, as, if they are left very long their general appearance deteriorates. If the weather is warm and dry, one can leave the plumes outside to dry naturally for a few days, with the aid of the sun. They are then taken into a dry shed or other suitable place and either hung up to continue the drying process or laid out to dry on some suitable flat surface, such as a bench or shelf.
Cultivation and propagation A deep sandy loam is the ideal for this plant, but it will grow satisfactorily upon a wide range of soils providing they are both deep and well drained. It needs a sunny sheltered site. *Cortaderia* could be planted in the lawn and would make a fine special feature in the garden if so positioned. Planting is best undertaken in the early spring, just when new growth is about to commence. Established clumps of this giant grass will multiply over the years if left undisturbed. The remains of the previous year's growth are trimmed back in the spring, each year. Propagation is by division of the clumps of grasses in the spring.
Uses Most people recognise *Cortaderia* by its more familiar name, Pampas grass. In the past it has been used in an unimaginative way often to merely fill up a quiet corner of the house or as something to stand at the bend of the stairs. Used in limited quantities it can be a very long lasting piece of outline material in pedestal or large-scale designs. I prefer to use it as fresh plant material when the plumes are a shining mixture of cream and green. It can be removed from the arrangement afterwards and dried.
Conditioning It requires very little conditioning ,an hour or two in deep water.
Preserving Pampas will dry on the plant, but is prone to continuous seed dispersal. Preserve the stem in glycerine at the point of maturity. It should be reasonably fluffy and display a silvery sheen. Preserving in this way will hold the seed firm without reducing the bulk of the plume.

Gypsophila

Baby's Breath
S. Europe and Asia Minor
Caryophyllaceae

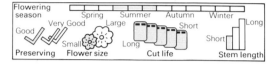

Gypsophila paniculata

Gypsophila is much used by the flower arranger both when it is freshly cut and when it is dried for winter decoration. It has loose panicles of small, star-like flowers on glaucous stems. *Gypsophila elegans* is an annual species that produces panicles of small dainty flowers which may be white, rose or pink in colour and grows to a height of 12 to 20in (30 to 50cm). This is an exceptionally popular cut flower and white is the colour most frequently grown.
G. e. 'Grandiflora Alba' has pure white flowers, height 1½ft (45cm).
G. e. 'Crimson' displays bright carmine flowers, height 1½ft (45cm).
G. e. 'Rosea' has fine rose pink flowers, height 1½ft (45cm).
The hardy perennial *Gypsophila paniculata* forms a mound of much branched panicles bearing tiny white flowers, throughout the summer, and has grey-green leaves.
G. p. 'Bristol Fairy' has a mist of double white flowers and is of a superior quality to the original *Gypsophila paniculata* upon whose roots it is in fact grafted.
G. p. 'Flamingo' produces a mist of tiny double pink flowers, later than the previous two. They all grow to a height of approximately 4ft (120cm). A shorter form well worthy of inclusion here is G. p. 'Rosy Veil', height 18in

(45cm), which bears a mist of tiny double flowers which are white but later become pink.
Cultivation and propagation Any well drained soil is suitable providing that it is not deficient in lime. This can be remedied with a top dressing of hydrated lime. Choose a sunny position for the plants and loosen the soil deeply as *Gypsophila* push their long fleshy roots way down into the ground so that they can withstand any long summer drought. Planting takes place during spring, when the taller varieties are set out 3ft (90cm) apart in each direction and the short ones 20in (50cm) apart each way.

Seeds of *G. elegans* may be sown in the open in autumn for plants which will flower the following spring. A second sowing may be made in spring in the open ground to flower later in the summer. It is particularly important that the soil should not be too rich for the autumn sown plants, otherwise they will not survive the winter. Earlier flowering from the autumn sown *Gypsophila* can be produced if one is able to provide it with some protection from December onwards. When the seedlings are large enough to handle thin them out to 8in (20cm) apart in the row.

Gypsophila paniculata may be propagated either by seeds or by cuttings. Seeds are sown in the open ground, during early summer taking care to sow the seeds as thinly as possible. When the seedlings are large enough to handle, thin the plants out to 8in (20cm) apart in the row. The resulting plants are transferred to their permanent positions in the early autumn. *G. paniculata* is also easily propagated from root and shoot cuttings, inserted in sand in a closed coldframe, any time in summer. Shoots are most suitable for rooting when they begin to harden.
Uses This flower has a lightening effect wherever it is used. The small widely spread flowers break up the outline of more solidly formed or deeper coloured material used with it. It is not a flower to be used to excess. Treat it like thin clouds in a summer sky as too much can make an arrangement look fussy and distracting.
Conditioning It has an exceptionally long cut life and it requires only the simplest of conditioning, 4 to 6 hours in water.
Preserving The flowers can be pressed or desiccant dried, an exquisite form for those of you who enjoy creating arrangements in miniature. Air drying is the easiest method of preserving. Pick when most of the flowers are open, and tie them in loose bundles. Suspend them in a light airy room until they look and feel dry, and slightly crisp to the touch.

Helleborus

S. Europe and Western Asia
Ranunculaceae

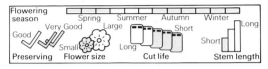

Helleborus niger

Helleborus is a herbaceous perennial of special value as it flowers outdoors at a time when other flowers are very scarce.
Helleborus niger (Christmas Rose) produces delightful trusses of saucer-shaped, white flowers which may also be faintly tinted pink, in midwinter, height 1ft (30cm).
Helleborus foetidus produces trusses of creamy-green flowers edged maroon, during spring, height 2ft (60cm).
Helleborus orientalis (Lenten Rose) is a very variable species with flowers from white to plum purple and spotted inside crimson and maroon. It has a long flowering period from autumn to spring, height 12 to 16in (30 to 40cm).
Cultivation and propagation Hellebores like a rich, moist, well-drained soil, in a shady location. If there is any doubt about the level of fertility give the soil a copious dressing of manure or well-rotted garden compost, at the time of cultivation. When once planted they resent being disturbed, so it is important that the soil conditions are correct from the start. Division of the roots should be infrequent, as this has a tendency to reduce flowering potential. Set the plants 1½ft (45cm) apart in each direction. The plants benefit from frequent watering during the spring and summer months, when they are in active growth. The application of a surface mulch of

Helleborus foetidus

Helleborus orientalis

Helleborus orientalis 'Bowles Yellow'

well decayed manure or garden compost is also useful.

Helleborus is best grown in a bed on its own, where it may be given some form of protection during the late autumn and winter. This produces earlier flowers with longer stems and will also prevent soil splashing upon the flowers in wet weather.

The normal method of propagation is by division as soon as flowering ceases. Great care should be taken not to damage any leaves for such injury weakens the buds and may result in no flowers being produced. The easiest way to divide the roots is with a sharp knife. They may be divided in two or three pieces each one of which must have one or more leaves attached to it together with some roots. These small sections are planted out in a shady coldframe, allowing 1ft (30cm) between these sections. Keep them cool and moist during the summer and plant them out into their permanent positions during the autumn.

Helleborus can be propagated from seed, but growth is slow and it takes some three years to get them to flower. The plants will be very variable. Seed sowing takes place in the autumn in a coldframe. Germination will take place during late spring. When the resulting seedlings are large enough to handle, they are pricked out 9in (22.5cm) each way in a nursery bed in a moist shady part of the garden. The plants are subsequently planted out in their permanent position the following spring.

Helleborus can also be forced in gentle heat, in the greenhouse. Choose plants that have been divided during the previous spring. When forcing has finished let the plants recover for two or three years in the garden before forcing again.

Uses *Helleborus* is a family of very showy flowers growing in the spring. Once the plant is established, it is very generous with flowers and foliage. *H. niger* flowers grow from the crown of the plant, separated from its foliage. Coming so early (or possibly late) in the season, it is a subject for landscape arrangements to herald the spring, or to group with snowdrops and crocus in a small basket. Hellebores with stem cluster flowers are unique in form and colour. Reserve them for something special, as a single fresh item in a modern design or as the focal area of a preserved foliage arrangement.

My fascination is with the colour forms, particularly seedlings of *H. orientalis*. The basic colour is cream overlaid with a freckle of crimson, but the seedlings will amaze you with their variations in colour. An added advantage is the stem length, anything up to 18in (45cm).

The leaves are just as important to the arranger as the flowers. *H. niger* has five leaves growing in a horseshoe design on a single stem, a fascinating inclusion for an all foliage arrangement. Equally attractive are the leaves of *H. foetidus*. The flowers are bell shaped, green with a margin of maroon. Its leaves grow from a single stem, deeply divided, like fingers, a deep black-green colour.

Conditioning *Helleborus* can be difficult to condition and it is advisable to cut the flowers only after they have set seed. Usually hellebores that flower on short stems are not temperamental, and will absorb moisture with the minimum of fuss. Thicker stemmed flowers are on the middle scale of reliability. If any wilting does occur they can generally be revived by floating or submerging them in water for about an hour.

H. orientalis is the most difficult, and must only be cut when the seed has set. I scar the flower stem with a pin from the cut end up to the level of the water that they are to stand in. Keep them cool at all times both during conditioning and when they have been arranged. Never put them in an over-heated atmosphere and at night move them to a cool area.

A number of rather odd recipes exist to help with the conditioning of hellebores. It is suggested that they are stood in a small amount of gin for a short period then transferred to water. Adding aspirin or sugar to the conditioning water is supposed to be as effective. If you follow the basic rules of conditioning you will not need to resort to the drinks or medicine cabinet. Cut the flowers at the coolest time of the day, preferably early morning when they have had time to recharge themselves. Float them on water for an hour making sure that the cut stem end is submerged, then stand them in water for at least 3 hours. Check them periodically and if any show signs of wilting re-cut the stem and repeat the process.

The leaves are much simpler and can be stood or floated in water until required.

Preserving Hellebore foliage will absorb glycerine greedily. The darker leaves of *niger* and *foetidus* adopt the brown/black colour of leather. They remain supple and once preserved last indefinitely. *H. orientalis* is particularly attractive when dried in dessicant. Remove the stem and place the flower in a depression of desiccant. Filter more preservative into the centre of the flower. The drying process is very rapid, but they can be left in the drying agent for a long period. Mount the flowers on to a short piece of *Corylus contorta* stem, with short pieces of *Garrya eliptica* catkins glued to the back of the hellebore flower. Arranged with delicacy and restraint this design has a truly oriental feel.

Iberis

Candytuft
Europe
Cruciferae

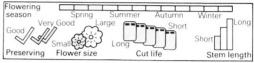

Iberis amara

The annual *Iberis amara* is useful as a cut flower very early in the spring when there is a shortage of fresh flowers.

I. a. 'Giant White' produces large showy clusters of white flowers, height 1ft (30cm).

I. a. 'Giant Pink' has large clusters of bright pink flowers, height 15in (37.5cm).

I. a. 'Red Flash' has vivid clusters of flowers, height 1ft (30cm).

I. a. 'Dwarf Fairy Mixed' is the shortest strain, but still produces some very attractive flowers for use in table decorations. The range of colour in the flowers is lilac, pink, maroon, carmine and white, and these in turn are followed by fine seed heads.

Cultivation and propagation Iberis grows very well on poor soils providing that it is given a sunny situation. When sowing the seeds in the autumn avoid over-rich soils, otherwise soft vegetative growth will be produced and the plants become susceptible to frost damage. Sow the seed in the place where flowering is to occur. Germination will take about 10 days. When the seedlings are large enough to handle, thin them out to stand 8in (20cm) apart. Protect the young plants with cloches during the winter to keep the plants dry. This protection will produce good plants and induce flowering in spring. The flowers will be of excellent quality and free from soil

splashings in wet weather. Iberis which is grown without protection will flower later.
Uses *Iberis* flowers early in the season when there is a shortage of flowers in the colour range. They are a welcome addition to small groupings of short-stemmed flowers in a basket or posy bowl. They are extremely tolerant of town and city pollution.
Conditioning Conditioning is simple. A drink of water for at least 3 hours is sufficient.
Preserving The fresh flowers may be pressed, but I prefer to wait until the seedhead develops. It will dry naturally on the plant and provides interesting texture and form in a small dried arrangement.

Lunaria

Honesty
Sweden
Cruciferae

Lunaria

Lunaria annua is treated as a biennial and thrives almost anywhere. While its purple or white flowers, height 2½ft (75cm), make a brave display during early summer, and these are sometimes used as fresh cut flowers, the real attraction of this plant is its moon-like seed-cases. These are borne along the well-branched stems and when dried turn a silvery-white colour. They may also be dyed.
L. a. 'Alba' has white flowers.

L. a. 'Munstead Purple', rich purple flowers.
L. a. 'Variegata', which is a less common form, has variegated cream and green leaves and purple flowers.
Cultivation and propagation *Lunaria* is shade tolerant and likes damp situations. Seed is sown in early summer where flowering is to take place. Germination usually takes 2 to 3 weeks. Once the plants are large enough to handle they should be thinned out to stand 9in (22.5cm) apart. These plants will flower the following year and, providing that one does not remove all the seed-heads, they will propagate themselves quite freely.
Uses As fresh plant material *Lunaria* may be considered quite dull, but as a dried component it is invaluable. The seed case will dry naturally on the plant. If you have no use for the entire stem, single seed cases can be removed with a pair of fine scissors. Check the plant daily for the right moment to harvest the seed, this must be done before the seed case splits and becomes brittle. Individual seed cases are useful for pictures or collages and their translucent quality can be utilized to advantage in making fantasy flowers by fixing them together on a false stem or gluing them on to a pine cone.

Polygonatum

Solomon's Seal
Northern temperate regions
Liliaceae

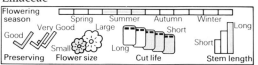

Polygonatum multiflorum

Our concern here is with just two of the hardy perennial species. They have fleshy, rhizomatous roots which spread and because of this they are best planted in an area where they are not likely to encroach on other plants which might be near. They have oval pointed leaves along their arching stems which also bear creamy white clusters of green tipped bell-shaped flowers about 1in (2.5cm) long, during early summer.

P. japonicum is the larger species which attains a height of 3ft (90cm). There is also a variegated form which has green leaves striped with white, *P. j.* 'Variegatum'.

P. multiflorum, a European native species, grows to a height of 2 to 2½ft (60 to 75cm).

Cultivation and propagation *Polygonatum* likes a moist soil and a shady position. Mulch annually. Plant in the winter. Propagation is by division of the roots during the dormant season.

Uses This is certainly a plant to recommend to the flower arranger. The arching stems are perfect for establishing the outline of any shaped design. The curving stems used in opposing directions create an 'S' shape, or used in the same plane they will establish a crescent shape. The leaves may be removed to reveal the hanging white bell flowers, which adds an unusual note to an arrangement.

Conditioning Allow the foliage to mature before cutting, then stand in water for 3 hours to condition.

Preserving The flowers can be carefully cut from the growing stem and preserved in desiccant. The ideal preserving material is the leaf. The time to preserve the leaves is once the flower has faded and the leaf is fully mature. Remove any lower leaves from the stem that are likely to come into contact with the glycerine solution. Stand the stem in the glycerine for about three days. The colour will change to a light biscuit brown. You should check them every day. Any that show signs of stem weakness should be given some support to allow the glycerine to reach the extreme tip.

MIXED COLOURS

Allium

Northern Hemisphere
Liliaceae

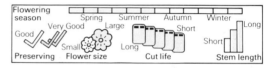

Allium siculum

We are all familiar with at least some of the edible species such as garlic, onion, leek and shallot. While the form of the garden flower is very similar to that of the onion it produces flowers in a wide range of colours and most do not have an oniony scent unless the leaves are damaged. Indeed, some are mildly fragrant and all the species recommended below are much sought after by the flower arranger as their flowers have a long vase life:

Allium aflatunense. Central China. Large umbels of rosy-purple flowers, early summer, height 2½ft (75cm).

A. albopilosum. Turkestan. Large umbels of deep purplish mauve flowers, with a metallic sheen, up to 18in (45cm) in diameter, early summer, 2ft (60cm).

A. coeruleum. Siberia and Turkestan. Cornflower blue umbels of flowers,

midsummer, height 2ft (60cm).
A. cowanii. Origin not known. Pure white umbels, early summer, height 2ft (60cm).
A. neapolitanum. Mediterranean. Umbels of white star-shaped flowers, spring, height 1½ft (45cm).
A. pulchellum. Mediterranean. Attractive reddish-purple umbels of flowers, late summer, height 1½ft (45cm).
A. siculum. Southern France and Sicily. Unusual, yet most attractive, greenish flowers, early summer, height 2ft (60cm), and is one of the best for drying for winter decoration.
A. sphaerocephalum. Western Europe and Britain. Dark purple flowers, late summer, height 2ft (60cm).
Cultivation and propagation *Allium* will thrive in any sunny place in well-drained soil. Plant the bulbs in the late autumn, twice their own depth and some 6 to 9in (15 to 22.5cm) apart, according to height of growth. Leave the bulbs to multiply over the years until their crowded conditions indicate that it is time to lift and divide them. Take this opportunity to cultivate the site and introduce some peat or well rotted garden compost, before replanting the bulbs. Apply a surface mulch of peat in the spring.

Propagation is by seed. Sow in the dormant season and leave the young plants in their seedtrays till the following spring. Some species can be divided in autumn or spring.
Uses This family provides a most interesting range of flowers that are generally grown by the arranger for the resultant seed head. Once the bulb has established itself in the garden it will soon produce offsets so that you have enough flowers to use fresh. The globular shape of the seed head is quite striking and has a long stem that will help to create height in a design or a bold focal area.
Preserving Let the seed develop in the garden until the head changes from green to biscuit brown, then gently tug the stem from the bulb. Any resistance is an indication that it is not ready, so leave it for a day or two and try again. The dried head may be used in most styles of arrangements, it is often seen lightly gilded with preserved foliage and the pods of *Physalis franchetti* at Christmas.

Alstroemeria

Peruvian lily
Chile
Amaryllidaceae

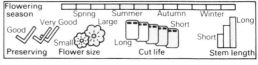

Alstroemeria ligtu

Umbels of trumpet shaped lily-like flowers are borne on straight stems in summer.
A. aurantiaca. Loose umbels of deep orange flowers, summer, height 3ft (90cm). The roots are tuberous and probe deeply into the soil; when once established, they spread quite widely, so plant them in a sunny sheltered part of the garden on their own where they can be contained. *A. ligtu* hybrids, in a variety of colours, pink, yellow, red, orange and white, height 2½ft (75cm). These need somewhat moister root conditions than *A. aurantiaca* and watering will be necessary during dry spells in summer.
Cultivation and propagation Most types of soil are suitable, provided they have been deeply cultivated and well supplied with manure or garden compost prior to planting. Plant the tubers in spring at least 6in (15cm) deep, so that they are not damaged by hard winter frosts. If you have space to spare in a greenhouse you can enjoy their flowers over an extended period, with a little heat to encourage them along. Their first flush of flowers will commence in spring and continue into summer. This will then be followed by a period of rest before a second and lighter flush of flowers are produced in the autumn.

Propagation of *A. aurantiaca* is best achieved by division of the tuberous roots in the spring.

A. ligtu cannot readily be propagated vegetatively and must be grown from seed sown in the early spring in seed-boxes containing a peat based compost, placed in a cool greenhouse. Prick the seedlings out in 3in (7.5cm) pots when large enough to handle and grow them on during the summer months in an open frame. Plant out the following spring. Young plants frequently succumb to winter damage.

Uses Given an adequate supply of water the *Alstroemeria* has a very long cut life, often up to a fortnight. It is like a lily in shape, with a cluster of flowers at the top of the stem and is generally used in massed traditional arrangements. *A. aurantiaca* is a vibrant orange, a startling companion to blue delphiniums arranged in a modern, upright container. The rainbow choice of colours of the *ligtu* hybrids has been expanded to include pink, flame, white, yellow and lilac, which provides a wide choice to use with flowers of pure hue or pastel shades. The large glowing white flower of *A. pelegrina 'alba'* is worth a special mention. Known as the Lily of the Incas, the flowers are large, often carried singly on a stem of about fifteen inches. If you can obtain this variety, do take advantage of it as it is excellent in an arrangement of white summer flowers.

Conditioning Condition the flowers in deep cold water for about 3 hours.

Preserving The thin flower petals will not absorb liquid preservative nor air dry properly. Individual blooms can be dried in desiccant.

Anemone 'St Brigid'

Anemone appenina

Anemone

Windflower
China
Ranunculaceae

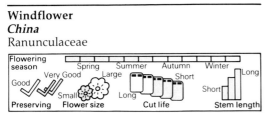

Flowering season	Spring	Summer	Autumn	Winter	
Very Good	Large		Short	Long	
Good					
Small	Long		Short		
Preserving	Flower size		Cut life		Stem length

Summer-flowering anemone Often referred to as *Anemone japonica*, this plant is listed more correctly as *Anemone hupehensis*. A herbaceous perennial from China, it makes bushy plants, and displays attractive, saucer-shaped, mauve or carmine flowers, which may be up to 2½in (6.25cm) across, autumn, height 2 to 3ft (60 to 90cm). There is also a white form *A. h. 'Alba'*. Many named hybrids are available.

'Bressingham Glow', very pretty rosy-red semi-double flowers, height 1½ft (45cm).

'Lady Gilmour', large pink almost double flowers, height 2ft (60cm).

'Louise Uhink', semi-double white flowers, height 32in (80cm).

'Profusion', deep pink flowers, height 2½ft (75cm).

'September Charm', single soft pink flowers which are 4in (10cm) across, with continuous flowering throughout the autumn.

A. × lesseri, rosy-purple flowers, early summer, height 2ft (60cm).

All the above produce flowers on sturdy stems and, while they are not particularly long-lasting as cut flowers, they are all very free flowering so fresh supplies of cut-flower material are readily available.

Cultivation and propagation Once planted, *Anemone hupehensis* and the various hybrids are best left undisturbed for many years. Therefore good soil preparation is important. Heavy soils should have coarse sand or other suitable gritty material introduced to open up the soil. Granulated peat can be forked into the surface. These anemones thrust their roots deep down into the soil and are very long lived. Plant in the early spring. They flower little during their first year of planting, but settle down to flower well in subsequent years. They will grow equally well in sun or shade, providing there is some moisture around their roots while they are in active growth. Give them an annual mulch of peat in spring.

One method of propagating these anemones is by lifting and dividing the plants in the late autumn when flowering has ceased. The divided plants take some time to re-establish themselves with the loss of flowering during the first year. Root cuttings can also be used, taken in the dormant period by excavating round the parent plant so as not to disturb it. These are then potted-up and given the protection of a coldframe through the winter and the early spring. Once new growth from the pieces of root has developed sufficiently the various pieces are potted up individually, in the early summer and placed back in the coldframe with the top glass removed. Transfer to the flowering position in the early spring of the following year.

Spring-flowering anemones There are several species of tuberous-rooted anemones that flower in spring.

Anemone apennina (Common Wood Anemone), Southern Europe. Clear blue flowers on 6in (15cm) stems, spring.

A. a 'Alba', white flowers.

A. blanda, Asia Minor. Small flowers, which may be blue, pink, red or white, on short 4 to 5in (10 to 12.5cm) stems, spring.

A. fulgens, Greece. Large scarlet, yellow-centred flowers, some 2½in (6.25cm) across, on 12in (30cm) stems, early summer.

St Bavo is a related strain, with flowers in a fine range of colours with stems 12in (30cm) or more in length, late spring.

Anemone blanda

A. coronaria, Greece and the Eastern Mediterranean. There are two types which are particularly popular: the single-flowered De Caen, large flowers up to 3in (7.5cm) across, on stems 9in (22.5cm) long; and the St Brigid, semi-double flowers, on stems of a similar length. Both these are available in a range of brilliant colours and are ideal for cutting from late spring to early summer.

Cultivation and propagation None are particularly difficult about soil, providing that it is well supplied with organic matter, so that it holds moisture well, and is in a sunny, sheltered situation. Fresh tubers must be planted each year to give good quality flowers, but otherwise need little attention.

Early flowering may be induced by giving plants the protection of a cool greenhouse, with a minimum night temperature of 42°F (6°C). Plant the tubers in early autumn. Soak them in water for 12 hours before potting them up in 6in (15cm) pots. Place them on the greenhouse bench and water just sufficiently to keep the compost slightly moist. When growth is in evidence begin to water more freely and apply a dose of a liquid fertiliser every 10 to 14 days.

Even anemones to be planted in the open ground should be soaked in water for 12 hours first, as this encourages the early development of roots. The tubers are irregular in shape and referred to as claws; it is particularly important that they are planted no more than 2in (5cm) deep. Upon close inspection one will see small buds surrounded with scales and these must be planted facing upwards. The rows of anemones should be some 6 to 8in (15 to 18cm) apart. Plant successively through the winter to give an extended flowering period. Mulch in late spring.

Uses The short-stemmed spring flowering species look most attractive simply arranged in a small glass vase or grouped with other flowers in a basket. Plants grown in pots are an advantage to the busy arranger, as they can be positioned in a suitable dish and the pots concealed with a little moss. The only maintenance they need is a little water every day. The more widely recognized pink *Anemone japonica* is a delightful flower for the late summer and early autumn. The stems are long and willowy, making them an ideal component as outline material. The foliage is carried on erect stems arranged in whorls of three. Once it has matured it is a long-lasting cut leaf.

Conditioning Condition the flowers when they are about to open. Some of the hybrids shed their petals so handle them carefully. Stand them in water for up to 4 hours. The spring anemones are prone to wilting. If this occurs score the stem with a pin from the cut end to the flower and recondition.

Preserving Individual flowers will dry

successfully in desiccant; single flowers are particularly useful for pressing.

Antirrhinum

Snapdragon
Europe
Scrophulariaceae

Antirrhinum

Although the antirrhinums grown in our gardens are treated as annuals you may be surprised to learn they they are in fact perennials. The ones we use for the summer bedding display are named cultivars of the species, *A. majus*. *Antirrhinum* has only recently become a serious contender for a place in the flower vase, thanks to the introduction of the modern F1 hybrids which have not only longer stems, but also larger flowers than those we associate with the bedding types. For cut flower cultivation in the open one requires the F1 Hybrid Butterfly Type: 'Bright Butterflies', penstemon-like flowers in the full range of colours normally associated with antirrhinums (bronze, crimson, pink, rose, yellow and white). These plants have sturdy stems, height 2½ft (75cm). 'Madam Butterfly', a double petalled form in similar colours, height 2½ to 3ft (75 to 90cm).
Cultivation and propagation *Antirrhinum* is fairly tolerant but prefers light, rich soils, in full sun. Seed should be sown in slight heat during early March. When the seedlings germinate give them plenty of light to keep them compact as they develop, thus producing

nice sturdy material for pricking out into seedboxes when they are large enough to handle. Grow on under a coldframe or cloche until they are planted out in early summer, spacing them 16 to 18in (40 to 45cm) apart. Flowering is continuous from midsummer to the first frosts.
Uses With their extensive colour range, long stems and pointed flower heads these are indispensable as outline material. Those with strong clean colours, crimson, yellow and orange, are ideal for modern and free-form arranging, where vivid and contrasting colour is needed. The lighter pastel shades of lemon, apricot and pink blend well in a scheme of mixed flowers adding a distinctive form and flowing line to delicate, less regimented styles. When cutting the first flush of flowers leave a number of leaves on the plant to encourage the side shoots to develop.
Conditioning Cut in the morning or afternoon. Remove the lower leaves and lightly crush the semi-woody stem. Stand the stems in water in a cool place for at least 4 hours.
Preserving Sadly this elegant flower is awkward to preserve. Pressing distorts the shape, and its form does not accommodate desiccant.

Aquilegia

Columbine
Temperate regions of the Northern Hemisphere
Ranunculaceae

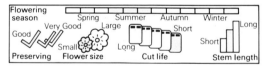

Some of the species have been hybridized to produce excellent named cultivars which are absolutely wonderful for cutting. They have long spurs and brightly coloured flowers. The colour range of the flowers covers crimson, pink, purple, blue, yellow and white. The best hybrids include:
'McKana's Giant Hybrids', large 4in (10cm) flowers and spurs not much shorter, available in a mixed blend of colours which embrace blue, pink, maroon, purple, red, deep yellow, light yellow, cream and white, with many bi-colours, late summer, height 2½ to 3ft (75 to 90cm).
'Coerulea F1 Hybrid Heterosis Olympia Red and Gold' is perhaps the best colour combination so far produced in aquilegias, and while the seed is fairly expensive it is well

Aquilegia 'McKana's Giant'

Aquilegia 'Nora Barlow'

worth the price. For a dwarfer aquilegia, try 'Dragonfly Hybrids', long spurred flowers in a fine blend of colours, summer, height 1½ft (45cm). Other good named cultivars include: 'Crimson Star', masses of crimson and white flowers, summer, height 20in (50cm). 'Nora Barlow', fully double flowers quaintly suffused red, pink and green, summer, height 28in (70cm).

Cultivation and propagation *Aquilegia* thrive in any cool, well-drained soil and can be grown in full light or partial shade. Although a perennial, it is not long-lived, so for top-quality flowers it is best to propagate annually from rootstocks purchased at nurseries, or by seed bought from a reputable seed merchant. Although *Aquilegia* sets seed very readily, it results in inferior plants in muddy colours not worth growing.

Sow seed in spring, preferably under glass. The aim is to give the plants the longest possible growing season, as all the development of these plants takes place in the first year. Germination is slow and irregular, so be patient. With the protection of cloches it takes about three weeks, but in the open ground it will take at least five weeks. When the seedlings are large enough to handle they are thinned out to 12in (30cm) apart. Under cloches ventilate the plants on warm sunny days in late spring. The plants are then hardened off ready for planting out in a nursery bed for the summer. In the autumn the plants are transferred to their flowering situation. None of these plants require any type of support.

Uses These flowers provide us with an almost unique distinctive form with graceful nodding flowers and long spurs, valued for their shape and interesting range of colour blends. They have long been associated with country cottage gardens and for this reason are often used in re-creating period styles of arrangements seen in the Dutch/Flemish flower paintings. While historically this is not accurate, as the majority of species were not introduced to Europe until the mid 19th century, they have that old-fashioned look and assist in establishing the period atmosphere which is so desirable.

Conditioning They will condition very easily. Stand them in deep water for about 4 hours.

Preserving Some of the smaller flowers and buds will dry in desiccant. If you are able to resist cutting all the flowers, you will be rewarded with an interesting cluster of seed heads, which may be lightly gilded for a fantasy style arrangement at Christmas.

Aster

Michaelmas Daisy
Eastern USA
Compositae

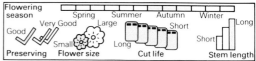

Aster novi-belgii has daisy-like blue flowers, slender-pointed deep green leaves and reaches a height of 4ft (120cm). Many hybrids are available in a great range of colours with the height varying with the cultivar from 9in (22.5cm) to 4ft (120cm).

For autumn colour the following selection has no equal:
'Audrey', violet, height 1ft (30cm).
'Blandie', pure white, height 3½ft (105cm).
'Coombe Margaret', light pink, height 3½ft (105cm).

'Countess of Dudley', deep pink, height 9in (22.5cm).
'Crimson Brocade', cyclamen purple, double, height 3ft (90cm).
'Little Pink Beauty', pink semi-double, height 15in (37.5cm).
'Marie Ballard', powder blue, double, height 3ft (90cm).
'Mistress Quickly', deep blue, height 4ft (120cm).
'Raspberry Ripple', carmine-red, double, height 2½ft (75cm).
'Rev Vincent Dale', deep purple, height 4ft (120cm).
'Sailor Boy', bright rich blue, height 3½ft (105cm).
'Snowsprite', white, height 1ft (30cm).
'The Cardinal', rosy-red, semi-double, height 3½ft (105cm).
'Winston S. Churchill', reddish purple, height 2ft (60cm).

Cultivation and propagation Any reasonable well-drained soil will do, provided it contains plenty of humus and is in full sun. Dwarf forms make neat compact growth, while taller ones will need some form of support to prevent them looking untidy. A few stakes with stout strings running between the plants provides the necessary support. This type of arrangement could also serve to support a sheet of clear polythene over the plants when they come into flower, preventing the autumn rains spoiling the appearance of the flowers, and thus extending their period of availability for cutting. Dwarf cultivars might also be given the protection of cloches or a portable cold-frame to extend the flowering period. *Aster novi-belgii* provides its best flowers from the young plants so they should be lifted and divided up every second year. In the autumn after they have ceased flowering cut down the dead stems to just above ground level and then lift and divide the clumps of roots. Discard the worn-out central portions and replant only the young vigorous outer portions (stolons), about 1 to 3ft (30-40cm) apart, depending on the height of the cultivar. At this time introduce some well-rotted garden compost and dig this into the soil as the work proceeds, supplementing this in the early spring with a surface mulch of peat or leaf mould between the plants.

Uses These flowers are an asset as intermediary flowers in traditional designs, large or small. The wealth of colour and ease with which they grow will allow you to use them in profusion. They have a distinctly rural atmosphere; though generally reserved for the traditional style of arranging *novi-belgii* 'Crimson brocade' used as a block of colour is an exciting flower for modern arranging.

Conditioning The flower stem can become woody. Lightly crush the end before standing them in water for 3 hours.

Aster 'Audrey'

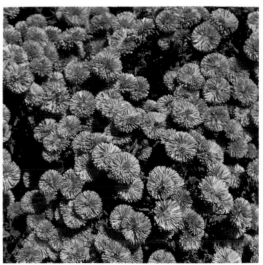

Aster 'Marie Ballard'

Aster 'The Cardinal'

Preserving Aster flowers with few petals will dry in desiccant. It is necessary to be selective when pressing the flower, a frill of petal that is too thick will bruise and discolour during the process.

Callistephus Chinensis

China Aster
China
Compositae

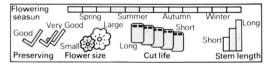

Callistephus chinensis 'Ostrich plume'

The most frequently grown China Aster for cutting has traditionally been Ostrich Plume, with Bouquet Powder Puffs coming a close second. Both have good long stems and early flowers, of substance, in a wide range of mixed colours, late summer to autumn. Other good strains include:
Duchesse, a medium to late-flowering vigorous strain growing to a height of 2ft (60cm). This has strong stems and produces flowers, with incurved petals, 5in (12cm) in diameter and resembling chrysanthemums, in a splendid range of colours.
New Giants Of California is another good late-flowering strain with flowers up to 6in (15cm) in diameter, height 2½ft (75cm).
Madeleine is possibly the finest single-flowered aster and it flowers mid-season. It is available in a good mixture of colours and grows 2ft (60cm) high.
'Pompon – Mixture', is a medium to late flowering strain, bearing small round flowers in a good mix of colours, height 1½ft (45cm).
Cultivation and propagation *Callistephus* flourishes on a wide range of soils, providing that some lime is present, and this is the key to success with this plant. The aster is a half hardy annual and the seed may be sown directly under a coldframe or cloche in spring. If sown thinly the plants will need no attention until they are transferred to their flowering places in early summer. Plant 12 to 16in (30 to 40cm) apart, according to height.
Uses These flowers are most welcome in their season of late summer and autumn when there is less alternative material in their colouring of pinks and blue. The single-flowered cultivars are best suited to informal designs, whereas the double and ostrich plume could find a place in the more sophisticated arrangement. The regular rounded forms of 'Powder Puff' are both unusual and striking in modern or free-form designs.
Conditioning Remove any excess stem foliage and condition them in cold water for up to 6 hours.
Preserving The single flowers may be pressed or dried in desiccant. Their bold colours introduce an eye-catching note to a picture of preserved material.

Centaurea

Europe including Britain
Compositae

Centaurea 'Polka Dot'

There are two species of Centaurea which are worthy of consideration for cut flower use. *Centaurea cyanus* (Cornflower), which in its wild form is just a common annual weed has been much improved with larger flowers available in a range of colours in addition to the original cornflower blue. *C. cyanus* is sold as a mixed blend of colours as *C. c.* Mixed and has flowers of mauve, blue, red, pink and white, summer, height 2½ft (75cm). *C. c.* 'Blue Diadem', intense deep blue, double powder-puff type flowers some 2½in (6.25cm) across, height 2ft (60cm). *C. c.* 'Red Ball' unusual scarlet to pink flowers 2in (5cm) across, early flowering, height 3ft (90cm).

There is also the much dwarfer, yet very desirable, *C. c.* 'Polka Dot Mixed', fully double flowers in shades of pink, carmine, blue and white, height 15in (37.5cm). *C. c.* 'Nana Jubilee Gem', large, dark blue, double flowers, height 1ft (30cm). *C. moschata* (Sweet Sultan) has fragrant vanilla-scented flowers, and is a native of the Eastern Mediterranean Region, and not entirely hardy. The flowers resemble those of the cornflower and may be white, crimson, pinkish-purple, rose or yellow in colour, height 1½ to 2ft (45 to 60cm). It is generally offered for sale in mixed colours, except in the case of the yellow which is sold as Moschata Yellow.

Cultivation and propagation *Centaurea* likes an open sunny situation and will grow in any well-drained soil. *C. cyanus* is quite hardy. Seed may be sown in autumn to give an early crop of flowers for cutting in the spring. It will grow quite happily in the open ground throughout the winter but for good quality early flowers it is well worth considering giving the plants some protection. A sowing of seeds in the open ground in spring will result in a crop of flowers being produced during the late summer. Seed should be sown in the flowering site, as seedlings do not transplant well.

Sow seed of *C. moschata* in spring where flowering is to occur. Germination will take 7 to 10 days. Thin out the resulting plants to stand 10in (25cm) apart. Flowering starts about 8 weeks after seed has been sown.

Uses In its season *Centaurea* provides a supply of intermediate or filler material and has a special use in wedding arrangements where 'something blue' is needed. For such an occasion they look especially attractive arranged in a basket with grey foliage carried by child bridesmaids. The length of stem will allow their use as outline material for large arrangements, but you may find that the stems are a little brittle and need support.

Conditioning Conditioning is simple. A drink of water for about 4 hours is sufficient. Remove any foliage that is likely to be submerged as it decays very rapidly.

Preserving Some attempt should always be made to dry the flowers in desiccant as there are few flowers of this colour for using in flower pictures or collages.

Cheiranthus

Wallflower
Europe
Cruciferae

Flowering season / Spring / Summer / Autumn / Winter / Good / Very Good / Large / Small / Long / Short / Long / Short / Preserving / Flower size / Cut life / Stem length

Cheiranthus 'Blood Red'

Cheiranthus 'Orange Bedder'

There are two species commonly grown.
C. allionii (Siberian Wallflower) is believed to
be a hybrid raised in 1846 by Mr J. Marshall.
This is a very attractive biennial plant which
flowers over a longer period of time and later
than the perennial species *C. cheiri*. Indeed,
the Siberian Wallflower will flower for getting
on for two months in late spring and grows to
a height of some 12 to 15in (30 to 37.5cm).
C. a. 'Orange Queen' has bright orange
flowers, while *C. a.* 'Golden Queen', has
golden yellow flowers.
C. cheiri (the true wallflower) is grown widely
as a bedding plant. It is also grown
commercially as a cut flower subject, as its
sweet-scented flowers are in great demand.
There are lots of named cultivars available in a
wide range of colours and the following
selection, flowering in late spring, are all
suitable for cutting:
'Blood Red', very fragrant dark red flowers,
height 15in (37.5cm).
'Cranford Beauty', syn. 'Cloth Of Gold',
golden yellow flowers, height 18in (45cm).
'Fire King', vivid scarlet flowers, height 15in
(37.5cm).
'Golden Bedder', clear golden yellow flowers,
height 12in (30cm).
'Ivory White', creamy white flowers, height
12in (30cm).
'Orange Bedder', rich orange shaded apricot-
yellow flowers, height 12in (30cm).
'Vulcan', rich crimson flowers, height 14in
(35cm).
Cultivation and propagation Wallflowers will
grow quite happily on a wide range of soils if
they are well drained. However, they are
subject to a disease commonly referred to as
'Club Root'. This is a fungus which attacks all
members of the brassica family, causing
swellings on the roots or stem base. This
fungus thrives in poorly drained acid soils and
it is important that one provides the plants
with a well-limed soil and that they do not
follow a previous crop of brassicas. So move
them from place to place each year and treat
any infected plants with 'Calomel Dust' both
when setting the plants out in the nursery bed
for the summer and when transferring them to
their flowering site in the autumn. It is also
worth while dusting calomel down the seed
drill. Earlier flowering can be induced if the
plants are protected through the winter with
cloches.
   Seed is sown in the open ground during late
spring. Germination takes 7 to 14 days. When
the seedlings are large enough to handle they
are planted out in a nursery bed allowing 6in
(15cm) between the plants. In the autumn the
plants are transferred to their flowering sites,
setting them out 12in (30cm) apart. Both
species are treated as biennials.
Uses As an added bonus to any arrangement,
wallflowers have an exquisite perfume which

seems to become more intense after the
flowers have been in a warmer indoor
atmosphere. The relatively short length of
stem somewhat limits their use to outline and
filler material in smaller designs. The colour
range has been much extended by the
hybridist and now includes a number of
unusual shades including reds/browns and
greys/purples much prized by the arranger
seeking the unusual in pursuit of recreating a
period atmosphere.
Conditioning It is essential to crush the
bottom of the woody stem before standing
them in water for up to 6 hours. The crushed
section should be cut away before arranging.
Preserving As the wallflower is so free
flowering any difficulties in pressing the
individual flowers can be overlooked.

Chrysanthemum

***Widely distributed in the Northern
Hemisphere***
Compositae

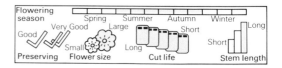

There are two species and many hybrids to
consider for cut flower work.
Chrysanthemum maximum (Shasta Daisy) has
large white daisy-like flowers, and comes from
the Pyrenees. By careful selection you can
have cultivars that flower from early summer
to autumn.
C. m. 'Esther Read', double, pure white,
flowers summer, height 2½ft (75cm).
C. m. 'Everest', large, single white flowers,
summer, height 3ft (90cm).

Chrysanthemum maximum 'Esther Read'

Chrysanthemum maximum 'H Seibert'

Chrysanthemum Korean hybrid 'Columbine'

Chrysanthemum rubellum

Chrysanthemum Korean hybrid 'Rosalie'

Chrysanthemum Korean hybrid 'Belle'

Chrysanthemum Korean hybrid 'Ruby Mound'

Chrysanthemum Korean hybrid 'Wedding Sunshine'

Chrysanthemum Korean hybrid 'Lorna'

Chrysanthemum Korean hybrid 'Betty'

C. m. 'H. Seibert', enormous, single white flowers, summer, height 2½ft (75cm).
C. m. 'Silver Princess', single white flowers, early summer, height 1ft (30cm). This subject is ideal for covering with cloches or a coldframe in early spring, as this will encourage flowering to commence some four to five weeks earlier than in the open ground.
C. m. 'Thomas Killin', semi-double, white flowers, summer, height 2½ft (75cm).
C. m. 'Wirral Pride', semi-double, large white flowers, summer, height 3ft (90cm).
C. m. 'Wirral Supreme', double, white flowers, with anemone centres, autumn, height 3ft (90cm).

Following on from the summer flowering kinds are these hardy autumn flowering ones, which are fairly resistant to early frosts. The first of these is *C. rubellum* from Japan. Height approximately 3ft (90cm). From this have arisen a number of very desirable cultivars such as *C. r.* 'Clara Curtis', single clear pink, *C. r.* 'Duchess of Edinburgh' (semi-double), clear red, *C. r.* 'Mary Stoker', soft yellow. The second is the Korean hybrid spray chrysanthemums and these provide the flower arranger with much valuable colour late in the season. There is a wide range of hues for autumn flowering. With the aid of a little protection from the rain, flowers of the following hybrids will even last well into early winter in most years:
'Apollo', salmon-bronze.
'Bright Eye', golden yellow.
'Ember', bronze.
'Orange Wonder', coppery-orange.
All the above Koreans grow to a height of about 2ft (60cm) and need no disbudding.

The pretty little Japanese pompom with its double pink flowers, 'Mei-kyo' is one of the very last hardy outdoor chrysanthemums to flower in late autumn, height 2ft (60cm). 'Bronze Elegance' is a browny-orange form of 'Mei-kyo' and flowers at the same time.

The popular florist's chrysanthemum *C. morifolium* syn. *C. sinense* comes originally from China and Japan. They are one of the longest lasting cut flowers and are available in a wide array of colours which include white, yellow, pink, red, bronze and purple. Furthermore flowers may be of various types and they are classified accordingly.
Incurved. Incurving florets which form a firm globe.
Incurving. Incurving florets which do not form a firm globe with the result that the flowers have a less definite shape to them.
Reflexed. Florets are of two types as the outer ones are reflexed while the inner ones are incurving.
Anemone flowered. Single flowered cultivars with just several rows of outer florets but with a central cushion of tubular florets.
Singles. Similar to the anemone-flowered type

but have a central daisy-like disc.
Pompoms. Small globular flowers of tightly packed incurving florets.

Cultivation *Early-flowering cultivars and species* Chrysanthemums can be grown successfully on any ordinary garden soil which is well drained and of reasonable depth. Heavy soils can have added grit or sharp sand. Choose an open sunny position for them. Give the ground a generous dressing of farmyard manure or well rotted garden compost prior to autumn digging. In spring break down the soil's surface to a fine tilth with the aid of a garden rake, then dress the surface with a good general fertilizer such as National Growmore at the rate of 4oz per sq yard (135.6gm per sq metre) and work this into the soil's surface with the garden rake.

If the weather is suitable early flowering chrysanthemums may be planted in the open ground in late spring. When growing them in a bed the plants should be set out 14in (35cm) apart each way with three rows of plants together with a gap of 30in (75cm) between each block of three rows of plants. This serves as a path for access. In exposed places one would be well advised to erect a hessian screen to afford some protection on the windward side. Tall growing cultivars may require support at an early stage either with individual canes or by 2in (5cm) mesh wire-netting stretched out over the chrysanthemum bed and held in place by a horizontal framework attached firmly to strong corner posts about 5ft (150cm) high. As the chrysanthemums grow taller the wire-netting can be raised up the posts while still remaining taut and giving suitable support to the plants. Shorter cultivars will not require any form of support until later.

Young chrysanthemums generally produce a single stem some 12-18in (30-45cm) long before they develop flower buds at the tips. Side shoots then develop from the leaf axils below, giving the plants a branched structure. The terminal bud on each plant is referred to as the *break bud* as it causes the plants to produce these side shoots. Subsequently these side shoots develop until they in turn produce flower buds at the tips of their stems and these are referred to as crown buds. In this particular instance they are *first crown buds*. In general early flowering chrysanthemums produce their best flowers from first crown buds, as do many of the mid-season cultivars too. However, some cultivars particularly of late flowering chrysanthemums such as the American Beauty Family produce their best flowers when stopped a second time and grown on to *second crown buds*. Once the crown buds can be seen developing, the process of *disbudding* should commence. The aim is to remove unwanted flower buds from a cluster, leaving just the one flower bud selected. All

leafy side-shoots from the leaf axils below should also be removed. All the energies of the plant should be directed to the task of producing top-quality flowers from the selected flower buds and disbudding should not be delayed. Indeed, even if sprays are grown, the side shoots should still be removed without delay. When growing chrysanthemums as sprays, remove the crown bud and leave all the other buds in the cluster, as this bud is inclined to open in advance of the other flower buds.

Some cultivars break into side shoots in early summer, while others are shy at doing so and may be left some two or three weeks longer in order to develop enough sideshoots. If they fail to do this naturally, stop the leading shoot and, as the side shoots develop, select two or three of the topmost side shoots and stop these again when they have developed their first pair of leaves. In this way each of these will produce a couple of extra side shoots which will furnish additional flowers in due season.

Chrysanthemums like some moisture about their roots and while the soil must never be over wet it pays to water the plants regularly if the weather is dry. The provision of a dilute liquid feed occasionally is also beneficial, particularly after periods of very heavy rain.

Choose varieties that are doing well, and are healthy plants to propagate from in future years. Stout labels should be placed against these so that they may be readily identified later. Once flowering has finished cut back the main stem of each plant to 6in (15cm) above ground level on those plants which have been selected to be retained. (Lift and destroy all the unwanted plants and their debris at the same time.) Then, with the aid of a garden fork, lift the stools, with as little soil as possible to enable the stools (roots) to be packed more closely together either on the floor of a greenhouse or in a garden frame. Some fine dry soil/compost is then spread over the roots to the original soil level to prevent them from becoming shrivelled during the winter dormancy period. This should then be given a light watering to settle it about the roots.

Ventilation of the greenhouse or garden frame should be given during mild weather to keep the temperature down. When garden frames are used the tops can be removed during the day, if the weather is dry and mild. When fresh growth commences the garden frame must be given additional protection on frosty nights and the covering removed each day if the weather permits.

Mid-Season Flowering Chrysanthemums Cultivation is as for early flowering chrysanthemums, but you need to erect a temporary structure clad with strong clear polythene to cover the plants from the beginning of October onwards. This is to prevent rain damage rather than frost.

Knock strong posts into the ground adjacent to the ends of the chrysanthemum bed, with intermediate posts along the sides of the bed if necessary too, of sufficient height to allow a gap of 1ft (30cm) above the top of the chrysanthemums when they are fully grown. Strong straining wire is then run down the sides of the chrysanthemum bed, from the top of each post and across the ends and between the intermediate posts. Galvanized staples are suitable for attaching the wire to the posts. The clear plastic is then rolled out over the top of this temporary structure, of sufficient width to enable it to hang down either side for a distance of approximately 2-3ft (60 to 90cm) and held securely in position by a number of 3in (7.5cm) long 'Bulldog' clips along the side wires and at the ends.

The alternative solution is to grow the chrysanthemums in 9 or 10in (22.5 or 25cm) pots in the open in the summer and move them into an unheated greenhouse in the autumn. This will necessitate several repottings during the course of cultivation. They will grow quite happily either in the traditional John Innes Potting Compost No. 2 or one of the peat-based potting composts. Spacing them out 18in (45cm) apart in the row. Each pot will require a cane to support the plant. The canes too will need to be tied to a straining wire stretched out along each row of pot plants and secured to a stout post at each end of the row to prevent the plants from being blown over and injured in strong winds. The plants grown in pots will need watering every few days. Once the chrysanthemums have become established in the final pots they should be given an application of dilute liquid feed every second week and this should continue until the flowers are showing colour. Move the plants into the greenhouse before the weather deteriorates and give as much ventilation as possible to keep the temperature down and prevent soft growth.

Once flowering has ceased and one has selected which plants are to be retained these should have the main stem cut back to 6in (15cm) above the top of the pot. The stools of these plants may be left in their pots and they can be given the protection either of a cold greenhouse or a garden frame during the winter months. If space is limited follow the procedure recommended for the early flowering cultivars.

Propagation C. *maximum* is propagated by root division in spring, either annually or biennially. C. *rubellum* is propagated either by root division in spring or by stem cuttings secured in spring and rooted in sandy soil in a garden frame.

In early spring, rising temperatures in the greenhouse or frame will stimulate the chrysanthemum stools into growth and some soft-wood cuttings can be taken from these. The cuttings should be some 2 to 2½in (5 to 6.25cm) long and cut just beneath a leaf joint. Remove the lower leaf. They should all be of a uniform size. So if there is a shortage of suitable shoots to secure as cuttings, it is better to wait a week or two before starting any propagation work. If the soil/compost is at all dry provide a light watering to encourage some root activity and shoot development. The ideal rooting medium consists of two parts by bulk of finely divided moist peat and one part sharp sand. When putting this compost in boxes or pots it is important to ensure that it is pressed down firmly. The cuttings are inserted into the compost to the depth of 1in (2.5cm) and spaced out 2in (5cm) apart, when rooted in boxes. If one is using pots for this purpose insert the cuttings around the rim. For speedy rooting the minimum night temperature should be 50°F (10°C). At lower temperatures rooting will take longer but sturdy plants can be produced. On bright sunny days it is important to shade the cuttings from the sun otherwise they may wilt. Once rooting has taken place no time should be lost in potting up the plants either in John Innes Potting Compost or one of the peat-based universal composts. The rooted plants should be grown on cold and merely be given the protection of a garden frame with extra protection given on frosty nights.

Once established in the pots ventilation should be given whenever possible and the plants hardened off prior to planting in the open ground.

Uses Unlike its sophisticated cousin the exhibition chrysanthemum, the Shasta daisy has an air of informality about it. The flower is round, white or creamy white and may be used almost to excess in a massed arrangement using the larger more perfect blooms as the focal area. Like so many simple flowers, they can look attractive placed in a deep vase. They are the perfect accompaniment to a foliage arrangement, but do not use many or you will lose the cool tranquil effect that green and white generates.

Conditioning Autumn-flowering chrysanthemums mix well with preserved foliage, and the warm colouring looks well in brass or copper containers. Given plenty of water they can last up to 10 days. Cut the flowers as they develop. The central disc should look fresh and not be discoloured. Stand them in deep water in a shaded position for 2 to 3 hours. If the stem is woody, this should be lightly crushed before conditioning.

Preserving Consider well what you would use a preserved flower for. I find them rather coarse for pictures or collage and much prefer to use them as fresh flowers. Simple flowers are best pressed, while double blooms need to be preserved in desiccant.

Cosmos

Mexico
Compositae

Flowering season	Spring	Summer	Autumn	Winter	

Good / Very Good / Small — Large / Flower size — Long / Short — Long / Short / Cut life / Preserving / Stem length

Cosmos sulphureus 'Bright Lights'

Cosmos bipinnatus

Cosmos (Cosmea) can be a very attractive cut-flower, providing one obtains the suitable strains and cultivars of the species available. *C. bipinnatus* has a number of named cultivars. *C. b.* 'Candy Stripe' is a relatively recent introduction, with flowers which are ice white in colour with each petal boldly edged and striped brilliant crimson. It is early flowering, height of 2½ft (75cm).
C. b. 'Klondyke Goldcrest', double flowers of

exquisite golden-orange, early flowering, and height 2ft (60cm).
C. b. 'Klondyke Diablo' fiery red flowers, height 2ft (60cm).
C. sulphureus is another highly desirable species, generally sold in a mixed blend of superb bright colours as *C. s.* 'Bright Lights Mixed'. It bears fully double flowers, height 2½ft (60 to 75cm). One may also find in the seed catalogues, if you search through them carefully, *C. s.* 'Sulphureus Sunset' with brilliant red, semi-double flowers, height 2½ft (75cm). Flowering is throughout the summer.
Cultivation and propagation Cosmos likes a dry, poor soil and does best in hot years. Dead head regularly. Sow seed either in a coldframe or under cloches in early spring, in boxes containing a peat based compost. When the seedlings are large enough to handle prick them out and grow them on under the coldframe. Harden them off for planting in their flowering positions in late spring. Where no protection can be provided delay sowing until late spring and sow where flowering is to take place. When the seedlings are large enough to handle thin them out to stand 1½ft (45cm) apart.
Uses This is a very showy flower that delights in the summer sunshine. The colours are extremely bright and the flower size can be up to 4in (10cm) across. This puts it in the range of the larger flower arrangement. Its rather flat face suits the focal area position, whilst any of the smaller blooms can be sprinkled through the design to continue the colour scheme.
Conditioning The flowers should be cut during the cool of the day as they flag slightly during conditioning if they are not charged with moisture. Stand them in deep water for 3 hours in a shaded area.
Preserving The finest flowers are the single varieties and these press extremely well. The colours are quite startling and make a fine centre for a pressed flower design.

Dahlia

Mexico
Compositae

Flowering season		Spring	Summer	Autumn	Winter	
Good / Very Good		Large		Short	Long	
Preserving	Small / Flower size	Long / Cut life		Short		Stem length

Dahlia 'Bellamour'

Dahlia 'Gerrie Hoek'

Dahlia 'Beechy'

Dahlia 'Doris Day'

Dahlia is a half hardy tuberous perennial. Not all types of dahlias are suitable for use as cut flowers. The type required should be closely petalled, have long stiff stems, take up water easily and be highly productive of flowers for cutting. The following selection of dahlias all satisfy these requirements:
Decorative Dahlias
'Arabian Night', dark red flowers, height 3½ft (105cm).

Dahlia 'Amelisweert'

'Duet', blood red tipped white flowers, height 4ft (120cm).
'Gerrie Hoek', pure pink flowers, height 4½ft (135cm). Very prolific.
'Glory of Heemstede', sulphur yellow flowers, height 4½ft (135cm).
'House of Orange', glowing orange flowers, height 4ft (120cm). Early.
'Lavender Perfection', deep lavender flowers, height 5ft (150cm).
'Peter', deep pink shading to light pink in the centre flowers, height 3½ft (105cm).
Pompon and Ball Dahlias
'Amusing' (Ball), yellow flowers edged orange, height 3½ft (105cm).
'Brilliant Eye' (Ball), brilliant scarlet flowers, height 3ft (90cm).
'Doxy' (Pom), ivory-white flowers, height 3ft (90cm).
'Potgeiter' (Pom), bright yellow flowers, height 3ft (90cm).
'Pride of Berlin' (Pom), lilac pink flowers, height 3½ft (105cm).
Cactus Dahlias
'Cheerio', purple-red flowers with small white tip, height 4ft (120m).
'Doris Day', cardinal red flowers, height 4ft (120cm).
'Hit Parade', signal red flowers, height 4½ft (135cm).
'My Love', creamy white flowers, height 3½ft (105cm).
'Preference', coral pink flowers, height 3½ft (105cm).
'Promise', pure yellow flowers, height 4ft (120cm).
'Purple Gem', glowing cyclamen purple flowers, height 2½ft (75cm).
Cultivation and propagation Dahlias like a sunny position. They are gross feeders, so the plot should be well cultivated, and a generous amount of farmyard manure or well-rotted garden compost incorporated, in the autumn. A dressing of a good general fertilizer should be sprinkled on the soil just prior to planting in early summer. Over-wintered or divided tubers may be planted in late spring as the buds will not be very developed and a covering of soil will protect them from frost. Rooted cuttings must not be planted until all danger of frost is over. Plant dahlias carefully, taking out enough soil in the planting hole to accommodate the plant's rootball. Lightly firm the soil. At the same time carefully insert stakes of a length to match the final height of the variety. Tie the plant to the stake as it develops. Mulch between the plants and water in dry weather.

The tips of the young plants should be pinched out about three weeks after planting, to encourage lateral growth. The aim should be 6 to 8 shoots per plant, for prime quality flowers. The stems should also be disbudded regularly to give single flowers on long stems

for cutting. Dead head as the blooms fade.

After flowering leave the dahlias until frost has blackened the stems. Lift carefully with a fork and shake the soil from the roots. Cut the stems back to 6in (15cm) and store the tubers for about a week in a frost-proof shed to dry. Shake any loose soil from the tubers and then pack in dry peat or straw in boxes. It helps to prevent fungus attack if the tubers are dusted with flowers of sulphur. Examine the tubers regularly and discard any that are showing signs of disease.

Dahlias may be propagated from seed, by division of the plants and by cuttings. Producing dahlias from seed is the method used for many of the bedding type dahlias each year but is not to be recommended for the other dahlias, as these do not come true to type from seed.

The easiest way of increasing plant stocks is by division of the dahlia tubers. This is best undertaken when the new buds begin to appear. Close examination will indicate that these new buds are usually situated at the base of the old stem and not on the tubers. Pieces of tuber which are to be used for planting must have attached to them some of the old stem, carrying one or more new buds, otherwise they will not grow. The division of the dahlia tubers is best undertaken with a sharp knife.

Start the tubers into growth in gentle heat 50°F (10°C) in early spring. If a greenhouse is not available perhaps one could start them into growth in a warm shed or some other suitable place. Light is not important at this early stage. Small numbers of dahlia tubers should be placed in boxes containing a layer of seed compost or peat. The plants need spraying with water once each day, in the first instance, more frequently as the buds begin to appear.

Dahlia cuttings may be obtained in one of two ways. When they are about 4in (10cm) long the cuttings may be taken, together with a piece of the old tuber, though this procedure limits the total numbers of cuttings which may be obtained from each tuber.

For a greater increase in numbers of plants it is far better to sever each cutting, with a sharp knife, about ½in (1.25cm) above the tuber. If you do this there is every likelihood that fresh buds will develop from the stump for further cuttings. Trim the cuttings by making a second cut just beneath a node (leaf-joint), as this is the place on the stem where rooting is best achieved. Dip into hormone rooting powder and insert several cuttings into seed trays or plant-pots containing a mixture of two parts peat to one part sand. This compost should be well watered prior to the cuttings being inserted and no further water should be given until the plants show some signs of growth. Place in a warm, light situation to encourage early rooting. The minimum air temperature should be about 55°F (12.5°C). Unrooted cuttings may wilt if not given some protection from the sun, such as a sheet or paper spread over the top of them. When the cuttings are well-rooted, pot up individually and keep in a frost free place until planting out.

Uses The petal shape of this generous flower often influences where it is to be used. The dramatic shape of the cactus dahlia adds considerable impact to a bold free form or a modern design. Decorative dahlias have more rounded petals and lend themselves more to the sophisticated traditional style of arrangement. They can be used at various stages of development allowing you to spread them throughout the design without losing continuity of form and colour.

Conditioning Cut the flower stem just above the leaf axil; remove any foliage that will come into contact with water and condition them for 3 hours in a shaded room. Aftercare is most important as they are gross drinkers, so top up the arrangement at least once a day.

Preserving A light spray with water will extend the cut life of the flowers. Dahlias are not easy to preserve. Small-flowered varieties can be dried in desiccant.

Digitalis

Foxglove
Europe, North Africa and Western Asia
Scrophulariaceae

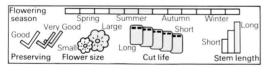

Digitalis purpurea 'Excelsior'

The species which is of particular interest to the flower arranger is *Digitalis purpurea*, a hardy biennial native to Europe. It is the 'Excelsior' hybrids with their tall spikes of tubular flowers which are most desired by the flower arrangers today. These have replaced the truly wild species to a great extent and they have a colour range which includes white, cream, primrose, pink and purple in summer, height approximately 5ft (150cm).

Cultivation and propagation *Digitalis* grows best in damp shady places under trees. However, it can grow successfully in a sunny situation providing that one keeps the soil about the roots moist at all times. The seeds are very small. Sow them very thinly in the flowering position, in early summer. Rake the soil to a fine tilth so that the seeds fall into the soil crumbs. They do not require covering with soil. Germination will occur within 2 to 3 weeks. When the plants are large enough to handle they should be thinned out to stand 6in (15cm) apart in each direction. Flowering will commence in midsummer the following year.

Uses The foxglove is a statuesque flower with a decided rural flavour. Used in limited numbers it will form a perfect foil for other unsophisticated flowers and foliages in a simple landscape arrangement. Because of its columnar growing habit it is often used to establish the height in a more formal design. As the flowers tend to clothe most of the stem it is particularly suitable for continuing the flower colour from the extremes of the design to the centre.

Conditioning The lower foliage should be removed before conditioning in water for at least 2 hours.

Preserving Always let a number of flowering stems set seed. These may be collected during the autumn and used almost immediately as dried material. Individual flowers can be removed from the flower stem and dried in desiccant, the tubular shape of the flower increases the three-dimensional quality of a dried flower picture.

Eremurus

Foxtail Lily
Asia
Liliaceae

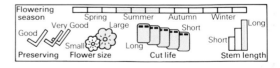

Eremurus provides some of the most stately spikes of flowers of all the herbaceous perennials which adorn the flower garden.

Eremurus bungei

Uses An extremely elegant flower to grow and arrange, the upright growth demands that it is used as height material in the large opulent designs of summer flowers and foliages. It is particularly useful in church arrangements when pastel shades are used. The height of the flower makes it very easy to be seen at a distance.

Conditioning Cut the stem when the lower flowers are open, it will continue to develop in a limited way once it is arranged. Stand the stems in deep water in a cool room for at least 3 hours to condition.

Preserving I have not been successful at preserving the entire flowering stem using any of the recognized methods. The small star flowers can be cut from the growing stem and dried in desiccant.

Eremurus robustus

Their tall spikes call for a spot sheltered from strong winds, as they attain a height of up to 10ft (300cm). They provide wonderful material for inclusion in floral arrangements either in their fresh state or as dried flowers.

E. bungei is native to Iran and produces bright yellow spikes of starry flowers, 3ft (90cm).

E. elwesii has fragrant spikes of pink flowers, height 7 to 9ft (210 to 270cm).

E. 'Highdown Hybrids' have flower spikes in shades of pink, orange, yellow and copper, height 5 to 6ft (150 to 180cm).

E. robustus is native to Turkestan and has spikes of flowers of soft pink or white, height 8 to 10ft (240 to 300cm).

All flower in the early summer.

Cultivation and propagation *Eremurus* will grow in any well-drained soil in sun. Propagation is by division of the roots during the dormant season.

Gladiolus

Sword Lily
S. Africa, Asia Minor, S. Europe
Iridaceae

Flowering season	Spring	Summer	Autumn	Winter	
Good / Very Good	Large		Short		Long
Small	Long			Short	
Preserving	Flower size		Cut life		Stem length

Gladiolus 'The Bride'

Gladiolus is a genus of herbaceous perennial flowering plants which produce spikes of flowers on stiff erect stems and have sword-shaped pointed leaves during the summer months. During their resting period in winter they survive in the form of corms (swollen bases of stems). In the late spring the corms develop fibrous roots and new shoots again to become one of the most popular of summer

Gladiolus 'Red Cascade'

Gladiolus 'Blue Conqueror'

Gladiolus 'Sweepstake'

flowering plants, providing the flower arranger with many highly desirable tapering spikes of flowers in a wide array of colours. They are too tender to survive the winter in the open ground in most places, so the corms are generally planted in spring each year. The following selection represents some of the best named hybrids currently available:

Gladioli Nanus, height 18 to 24in (45 to 60cm). Early summer flowering.
'Amanda Mahy', deep pink.
'Albus', white.
'Charm', magenta rose.
Colvillii 'The Bride', white veined greenish yellow.
'Guernsey Glory', coral red with creamy blotch.
'Peach blossom', rose pink with a white eye.

Large flowered gladioli, height 36 to 60in (90 to 150cm), summer flowering. Flowering period: 1, early; 2, mid-season; 3, late.
Red Shades
3 'Aristocrat', carmine-red, shaded crimson-orange.
1 'Carmen', brilliant scarlet blotched white.
2 'Oscar', blood-red.
Orange Shades
1 'Nicole', deep orange blotched red.
2 'Queen of Holland', pure orange.
2 'Tiger Flame', bright orange with yellow marks.
White and Creamy-White Shades
2 'Classic', ivory white with rose striped markings.
2 'Mary Housley', creamy-white with scarlet blotch.
2 'Snow Princess', creamy white.
1 'Tequendama', pure white.
2 'White Friendship', white with a pale yellow blotch.
Pink and Salmon Shades
2 'Albanberg', salmon rose.
1 'Deciso', shell pink with scarlet blotch.
1 'Frosty Pink', lilac pink.
2 'Wine & Roses', rose pink blotched purple.
3 'Sweepstake', shell pink and carmine.
Blue and Purple Shades
1 'Blue Conqueror', deep blue.
2 'Fidelio', cyclamen purple.
2 'Mr. W. E. Cobley', lavender blue with white blotch.
Yellow shades
1 'Aldebaran', yellow with blood red blotch.
2 'Green Woodpecker', lime-yellow with purple blotch. (Perfect for green displays).
2 'Nova Lux', rich yellow.
Gladioli Primulinus Hybrids, height 30 to 36in (75 to 90cm), late summer flowering.
2 'Carioca', brilliant orange.
2 'Columbine', carmine rose with creamy-white centre.
2 'Leonore', pale yellow.
2 'Piquant', deep purple.
1 'White City', pure white.

Dutch Butterfly Gladioli, height 36in (90cm), late summer flowering.
1 'Eastbourne', violet.
2 'Green Bird', uranium green.
1 'Ivanhoe', yellow with red blotch.
2 'Merry', coral pink.

Cultivation and propagation *Gladiolus* will grow in any ordinary well-drained garden soil providing it is in sun. Planting should take place in the open garden as soon as the first leaves on the trees begin to appear. If one plants small batches of corms at 14 day intervals from then to early summer, steady supplies of flowers can be had over a long period. If one has a garden frame, then gladioli can be started into growth a month earlier, in pots, and planted out in the open ground when all fear of frost has past. The time from planting to flowering is about 90 days for the early flowering gladioli; 100 days for the mid-season ones and 120 days for the late-flowering types. Corms planted in the open ground should be 4in (10cm) deep and 6in (15cm) apart. Once flowering has ceased and the stems have become brown, the gladioli are forked from the ground. Upon close inspection, it will be seen that the old corm has withered and a new one has been produced to replace it. There are usually small cormlets attached. The large corms are stored in a cool, frost-free place until the following year, when they are planted and produce a fresh crop of flowers. The small cormlets are also planted, but in a nursery bed in an out-of-the-way place, as they will need several years' more growth before reaching flowering size.

Uses The list of *Gladiolus* in the text will enable you to grow tall spiky flowers to suit any occasion. It is a flower that will fit into all categories of design. As outline material in a formal design I prefer to use it to establish the height of an arrangement. Used at the lower, outer edges it tends to look stiff and unyielding. In more modern, even abstract, work it may be used for its form, texture or as blocks of colour.

Conditioning Cut the stem when the lower flowers are beginning to develop. It will continue to open once it has been arranged. Stand the cut stems in water until you need to arrange them. The flowers can be advanced or retarded depending on the amount of heat they are subjected to, during the conditioning process.

Preserving The form of the flower precludes its preserving in the flower press. Some of the smaller flowers may be preserved in desiccant.

Godetia

North West America
Onagraceae

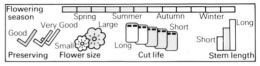

Godetia 'Sybil Sherwood'

Godetia 'Azalea flowered'

There are two species which provide valuable flowers for cutting. These are *G. amoena* which attains a height of 2ft (60cm) and *G. grandiflora* which only grows about 1ft (30cm) high.

Godetia is available in both single and double or azalea-flowered forms and they are all extremely showy, with flowers available in a splendid array of colours. Seed catalogues tend to offer strains of mixed colours but you can find straight colours being offered in the form of named cultivars:

'Kelvedon Glory', salmon orange, height 1½ft (45cm).

'Orange Glory', scarlet orange, height 1ft (30cm).

'Sybil Sherwood', brilliant pink, edged white, height 1½ft (45cm).

'Whitnevi Duchess of Albany', white, height 1ft (30cm).

'Vivid', shiny cherry rose, height 1ft (30cm). Among the mixed strains of Godetia there is 'Grandiflora Double Flowered Mixed', with flowers of various shades of pink, mauve, carmine, crimson and white, height 2ft (60cm). There is also the 'Grandiflora Azalea Flowered Mixed' which has semi-double azalea type flowers with wavy edges to the petals; height 15in (37.5cm). These are available in an exotic range of colours and provide a breath-taking display both in the garden and when cut.

Cultivation and propagation *Godetia* needs a sunny position and not too rich a soil. Seed of both species may be sown in the open ground either in the spring or the early autumn. After germination the plants are thinned out to stand 1ft (30cm) apart. Flowering commences in late spring from early autumn-sown seed and continues throughout summer with the aid of spring sowing. Autumn-raised plants may need protection in cold areas.

Uses Both the single and double flowered kinds are spiky, ideal for creating an outline. Their flexible stems allow them to flow in a downward direction. The taller cultivars are perhaps the most useful, as the flowers are more widely placed on the stems giving a lighter appearance. The dwarf varieties tend to form a solid clump, discordant as outline material but very useful as an intermediate flower.

Conditioning Remove the lower foliage and crush the stems before conditioning them for 4 hours.

Preserving The brightness of the flower colour is well worth preserving. Do this by pressing when the flower is fully open.

Helichrysum

Straw Flower
Australia
Compositae

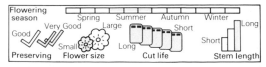

For the flower arranger one species is of considerable importance in the composition of floral displays, during the winter months. This

Helichrysum bracteatum mixed

Helichrysum bracteatum 'Sulphur Light'

is *Helichrysum bracteatum*, one of the best known dried flowers. It bears large daisy-like flowers in summer which are noted for holding their colour well and may be dried easily. *H. bracteatum* is a half-hardy annual plant which has both dwarf and tall growing forms bearing flowers in a wide array of colours.

H. b. 'Swiss Giants' has flowers of copper red, orange, rose, scarlet, white, wine red or yellow, height 3ft (90cm). One can obtain it in separate colours or as mixed seed.

Helichrysum 'Monstrosum' is a cultivar of *H. bracteatum* and there is a fascinating dwarf form in *H.* 'Monstrosum' 'Dwarf Hot Bikini' with a mass of glistening scarlet flowers, height 1ft (30cm).

'Bright Bikini' is available in a blend of mixed colours and in straight colours, bright yellow, rose, salmon rose, terracotta and white, height 1ft (30cm). These form neat compact plants which look very nice when in full flower. When used as dried flowers they retain the same bright colours even in the depth of winter. Another good strain is *H. b.* 'Sulphur Light', clusters of sulphur yellow fluffy flowers which become bright orange later, height 15in (37.5cm).

Cultivation and propagation The most suitable soil for these plants is a light sandy one, but they will grow equally well on heavier soils providing some sharp sand is introduced to improve drainage. Choose a sunny situation and sow the seeds in the open, where flowering is to occur. Germination takes about two weeks. When the seedlings are large enough to handle they should be thinned out to stand 1ft (30cm) apart. Dwarf strains will not need any support but in the case of the 'Swiss Giants' it is advisable to use canes and string or twiggy branches to keep the stems straight.

Uses *Helichrysum* is probably the most well-known flower for preserving, but because of this it is seldom used in its fresh state. The flowers will dry naturally on the plant, but when fully developed expose a large yellow daisy centre which makes the flower look very flat and is often at odds with the petal colour. When the flower is younger, the undeveloped petals form a cone in the centre making a much more attractive shape. Sometimes the colour on the reverse side of the petal is a different shade, which adds to the interest. It is in this cone stage that they should be gathered for drying. It is a continuous process, so you may have to collect them daily. Pick the flower heads only and immediately mount them on to stub wires. Bend a small hook shape in the wire and insert it in the top of the flower concealing the hook in the petals. The residual sap in the fresh flower will slightly rust the wire and create a strong bond. Once the head is wired, hang them upside down or push them into a block of oasis to complete the drying process which will take up to three weeks in a warm but dry atmosphere.

Iris pumila

Iris germanica 'Jane Phillips'

Iris

North Hemisphere
Iridaceae

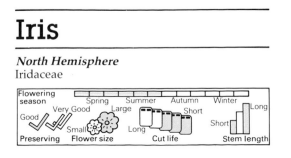

Iris unguicularis

The Iris is a large genus of some 200 different species of plants. There are two quite distinct types of root system. In the one type there is a bulb or bulb-like structure, as is witnessed in the early flowering *Iris reticulata*. In the other type there is an underground stem or rhizome which stores food through the dormant season and sends up shoots annually which terminate in flowers. For cut flowers we grow seven of these species of Iris, all of which have rhizomatous root-stocks, and we will deal with them in order of their flowering period.

The very earliest to flower is *Iris unguicularis* syn. *stylosa*. This is a native of Algeria which bears large, scented, lavender blue flowers, on short stems in winter and early spring. It likes poor limy soil and flowers best in full sun which provides dry hot conditions for its rhizomes during the summer months.

I. u. 'Mrs Barnard' is an improved cultivar with larger flowers which are more freely produced. Both grow to a height of 1ft (30cm) Heavy soils will need the addition of large amounts of sharp sand and other gritty material.

I. pumila 'Aurea' from S.E. Europe has delightful pale yellow flowers in spring and grows 10in (25cm) high. Here is a cut flower subject ideal for the small posy-vase or table bowl. This miniature iris should be planted in a sunny position in a rockery or in the front of the herbaceous border.

I. warlsind is a delightful hybrid with deep blue and yellow flowers during spring, height 12in (30cm).

I. willmottiana comes from E. Turkestan and has a very pretty cultivar in *I. w. alba* with pure white flowers blotched orange, appearing during late spring, height 10in (25cm).

Iris pallida dalmatica is an old favourite, one of the few iris of the Bearded type to have magnificent foliage. It bears clear lavender-blue/golden, fragrant, flowers in early summer, height 2½ft (75cm). This is a native of Southern Europe. *I. p.* 'Argentes-Variegata' has cream and glaucous foliage and blue flowers, height 2ft (60cm).

Iris germanica (Bearded Iris) is the 'Common Iris', which grows some 2½ft (75cm) high and has fragrant, purple and yellow flowers during early summer. It has been very long in cultivation and its origin is uncertain. There are many hybrid forms and they are all attractive cut flower material, because they are of stiff habit and available in such an extensive range of colours. The following selection is provided to give an indication of the range of material available. It also represents my own particular preference among the Bearded Iris which are readily available from the garden centres and nurserymen, and all are early summer flowering:

'Arabi Pasha', cornflower blue, height 40in (100cm).

'Berkeley Gold', bright yellow, height 3ft (90cm).

'Black Hills', excellent very dark blue/black flowers, height 40in (100cm).

'Buterscotch Kiss', glistening caramel, height 3ft (90cm).

'Golden Alps', ivory white and greenish-yellow, height 3ft (90cm).

'East Indies', light bronze, mauve and yellow, height 4ft (120cm).

'Edward of Windsor', pastel pink, height 40in (100cm).

'Jane Phillips', an outstanding iris with large rufled intense blue flowers, height 3½ft (105cm).

'Ola Kala', rich orange/yellow, height 40in (100cm).

'Pearly Dawn', exquisite pearly pink, height 3ft (90cm).

The Bearded Iris will succeed on a wide range of soils providing that they are well drained and limy. If there is any doubt about the lime content it is wise to provide a dressing of carbonate of lime, in late winter. The main source of sustenance is an annual top dressing of bonemeal, which is applied during late spring. The only other requirement is a sunny situation. Once established the plants should be lifted and divided every 3 years, immediately flowering ceases.

Iris acutiloba is native to Transcaucasia and has creamy-white flowers in midsummer, height 6-8in (15-20cm).

Iris foetidissima is a native British and European species and prefers a dry, shady, limy soil even pure chalk. It has yellowish-green and lilac flowers during early summer, height 2ft (60cm). The real importance of this iris is its large orange seeds which are produced in the autumn, as these are marvellous for use in winter decorations.

Iris sibirica is a native of Central Europe and Russia. This is a moisture loving pant which can be planted near the edge of a pond, or some other moisture retentive spot in the garden. Improve dry soils by the incorporation of lots of peat and old well-decayed garden compost, when preparing the soil for planting. Choose any open sunny position if possible, although *I. sibirica* will tolerate partial shade.

This species forms rushy clumps of foliage and wiry stems which bear flowers during midsummer. The flowers are among the longest lasting of all cut flowers used for vase work. They also produce seed pods of an ornamental nature which can be dried for use in the winter decorations. There are a number of cultivars:

Iris sibirica 'Blue King', deep blue flowers, height 3ft (90cm).

I. s. 'Ottawa', clear blue flowers, height 3ft (90cm).

I. s. 'Snow Queen', pure white flowers, height 32in (80cm).

Iris reticulata 'Harmony'

Iris kaempferi

Iris germanica 'Golden Alps'

I. s. 'Tropic Night', dark violet blue flowers, height 3ft (90cm).

Iris kaempferi is a native of Japan and flowers in high summer. It likes moist, lime-free soil. The flowers are very orchid-like and quite large in the cultivars, but not so long lasting as *I. sibirica*. It has mauvish-purple flowers, height 2½ft (75cm).

I. k. 'Snowdrift', pure white flowers, height 3ft (90cm).

I. k. 'Rose Queen', soft pink flowers and may be grown in very moist soil or even shallow water and still remain winter hardy, height 2ft (60cm).

Propagation Propagation of rhizomatous iris is by division of the rhizomes into smaller pieces after flowering ceases during the summer months. Growth buds may also be removed from the sides of the rhizomes when about as big as a garden pea. A sharp knife is needed for their removal and they are then inserted as cuttings, and given the benefit of a closed shaded coldframe or cloche to encourage rooting. One can also propagate irises from seed in order to obtain additional plants. This is particularly useful for obtaining *I. k.* hybrids and *I. s.* hybrids. Soak the seeds in water for 24 hours and then sow in a well-drained compost, in a closed coldframe, in the early summer. Propagation from seed is slow as the plants take 2 or 3 years to reach flowering size.

Uses The form of this flower is both dignified and individual. It is at home in a massed traditional design or as a focal flower in a stark modern arrangement. Those that flower in the early spring add a welcome touch of blue to a basket of mixed spring flowers. The soft stems can be put into small plastic phials then placed in the water-retaining foam. The larger bearded iris with its strong upward movement is a handsome flower to use in a vertical design where little plant material is needed.

Conditioning The flowers can be cut as the bud is about to open, as they will continue to develop after they have been arranged. Condition them in deep water for 3 hours.

Preserving Sadly the flower does not preserve well, but some seed pods are worth collecting. The best of these is *I. foetidissima*. The seeds are bright orange and revealed once the pod has burst, making an exciting complement to preserved *Choisya ternata* and *Mahonia* foliage.

Lathyrus

Leguminosae

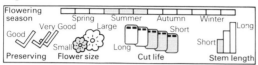

Lathyrus odoratus

This is a large genus of climbing plants.
Lathyrus odoratus (Sweet Pea) comes from Italy
and Sicily. There is a huge variety of different
cultivars – the Spencer Range is the most
widely used for the provision of cut flowers
and all the following are recommended:
'Cream Delight', rich cream.
'Firebrand', prolific, deep scarlet.
'Gigantic', very large, pure white.
'Hunters Moon', large creamy-primrose frilly
flowers.
'Leamington', frilly lilac flowers.
'Monty', deep creamy pink.
'Noel Sutton', rich blue.
'Olympia', large deep purple flowers.
'Rosy Frills', large frilled flowers of white with
a broad picotee rim deep rose.
'Southbourne', almond blossom pink, white
base.
'Winston Churchill', frilled and fluted brilliant
crimson.
Cultivation and propagation The sweet pea,
unlike other annual flowering plants, is a gross
feeder. While it will grow quite happily in a
wide range of soils it will only do so if they are
deep, well-drained and well supplied with
bulky organic matter in the form of manure or
well rotted garden compost. Deep cultivation
is essential if good results are to be obtained.
Ideally the ground should be double dug in 2ft
(60cm) trenches. If this is not possible, liquid
feed will be necessary every 14 days through
the flowering season.

Towards early spring, when soil conditions
will permit, a good dressing of bone meal
should be forked into the soil's surface along
the line of the trench. Each of these trenches
will accommodate two rows of sweet peas and
where more than one trench is to be dug they
should be some 4ft (120cm) apart. Round holes
about 4ft (120cm) in diameter are better than
trenches on heavy soils.

Sweet peas may be sown at three distinct
times of the year. They may be sown during
late spring outdoors in their flowering
positions to flower in late summer and
autumn. They may also be sown in the
autumn in a coldframe or under cloches. Once
the seeds have germinated they are grown on
cold, with ventilation, but sheltered from rain.
Once the plants have developed their second
pair of leaves, they are transplanted 3in
(7.5cm) apart into other boxes or singly into
3½in (8.75cm) pots containing potting
compost. Once the plants have recovered from
this move they should have their shoots
removed, as this induces the development of
basal growths which are much stronger than
the original shoots. The plants are grown
throughout the winter without any heat, with
ventilation being given whenever the weather
will permit, keeping the compost on the dry-
side. The resulting plants may be transferred
to their flowering positions in early spring to
flowering in early summer. It is also possible
to sow seeds in a warm greenhouse in early
spring, following the general advice on
pricking out and shoot removal just given.
Growth will be fairly rapid under these
conducive conditions and by late spring the
resulting plants can be hardened off in a
coldframe or cloches before planting in their
flowering positions. These plants will then
flower during midsummer.

Sweet peas need the support of netting or
stakes. Canes will prove the most economical
as they last for years. The aim is to produce
good quality flowers on long stems and the
best way of achieving this is by growing the
sweet peas on the cordon system, though it
reduces the quantity of blooms. For this the
plants are set out 8in (20cm) apart in the row.
Each one of these plants is then trained up a
single cane or string as the case may be. All
side growths and tendrils are removed so that
all the energies of the plant are devoted into
the development of larger flowers and longer
stems than normal. No flowers should be
permitted to develop until the plants are about
3ft (90cm) high or it is clear that the flower
stems have at least four flower buds on them.
When the sweet pea plants reach the top of
their canes or other supports, they are untied
and laid along the ground for some distance
down the row before being trained up another
support. This encourages the strong growth of
the terminal shoot.

Sweet peas grown in a less intensive way are still useful for cut flowers. Just give them something to climb up and allow to grow naturally.

Uses Surely here we have the most feminine of flowers. The slender stems, soft texture, sensitive perfume and delicate colour is sufficient to justify its claim as queen of the annuals. The flowers are well spaced on the stem, giving it a light, airy appearance for outlining a medium-size arrangement or as an adjunct to the focal flowers in a large design. The flowers are elegant and sophisticated and on occasions deserve to be arranged by themselves in an equally elegant container, crystal or silver. They need no added foliage, though a little light grey *Artemisia* or *Senecio* will enhance the pink shades. It is essential to cut sweet peas at least twice per week to encourage further flowering. At the same time any seed pods should be removed, for if left on the plant they make the plant give up producing flowers.

Conditioning Cut the flowers when the top two buds are displaying colour and are beginning to unfurl, as this will prolong the flower's cut life.

Sweet peas have the most amenable habit of going to sleep after cutting, resuming development when placed in water. They can therefore be cut and left in a cool place for a day until you need them. Re-cut the stem and stand them in deep water; they will fully recover within 3 hours.

Lilium henryi

Lilium regale

Lilium

Lily
Northern Hemisphere
Liliaceae

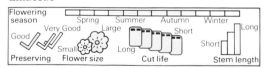

Lilies all have beautiful flowers and some are of considerable fragrance. The following selection of *Lilium* species are recommended:
L. auratum (Lily of Japan), large very fragrant white flowers with each petal banded with gold and speckled crimson, early autumn, height 5ft (150cm). A native of Japan.
L. candidum (Madonna Lily), is one of the most beautiful and best-loved of all the *Liliums* with its ivory white flowers and yellow anthers, midsummer, height 4ft (120cm). This is a native plant of the Eastern Mediterranean region. It requires a warm sunny situation and likes some lime in the soil.

Lilium speciosum **hybrid**

Lilium auratum

Lilium candidum

Lilium hansonii

L. hansonii, bright golden yellow flowers speckled maroon, early autumn, height 3ft (90cm). This is a *Lilium* of vigorous growth and its clumps of bulbs will need dividing up every three to five years. Ideally one should grow this species in a slightly shady situation such as on the edge of a shrubbery or where a building will cast a shadow in the hottest part of the day as it likes to keep its roots shaded and cool. It is a native of Korea and Siberia.

L. henryi, very floriferous and has bright orange flowers, early autumn, height 5 to 6ft (150 to 180cm). This is a native of China.

L. longiflorum, very fragrant, glistening white flowers, midsummer, height 2ft (60cm). This species can also be forced into flower in spring, in a cool greenhouse. Plant this *Lilium* in a sunny sheltered place in the open and if possible provide it with the protection of a cloche to prevent its shoots being damaged by late frosts. It is a native of Formosa and Ryukyu Islands of Japan.

L. regale, large white flowers, flushed yellow, with the back of the petals flushed maroon, midsummer, height 4 to 5ft (120 to 150cm). It should be planted in a sheltered sunny place and should be given the benefit of some protection from late frosts. *L. regale* is a native of Szechwan Province of China.

L. speciosum is of very easy culture and is recommended for the beginner growing *Liliums* for the very first time. It bears brilliant white flowers which are speckled pink or crimson, early autumn, height 3ft (90cm). It prefers a lightly shaded situation in a lime free soil and it can be forced in spring, if grown in a cool greenhouse. It is native to China and Japan.

There are some very good new hybrids:
'Black Dragon', creamy-white flowers. The outside of the petals are dark purple, fragrant, late summer, height 4ft (120cm).
'Fiesta Hybrids', pale yellow to bright red and vivid orange, summer, height 3–5ft (90–150cm).
'Golden Clarion Strain', excellent golden-yellow flowers, summer, height 3–5ft (90–150cm).
'Moonlight', exquisite greenish coloured flowers, summer, height 5ft (150cm).
'Pink Perfection', clear deep pink flowers, summer, height 5ft (150cm).
'Stargazer', red with a white border, late summer, height 3ft (90cm).
'Yellow Blaze', yellow flowers, early autumn, height 3ft (90cm).

Cultivation and propagation Many *Liliums* are stem-rooting, that is to say they grow roots on that section of the stem immediately above the bulb, in addition to the roots which grow from the base of the bulb in the customary manner. *L. candidum* is of this type and should be planted so that the tip of the bulb is just 1in (2.5cm) below the soil surface. All the other species are stem-rooting and require planting 8in (20cm) deep in the soil, so that there is at least 4in (10cm) of soil above the tip of the bulb. They are planted some 6 to 12in (15 to 30cm) apart according to the height of growth of the species concerned, in the late autumn.

The ground in which *Liliums* are to be grown needs to be well drained and not too rich in organic matter, as this causes losses from fungoid diseases and encourages pests which attack and destroy the bulbs. The ideal soil is a light sandy soil. However, heavy soils can be made suitable providing that sand or other suitable gritty material is incorporated. Poor soils can be enriched with either leafmould or peat. Do not use fresh manure. A surface mulch of peat should be applied each spring and forked in each autumn. Some watering will be required during the summer.

Support the taller growing *Liliums* with canes to prevent wind damage.

Lilium species may be increased by seed, but the time it takes for them to germinate varies amazingly as some remain dormant for many months and a great deal depends on the species involved. *L. regale* seed germinates in a matter of weeks, sown in a garden frame or greenhouse, and the resulting seedlings develop into bulbous plants which will flower during the second year. Some other species will take several years more before flowering. Hybrids do not come true from seed and it is necessary to wait for them to multiply naturally, which can be a slow business. It is possible to speed this up by pulling the scales off mature bulbs in the autumn and planting these, with their tips just visible, in sandy soil within a garden frame. These scales will, given time, develop into new flowering bulbs. Bulbils are another means of propagation. Bulbils may be found on the stem of a plant either above or below ground level depending upon the species concerned. These can be removed when they are mature enough to drop off when touched. They should be sown just like one would sow seed, immediately they are collected. They vary in the length of time it takes to reach flowering size.

Uses I hope that I can do sufficient justice to the beauty of this flower in such a short space. Always plan an arrangement around the lily flower. The foliage is stem borne and some must be left to feed and strengthen the bulb. Cutting the flower to the correct length will enable you to enjoy it in an arrangement and ensure a future supply. There are many ways to arrange lily flowers. The splendid form sets it apart as a flower for the centre of a formal design. Those that grow on very long stems can be placed at the sides of a large arrangement to emphasize the bell shape of the flower. They are equally at home in a modern design.

Conditioning Cut the stems when most of the flowers have opened. Remove the stamens to prevent the inner surface being marked by disturbed pollen. Condition them in water in a cool place for up to 4 hours. Once the conditioning process is underway, resist any temptation to handle them as they bruise and discolour very easily.

Preserving It is possible to dry the smaller flowers in desiccant. Some of the larger-flowered types display an exciting arrangement of seed pods that resemble a candelabra. If you are not saving the seed these should be collected as the pod changes to a brown colour and allowed to continue to dry suspended from a line in a light, dry atmosphere.

Limonium

Sea Lavender syn. *Statice*
S. Europe, N. Africa
Plumbagiaceae

Limonium sinuatum

Three species of *Limonium* are widely grown for cut flower production and are particularly important as dried flowers.

L. bonduellii is a perennial species with yellow flowers, height 18in (45cm).

L. sinuatum is another perennial species with blue flowers, height 18in (45cm). It also has cultivars with flowers which may be light pink, dark pink, light blue, dark blue, yellow or white in colour. Indeed, where the white form is grown, it is sometimes dyed various colours before it is dried. Both the above species are treated as annuals and their flowers may be used fresh cut throughout the summer, as well as dried for winter display. *L. suworowii* is an annual which bears long spikes of rosy pink flowers, height 18in (45cm). By making timed sowings one can have a continuous supply of flowers for cutting from late spring to autumn.

Cultivation and propagation All these species do well in an open sunny place in any ordinary well drained garden soil.

The earliest flowers are obtained from seeds sown under coldframes and cloches during early spring for transplanting to the open ground during early summer. In late spring further sowings are made in the open to produce later flowers for cutting. Germination takes 14 to 21 days. When the seedlings are large enough to handle they are pricked out into seed boxes containing seed compost and the young plants are hardened off for transferring to the open. Plant out 10in (20cm) apart. Seed may also be sown directly where flowering is to occur.

Uses *Limonium suworowii* and to a lesser extent *L. sinuatum* may be used fresh as outline material for any arrangement. It is as material for drying that these have a much greater value. The stems are strong enough to support the flower head after drying and the flower colour is retained with little or no fading. A favourite area for arranging these flowers is in a seascape. They have an association with the shoreline and certainly add authenticity to a maritime theme. The stems should be cut when the flowers are fully developed, showing maximum colour. Collect them when they are dry and tie them into very loose bundles. Suspend them in a warm room for 2 to 3 weeks. Once they are dry, they can be stored in a box for later use.

Lupinus polyphyllus

Lupinus polyphyllus 'Lulu' strain

Lupinus

Lupin
North America
Leguminosae

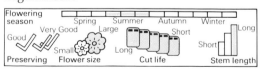

Lupinus polyphyllus is the commonest and best known of all the species. George Russell, a private Yorkshire gardener, transformed *L. polyphyllus* from a rather unpretentious herbaceous perennial, with blue flowers, into a stronger plant bearing spikes of flowers in a whole range of colours. The following selection contains some of the best modern cultivars which are readily obtainable. All

Lupinus polyphyllus 'Lulu Mixed'

flower in midsummer unless indicated.
'Chandelier', golden yellow flowers, height
40in (100cm).
'Fireglow', orange-flame flowers, height 3ft
(90cm).
'Harlequin', a striking bi-colour of bright pink
and yellow, height 3ft (90cm).
'Lady Fayre' a dwarfer cultivar, height 2½ft
(75cm) and delightful pink and white flowers,
late summer.
'Noble Maiden', exquisite ivory white flowers,
height 40in (100cm).
'The Governor', blue and white flowers,
height 40in (100cm).
'The Pages', carmine red flowers, height 40in
(100cm).
'Thundercloud', violet-purple flowers, early
summer, height 3ft (90cm).
Cultivation and propagation Lupins grow best
in a light, lime-free soil, which is given a
dressing of peat at the time of cultivation.
Choose a sunny position for these plants and
set them out 15in (38cm) apart in each
direction. Established lupins require an
application of bonemeal in spring. Mulch with
well rotted garden compost or peat in late
spring. Lupins are not long lived plants and
will need to be lifted and divided every 3 years
early in the spring. Stake early in the season
before much growth has developed. A second,
light crop of flowers can be encouraged by
deadheading regularly.
  Propagation of named cultivars is always by
division of the roots in spring or by root
cuttings. Basal cuttings may also be taken in
late spring. Lupins can also be propagated
from seeds e.g. 'Russell Dwarf Lulu Mixed',
height 2ft (60cm) and 'Russell Hybrid Mixed',
height 3ft (90cm). These are sown in the open
deep, in late spring and when the plants are
large enough to handle they are pricked out
6in (15cm) apart and transferred to their
flowering positions in the autumn to flower
the following year.
Uses This elegant flower is most evocative of
cottage gardens and is often simply arranged
in a vase without accompanying flowers or
foliage. It is not reliable as a cut flower, though
this is not to say that you should not try.
Conditioning The stems are hollow and
should be filled with water and plugged with a
tiny amount of wet oasis and immediately
placed in deep water for 3 hours. They can
then be arranged in water-retaining foam with
confidence, removing the plug before
arranging. If they are placed directly into a
vase they should still be filled with water and,
with your finger covering the end, stood in the
vase to prevent an airlock forming.
Preserving It is distressing that a plant as
generous in its colour forms will not preserve
to any degree. With a little care individual
flowers can be removed and dried in
desiccant. If the seed head is left, it will prove

useful for a limited time as a component for
both fresh and dried designs before it finally
sheds its pods.

Matthiola

Stocks
Europe and West Asia
Cruciferae

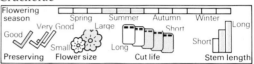

Matthiola 'Ten-week Stocks'

Matthiola incana is a native of Southern Europe
and it is from this species that most of the
garden stocks are derived, and all are fragrant.
  For summer flowering the 'Ten-week Stock'
and the column type Stocks are chosen and
treated as annuals. These are available in both
straight colours and mixed blends of colour.
'Trysomatic Giant Imperial Mixed' is
particularly good with a fine blend of colours,
height 1½ft (45cm). It contains about 80 per
cent double flowered and 20 per cent single
flowered plants. Select them at pricking out –
the stronger growing seedlings are the
doubles and the weak ones the single. 'Giant
Rocket Mixed' is a vigorous column type Stock
available in a good range of colours, height 2ft
(60cm). Another equally good strain which
grows taller is 'Pacific Column Mixed', height
2½ to 3ft (75 to 90cm). Column type Stocks are
capable of pre-selection for double flowers but
at least 65 per cent will be double.
Cultivation and propagation Any ordinary
garden soil will do providing it contains some
lime and is well drained. Choose an open
sunny position. Where a warm greenhouse is
available, seed may be sown very early in

spring and subsequently pricked out into seed boxes which are placed in a coldframe or cloches to harden off before planting. A second method is to sow the seeds thinly where they are to flower in spring, and provide protection with cloches. Seed may also be sown in the open ground where flowering is to occur in late spring. Germination takes 10 to 14 days and the resulting plants should be thinned to stand 10 to 12in (25 to 30cm) apart. They flower throughout the summer.

Uses In their season these are standard material for the arranger. *M. incana* channels its energy into producing a single imposing flower spike. The form is most impressive and the colour range sufficiently wide to warrant a considerable space in the garden. Their bold form makes them highly suitable for the largest of arrangements, flowering at a time when the garden is at its most bountiful and allowing you to compose an arrangement that will be both opulent and heavily perfumed.

Conditioning The stems are woody and should be lightly crushed before conditioning them for up to 6 hours. If it is possible remove the whole plant, wash the soil from the roots and condition the complete plant as usual. The plant can then be arranged in a cone of water. I use both methods and find that the cut life of the flower is not affected by either.

Preserving *M. bicornis* will press. The dull lilac colour is an exciting foil to preserved materials in darker colours.

Nicotiana F1 hybrid 'Nicki'

greenhouse. In early summer transfer the plants to a garden frame and harden them off for planting 12in (30cm) apart in the open ground in midsummer.

Uses This is an annual flower that comes in a wide range of colours including that much-sought-after green. It is not sophisticated in appearance, though it is more suited to the full traditional styles of arrangement. The medium size allows its use throughout the design.

Conditioning The leaves are slightly sticky and should be removed before conditioning to prevent them sticking to each other. Stand the stems in water for up to 3 hours.

Preserving *Nicotiana* can be dried in desiccant. To do this, collect the individual flowers just as they open. Any that develop a short tubular back to the flower may be pressed in the usual way.

Nicotiana

Tobacco Plant
Tropical America
Solanaceae

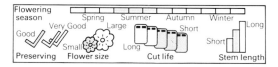

The species which is of concern to us here is *Nicotiana affinis* and this is a half-hardy annual which bears tube-shaped fragrant flowers in a wide range of colours. The F1 hybrid 'Nicki Mixed' provides a good selection of all the available colours which include various shades of pink, rose red, lime green (yellowish green) and white, height 16in (40cm).

Cultivation and propagation *Nicotiana* can be grown successfully either in full sun or partial shade. Sow the seeds in spring in a greenhouse with a temperature of 60°F (16°C). Germination will occur in 2 to 3 weeks. Once the seedlings are large enough to handle, prick them off 2in (5cm) apart into seedboxes and grow them on in the first instance in the

Papaver

Poppy
Northern sub-Arctic
Papaveraceae

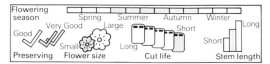

Papaver nudicaule (Iceland Poppy) is a perennial plant which is best grown as a biennial. It bears large fragile paper thin flowers in a range of colours which embraces red, pink, orange, yellow and white, on long leafless stems, from early summer to autumn.
Papaver nudicaule 'Champagne Bubbles' is an F1 hybrid which has large flowers in shades of

Papaver nudicaule

apricot bronze, orange, scarlet and yellow, height 1½ft (45cm).
P. n. 'Garden Gnome' has a tidy habit and brightly coloured flowers of scarlet, salmon, orange, yellow and white, on sturdy stems, height 1ft (30cm).
P. n. 'Goodwins Victory' is another large flowered strain in a range of pastel shades, height 2ft (60cm).
P. n. 'Matador' has large scarlet flowers, height 2ft (60cm).
P. n. 'Tasman Strain' provides a fine mixture of bright colours, height 15in (37.5cm).
Cultivation and propagation These plants like a sheltered sunny situation in any well drained fertile soils. They need plenty of water in hot dry weather.

Iceland poppies are raised from seed sown during late spring in the place where they are to flower. Sow in the open ground. Germination will take some 10 to 14 days. Once the plants are large enough to handle thin out in two stages. In the first thinning, leave the plants spaced 6in (15cm) apart and about four weeks later go back and make a second thinning choosing the strongest of the remaining plants and discarding the remainder so that they are spaced out 12in (30cm) apart in each direction. In cold areas it may be better to sow earlier in individual pots in the greenhouse to transplant after the last frost.
Uses These flowers, with their interesting cup-shaped bloom and long stems, provide us with useful material for all but the smallest of arrangements. The colours are solid and clear; flowers from a mixed packet of seeds will give an exciting wide range to blend with most other garden colours. The pastel shades of apricot and pink are ideal for delicate designs that are based on flowing lines. The bright yellows and oranges are a striking note when used in modern work or when associated with driftwood. For me, the most attractive

arrangement is a simple collection of harmonious colours in an earthenware jug.
Conditioning It is essential to cut the flowers as the buds are about to open. This will prolong the cut life as they continue to develop once they have been cut. At the same time, remove any seed heads that are developing on the plant as this weakens the flower production. As they exude a milky sap, the end of the stem must be sealed. Do this over a naked flame until the tip has turned to charcoal, then stand them immediately in water for up to 4 hours. Alternatively stand the bottom 1in (2.5cm) of stem in boiling water for 20 seconds.
Preserving Allow a number of the flowers to go to seed. The head will dry on the plant and should be collected before it is damaged by adverse weather. Individual petals can be carefully removed from the flower and pressed.

Phlox

E. North America
Polemoniaceae

Flowering season	Spring	Summer	Autumn	Winter

Flower size: Very Good, Good, Small, Large, Long
Cut life: Short, Long, Short
Stem length: Long, Short
Preserving

Phlox paniculata 'Sandringham'

The herbaceous phlox provides the flower lover with gay panicles of fragrant flowers all summer. By careful selection of cultivars one can have flowers available in a delightful range of colours, throughout their period of flowering. The following selection of popular cultivars will provide a good indication of the colour range.
P. maculata 'Alpha', fine tapering spires of pink flowers, height 3ft (90cm). One of the earliest to flower.

Phlox paniculata 'Starfire'

P. m. 'Omega', white tinged violet, height 2½ft (75cm).
P. paniculata 'Border Gem', deep violet blue flowers, height 3ft (90cm).
P. p. 'Brigadier', brilliant orange-red flowers, one of the most popular cultivars, height 3ft (90cm).
P. p. 'Cherry Pink', exquisite bright carmine rose flowers, height 3ft (90cm).
P. p. 'Fujuyama', a very outstanding cultivar with flowers of the purest white, height 2½ft (75cm).
P. p. 'Mother of Pearl', white flowers suffused pink. This is a weather-resistant cultivar which flowers over a long period, height 2½ft (75cm).
P. p. 'Pinafore Pink', light pink flowers, height 2ft (60cm).
P. p. 'Prince of Orange', beautiful, brilliant orange flowers, height 3ft (90cm).
P. p. 'Prospero', pale lilac flowers, height 3ft (90cm).
P. p. 'Sandringham', striking cyclamen pink flowers with a darker centre. This is another very popular old cultivar, height 2½ft (75cm).
P. p. 'Starfire' by far the best deep red flowered cultivar, height 32in (80cm).
Cultivation and Propagation *Phlox* likes to grow in a rich loam and is most long flowering in a shady situation. Soils which are lacking in humus should be given a generous dressing of bulky organic matter in the form of farmyard manure, if obtainable. If this is not available well-rotted lawn mowings are the next best material. The secret to obtaining a long flowering season is plenty of humus in the soil and plenty of moisture around the roots during the growing season. A mulch is also beneficial.

Flowers cut from plants grown in a sunny situation generally have a shorter vase life than those grown in the shade with their roots enjoying a moist cool root run. Planting may take place at any time while the plants are dormant, and the plants should be spaced out 15 to 18in (38 to 45cm) apart in each direction according to the vigour of growth.

Established beds of *Phlox* should be lifted and replanted every third year, as beds left undisturbed longer than this very quickly deteriorate in vigour. If possible choose a new site each time they are lifted. Divide the plants in the late winter, just before new growth is due to commence. Choose young fibrous roots as free as possible of the older woody bases of the stems. Do not replant too deeply. If eelworm is a problem it is better to propagate by root cultures in the dormant season. For the best flowers, thin out the weaker shoots in spring when they are a couple of inches (a few centimetres) high.
Uses These are flowers for opulent arrangements of mixed summer flowers. *P. maculata*, with its fine tapering flower spike, is a good flower for establishing the height of a massed design. *P. paniculata* has a domed head, carrying multiple flowers on one stem. If the sizes of the heads can be graded they can be used as transitional material or for the focal area. They are very thirsty flowers and should never be without a constant supply of water.
Conditioning To condition them remove a good quantity of foliage and stand the stems in water for at least 4 hours.
Preserving Pressing the individual flowers is the most effective way of preserving them. The petals reflex from a small but significant tube formation, which prevents them from lying flat. Place the flower face down on the paper and crease the tube with a pair of tweezers to fold it out of the way.

Primula

Primulaceae

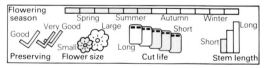

Primula is a large genus of well over five hundred species of herbaceous perennials and monocarpic herbs which are to be found very widely distributed throughout the world. *Primula polyanthus* is a hybrid which has resulted from crosses between the cowslips and the primroses, and it is known to have been grown since as early as the 16th century. Originally all the flowers were yellow but about the mid-17th century other coloured forms appeared. Today we have a number of strains suitable for cut-flowers.
'Pacific Giants' is an excellent strain with long stems and large flowers in a wide range of delightful colours, blue, red, pink, white, yellow, height 10in (25cm). There is also another completely winter hardy F1 Hybrid of

Primula hybrids

the Pacific type which is very free flowering
and ideal for cutting. This is 'Crescendo F1
Hybrid Mixed' and it is particularly useful for
growing in cold frames and cloches for early
flowering. It has the same large flowers and
delightful colours as the 'Pacific Giants' and is
equally good for cutting, height 12in (30cm).
When given protection both these hybrids may
be in flower from early spring onwards and
when grown in the open the flowering period
is spring and early summer.

Cultivation and propagation Any reasonably
fertile soil will be suitable, and the *polyanthus*
prefer sun or partial shade. While these plants
are perennials they are generally treated as
biennials, with the seed sown one year
resulting in plants that flower the following
year. The seed is sown on the surface of seed-
boxes containing seed compost, in spring, and
these are then given the protection of a
coldframe or cloche, which during bright
sunny days is provided with some temporary
shading. A second sowing may also be made
in the open in summer, in a moist shady part
of the garden. The resulting seedlings are
planted out in a nursery bed, in a cool moist
place, 6in (15cm) apart in each direction. The
nursery bed will need frequent watering in
summer. The plants are transferred to their
flowering places in the autumn, and should be
set out 9in (22.5cm) apart each way. When the
planting has been completed dust some bone
meal between the plants. Where used, cloches
should be placed in position in late autumn.

Uses Here are flowers that have been
improved out of all recognition in the last few
years. The hybridists have increased the
vigour of the plants, giving us flower trusses
of up to 9in (22.5cm) across. Perhaps of greater
importance is the colour range. Apart from
black, all shades can be obtained. The clear
colours of red, orange and yellow are a

striking inclusion in a modern design, while
the softer shades add charm to traditional
styles. Small plants can be lifted from the
garden and used wrapped in polythene in a
landscape design or added to a basket
arrangement.

Conditioning Cut the flower head when most
have opened and stand them in deep water for
3 hours. Where it is possible, arrange them
directly in water as they sometimes react badly
to oasis. Some people like to burn the lower
end of the cut stem before conditioning.

Preserving Individual flowers are ideal for
pressing and drying in desiccant, providing an
exquisite source of delicate flowers in bright or
subtle colours for dried flower pictures.

Ranunculus

Asia Minor
Ranunculaceae

Flowering season	Spring	Summer	Autumn	Winter	
Good / Very Good / Large / Short / Long					
Preserving	Flower size		Cut life		Stem length

Ranunculus

R. asiaticus has been cultivated from very
ancient times and has been the subject of
much selection and hybridization, with the
result that there are four distinct types now
available. They all range in colour from white,
yellow, orange, red to pink.

The 'French' *Ranunculus* is best planted in
early spring. It produces large double flowers,
red, pink, yellow, white with a distinct black
central blotch. The flowers appear in early
summer, height 10 to 12in (25 to 30cm).

The 'Paeony-flowered' *Ranunculus* has large
double or semi-double flowers in early

summer but is not so floriferous as the former type. It does tend, however, to produce slightly longer flower stems. In mild districts or under cloches planting may take place in early winter. Available in a varied range of colours.

The 'Persian' *Ranunculus* is far more tender and susceptible to weather damage, even in the mildest districts, and should not be planted until spring. Flowers may be double, semi-double or single, and they have a wider range of colouring than the French *Ranunculus*. Flowering commences in midsummer, height 12 to 16in (30 to 40cm).

The 'Turban' *Ranunculus* is somewhat hardier than the other types of *Ranunculus* and may be planted either in the autumn or spring. It bears large double or semi-double flowers in midsummer in a brilliant range of colours, height 9 to 12in (22.5 to 30cm).

Cultivation and propagation If possible choose a site in the garden in an open sunny situation. Good drainage is essential, so raised beds may be best. Coarse sand and gritty material should be introduced at the time of cultivation. The peculiar claw-like tubers are planted claws down, 1½in (3.75cm) deep and some 6in (15cm) apart in the row, with the rows set some 6 to 8in (15 to 20cm) apart. A mulch of peat between the plants at the time they peep above the soil is very beneficial to them as this helps to maintain moist conditions around their roots without interfering with the general drainage.

Vary the time of flowering by making several separate plantings of *Ranunculus* in the open so that there is a steady supply available for cutting through the summer. With the aid of a cool greenhouse or perhaps a coldframe or cloches flowering may be induced even earlier. All the above *Ranunculus* last well as cut-flowers. Tubers are lifted for storage when the leaves turn yellow. Store in a dry, frost-free place until spring.

Propagation is by offsets from the old tubers when they are lifted for storage, or from seed germinated in a coldframe.

Uses The bulbous and creeping buttercups are a natural flower to include in a landscape arrangement with other flowers and grasses from the wild area of your garden. The cultivated *Ranunculus* is much taller, with a wider range of colours. Peony-flowered, double or semi-double, they look as though they are made from the finest silk. They grow on fine slender stems and are an elegant component in a formal arrangement. I prefer the arrangement to be small so that each flower is seen and appreciated clearly.

Conditioning Cut them at a cool time of the day and condition them for 2 hours in a cool position.

Preserving The double and semi-double flowers will be spoiled by pressing, so it is wiser to dry them in dessicant. Buttercups and buttercup types may be pressed successfully, to be used in a collage or picture of other wild flowers and grasses.

Rosa

Rose
Northern Hemisphere
Deciduous
Rosaceae

Rosa 'Blue Moon'

There are varying estimates as to the numbers of rose species which exist, but the genus is known to have at least 130 species, and a vast multitude of garden hybrids have been produced over the years. Roses are extremely popular garden flowers and cut flowers as their range of colour is so wide and many are of considerable fragrance. Even their deciduous pinnate leaves are found to be aromatic in many instances when bruised. Readers are strongly advised to see different varieties for themselves during the flowering season, in order to choose. They flower from early summer to late autumn. The following selection is of some of my favourite among the Hybrid Tea Roses (HT) and Floribunda Roses (FL) and they are grouped together here according to colour for convenience:
Red shades
'Alec's Red' (HT), large bright red flowers of considerable fragrance, sturdy growth, height 32in (80cm).
'City of Belfast' (FL), clusters of brilliant orange

Rosa 'Peace'

Rosa 'Iceberg'

Rosa 'Wendy Cussons'

scarlet flowers, height 2ft (60cm).
'Josephine Bruce' (HT), very large, richly
fragrant, deep velvety crimson flowers, height
32in (80cm).
'Wendy Cussons' (HT), large cherry red
flowers with paler red reverse, vigorous
growth, height 32in (80cm).
Pink shades
'Blessing' (HT), large soft coral-pink flowers in
clusters, upright habit, height 32in (80cm).
'Congratulations' (HT), large deepish pink
flowers which become soft pink later, borne in
clusters, sturdy erect growth, height 40in
(100cm) plus.
'Elizabeth of Glamis' (FL), intense orange
salmon, richly fragrant flowers in clusters,
height 32in (80cm).
'Queen Elizabeth' (FL), large clear pink flowers
which are borne both singly and in clusters on
sturdy vigorous, almost thornless stems, height
5ft (150cm) plus.
Yellow shades
'Arthur Bell' (FL), clusters of highly fragrant
buttercup yellow flowers which become pale
yellow as they age, height 32in (80cm).
'Grandpa Dickson' (HT), large lemon yellow
flowers borne in great profusion on long sturdy
stems, erect growth, height 32in (80cm).
'Peace' (HT), very large deep yellow flowers
with a reddish flush borne in great profusion,
vigorous erect growth, height 5ft (150cm).
'Troika' (HT), large orangey-yellow, richly
fragrant, flowers, upright habit, height 32in
(80cm).
Lilac
'Blue Moon' (HT), large ice-blue strongly
fragrant flowers on long sturdy stems; freely
produced, erect habit, height 32in (80cm).
Whites and Creams
'Iceberg' (FL), large pure white sweetly fragrant
flowers in clusters. These have a tendency to
become tinted pink in the autumn, very
prolific, erect vigorous habit, height 32in
(80cm).
'Pascali' (HT), medium-sized creamy-white
flowers on long stems, produced in a steady
stream as fast as the old flowers fade, height
32in (80cm).
Bi-colours
'Chivalry' (HT), well-shaped bright red and
ivory-white flowers on sturdy stems, vigorous
erect habit, height 40in (100cm) plus.
'Court Jester' (FL), well-shaped golden-orange
and yellow flowers borne singly and in clusters,
upright habit, height 40in (100cm) plus.
'Matangi' (FL), clusters of orange vermilion and
silver flowers, moderate vigour, height 26in
(65cm).
'Piccadilly' (HT), large scarlet and gold flowers
produced in a steady stream throughout the
summer, early flowering, height 32in (80cm).
'Rose Gaujard' (HT), large magenta and silvery-
white flowers on stiff erect stems, height 32in
(80cm).

Cultivation and Propagation Roses can be grown successfully on a wide range of soils providing they are not subject to water-logging during the winter. Contrary to general belief roses do not like heavy clay soils. Choose an open sunny site. Light soils will require the incorporation of some bulky organic matter to improve their fertility and moisture retention. Clay soils will need the incorporation of coarse sand or other suitable gritty material to improve their drainage. Where the soil is shallow, raised rose beds can be constructed by the introduction of suitable soil from elsewhere to provide the appropriate depth. This is also a suitable solution when confronted with heavy wet clay soils. Planting is best undertaken during autumn or spring.

Pruning of newly planted roses should be fairly severe and this is best done in late spring. The weaker shoots are cut back to two buds while the strong shoots are cut back to four buds. Prune established roses in mid-spring, in a similar way. Dead and diseased shoots are also cut out at this time. The aim is to create an open vase-shaped bush and the pruner should endeavour to cut to an outward facing bud. Established roses of vigorous growth such as 'Peace' (HT) and 'Queen Elizabeth' (FL) should have their long stems shortened by up to half in late autumn, to prevent damage from wind-rock during the winter. Summer pruning consists of removing dead flowers by cutting back to a wood bud, and not simply cutting off the flower heads.

Hybrid Tea roses and Floribunda roses are increased in number by budding them on to rootstocks of wild species of roses such as *R. canina, R. laxa, R. rugosa* etc., during late summer and this is a job best left in the hands of the commercial nurseryman.

Uses No flower arranger would want to be without roses. They are not flowers to be arranged in the accepted fashion, and there will be times when the flowers will be best displayed in a simple glass or silver vase. As a feature in a design of mixed summer flowers arranged in a traditional style they are beyond compare. Roses that are of a particularly striking colour or size should be restricted to the focal area. Those that have not been disbudded and are on a slender stem can be used throughout the design. 'Peace' will grow to a considerable size and looks most effective arranged with wood in a simple modern container. One of the most traditional styles is the basket of roses. This need not contain masses of roses, as other flowers like *Alchimella mollis* or *Astrantia* may be included. The flowering period is often long, and sometimes roses flower twice a year which makes them useful in September for arranging with dahlias and chrysanthemums.

Conditioning Cut the flowers in bud, remove the lower thorns and leaves, and stand the stems in deep water in a cool area for at least 2 hours. Any that show signs of wilting should be removed. Recut the stem and stand the tip in boiling water for 10 seconds before returning the flower to the conditioning bucket.

Preserving The rose is an ideal flower to preserve. It can either be pressed or dried in desiccant. I favour the latter method to maintain the shape of the flower.

Tulipa

Tulip
Spain, the Mediterranean region, Asia Minor, Asia and Russia
Liliaceae

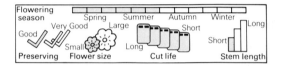

Tulipa 'Sorbet'

Tulips are hardy bulbous plants. The species have, for the most part, been superseded by hybrids. All the following are good for garden display as well as cut flowers. The approximate flowering times given are the natural ones, grown in the open ground, but unless otherwise stated all the tulips listed may be forced into flower earlier in the year.

Single early tulips (spring):
'Bellona', deep golden yellow, fragrant flowers, height 16in (40cm).
'Christmas Marvel', cherry-pink, height 14in (35cm).
'Ruby Red', scarlet, height 14in (35cm).

Triumph tulips (late spring):
'Grevel', rose-pink edged ivory white, height 16in (40cm).
'Sorbet', exterior feathered red with creamy white interior, height 2ft (60cm).

Tulipa Darwin hybrid

Tulipa 'Sunshine'

Tulipa greigii 'Marjoletti'

'Paul Richter', bright geranium red, height 20in (50cm).

'Prince Charles', purple violet, height 18in (45cm).

Darwin hybrids (late spring):

'Ad Rem', scarlet (not recommended for forcing), height 24in (60cm).

'Gudoshnik', creamy-yellow with red and rose, height 24in (60cm).

'Striped Apeldoorn', red striped yellow, height 24in (60cm).

Lily Flowered tulips (early summer):

'Aladdin', rich crimson edged yellow, height 20in (50cm).

'China Pink', satin-pink, height 22in (55cm).

'Lilac Time', violet-purple, height 22in (55cm).

'White Triumphator', large pure white flowers, height 28in (70cm).

Parrot tulips (early summer):

'Blue Parrot', bluish-purple (not recommended for forcing), height 24in (60cm).

'Orange Favourite', fragrant orange flowers (do not force), height 22in (55cm).

'Red Champion', rich scarlet, height 22in (55cm).

'Texas Gold', deep yellow with narrow red edge to the petals, height 20in (50cm).

'Sunshine', golden yellow, height 18in (45cm).

'White Parrot', large pure white flowers (do not force), height 20in (50cm).

Cultivation and propagation Tulips can be grown on any ordinary well-drained garden soil either in full sun or slight shade. Plant in the open garden in late autumn, 8½in (22.5cm) apart and 4in (10cm) deep.

Propagation is by the removal of the small bulblets which develop on the base of the mature tulip bulbs. These are removed when the bulbs are lifted after flowering. These are then stored until replanted in the late autumn. It takes several years to produce flowering bulbs of a suitable size.

Uses Choosing which tulips to grow in the garden can be as exciting as seeing them grow and subsequently arranging them. The colour range is vast and as the form of the flower is pleasing in itself there is no need to worry about what to associate them with. As a component in a massed design of spring flowers they can be used throughout the arrangement. One or two self-coloured flowers look very striking arranged with a bare branch in a modern container.

Conditioning The cut flower will last a considerable time. Cut the flower as it is showing colour, as it will continue to develop once it has been arranged. The main problem is that the stem continues to grow after cutting, which usually means that the stem becomes bent. To reduce this, wrap a small number of stems in newspaper, secure with an elastic band and condition them in deep water for at least 3 hours. Once the flower has been arranged it will still be attracted to the light and those that have been arranged at a downward angle usually turn upwards like candelabra. It is best to accept this and leave room in the arrangement to compensate. **Preserving** Unfortunately they do not preserve easily. The best method is to press each petal separately and reassemble them on to a seed head.

Zinnia

Mexico
Compositae

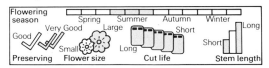

Zinnia 'Dahlia Flowered'

Zinnia 'Ruffles' hybrid

Zinnia elegans is a half-hardy annual suited to sheltered places. The 'Dahlia Flowered' Zinnias have been grown for cutting over the years and these are still very popular. They have very large double flowers up to 5in (12.5cm) across, which may be of yellow, gold, salmon, crimson or white, with a contrast of one of the other colours, height 2 to 2½ft (60 to 75cm). Generally these are available in mixed colours but one can occasionally find straight colours such as 'Big Snowman Double' being offered in the seed catalogues. Modern F1 hybrids are in single colours:
'Golden Sun', golden yellow flowers, height 4in (10cm) across.
'Red Sun', flowers of the same size which are brilliant scarlet. Both of these grow to a height of 2ft (60cm).

Zinnia 'Red Sun'

Zinnia 'Pacific Yellow'

Zinnia 'Golden Sun'

'Pacific Yellow' is another F1 hybrid of the dahlia-flowered type. This produces soft yellow flowers early and is noted for its weather-resistant qualities, height 2ft (60cm).

For large cactus-flowered Zinnias choose the F1 hybrid 'Zenith All Colours Mixed'. The flowers are 5 to 6in (12.5 to 15cm) across and have a thick ball-shaped form. These are excellent for use as cut-flowers and grow to a height of 2½ft (75cm). Flowers in a wide range of colours are found in 'Ruffles Mixed'. This has flowers which are 2in (5cm) across and grows 2ft (60cm) high. Some seed catalogues have it on offer in straight colours of rose pink, deep yellow, deep scarlet, light pink and creamy white.

Of particular importance to the flower arranger is the Giant Dahlia Flowered hybrid 'Envy' with pale apple-green, double and semi-double flowers, some 3 to 4in (7.5 to 10cm) across, height 2ft (60cm).

Cultivation and propagation *Zinnia* likes a deep fertile soil which has been well prepared. The soil must contain adequate humus and it is necessary for some manure or well rotted garden compost to be incorporated at planting time. Heavy soils will also benefit from the incorporation of sharp sand or other gritty material to improve their drainage. Choose an open, sunny, yet sheltered situation for these plants.

If good-quality flowers are to be produced it will be necessary to remove all side buds as they develop. Some watering of the plants may also be required during periods of dry weathery They flower in summer and autumn.

The seed is sown either in a cool greenhouse or in a coldframe, in spring, in seed boxes containing seed compost. Germination may take 9 to 16 days. When the seedlings are large enough to handle, they are pricked out into other seed boxes containing potting compost and grown on in the protection of a coldframe. Ventilation is given during the warmer spring days and the plants are hardened off in readiness for transferring to their flowering positions after the frosts. Seed may be sown later, where it is to flower. When the plants are large enough to handle they are thinned out to stand 12in (30cm) apart. Once established in their flowering positions, in the open, Zinnias should have a mulch of peat spread about their roots to help conserve soil moisture.

Uses If any flower adds distinction to an arrangement it must surely be the *Zinnia*. The multi-petalled round form comes in such a variety of sizes, that it is possible to grow sufficient to meet the needs of any scale of arrangement. The texture is slightly coarse without affecting the beauty of the colour so it can be used in both traditional and modern styles of design. The smaller blooms can be used as intermediate flowers to establish a framework of colour and form. While the larger blooms may be used to create a focal area. One exciting colour form for this position is 'Envy', a clear green colour which darkens slightly as it ages. Never cut many to use with mixed flowers, but reserve one or two as a highlight for an all-foliage arrangement – the effect is quite breathtaking.

Conditioning The flowers have thin, tough petals, so little wilting takes place after cutting and about 3 hours in water is all they need to condition them. Occasionally the stem will kink just below the flower head as it conditions, but a small length of wire inserted through the top of the flower down into the stem will correct this with no detrimental result to its cut flower life.

Preserving The layered effect of the petals reduces their suitability as pressed flowers, though it can be done. I much prefer to dry them in desiccant, as the colour remains sharp and the exquisite form is not affected. They are very easy to mount on to false stems or wires. If wire is used a spray effect can be achieved by binding several flowers together. Arrange them with preserved foliage and seed heads, where the Zinnias will introduce a change of colour without the need to use any other flowers either fresh or dried.

SHRUBS AND TREES

Acer

Maple
Northern Hemisphere
Deciduous
Aceraceae

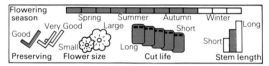

Acer palmatum 'Dissectum'

Acer japonica is native to Japan and forms a large bush with soft green lobed leaves with good autumn tints before leaf-fall. However, it has even more attractive cultivars which are particularly useful in floral arrangements.

A. j. 'Aconitifolium' has green deeply lobed leaves which turn brilliant crimson in the autumn before leaf-fall. This too is a rounded shrub, height 6ft (180cm).

A. j. 'Aureum' has golden yellow lobed leaves which are useful for floral displays from spring to autumn leaf-fall. It makes a delightful rounded, slow-growing, bush which benefits from being in a slight shade so that its leaves are not scorched by hot sun and sheltered from cold winds which can delay it coming into leaf in spring, height 3 to 4ft (90 to 120cm).

Acer palmatum (Japanese Maple) forms a delightful ornamental tree, height 12 to 14ft (360 to 420cm). It has large palmate deeply lobed bright green leaves which turn orange-red in the autumn prior to leaf-fall. It has quite a few cultivars which vary in habit and leaf form.

A. p. 'Dissectum' forms a low rounded bush of slow growth. It has finely divided leaves, consisting of five to eleven pointed lobes, fresh green in colour becoming bronzy-yellow in the autumn, height 2½ to 4ft (75 to 120cm).

A. p. 'Dissectum Atropurpureum' has rich purple leaves during the summer and these turn crimson before leaf-fall.

A. p. 'Dissectum Garnet' has the same finely divided leaves and these are deep crimson all summer but it is of more vigorous growth, height 4½ft (135cm).

Acer pseudoplatanus 'Brilliantissimum' is a cultivar of *A. pseudoplatanus* the Sycamore, which is native to Europe. This is a small slow-growing tree of mop-headed habit, which in time reaches 12ft (360cm). The young leaves are coral pink in colour and later turn yellowish-green before finally becoming green.

Cultivation *Acer* will grow in any fertile moist soil in sun or partial shade.

Uses A striking leaf to use in a foliage arrangement. The autumn colour that the foliage adopts late in the season is particularly attractive when used with dried seed pods and chrysanthemums.

Conditioning Immature foliage must be floated in water for 1 hour, then allowed to stand for a further 2 hours in cold water.

Preserving Sprays of leaves do not absorb glycerine, so the best method of preserving is to press the individual leaf. This can be done at any stage of development.

Artemisia

Deciduous
Compositae

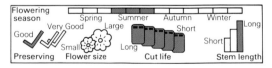

Artemisia arborescens is a sub-shrub native to Southern Europe and it has a cultivar *A. a.* 'Powis Castle' which provides the flower arranger with valuable foliage. It has finely divided silvery leaves and is of compact rounded habit, height 2 to 3ft (60 to 90cm). Another desirable species is *A. ludoviciana*. This is a herbaceous perennial which comes from North America and it has a very attractive cultivar in the form of *A. l.* 'Silver Queen' with downy stems and silvery-green divided leaves, height 2 to 3ft (60 to 90cm).

Cultivation and Propagation Artemisia

Artemisia ludoviciana

Aucuba japonica

requires a poor, not rich, well-drained soil. It is particularly suited to growing on the rock garden or a dry sunny bank. Plant in spring. Propagation is by stem cuttings secured in summer and rooted in a sandy soil in a closed and shaded garden frame or cloche. Roots may also be divided during spring.

Uses This is a valuable grey foliage for arranging with pink and blue flowers. The leaves clothe the entire stem and are light and delicate in appearance. The plant produces sufficient material to make a complete outline of foliage for a traditional design.

Conditioning As the stems are woody they will need to be lightly crushed before conditioning in water for 2 hours. Remove any leaves that are likely to be submerged as they deteriorate quickly.

Preserving Sadly, as with most grey foliages, *Artemisia* does not preserve well. Individual leaves may be pressed. These will increase the textural quality of a collage or picture.

Aucuba

Spotted Laurel
China and Japan
Evergreen
Cornaceae

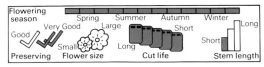

Aucuba japonica forms a rounded bush, height 5 to 6 ft (150 to 180cm) and has narrow oval, pointed slightly toothed leathery, shiny green leaves about 2 to 3in (5 to 7.5cm) wide and some 4 to 7in (10 to 17.5cm) long. There are

both male and female bushes. After flowering (the flowers are of no significance) suitably pollinated female plants produce bright scarlet berries, which retain their colour late into the autumn. Of more attraction are the many cultivars which have been introduced, some of which have attractive variegated leaves.

A. j. 'Crotonifolia' has large leaves generously blotched and spotted bright yellow. This is a male form and has no berries.

A. j. 'Fructoluteo' has leaves which are spotted and blotched pale green and yellow. It also bears whitish berries.

A. J. 'Gold Dust' is a female form with leaves boldly speckled and blotched golden yellow.

A. j. 'Picturata' has leaves which are generously splashed with pure gold down the centre and have rich green margins. This is a male form and has no berries.

Cultivation and Propagation No regular pruning is required. Any shaping which may be necessary can be achieved when cutting material for use, over the course of the year.

Propagation is by hardwood cuttings 8in (20cm) long taken in the late autumn. These may be rooted in a nursery bed in the open ground or given the protection of a frame.

Uses This is an all-purpose foliage, useful in concealing mechanics or as a focal area in a foliage arrangement. As the bush matures the leaves get bigger, an asset for large arrangements in the winter when little else is available. The flowers are insignificant, but the resulting fruit is an interesting addition to an autumn arrangement of berries and foliage.

Conditioning Stand them in deep water for up to 3 hours.

Preserving The leaves will absorb glycerine, though the variegation will be lost.

Ballota

Mediteranean Region
Evergreen
Labiatae

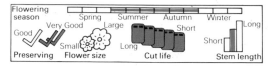

Ballota pseudodamnictus

Only one species is of any real importance as a garden plant, and that is *Ballota pseudodictamnus*. This is a small sub-shrub which only grows about 2ft (60cm) high and it is a native of Crete. If one has any difficulty in finding it in the shrub catalogues try looking it up in the herbaceous perennial catalogues, as it is often listed there. It has arching stems which are woody at their base and obovate, greyish-white, woolly leaves about 1in (2.5cm) long. Whorls of lilac-pink flowers appear in summer.

Cultivation and Propagation Cultivation is quite easy, as it will grow in any ordinary well-drained soil, providing it is given a sunny situation. The best time to plant it is in spring. Established shrubs should be pruned in spring to encourage the production of new stems.

Propagation can be achieved by either division of the roots in the spring or by stem cuttings which are taken during the summer and rooted in a shaded garden frame. Rooted cuttings are planted out in the open ground the following spring.

Uses This green/grey plant can be arranged in so many ways. The arching growth is a useful outline material. As the plant matures, the colour is a more distinct grey with a soft texture. It relates perfectly with pastel colours especially pale pink.

Conditioning Use only the mature stems. Burn the stem ends over a flame and stand them in water for up to 2 hours.

Preserving It is the stem and bract that preserve; the flower is small and quickly shrivels. Remove the stem foliage, leaving the bracts intact; stand the stems in glycerine. The colour will change to a soft beige.

Berberis

Barberry
Wide distribution
Evergreen and deciduous
Berberidaceae

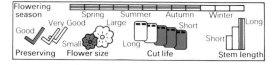

Berberis thunbergii 'Atropurpurea'

The majority of the species are quite hardy. *Berberis aggregata* is a deciduous species which is native to W. China. It forms a dense bush height 4ft (120cm), and it has the characteristic spines of the barberies. It bears clusters of small pointed green leaves some ½ to 1in (1.25 to 2.5cm) long which produce good autumn hues. This shrub is covered in clusters of pale yellow flowers in summer and these are followed by red berries covered in bloom. The purpose of the bloom is to protect them from strong autumn sunshine. The berries last into late autumn. Among the many hybrids available is *B. a.* 'Barbarossa' which has so many red berries in the autumn that their weight causes the branches to arch under the burden. This is a vigorous shrub attaining 6ft (180cm).

Berberis candidula is an evergreen species of dwarf habit from China. This is an excellent ground-cover subject of slow growth. It has spiny arching branches clothed in small oblong elliptic shiny dark green leaves with silvery-blue lower surfaces. In spring its branches are studded with single bright yellow flowers and these are followed by small oval purple berries. Height 2ft (60cm).

B. c. 'Armstelveen' is of similar habit but the upper surfaces of its leaves are fresh green and it is of faster growth.

Berberis thunbergii is native to Japan and this is a deciduous shrub of compact erect growth, height 4ft (120cm). Its spiny stems bear small obovate green leaves which turn brilliant orange-red in the autumn. Small pale yellow flowers appear in the spring and these are followed in the autumn by bright red berries.

B. t. 'Atropurpurea' is of a similar height and has rich reddish-purple leaves.

B. t. 'Atropurpurea Nana' is a beautiful purple leaved dwarf form of this shrub of slow growth which has few if any spines, height 2ft (60cm).

B. t. 'Aurea' is a very striking golden-yellow-leaved small shrub, height 3ft (90cm). Its leaves become pale green in the autumn.

B. t. 'Helmond Pillar' is of stiff erect habit with large reddish bronze leaves. This can be used to make a fine ornamental boundary hedge. It grows about 5ft (150cm) high by 1½ft (45cm) wide..

B. wilsonea is a beautiful, low, densely branched, semi-recumbent shrub, with tiny soft oblong, grey-green leaves, height 2 to 3ft (60 to 90cm), and comes from Western China. It bears clusters of tiny yellow flowers in spring, and these are followed in the autumn by quantities of soft, coral-red berries. The leaves by this time have taken on their red and orange autumn hues.

Cultivation and Propagation Berberis grows on a wide range of soils, provided they are well-drained, in sun or partial shade. No regular pruning is required and the removal of material for floral arrangements over the year will serve to keep individual shrubs in shape. Hedges are best trimmed in the winter after fruiting in the case of deciduous species. Evergreen species are best trimmed in the early spring.

Propagation is by half-ripe cuttings secured in the summer and rooted in a closed and shaded garden frame.

Uses A splendid range of shrubs that offer exquisite leaf colour during the growing season with an abundant crop of berries to use in the autumn. The fruiting branches can be arranged with the ripening pods of Physalis and dahlias to excellent effect.

Conditioning Avoid using immature foliage as it tends to wilt. Mature stems should be lightly crushed and stood in water for 2 to 3 hours.

Preserving Preserve very early foliage in desiccant. The process is rapid and the brilliant colour is retained.

Buddleia

Butterfly Bush
Asia, South Africa and South America
Evergreen and deciduous
Loganiaceae

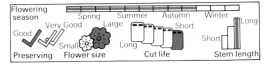

Buddleia fallowiana

Buddleia is noted for its vigorous growth and fragrant flowers.

Buddleia alternifolia, from Kansu, China, can be grown either as a large shrub or a small tree. It has a weeping-willow-like habit and has small willow-like, alternate, lanceolate, dark green, deciduous leaves, the lower surfaces bluish-grey. In summer its branches are abundantly covered in clusters of tiny bright purple flowers which have the fragrance of heliotrope. The cultivar B. a. 'Argentea' has leaves covered in silvery down, height 8ft (240cm). Prune by removing the branches bearing the old faded flowers as soon as flowering ceases.

Buddleia fallowiana is another deciduous species of shrub from Yunnan China. This is of more vigorous growth and, given the protection of a south-facing wall, it can attain a height of 10ft (300cm) or more. When grown as a shrub it grows about 5 to 6ft (150 to 180cm) in height. It has long pointed silvery grey leaves which are covered in white felt on their lower surface. The leaves vary in length from about 4 to 8in (10 to 20cm) and it has terminal panicles of pale lavender-blue fragrant flowers 8 to 12in (20 to 30cm) long during late summer.

B. f. 'Alba' has the same silvery grey leaves but has fragrant white flowers with an orange eye. It is of somewhat less vigorous growth, height 4 to

5ft (120 to 150cm). This flowers on the current year's growth and should be pruned in early spring, as renewed growth commences. *Buddleia globosa* is a semi-evergreen species of shrub from Chile and Peru. It has long, pointed leaves. In this species they are dark green on the upper surfaces with tan-coloured felt on the lower surfaces. This is commonly referred to as the 'Orange Ball Tree' due to its bright tangerine balls of flowers which appear in early summer and have a sweet fragrance of honey. The flowers are borne both on the old wood of the previous year and the new shoots of the current year's growth, therefore any pruning to shape the shrub should take place immediately flowering ceases.

Cultivation and Propagation *Buddleia* is easy to grow in any fertile soil in sun. Propagation is possible in either of two ways. The one is by seed sown in the open ground in the spring, and the other is by cuttings taken in the late summer. Cuttings root quite easily at this season of the year but need protecting with a garden frame until the following spring.

Uses A firm favourite with arrangers is *B. alternifolia*, as its weeping habit makes it a suitable outline material. Most of the varieties may be used in the same way for both large and small designs.

Conditioning The flowers are long lasting, so pick them when most are open. Remove any excess foliage and stand the stems in water for 3 hours.

Preserving The flowering branches will not absorb preserving liquid. *B. globosa* may be dried in desiccant, when the majority of flowers are open. The brilliant orange colour will associate well with the pressed leaves of *Acer*.

Buxus

Box
North Africa, Asia and Central America
Evergreen
Buxaceae

Flowering season	Spring	Summer	Autumn	Winter	
Very Good	Large		Short		Long
Good					
Small		Long		Short	
Preserving	Flower size		Cut life		Stem length

Buxus sempervirens is native to Europe. One sport which has evolved from that species and is very attractive is *B. s.* 'Aurea Marginata'. This has glossy medium-sized, oblong, pointed, dark green leaves which are both margined and splashed yellow. This is an erect growing shrub which can attain 6ft (180cm) in height. It responds well to cutting and can be used as a garden hedge very effectively.

Buxus sempervirens

Cultivation and Propagation Box is not particularly fussy about the soil in which it may have to grow, providing it is reasonably well drained, and it is a useful shrub for growing on chalky soils. It will even flourish on exposed sites or in the shade of trees. No regular pruning is necessary other than for the removal of dead or diseased branches. However, one should keep a watch out for variegated branches which may revert to the common dark green of *Buxus sempervirens* and remove these as soon as they appear, otherwise the whole shrub may revert in due course!

Propagation is by cuttings of mature shoots, during autumn and these are rooted in a shaded garden frame and planted out in the open ground the following spring.

Uses The virtue of this foliage is its longevity. It is both a background foliage and medium for concealing small areas of mechanics. The shiny surface is an excellent complement to dried foliage with a matt finish.

Conditioning Stand the cut sprays in water for up to 2 hours.

Preserving On occasions the foliage will dry in the arrangement if it is left that long. Preserving it in glycerine will give it a longer dried life. The time will vary for the process to be completed, but the colour will change to beige.

Camellia

Asia
Evergreen
Theaceae

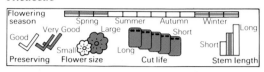

Camellia japonica 'Mathotiana Rosea'

The *Camellia* is one of the finest late winter and early spring flowering shrubs. *Camellia japonica* (Common Camellia) from China and Japan, together with its many cultivars, provides some of the most scintillating flowers and foliage. *C. japonica* is quite hardy. It forms a large shrub or small tree with age, some 10ft (300cm) in height. It has glossy, olive green, leathery, elliptic, pointed, slightly toothed leaves, the lower surfaces shiny and fresh green in colour. The wild species bears red five-petalled flowers and from this parent shrub a large number of cultivars have been evolved; the following selection will serve to give a general indication of the wealth of material from which one may choose:

C. j. 'Adolphe Audusson', vigorous yet compact growth, large blood-red, semi-double flowers with prominent yellow stamens.
C. j. 'Alexander Hunter', more erect habit medium-sized crimson single flowers.
C. j. 'Apollo', open vigorous habit with medium-sized rose red semi-double flowers.
C. j. 'Lady Vansittart White', of slow growth and bushy compact habit, with medium-sized white, semi-double flowers, which have wavy edged petals.
C. j. 'Mathotiana Alba', open vigorous habit with large white double flowers.

C. j. 'Mathotiana Rosea', large clear pink double flowers.
C. j. 'Nagasaki', vigorous growth and spreading habit with large rose-pink, white marbled, semi-double flowers. The leaves are often mottled yellow.
C. j. 'Nobilissima', one of the earliest camellias to come into flower. It is of vigorous compact habit with medium-sized, creamy white, paeony-form, semi-double flowers.
C. j. 'Pink Perfection', vigorous erect habit with small shell-pink double flowers.
C. j. 'Tricolor', sometimes listed as *C. j.* 'Sieboldii', is of erect compact habit with medium-sized, blush pink streaked red, semi-double flowers.

Cultivation and Propagation Camellias are not fond of limey or chalky soils but prefer acid, peaty soils. Nevertheless, they can flourish in loamy soils if a good dressing of peat or leafmould is added when preparing the ground. Once established the camellias should have a peat mulch spread about them each spring to keep roots cool and retain moisture. *Camellia japonica* is quite hardy providing it is grown in a reasonably well-drained soil which is not liable to flooding during the winter. Flowering is encouraged in an open sunny situation but plants need shelter from cold north-east winds. Partial shade offers flowers a little protection from the spring frosts. *Camellia* is a particularly good subject for growing in a large tub where space is strictly limited or ground conditions are not satisfactory. Try growing them in a cool greenhouse and ventilate well on sunny days to prevent the temperature rising above 65°F (18°C). Keep the atmosphere from drying out by damping the greenhouse floor as necessary. Flowering will then commence in late autumn and continue until well into the spring of the following year, providing the roots of the camellias in the tubs are not allowed to become dry. Once all flowering has ceased the tubs may be placed outside in a shaded spot during the summer before bringing back into the greenhouse the following autumn again. Give tub-grown plants a weak solution of a liquid fertilizer once every two weeks, during the growing season. Provide a peat mulch each spring. The best time to plant young camellias, either in the open ground or in tubs or large pots, is in the autumn just when growth has ceased and before the flower buds have developed very much, otherwise bud drop may result. No regular pruning is required, other than the removal of damaged or unwanted branches, during the dormant season.

Propagation is by half-ripe cuttings secured in summer. These are inserted 4 per 3in (7.5cm) pot containing equal parts of peat and sand. The cuttings are set out around the sides of the pot and then placed in a closed propagation case in the greenhouse to root. If this has

bottom heat set it at 60°F (16°C). Alternatively branches could be layered during late summer.
Uses This must be the most elegant flower the arranger can grow. The texture of the petal is soft and delicate, which gives the flower a classical beauty. The shrub is slow growing so you may have to limit the number of flowers picked per year. Choose an elegant container and arrange the branch with a limited quantity of suitable foliage that will enhance the design without overpowering the flower.
Conditioning Crush the woody stem and stand in deep water for 2–3 hours.
Preserving The beauty of the flower fades very quickly and the tragedy is compounded with its inability to preserve. However the leaf will absorb glycerine. To prevent damaging the shape of the shrub, remove individual mature leaves and float them in a dish of glycerine. The leaf will change to an olive green and feel quite pliable, in up to 3 weeks. The foliage can then be mounted on to wires and wired into a spray.

Carpinus

Hornbeam
Temperate regions of the Northern Hemisphere
Deciduous
Carpinaceae

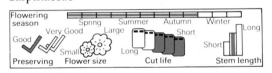

Carpinus betulus 'Fastigiata'

Carpnius looks similar in appearance to a beech tree and people often mistake it for this tree but it grows to more modest proportions.
However, like the beech it can be used as a

hedging subject and will retain its dead leaves until the spring in a like manner. It has oval, pointed, toothed, green leaves often with unequal leaf bases. Leaves may be from 1½ to 3½in (3.75 to 8.75cm) long and 1 to 2in wide.
Carpinus betulus (Common Hornbeam) generally grows too large for inclusion in a town garden. It is better to plant either *C. b.* 'Columnaris' or *C. b.* 'Fastigiata'.
C. b. 'Columnaris' is of slow growth and compact spire-like habit which later becomes columnar, height 15ft (450cm).
C. b. 'Fastigiata' is of larger growth and while it is fastigiate when young it becomes broader when mature, height 21ft (630cm) or more. These trees bear green catkins in the spring which are followed in the autumn by fruiting clusters or keys as they are commonly called. The keys generally remain on the branches long after leaf-fall. The leaves taken on good autumn hues of yellow and orange.
Cultivation and Propagation *Carpinus* thrives on poor wet clays and on chalky soils too, either in a sunny or partially shaded situation.
Propagation is by seeds sown in the spring either in the open ground or in a garden frame in the case of *C. betulus*. Propagation of the named cultivars is best left in the hands of the skilled nurseryman as these are grafted on to other wild species.
Uses The Hornbeam can be used for arranging at most times of the year. The spring growth is a delightful pale green. Small branches are most useful for landscape arrangements. The mature leaves during the summer form the outline for traditional styles of mixed garden flowers. It is in the autumn that it really comes into its own, when the leaf colour changes to a bronzed yellow, with clusters of keys, to arrange with other autumn fruits and flowers.
Conditioning The spring foliage should be submerged in water for at least 1 hour then allowed to condition in deep water for a further 2 hours. Mature foliage requires only a deep drink for about 2 hours.
Preserving The leaves can be preserved in glycerine, when they are fully developed. It is possible to preserve the keys in the same way, though the autumn leaves may fall.

Chamaecyparis

Cypress
North America, Japan and Formosa
Evergreen
Cupressaceae

cut material so it is not worth preserving it, though pieces can be pressed between sheets of newspaper under the carpet.

Chamaecyparis lawsoniana 'Pembury Blue'

Its distinguishing characteristics are flat branches and small cones. Our concern here is with several of the numerous cultivars of *Chamaecyparis lawsoniana*, a species native to Oregon and California:

C. l. 'Elegantissima', clothed in silvery grey foliage and of a broadly conical habit. It is of moderate growth, height 15ft (450cm).

C. l. 'Kilmacurragh', a narrow columnar tree of dense habit and has dark green foliage, height 15 to 20ft (450 to 600cm).

C. l. 'Pembury Blue', an outstanding cultivar of conical habit clothed in silvery-blue foliage, height 10ft (300cm).

C. l. 'Stewartii Erecta', compact conical erect habit and its foliage changes colour according to the seasons. During the spring and summer the foliage is bright yellow while in the late autumn and winter months it turns yellowish-green, height 10 to 14ft (300 to 420cm).

Cultivation and Propagation *Chamaecyparis* flourishes on loamy moist soils and does not grow so vigorously on dry soils. Choose a site not exposed to strong winds. They may be planted either in a sunny or shady place. Purchase container-grown stock. Planting is best undertaken during autumn or spring. No regular pruning is required.

Propagation is by cuttings secured in the autumn and inserted in a heated propagation case in a greenhouse.

Uses This has useful foliage for creating a background for flowers. The foliage is arranged in a flat spray which you will find indispensable for concealing mechanics and for creating a foil for focal area flowers. 'Stewartii Erecta' is a light foliage to use with summer flowers; it will provide sufficient visual weight without causing the design to look dark and heavy.

Conditioning Cut branches should be stood in water for at least 2 hours.

Preserving The shrub will provide lots of fresh

Choisya

Mexican Orange Blossom
Mexico
Evergreen
Rutaceae

Choisya ternata

Choisya ternata is of rounded bushy habit and bears glossy bright green trifoliolate leaves. The leaflets are oblanceolate and some 1½ to 3in (3.75 to 7.5cm) long and meet together at their leaf bases on a leaf stalk which is 1½ to 2in (3.75 to 5cm) long. These compound leaves give the impression of being small fans. The white fragrant flowers are borne in clusters at the ends of the shoots mainly during late spring but spasmodically through to winter. The individual flowers are about 1in (2.5cm) across and composed of five rounded petals.

Cultivation and Propagation This shrub does well in any ordinary garden soil which is freely drained. While it is suggested that this shrub is not entirely hardy this is usually when it is grown in over-rich damp conditions. It prefers a sunny situation which is sheltered from the cold north-eastern winter winds, but can be grown in partial shade at the risk of reduced flowering. The best time to plant it out is during autumn or spring. No annual pruning is necessary except for the removal of the occasional damaged branch.

Propagation is by stem cuttings taken during summer rooted in a closed and shaded frame.
Uses A very valuable foliage. Long sprays can be used to outline a design, while terminal rosettes can make alternative focal areas or they may be used to conceal the mechanics. The white flowers look most effective in a design of early summer pastel flowers.
Conditioning Stand the cut stems in cool water for 2 hours in a shaded area.
Preserving The special quality of *Choisya* is that in preserving, the leaves turn an exquisite shade of beige. The process takes a variable length of time, so check them each day. A lighter shade can be attained by standing them in direct light.

Cornus

Dogwood
Northern Hemisphere
Deciduous
Cornaceae

Cornus kousa

Cornus alba is a deciduous shrub from Siberia and China which is much valued for its current year's shoots, which turn deep red in the winter, and is generally referred to as the 'Red Barked Dogwood'. It is of very vigorous growth and will succeed on all types of soils.
C. a. 'Sibirica' is of less vigorous growth and has thinner shoots than *C. alba*, but they are brilliant crimson in colour and provide a very

worthy contribution to the winter display. Both have leaves which provide good autumn hues. Height depends on frequency of pruning, which may be done either annually or biennially. To maximize the production of coloured stems for winter usage pruning should take place in spring each year, when the shrubs should be cut back close to the ground. Established shrubs pruned in this way will make about 5ft (150cm) of growth each year.
Cornus stolonifoia is a far more vigorous species native to North America. The true species has dark purplish red shoots and its cultivar *C. s.* 'Flaviramea' has attractive yellow stems. Its leaves turn pale yellow in the autumn before leaf-fall. It can easily attain 7ft (210cm) in height when it is pruned in spring each year. The pruning of these shrubs can be done gradually during the winter as stems are required for displays.
Cornus kousa is a large shrub of slow growth and bushy habit which is native to Japan and Korea. It has ovate pointed green leaves 2 to 3in (5 to 7.5cm) long and 1 to 1½in (2.5 to 3.75cm) wide, which turn bronze and crimson in the autumn prior to leaf-fall. It is also noted for its beautiful white bracts (modified leaves), which and surround the inconspicuous flowers. These are followed by strawberry-like fruits which hang from the branches. Height 6 to 9ft (180 to 270cm).
C. k. chinensis is a larger growing shrub of more open habit native to China, and it has white bracts which are slightly larger, as are its green leaves noted for turning brilliant crimson in the autumn before leaf-fall.
Cornus mas (Cornelian Cherry) is a deciduous shrub or small tree which is native to Europe. It is valued for producing masses of tiny yellow flower clusters along naked stems in early spring each year. These are followed by small bright red fruits which never seem to be borne in any great quantity unfortunately. It has ovate dark green leaves similar in sizes to those of *C. kousa* and these turn reddish-purple in the autumn.
Cultivation and Propagation The species of *Cornus* which are recommended for flowering prefer a rich fertile, well-drained soil of some depth, and are not suitable for growing on shallow chalky soils. They will flourish equally well either in a sunny or partially shady situation and do not need any regular pruning.

Propagation of *C. alba* and *C. stolonifera* is by hard-wood cuttings taken in autumn and rooted in the open ground. *C. kousa* and *C. mas* are best propagated from half-ripe cuttings secured in summer and inserted in a closed shaded garden frame.
Uses For winter arranging there is nothing finer than the bare brilliant red stems of *C. Alba*. They can be used in both traditional and modern styles. If the container will allow, many intricate and interesting geometric patterns can

be created. The bracts of *C. kousa* are outstanding if used in a large traditional arrangement, as the long arching sprays hang down in a most graceful manner.

Conditioning The young foliage needs to be submerged for an hour then transferred to deep water for a further 2 hours. Once the plant is mature, the bracts and leaves can be stood in deep water for about an hour. Stems cut in winter can be arranged without conditioning.

Preserving As the plant produces so much new growth, this compensates for its lack of preserving ability.

Corylus

Hazel
Northern Hemisphere
Deciduous
Corylaceae

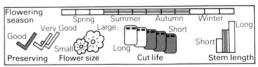

Corylus maxima 'Purpurea'

Two shrubby species are important to the flower arranger. The first of these species is *Corylus avellana* and this is native to Europe, West Asia and North Africa. Particularly attractive is the cultivar *C. a.* 'Contorta' (Corkscrew Hazel) with curiously twisted stems and attractive yellow male catkins about 2in (5cm) long, in early spring. It has somewhat rounded heart-shaped toothed leaves green in colour and downy on the lower surfaces. In the autumn these take on an attractive soft yellowish hue. Height 6ft (180cm).
The second species is *Corylus maxima* and this is

a native of southern Europe. The cultivar *C. m.* 'Purpurea' has dark purple somewhat rounded leaves and purplish-red male catkins in the early spring. This attains a height of 8ft (240cm).

Cultivation and Propagation Both may be grown quite successfully on any well-drained soil either in full sun or partial shade and they are particularly useful for planting in windswept situations where little else will succeed. Dead and diseased branches, together with branches which are more than 4 years old, should be pruned from these shrubs in spring, thus stimulating new more vigorous growth to be produced.

Propagation is by layering shoots in summer.

Uses The twisted stem of the *Corylus*, dripping with golden yellow catkins, is a traditional representational tree in a landscape design. Stripped of its leaves, it may be painted and gilded for Christmas designs or used for linear balance in a modern arrangement. The leaf tends to crowd the stem giving it a rather heavy appearance, one reason why it should be used for its contorted effect only.

Conditioning Split the stem end and stand it in water for up to 2 hours.

Preserving The branch, once cut, continues to dry and should last a number of years.

Cotinus

Smoke Free
Temperate regions
Deciduous
Anacardiaceae

Cotinus coggyria 'Foliis Purpureis'

Cotinus coggygria (formerly *Rhus cotinus)* is a
deciduous shrub from southern Europe and
Caucasus, which is well noted for large panicles
of pinkish beige flowers and rounded green
leaves some 2 to 3in (5 to 7.5cm) long. These
panicles last for a long time and finally turn a
smoke grey colour. Leaves turn an attractive
yellow in autumn. This forms a well rounded
bushy shrub about 9ft (270cm) in height.
C. c. 'Flame' has leaves which turn bright
orange-red in the autumn prior to leaf-fall.
C. c. 'Foliis Purpureis' is a purple-leaved
cultivar which has light red autumn tints.
Cultivation and Propagation *Cotinus* grows
very well in any ordinary well-drained garden
soil providing it is placed in a sunny situation.
No special effort should be made to add
manure or garden compost to the soil. The
poorer the soil the more brilliant will be the
autumn colouration of the leaves.

Propagation is by removal of rooted suckers
during the dormant season or by half-ripe
cuttings secured in summer and inserted in a
closed shaded garden frame.
Uses Purple foliage can be most useful for
arranging with certain pure colours. I always
feel that reds and blues become vibrant when
associated with foliage like *Cotinus*. The
autumn colour of the leaf is a warm addition to
designs of preserved leaves and dried grasses.
Conditioning Once the leaves are mature it
conditions very easily; just stand the cut stems
in water for a minimum of 2 hours.
Preserving Branches of foliage will absorb
glycerine. Do this in the summer but do more
than you need as it is notorious for objecting to
the preserving process. Leaves that have
adopted their autumn shades may be pressed
with much more success.

Cupressus

True Cypress
*Asia, Southern Europe and Central and North
America*
Evergreen
Cupressaceae

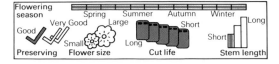

This genus of conifers is related to
Chamaecyparis. Two cultivars are useful for cut
material.
C. arizonica 'Conica' is of broadly conical habit
and it has silvery-blue foliage, height
eventually 20ft (600cm).

Cupressus arizonica

C. macrocarpa 'Gold Crest' is a cultivar
introduced in England. It is of narrow conical
habit and is clothed in rich yellow foliage which
looks quite striking during the dull winter
months. Height 20 to 25ft (600 to 750cm).
Cultivation and Propagation *Cupressus* needs a
deep moist soil. Both these varieties need a
sunny sheltered position. Plant container-
grown stock in autumn or spring.

Propagation is by autumn cuttings inserted
in a heated propagation case in a greenhouse.
Uses The foliage of the closely pressed almost
fleshy scales is borne on longer branches than
the *Chamaecyparis.* It is an outline material for
traditional designs that can be used all year.
The cones that are produced in the autumn are
an interesting foil for preserved foliage and
berries with one or two fresh flowers.
Conditioning Like most evergreen leaves they
are easy to condition, just stand them in water
until you need to arrange them. They have a
very long cut life.
Preserving I have found that they will absorb
glycerine, but it is not always successful.

Cytisus

Broom
Europe, Asia Minor and North Africa
Deciduous and Evergreen
Leguminosae

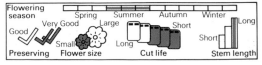

Cytisus 'Lord Lambourne'

Cytisus albus (White Portugal Broom) is a deciduous shrub found in Portugal, Spain and North Africa. It bears masses of small white flowers on slender branches during early summer, height 6ft (180cm).
Cytisus battandieri is a deciduous shrub of vigorous growth from Morocco, unlike all the other brooms in appearance. It is of upright habit and bears silky greyish-green trifoliolate leaves with leaflets oblanceolate and some 2 to 3in (5 to 7.5cm) long. It displays erect terminal racemes of fragrant bright yellow flowers in midsummer. Height about 9ft (270cm) when grown against a warm sunny wall.
C. nigricans is a native of Central and South Eastern Europe. It is valued for its display of bright yellow, fragrant flowers, which are borne on shoots of the current year's growth, during late summer. Prune this species in the spring just before new growth commences. This makes a rounded shrub 3ft (90cm) high.
Cytisus praecox (Warminster Broom) is a shrub of rounded habit which bears masses of creamy-yellow flowers in early summer, height 4ft (120cm).
C. p. 'Allgold' has deep yellow flowers.
Cytisus scoparius (Common Broom) is native to western Europe. It is a deciduous shrub which bears a great profusion of bright yellow flowers during early summer, height 5ft (150cm). This species has been subjected to a good deal of hybridization with excellent results as the hybrids are equally floriferous and are available in an array of attractive colours:
C. 'Andreanus', yellow and crimson flowers.
C. 'Cornish Cream', ivory white and pale yellow flowers.
C. 'Crimson King', large crimson flowers.
C. 'Criterion', orange and apricot flowers.
C. 'Dorothy Walpole', rich crimson flowers.
C. Killiney Salmon', salmon and bright orange flowers.

C. 'Lord Lambourne', crimson scarlet and pale cream flowers.
C. 'Zeelandia', creamy pink flowers.
Cultivation and Propagation Good drainage and ample sunshine are the only prerequisites to their successful cultivation. However, once they are planted in the selected site they resent having their roots disturbed. Buy containerized plants from garden centres or shrub nurseries, so as to avoid this problem when introducing them to the garden initially. They all have pea-shaped flowers and some are of considerable fragrance. *Cytisus* is best planted in late autumn. With the exception of *C. nigricans*, pruning should be undertaken by cutting back stems which have flowered by approximately half their length, immediately flowering ceases.
   Propagation of the species is by seed which may be sown in a garden frame in early spring or in the open ground during late spring. Stem cuttings should be taken during late summer and inserted in a closed and shaded garden frame, containing sandy soil. The frame should remain in position until the following spring. *Cytisus* hybrids are propagated by cuttings.
Uses A truly lavish flower for the arranger. It is a late spring-early summer blossom that should be used in profusion in massed arrangements of flowers. The colour range is so wide that you can choose several to go with a predominant garden flower colour. I favour *C. battandieri* for its pineapple fragrant flowers and silky grey-green foliage. The pendulous habit of the flowers looks effective in a formal design.
Conditioning Cut when the flowers are just showing colour. Crush the woody stems and stand in deep water for 2 hours.
Preserving The small individual flowers can be removed and dried in desiccant. Once the flowers have faded, the multi-stemmed branches can be preserved in glycerine; they darken in colour as an indication of readiness. To give a curving shape to the fresh or dried stem, carefully wrap it around a bottle and submerge it in water. After 2 to 3 hours it can be removed and the curve will dry and straighten slightly, but still retain a graceful curving line.

Deutzia

Asia and America
Deciduous
Philadelphaceae

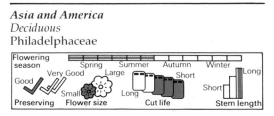

Deutzia × elegantissima

Deutzia is a genus of early flowering shrubs which have eloquent clusters of star-like, fragrant flowers in summer.

Deutzia chunii is of Chinese origin and its arching branches present a fine array of fragrant white flowers, whose reflexed petals have a pink exterior in summer. The foliage is greyish-green and willow-like, height 4 to 5ft (120 to 150cm).

Deutzia × elegantissima is of garden origin and it bears fragrant rose-tinted flowers in summer. It has dull green, oval pointed leaves, about 3in (7.5cm) long, and forms a graceful shrub of bushy habit a height of 5ft (150cm).

Deutzia gracilis is a native of Japan and has strongly fragrant white flowers in summer and lanceolate dark green leaves up to 3in (7.5cm) long, height 4ft (120cm).

D. g. 'Rosea' has rose pink flowers.

D. monbeigii is native to China and it bears glistening white star-shaped flowers unusually late in the summer. It has small oval pointed leaves which are white on the lower surface. It forms a compact shrub some 4 to 5ft (120 to 150cm) in height.

D. pulchra comes from Formosa and it is a vigorous shrub which can grow 8ft (240cm) or more in height, but it responds well to pruning where there is a need to contain its growth. It bears drooping racemes of white flowers in early summer and has lanceolate leaves some 2 to 4in (5 to 10cm) long.

Deutzia scabra is a very vigorous growing species from China and Japan. This is of erect growth and can attain a height of 10ft (300cm). It has flowers in summer which may be either pure white or suffused pinkish outside.

D. s. 'Pride of Rochester' is of the same erect habit but less vigorous attaining a height of 6ft (180cm).

Cultivation and Propagation Deutzias thrive on any ordinary, well-drained soil either in sun or in partial shade. They are pruned as soon as flowering ceases, as flowers are borne on shoots of the previous year's growth. This is the time too to remove some of the older wood to encourage new growth from the base of the shrubs. Planting of new shrubs may take place at any time during the dormant season.

Propagation of the species may be accomplished by seeds sown in a garden frame in spring or by cuttings of half-ripe shoots in summer which are rooted in a closed and shaded garden frame. They can also be rooted from hardwood cuttings taken outdoors in the autumn. The various cultivars mentioned are best rooted from cuttings as they do not necessarily come true from seed.

Uses *Deutzia* produces masses of delicate small flowers to enhance any traditional design of summer materials. The sprays are an asset used as outline material or as a grouping for a focal area. The fragrance is a bonus.

Conditioning It conditions remarkably easily. Lightly crush the end of the branch and stand it in water for about 2 hours.

Preserving Small sprays of flowers can be dried in desiccant.

Eleagnus

Europe, Asia and North America
Evergreen and Deciduous
Elaeagnaceae

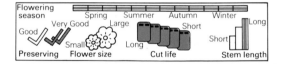

Eleagnus pungens 'Maculata'

Our interest here is confined to species and cultivars which have evergreen leaves desirable for floral arrangements. *Elaeagnus ebbingei*, is a fast-growing hybrid shrub with large broadly elliptic, pointed, leathery, glossy, mid-green leaves which have silvery lower surfaces. The leaves are up to 5in (12.5cm) in length. It bears small insignificant, yet fragrant flowers, in the autumn, on the older wood, height up to 10ft (300cm).
Elaeagnus pungens comes from Japan and it has elliptic pointed, leathery, wavy-edged, glossy dark green leaves some 2 to 4in (5 to 10cm) long. It also has a couple of good cultivars and it is these which are in great demand for their attractive foliage.
E. p. 'Maculata' has glossy dark green leaves with a generous splash of gold in the centre of each leaf, of moderate growth, height 5ft (150cm).
E.p. 'Dicksonii' is of erect habit and slow growth, dark green glossy leaves are irregularly margined rich yellow, height 5ft (150cm).
Elaeagnus 'Limelight' is a cultivar of more vigorous growth. It has leaves up to 5in (12.5cm) long which are mid-green in colour with a central splash of deep yellow and a silvery lower surface, height 10ft (300cm).
Cultivation and Propagation *Elaeagnus* are very tough shrubs which will grow in a wide range of soils, either in full sun or partial shade. Any pruning which may be necessary to shape the shrubs can be done when removing foliage for display or in spring, when new growth commences. Planting of new shrubs should take place in autumn or spring.
   Propagation is either by stem cuttings, in a closed shaded garden frame in late summer, or by rooted suckers removed during spring.
Uses *Eleagnus* is essential foliage for using with yellow and orange flowers, creating a light effect when used in massed arrangements. Most produce long sprays of leaves, which can be used to establish the outline of the design.
Conditioning When the leaves have matured the stems are easy to condition. Stand them in deep water for about 2 hours. Immature foliage should be floated in water prior to this.
Preserving *Elaeagnus* will preserve very well in glycerine, even the variegated types. The variegation will be lost, but the resultant colour compensates.

Enkianthus

North Eastern Asia
Deciduous
Ericaceae

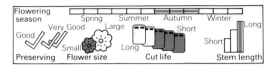

Enkianthus campanulatus

Enkianthus campanulatus is an erect-growing shrub, native to Japan, which has elliptic, pointed and finely toothed, dull green, leaves, some 1 to 2½in (2.5 to 6.25cm) long. In the autumn these leaves turn yellow and then finally bright red. Pendulous racemes of tiny, urn-shaped, creamy-yellow and red tipped flowers are borne during late spring. These make a splendid display lasting several weeks in extent. This is a beautiful garden shrub which will furnish lots of colourful autumn foliage, height 8ft (240cm).
Cultivation and Propagation This shrub likes moist, lime-free soil containing humus, in a lightly shaded situation. It is a good idea to apply a dressing of peat to the soil when preparing it for planting and to apply a mulch of peat around the roots of this shrub each spring. *Enkianthus* needs no regular pruning. The removal of autumn foliage for display will stimulate the production of new shoots. The flowers are produced on the previous year's growth, so any shaping of this shrub should be done as soon as the flowers begin to fade. Planting of new shrubs can be undertaken at any time during the dormant season.
   Propagation is either by seed sown in a cool greenhouse or garden frame during early spring or by cuttings taken in summer and inserted in a closed and shaded garden frame.

Rooting cuttings is a slow process, as it takes about 18 months and propagation by seed is to be preferred.

Uses This interesting foliage plant carries its leaves on the upper side of the branch with the pendulous flowers slung underneath like bell-shaped earrings. Branches that show individual beauty in shape should be arranged by themselves in a low dish with sufficient extra foliage to conceal the mechanics. To prolong the cut life of the autumn foliage, cut the stem when the leaf is turning from yellow to red.

Conditioning Condition it in the ordinary way for about 2 hours.

Preserving The fresh foliage can be preserved in glycerine, but then you are denying yourself the magnificent autumn coloration.

Escallonia

South America
Evergreen
Escalloniaceae

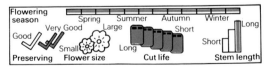

Escallonia 'Slieve Donard'

There are numerous cultivars of this flowering shrub:

Escallonia 'Donard Brilliance' has smallish shiny leaves on arching branches which bear large rosy-red flowers on mature wood of the previous year's growth through the summer and autumn, height 5 to 6ft (150 to 180cm).

E. 'Slieve Donard' has the same shiny green leaves and grows to a similar height, but it is of more compact habit and bears apple-blossom-pink flowers.

Cultivation and Propagation *Escallonia* will grow on any ordinary well-drained garden soil in either a sunny or partially shaded place. In cold districts it should be given the protection of a wall with a southern aspect. In milder districts and in proximity to the coast *Escallonia* makes a fine hedging subject. Any pruning should be undertaken in the autumn as flowering ceases. Plant in autumn or spring.

Propagation is by stem cuttings secured in midsummer and rooted in a sandy soil in a closed and shaded garden frame or cloche.

Uses The flowers extend along the full length of the branch which arches in a most attractive manner. Its obvious use is for outlining traditional styles of arrangements; it is a little too delicate to be used in a modern design. Once the flowers have faded it can still be used for its foliage, again as outline material.

Conditioning Cut the branches as the flowers are beginning to open, and stand them in water for 2 to 3 hours.

Preserving The flowers will preserve in desiccant or they may be pressed, *Escallonia's* real value is as preserved foliage. Select the stems when the flowers have dropped, crush the end of the stem lightly to allow the glycerine solution to be absorbed easily. The process will take from one to two weeks. The colour change will be variable depending on the variety used, but generally it is towards the dark brown shades.

Eucalyptus

Gum Tree
Australia and Tasmania
Evergreen
Mytaceae

Eucalyptus provides good grey foliage.

E. gunnii has obicular (rounded), silvery-grey, juvenile leaves up to 2½in (6.25cm) wide, it comes from South Eastern Australia and Tasmania; *E. parvifolia* has ovate-lanceolate, greenish-grey, juvenile leaves 1½in (3.75cm) long. This latter species is native to New South Wales and it is the hardier of the two, once established. While they are both capable of making substantial trees, their leaf characteristics alter when they become adult and they are no longer suitable for floral artistry. This change of leaf character can be prevented, however, by cutting the stems back annually, in spring to create a stool-bed which will keep on producing strong stems with attractive juvenile leaves.

Eucalyptus gunnii

Cultivation and Propagation They will both grow quite happily on a wide range of soils providing the winter drainage is satisfactory. Plant in a very sunny spot. Water during the drier summer months to encourage fast growth. Purchase only pot grown plants as they resent having their roots disturbed when being planted out in the garden. These species have been found to be reliable in cooler climates, if provided with some shelter during the first few years until they become fully established. The shelter should be in the form of a section of wattle fencing or a screen made from stout hessian on a wood frame. This should be placed in position on the windward side of the *Eucalyptus*, before the onset of winter and it may be removed again in the spring each year. Better still, plant them in a sunny sheltered spot near a wall which will give them permanent protection.

The propagation of *Eucalyptus* is by seeds sown in a seed-tray containing a sandy soil in a greenhouse in spring. To obtain a fairly even germination the soil temperature should be 65°F (18°C), so a heated propagation case with temperature control is desirable but not essential. Seeds should be barely covered when sown. Germination will take some 21 to 28 days. Once the seedlings are large enough to handle, they should be pricked out individually in 3in (8cm) pots and grown on in the same manner as half-hardy annuals.

Uses This foliage can be cut frequently, for the bush will benefit, producing more cutting material and keeping it at a manageable height. Its silvery blue colour is a perfect foil for pink flowers. The long sprays almost demand a traditional setting.

Conditioning It is simple to condition; stand it in water for 2 hours.

Preserving Its finest quality is for preserving — it absorbs glycerine as though it had a thirst for it. There is very little colour change, sometimes it will go a shade darker, if stood in strong light. The preserved leaves last almost indefinitely, and look equally attractive arranged with fresh or dried flowers.

Euonymus

Spindle Tree
Widely distributed
Deciduous and Evergreen
Celastraceae

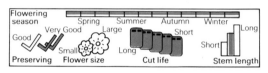

Euonymus europaeus is a European species to be found growing either as a shrub or small tree in the hedgerows or in woodlands, particularly on chalky soils. It has oval pointed green leaves some 2 to 3in (5 to 7.5cm) long, which in the autumn, prior to leaf-fall, produce brilliant pink or red hues. Furthermore, its branches carry an enormous crop of rosy-red fruits. Height 10 to 20ft (300 to 600cm).

E. e. 'Red Cascade' is a cultivar with arching branches, height 8 to 10ft (240 to 300cm). It has the same rosy-red fruits in abundance and brilliant autumn hues.

E. fortunei native to China, is an extremely hardy species of prostrate ground-covering evergreen shrub or climber with oval, slightly toothed, leathery, glossy green leaves, which in their juvenile state are about 1in (2.5cm) long. However, in their adult state when growth becomes more erect and bushy, the leaves attain a length of approximately 2½in (6.25cm).

E. f. 'Colorata' has a climbing or trailing habit with shiny green leaves all summer which develop purplish tints in the autumn and winter.

E. f. 'Emerald 'n' Gold' is particularly valuable for use in arrangements late in the year. This is a small shrub of somewhat open erect habit growing about 18in (45cm) high. This has fine golden yellow variegated foliage which develops exquisite reddish tints in winter.

E. f. 'Gold Tip' has somewhat larger leaves than the previous cultivar and these are dark green with golden yellow margins which change to a delightful creamy-white later in the year.

E. f. 'Silver Pillar' is rather less hardy than the other cultivars and should be grown in the

Euonymus europaeus 'Red Cascade'

Euonymus fortunei 'Emerald 'n' Gold'

Euonymus japonicus

open ground only in milder districts. Elsewhere it is advisable to grow it as a pot-grown subject and give it the protection of a greenhouse until all fear of frost has past. This forms a compact shrub of erect habit and its narrow, dark green leaves have broad white margins.

E. f. 'Silver Queen' is a compact shrub of slow growth which in time attains a height of 6ft (180cm) when planted near a wall. Its young spring foliage is at first a creamy-yellow in colour. During the summer these leaves change to become green with an attractive generous creamy-white margin to them. As winter approaches leaves develop pretty rose tints.

Euonymus japonicus (Evergreen Spindle Tree) native of Japan, will grow either as a shrub or small tree and is useful for growing in coastal districts as a hedging subject. It has glossy oval dark green leaves but it is the variegated forms which are mostly required.

E. j. 'Aureopictus' has emerald green, broad, leaves which have a generous splash of golden yellow in their centre.

E. j. 'Ovatus Aureus' is of slow growth and its leaves are margined and suffused yellow.

E. yedoensis is a deciduous shrub or small tree which is native to Japan. The leaves of this species are about 4 to 5in (10 to 12.5cm) long and broadly obovate in shape and these develop brilliant red autumn tints. It also carries attractive pink fruits.

Cultivation and Propagation All the above species and named cultivars can be grown on any ordinary garden soil either in a sunny or partially shaded situation. Deciduous species can be planted at any time while they are dormant. Evergreen species are best planted either during autumn or spring.

Propagation of prostrate forms presents no difficulty as they usually root themselves quite freely. Bushy evergreens are best struck from cuttings taken in the summer and inserted in a closed and shaded garden frame, while deciduous ones are best struck from hardwood cuttings inserted in the open ground shortly after leaf-fall. No regular pruning is required.

Uses *Euonymus* covers the spectrum of arranging needs. It will act as outline material or as a focal area in an all-foliage design. The smaller varieties will help to conceal the mechanics without darkening the centre of the arrangement. The fruits of *E. europaeus* look quite startling cascading from the centre of an arrangement of leaves or preserved material.

Conditioning To condition *Euonymus*, simply stand it in water until you need it.

Preserving I have had very little success with preserving the foliage or the fruits. As both are generously supplied I am not too disappointed.

Fagus

Beech
Asia, Europe and North America
Deciduous
Fagaceae

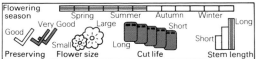

Fagus sylvatica 'Zlatia'

The flower arranger is particularly interested in foliage from two cultivars of the species *Fagus sylvatica*, a European native tree.

F. s. 'Tricolor' has coppery leaves striped rose and pinkish white and *F. s.* 'Zlatia' has leaves which are at first bright yellow and become green in late summer. Both these trees would grow large if allowed to do so but can be controlled by annual pruning.

Cultivation and Propagation *Fagus* may be grown in any ordinary well-drained garden soil. Choose a sunny position. Plant during the dormant season.

Propagation is for the experts.

Uses Don't be put off by the ultimate size of this tree. I am sure that you will be able to keep it well trimmed by using the foliage as fresh cutting material and for preserving. The long sprays of leaves are an invaluable source of material to create the shape of any arrangement.

Conditioning Immature leaves should be floated in water before being conditioned in deep water for about 4 hours. Full mature leaves may be stood in deep water for 2 hours.

Preserving It is probably the most popular preserved piece of plant material used by the arranger. Select the branches carefully, making sure that you have the shape you want.

Remove any damaged leaves and trim away any that are crowded. Stand the branch in glycerine solution. The process is fairly rapid so check them each day. The colour varies slightly but generally it will turn to a delightful golden brown. Once the branch has been preserved it will last a long time. Any leaves that get squashed during storage can be revived and flattened in a jet of steam.

Fatsia

Eastern Asia
Evergreen
Araliaceae

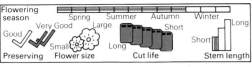

Fatsia japonica

Fatsia japonica syn. *Aralia japonica* syn. *Aralia sieboldii* is an exotic-looking subject from Japan. It will grow 8 to 12ft (240 to 360cm) or more in height and it has large, leathery, palmate, deeply lobed, glossy dark green leaves some 6 to 12in (15 to 30cm) or even more wide on stiff stalks 4 to 10in (10 to 25cm) in length. It also displays umbels of creamy-white globular flowers in branched terminal heads some 10 to 15in (25 to 37.5cm) in length, in late autumn. *F. j.* 'Variegatus' has leaves whose lobes are elegantly tipped creamy white. This cultivar produces only a few thick stems and forms a shrub of open spreading habit.

Cultivation and Propagation This is an ideal evergreen for growing in coastal areas. It is quite hardy and can be grown successfully on a wide range of soils. However, it does prefer a sheltered, partially shaded situation. No annual pruning is necessary. Sometimes it must be cut back to more moderate proportions. Do this in spring as new growth is about to commence.

Propagation is by seed in a warm greenhouse in the spring or in a heated propagation case with the bottom heat set at 65°F (18°C). Alternatively half-ripe stem cuttings some 4 to 6in (10 to 15cm) long can be taken during late summer and rooted in a heated propagation case with the bottom heat set at 65°F (18°C).
Uses The *Fatsia* leaf is in the realm of sculptured foliage. It grows to quite a large size and is often seen as an element for modern and abstract designs. As part of the linking foliage in a pedestal or a large arrangement, it is beyond compare. To bring out the best in the plain and the variegated leaf, lightly wash them with a very mild vegetable oil.
Conditioning The immature leaf will not condition well, so select the leaves when they have fully developed and stand them in water for about 2 hours.
Preserving This leaf will preserve perfectly in glycerine, but the stem and leaf joint will need a little support. This can be achieved by taping a light wire up the stem and the back of the leaf. The process takes anything up to 3 weeks to complete. It turns a dark leathery brown.

Forsythia

Southern Europe and Eastern Asia
Deciduous
Oleaceae

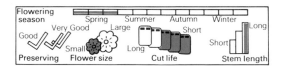

Forsythia 'Beatrix Farrand' is a tall growing hybrid of erect dense habit and vigorous growth which, if left unpruned, will attain a height of 10ft (300cm). This is an American introduction which has large canary yellow flowers up to 1in (2.5cm) across in late spring
Forsythia 'Lynwood Gold' is noted for the production of lots and lots of large broad-petalled flowers which are deep yellow in colour, in late spring. It is of erect habit and attains a height of 6ft (180cm).
Forsythia ovata comes from Korea and is one of the earliest flowering species with dainty primrose yellow flowers in early spring. Its branches are of a somewhat spreading lax habit and are clothed in large ovate leaves up to 4in

(10cm) long which provide good autumn tints. Height 4ft (120cm). This is a particularly useful subject to plant near a sunny south-facing wall. *Forsythia suspensa* is native to Eastern China and it is a shrub of rambling habit which is very useful for clothing walls and trellis where its stems will be covered with masses of slender primrose yellow flowers in late spring.
F. s. 'Fortunei' is of a similar habit to *F. suspensa* but has somewhat more arching branches and is of more vigorous growth, height 8 to 10ft (240 to 300cm) but much more than this if trained against a wall or trellis.

Forsythia 'Lynwood Gold'

Cultivation and Propagation Forsythias do well on any ordinary soil containing some humus While they will tolerate some partial shade they are most floriferous and commence flowering earliest when planted in a sunny yet sheltered situation. No regular pruning is called for and should be strictly limited during the first few years after planting, to enable the shrubs to develop naturally. When shrubs are becoming too large for their location, pruning should take place immediately their flowering ceases. The flowers are borne on wood of the previous year's growth.

Propagation is by hardwood cuttings inserted in the open ground in the late autumn, once the leaves have fallen.
Uses *Forsythia* is one of the earliest spring blossoms. It can be brought indoors in its bud stage and encouraged to open with indoor heat. The long arching sprays of yellow flowers may be used in any traditional style. Small branches in full flower will dictate an attractive outline in a basket of spring material.
Conditioning Conditioning is simple; stand the cut stems in water until you need them.
Preserving Individual flowers may be pressed or dried in desiccant.

Garrya

Mexico and Western North America
Evergreen
Garryaceae

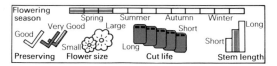

Conditioning Allow the catkins to reach their maximum length before you cut stems and stand them in water for 2 hours.
Preserving The joy of this fascinating material is that it can be made to last. It will preserve in glycerine quite readily. Stand the branch in glycerine, removing only any foliage that is damaged. The time will vary for completion, but usually takes from one to two weeks. The leaves darken to an olive green and the catkins go a metallic grey.

Garrya elliptica

Most of the species are not frost hardy. The one notable exception is *Garrya elliptica*, a species which is native to California and Oregon. This is a strong growing shrub of rounded habit with broadly oval wavy edged dark green shiny leaves which have a grey felty lower surface. Individual leaves are between 2 and 3in (5 to 7.5cm) long. It flowers in winter and displays clusters of beautiful silvery green silky catkins. There is also a cultivar with longer catkins which is worth seeking out and this is *G. e.* 'James Roof'. Height 10ft (300cm).
Cultivation and Propagation This shrub grows quite happily even in the poorest of soils and is at home in either a sunny or partially shaded situation. It may need the shelter of a wall in cold districts. It does not transplant very easily and should only be purchased as container-grown stock. The best time to plant is in autumn or spring.
   Propagation is by layering of the stems in summer or by seeds sown in a warm greenhouse during early spring.
Uses As *Garrya* is a special feature shrub in the garden, it should also be in an arrangement. The tassels are elegant with a silky sheen to them. They suit both formal and informal styles of arranging, as a focal point in an all-foliage design, or cascading at the edge of a large formal arrangement.

Griselinia

New Zealand and the southern part of South America
Evergreen
Cornaceae

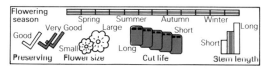

Griselinia littoralis 'Dixon's Cream'

Griselinia littoralis is a shrub which comes from New Zealand. Two cultivars of this particular species provide valuable foliage. *G. l.* 'Dixon's Cream' has apple-green oval leaves about 3in (7.5cm) long which are generously splashed and mottled creamy-white. This is a sport taken from *G. l.* 'Variegata' which has apple green leaves with attractive white variegations. They both form compact densely leafed shrubs of erect habit, height 6ft (180cm).
Cultivation and Propagation *Griselinia* thrives in a well-drained soil in either a sunny or partially shaded place in milder parts and by the coast. Individual shrubs make useful special feature subjects in small gardens.

Griselinia may also be used to make an evergreen hedge near to the sea as it is tolerant of salt-laden air. In cold districts it should be grown in a warm sheltered place as it is slightly tender and is liable to damage by frost. No regular pruning is necessary. However some shortening of long branches may be considered necessary in order to maintain shapely shrubs and this work should be undertaken during late spring. The best time to plant new shrubs is during autumn or spring.

Propagation may be hardwood cuttings taken in autumn and inserted in a sandy soil in a closed garden frame or young shoots may be taken as half-ripe cuttings in midsummer and rooted under a mist propagator.

Uses This is truly a flower arranger's foliage. Both the plain green and variegated forms are an ideal foil for any colour scheme. The variegated leaves are especially attractive outline material in a foliage arrangement.

Conditioning Simply stand the cut mature branch in water for 2 hours.

Preserving Its ability to preserve without problems is an asset not to be ignored. This may be done at any time during the growing season. Select a well formed branch, discard any damaged leaves and stand it in a solution of glycerine and water. The process may take up to a fortnight to complete, and the leaves will change colour to almost black/brown.

Hamamelis

Witch Hazel
Eastern Asia, North America
Deciduous
Hamamelidaceae

Flowering season	Spring	Summer	Autumn	Winter	
Very Good	Large			Short	Long
Good					
Small		Long		Short	
Preserving	Flower size		Cut life		Stem length

This is a very tiny genus of shrubs or small trees, with hazel-like leaves, which have good autumn tints, and spidery petalled fragrant flowers which appear on the leafless branches during the late winter or early spring. There are also a number of cultivars worthy of note and both they and the species are all frost hardy.
Hamamelis × *intermedia* (*H. japonica* × *H. mollis*). The following all form large shrubs about 9ft (270cm) high:
'Diana', large deep coppery red flowers and good autumn tints in large leaves.
'Jelena', large yellow flowers which are suffused coppery orange, appear very early. Autumn leaves tinged orange, red and scarlet.
'Moonlight', medium to large sulphur-yellow flowers which are tinged red at the base. The

Hamamelis × *intermedia* 'Jelena'

autumn leaves turn yellow.
Hamamelis japonica starts flowering early, sometimes in autumn and continues to spring. It has medium-sized deep yellow flowers and attains a height of 7 to 9ft (200 to 270cm). This species is native to China and Japan.
H. j. 'Zuccariniana' has small pale sulphur yellow flowers which appear in spring, and both the cultivar and *H. japonica* have yellow tinted autumn leaves.
Hamamelis mollis is a native of China and it is one of the most popular witch hazels in cultivation. It can grow to a height of 10ft (300cm) or more and bears large very fragrant golden yellow flowers from winter to spring. Its leaves turn yellow in the autumn.
H. m. 'Brevipetala' has short-petalled deep yellow flowers while *H. m.* 'Pallida' displays very large sulphur yellow flowers.
Hamamelis virginiana is native to Eastern North America and has yellow fragrant flowers which appear in the autumn, but these are hidden from sight by the yellow autumn tinted leaves, height 12ft (360cm) or more.

Cultivation and Propagation *Hamamelis* prefers a lime-free, loamy, moist soil, which is well drained. Heavy soils should be improved by the addition of leafmould or peat. Plant during autumn in either a sunny or slightly shaded situation. No regular pruning is necessary.

Propagation of *Hamamelis* is by layering the ripened shoots which were produced in the previous year. This should be undertaken in spring just before new growth commences. Bury the layered shoots some 4in (10cm) into the soil and place canes close to the tips of the shoots appearing above the soil and secure them.

Uses The flowers that clothe the branches of this plant are light and spidery in appearance. It is the type of flower that requires very little extra material to make a fine arrangement. One or two stems with a little sculptural foliage in a

Hamamelis × intermedia 'Jelena' – flower

suitable container creates an arrangement that will last for many days.
Conditioning The flowers can be encouraged to open if they are cut in the bud stage. A short time in deep water will condition them.
Preserving Sadly the flowers will not preserve successfully but the autumn foliage is well worth collecting and pressing.

Hedera

Evergreen
Araliaceae

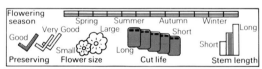

Hedera canariensis 'Variegata'

There are many varieties which provide the flower arranger with some wonderful foliage material for display work. *Hedera canariensis*, Canary Islands and North Africa, has an attractive sport *H. c.* 'Variegata'. This has large shiny olive green shield-like leaves with broad creamy-white margins and red leaf-stems. There is a tendency for older leaves to become flecked deep red. This climber is not entirely hardy and should be planted against a sunny sheltered wall. In mild districts it will flourish to a height of 12ft (360cm) with a similar spread. *Hedera colchica* is from the Caucasus and Asia Minor. Among its many sports is *H. c.* 'Dentata Variegata' which has large broadly elliptic pointed glossy leaves emerald green, shading to greyish-green, with a rich creamy yellow margin. This is quite a hardy climber and grows to a height and spread of 10ft (300cm).
H. c. 'Sulphur Heart' syn 'Paddy's Pride' has large broadly ovate, shiny leaves, boldly splashed bright yellow fading away to light green and margined emerald green. The intensity of the yellow splash fades as the leaves age. Individual leaves vary in the amount of yellow they display. Height 10ft (300cm) with a spread of a similar amount.
Hedera helix (Common Ivy) is a native of Europe and is the source of a great many sports.
H. h. 'Conglomerata' is a slow growing form, of a creeping habit, which is more suited to a spot in the rock garden than trying to ascend walls. It has small dark green shiny leaves, with wavy margins and stiff stems which invariably form a lowish hummock.
H. h. 'Golden Heart' is a particularly beautiful form with medium-sized rich green glossy leaves which are generously splashed a rich golden yellow down their centres. When first planted it takes a couple of years to become established but ultimately attains a height of 10ft (300cm) and a spread of a similar amount.
H. h. 'Glacier' has delectable small silvery-grey, heart-shaped shiny leaves which are narrowly margined white. This is of only moderate growth and attains a height of 6ft (180cm) and similar spread.
Cultivation and Propagation *Hedera* can be grown quite successfully on a wide range of soils, but a poor one is best suited to the variegated forms as it brings out their leaf colouring more clearly. The best time to plant is in spring as new growth is commencing.
   Propagation is by half-ripe cuttings taken during late summer and inserted under a closed and shaded garden frame. Another method of propagation is by hardwood cuttings taken during late autumn and inserted in an open garden frame. This simply serves the purpose of sheltering them from the wind.
Uses The arranger should grow at least one variety of *Hedera*. The small-leaved varieties will provide delicate arrow-shaped leaves to emphasize the focal flowers. Any branches that

need pruning from the plant will prove invaluable for establishing an outline to a design. Those with much larger leaves (and I strongly recommend *H. c.* 'Sulphur Heart') act in the same way for much larger arrangements. Those of you that favour modern arranging will find them terribly useful for hiding mechanics as well as adding impact to the design.

Conditioning Stems should be cut when mature, as new growth will invariably let you down. Float or stand them in water for 2 hours.

Preserving To preserve them stand freshly cut stems or float individual leaves in glycerine. Any variegation is generally lost but the resulting range of preserved colours will compensate.

Hydrangea

Eastern Asia and North America
Deciduous
Hydrangeaceae

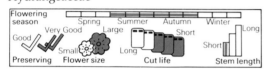

Hydrangea macrophylla

Several of these species provide us with some wonderful material for flower arrangements. *Hydrangea arborescens* is a native of the Eastern United States and has pointed leaves about 4 to 6in (10 to 15cm) long and 2 to 5in (5 to 12.5cm) wide. Its cultivar *H. a.* 'Grandiflora' is noted for its display of elegant, globular, creamy-white flower heads, about 8in (20cm) across, which are borne on shoots of the current year's growth, from summer and autumn. This should be pruned in the spring, height 4ft (120cm).

The familiar mop-headed *Hydrangea macrophylla*, syn. *H. hortensia*, is native to China

Hydrangea paniculata 'Grandiflora'

and Japan. It flowers in late summer and autumn. It is available in the colours white, pink, red and blue. However, blue flowered Hydrangeas need an acid soil in order to produce blue flowers. In an alkaline soil a blueing powder will have to be added at about 10-day intervals, prior to flowering. This method of controlling the colour is best achieved when Hydrangea are grown in tubs.

White Cultivars:
'Madame Emile Mouilliere'
'Soeur Therese'
Pink Cultivars
*'Europa,' dark pink (Fine Blue)
'Gerda Steiniger', bright pink
*'Neidersachsen', pale pink (Fine Blue)
'Wilhelmina', deep pink
Red Cultivars:
'Col. Lindberg', light red
*'Hamburg', red (Blues well)
'Sibilla', deep rosy-red
The cultivars with an asterisk (*) will produce good blue flowers providing they are treated with the blueing powder during the growing season. These cultivars need no regular pruning other than the removal of their old mop-heads of flower in the spring just before new growth commences.

Hydrangea paniculata is of fairly wide distribution in China, Formosa and Japan. One of its cultivars, *H. p.* 'Grandiflora', is a truly graceful shrub which produces great panicles of creamy-white flowers in early autumn, up to 12in (30cm) long, which fade pink as they age. It has oval pointed leaves some 4 to 6in long and is of vigorous erect habit, attaining a height of 6ft (180cm). This species is pruned in the spring just before new growth commences.

Hydrangea petiolaris is a climbing species from Japan. This is a particularly tough subject of vigorous growth which will readily clothe any wall even in shade. It is self-clinging and does not need any support. It has rich green, oblong-oval, pointed leaves about 2 to 4in (5 to 10cm) long and bears saucer-shaped clusters of white flowers, up to 9in (22.5cm) across, during midsummer. It attains a height of about 10ft (300cm) and has a spread of perhaps 14ft (420cm).

Cultivation and propagation All the Hydrangeas like a fertile well-drained soil and benefit from the introduction of some peat when the ground is being prepared. Planting may be undertaken at any time during the dormant season, preferably in a lightly shaded situation.

Propagation is by cuttings, some 4in (10cm) long taken in the early summer and rooted in a closed, shaded garden frame or a greenhouse. Half-ripe cuttings may also be taken late summer and rooted in a closed, shaded garden frame.

Uses You will find both the flower and the leaf of the *Hydrangea* of use. The range of sizes is considerable in both leaf and flower so it will adapt to any type of arranging style. Individual heads with intense colour look most striking arranged in a modern container with a piece of driftwood or several *Fatsia* leaves. The flowering form of *petiolaris* is particularly effective in pedestal designs.

Conditioning If the bract is used before it has begun to dry naturally it should be floated in water for 1 hour. Split the stem if it is woody and stand it in deep water for a further 2 hours.

Preserving The foliage will, in some instances, preserve in glycerine. The bracts preserve better. Cut them in the late summer as they are changing colour, remove any leaves and stand them in 1in (2.5cm) of water. Don't top up the water, allow them to drink it and continue to dry. Let one or two heads remain on the bush throughout the autumn and winter. Often the bract will naturally skeletonize.

Ilex

Holly
Europe, North Africa and Asia
Evergreen
Aquifoliceae

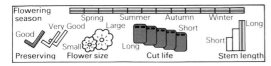

Ilex aquifolium (Common Holly) is of fairly wide distribution. Over the years it has been the parent of a large number of cultivars, some of which are of interest here.

I. a. 'Ferox' (Hedgehog Holly) not only has the traditional spiny toothed leaves, it has puckered leaves which also have spines on

Ilex aquifolium 'Golden King'

their upper surface! The leaves are small and dark green in colour.

I. a. 'Ferox Argentea' has the same sized spiny leaves but here the margins and spines are creamy-white and this looks most effective against the dark green. Both these cultivars are of slow growth and in time attain 8ft (240cm).

I. a. 'Golden King' has very few if any spines on its large, oval pointed, rich green leaves which have bright yellow margins. This grows to be a large shrub exceeding 10ft (300cm) in height, and is one of the best golden variegated forms with red berries.

I. 'Silver Queen' is a handsome subject with dark green leaves marbled grey and exquisitely margined creamy-white. Its young shoots are purplish green in colour. This is of slow growth and attains a height of 6 to 8ft (180 to 240cm).

Cultivation and propagation Ilex will grow on any well-drained soil in either a sunny or shaded situation. Putting a little peat into the soil, when planting, helps them to get established. Prune in the spring when new growth commences or as one requires material for display work. Plant in autumn or spring.

Propagate by layering in the spring or by hardwood cuttings, in an open garden frame, in the autumn.

Uses By tradition *Ilex* is a foliage for winter arrangements. As cut material it will last for many weeks, and this quality should be exploited. Create an arrangement of sprays of the holly foliage and add it to any late flowers that appear in the garden. When they have faded they can be replaced with flowers bought from the florist. Carnations are an attractive addition. If the *Ilex* is a dull green, red carnations will introduce a note of brightness.

Conditioning As the foliage is usually cut late in the year it is already mature. Often it needs only the barest of conditioning times, though it should be given at least 1 hour. Most of us

associate Holly with its red or sometimes yellow berries. Late in the year when there is virtually nothing else to arrange them with, make them a feature of the design. Carefully cut away extra leaves to expose the fruit.
Preserving It is not often seen as preserved foliage, but in fact it will absorb glycerine readily. This can be done from late spring onwards. Trim the cut branch of any crowded leaves and stand the stem in glycerine. It can take up to a fortnight to preserve fully, and the colour will vary depending on type, usually becoming a mid beige.

Ligustrum

Privet
Japan, China, the Philippines and Australia
Deciduous and Evergreen
Oleaceae

Ligustrum ovalifolium 'Aureum'

Ligustrum is very widely grown as a hedging plant and the species used is *L. ovalifolium*, a native of Japan. However, one should not be too ready to dismiss privet as a source of material for floral artistry as there are a couple of hardy species which provide useful foliage. *L. lucidum* is an evergreen species of shrub or small tree and has a form with large leaves some 3 to 6in (7.5 to 15cm) long, which when young are a beautiful yellow and as they age gradually become yellowish-green in colour. This is *L. l.* 'Golden Wax' and it produces terminal panicles of white flowers about 6in (15cm) long during late summer.
Another form is *L. l.* 'Excelsum Superbum'

which has large green leaves, mottled and margined rich yellow and creamy-white. It also has the same white panicles of flowers. *L. ovalifolium* 'Aureum' (Golden Privet) has bright yellow leaves, usually with a splash of green in the centre but occasionally entirely bright yellow all over and these are 1 to 2½in (2.5 to 6.25cm) long. Terminal panicles of white flowers, are borne in late summer.
Cultivation and Propagation All the above privets will grow about 6ft (180cm) high, if left untrimmed. They will grow in any type of soil and in either sun or shade. Plant in either autumn or spring. For floral work you will need to grow specimen shrubs. Any necessary shaping can be undertaken when material is removed for use.
Propagation is by hardwood cuttings secured in autumn and rooted in a nursery bed in the open ground.
Uses *Ligustrum* is considered to be the arrangers' stand-by foliage. The leaves clothe the stem in a uniform manner from the tip to the main stem. The plain green and variegated types have a slightly glossy surface. As the stems are long and regular in shape, they are ideal for creating an outline, mainly in traditional and formal styles.
Conditioning Stand the stems in water, removing any leaves that are likely to be submerged, for up to 2 hours.
Preserving The foliage will preserve in glycerine, the dark green form usually does best. Select the leaves when they are mature and place them in the solution. I tend to cut more than I need as the success rate is dubious.

Mahonia

Central and North America, Asia
Evergreen
Berberidaceae

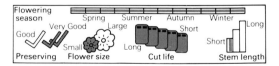

This small genus of delightful shrubs provides some of the best material for flower arranging, as it has fine glossy pinnate leaves, fragrant yellow flowers and attractive berries.
Mahonia aquifolium (Oregon grape) is a very hardy subject from Western North America. It is a shrub of suckering habit. Its pinnate leaves some 6 to 12in (15 to 30cm) long are composed of between 5 and 9 holly-like, spiny, glossy green leaflets, each being some 2 to 3in (5 to 7.5cm) long and between 1 to 1½in (2.5 to 3.75cm) wide. The actual colour of these pinnate leaves varies with the season of the year. In the late autumn and throughout the

Mahonia aquifolium

winter the older leaves turn purple or bronzy-green and some have splashes of bright red on their upper surfaces. In the spring the older leaves become dark green, in stark contrast to the emerging reddish-yellow new shoots. Terminal clusters of yellow flowers begin to appear during early spring, but the main flush of flowers usually appear in late spring. These are followed later in the year by blue-black edible berries which often stay on the shrub right through the winter. Height 2 to 3ft (60 to 90cm). This particular species is a parent of a number of hybrids.

M. a. 'Charity' is one of the best, both as a garden shrub and as a source of material for floral work. It is of strong erect habit and handsome appearance. It has fine pinnate foliage of glossy green, with individual leaves some 18in (45cm) or more long, and deep yellow terminal spikes of fragrant flowers from mid winter to early spring, height 6ft (180cm).

Mahonia beali is native to China and is very hardy indeed. It has large leathery glossy grey-green leaves which are yellowish-green on their lower surface. The pinnate leaves are 12 to 18in (30 to 45cm) long and individual leaflets tend to overlap each other to some extent. The short erect, light yellow flower spikes, some 3 to 5in (7.5 to 10cm) long, appear from winter to spring, and these are followed later by small ovoid, bluish-black berries. Height 6ft (180cm).

Mahonia japonica has dark green, oblong, glossy leaves with many spiny leaflets. Its pale yellow racemes of flowers are produced from winter to spring and are sweetly scented. Height 8 to 10ft (240 to 300cm).

Cultivation and Propagation Mahonias will grow on a wide range of soils and do well even on chalk. They are fond of a partially shaded place either beneath trees or near buildings, providing there is some moisture about their roots. Planting of new shrubs should take place either in autumn or spring. There is no need for annual pruning, but any that proves necessary should be undertaken in the early spring, when new growth is about to commence.

Propagation can be achieved by seeds which are sown in the spring. It is necessary to collect the berries in the autumn and stratify these in sand until the time comes for sowing. Another satisfactory method of propagation is by rooted suckers removed in the early spring or by division of roots at that time. One can also take half-ripe cuttings of shoots of the current year's growth, during late summer, and insert these in sandy soil in a closed and shaded frame.

Uses This plant has so many admirable qualities. The arrangement of the leaf and stem formation is unique. In large designs a rosette of reasonable proportions can be used as the focal area. The herring bone formation of the leaves is a fascinating shape to include in a foliage arrangement.

Conditioning They are quite tough and will condition without problem. Stand the stem in water, the leaves may be partly submerged.

Preserving Amongst the most reliable of the preserving foliages. Whole stems can be cut and stood in glycerine as well as individual sprays. The process should take up to 2 weeks. The colour will vary a little, but in general it will be medium brown.

Parrotia

Northern Iran and Caucasus
Deciduous
Hamamelidaceae

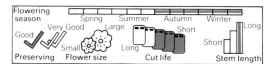

Parrotia persica – autumn foliage

P. persica is a tree much loved for the autumn colouring of its large beech-like leaves which are some 3 to 5in (7.5 to 10cm) long. These change from their customary dark green to become brilliant crimson and gold before leaf-fall. This is undoubtedly one of the finest trees for autumn hues. This species is also interesting for its flowers, which consist of tufts of small red stamens (these are the male organs of the flower), which appear on the bare branches during the late winter. Another interesting feature is its grey flaking bark. This is a strong growing tree which, if not pruned would attain a height of 24ft (800cm) or more. However, with some regular pruning and shaping annually, it need never become more than a large shrub of a broadly spreading habit.
Cultivation and Propagation *Parrotia* likes a moist yet well-drained soil and, for best autumn colour, a sunny situation. Light soils will need a generous application of well rotted garden compost or peat to improve their moisture-holding capacity, when preparing the ground. Planting may be undertaken at any time during the dormant season.

Propagation can be achieved either by layering of branches in the spring or by seeds sown in a sandy compost in spring and placed in a garden frame.
Uses Noted for its autumn foliage in tints of amber, crimson and gold. The stems grow to varying lengths and can be used throughout the design. They may be used with fresh autumn flowers and leaves, but I favour its use as a highlight arranged with preserved foliage and berries. As you will only be using the foliage in the autumn it will be fully matured.
Conditioning A short drink of water will be sufficient to condition it.
Preserving As with most striking autumn foliages, leaves that are interesting colour combinations should be pressed for use in collages.

Pernettya

Prickly Heath
Southern Hemisphere in New Zealand, Australia, Tasmania, the Falkland Islands and South America
Evergreen
Ericaceae

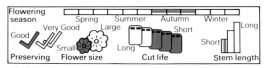

Pernettya mucronata is the species which is of interest to us here and this is native to Chile and the Southern Argentine. This is a very hardy ground-cover shrub with oval shiny small dark green, spiny pointed leaves. During

Pernettya mucronata

early summer it display small white, heath-like flowers and these are followed in the autumn by the finest display of berries any shrub could produce. The berries on individual shrubs may be white, various shades of pink, lilac, purple or crimson. It is a good idea to plant *Pernettya* where it can be seen readily from the house windows as the berries persist throughout the winter and are not affected by the weather. However to ensure the mass display of these berries one requires, in most instances, a male shrub to pollinate the berrying forms. Height 2 to 3ft (60 to 90cm). Except where stated all the following *Pernettyas* require a male shrub for berries to be produced:
P. m. 'Bells Seedling', large dark red berries (self-fertile).
P. m. 'Cherry Ripe', bright cherry-red berries.
P. m. 'Crimsoniana' crimson red berries.
P. m. 'Davis's Hybrids', a selection of berried forms which have large berries of mixed colours.
P. m. 'Lilian', pink berries.
P. m. mascula (male form).
P. m. 'Snow White', white berries speckled pink.
P. m. 'White Pearl', large brilliant white berries.
Cultivation and Propagation *Pernettya* requires a cool moist lime-free soil, preferably in a sunny place, but will succeed in a lightly shaded situation. It likes soils of a peaty nature and where necessary peat should be added to the soil when preparing the ground for planting. Where one is faced with a limey soil *Pernettya* can be grown in large tubs filled with lime-free compost. Always purchase pot-grown stock so as not to disturb the roots when transplanting. Planting is best undertaken during autumn or spring. No regular pruning will be necessary. If growth is getting out of hand, some light pruning may be undertaken in the early spring when new growth is about to commence.

Propagation of the species can be achieved by seed which is sown during early spring, in seed-trays or seed-pans containing a peaty compost. The seeds are then placed in a closed garden frame. The named cultivars listed here may be propagated by layering them into specially prepared peaty soil, in the spring, or by half-ripe cuttings secured in late summer and inserted in a closed and shaded garden frame containing a compost consisting of equal parts, by bulk, of peat and sand.

Uses The autumn berries of the *Pernettya* will console the passing of summer and its glorious bounty. This is an ideal subject to arrange with preserved foliages and flowers that linger past their flowering time. As the berries persist almost into the winter it is a subject to arrange with holly in a traditional manner.

Conditioning It needs only a slight amount of time to condition, and the berries rarely fall.

Preserving It is a generous shrub with its berries, which compensates for the inability to preserve them. Summer foliage may be preserved in glycerine but this will reduce the supply of an interesting fresh piece of material.

Philadelphus

Mock Orange
Widely distributed in the Northern Hemisphere
Deciduous
Philadelphaceae

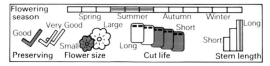

All the species discussed here are quite hardy and bear fragrant flowers which appear during midsummer. Today we have *Philadelphus* hybrids ranging in height from 3 to 10ft (90 to 300cm) with forms suitable for all types of gardens and with flowers which may be single, semi-double or fully double. The following selection gives a good indication of the forms which are available and there are many more to choose from:

P. 'Beauclerk' is a shrub of curving habit which has single white very fragrant flowers about 2in (5cm) across. The bases of the petals are flushed rosy-pink, height 6ft (180cm).

P. 'Belle Etoile' is of a semi-arching compact habit and it bears single white flowers which have fringed petals, the bases of which are flushed maroon. These are 2in (5cm) across and of considerable fragrance, height 5ft (150cm).

P. coronarius is a species thought to originate in Central and South Eastern Europe. This is a vigorous shrub of a spreading rounded habit with creamy-white strongly fragrant flowers

Philadelphus coronarius 'Aureus'

Philadelphus coronarius 'Sybille'

Philadelphus 'Virginal'

which appear early in summer. Height 10ft (300cm). It also has a form with leaves which are green with a creamy-white margin *P. c.* 'Variegatus'; and yet another in which the leaves are rich yellow at first and become greenish-yellow as they age is *P. c.* 'Aureus'. This species and its hybrids are well suited to growing on dry soils.

P. 'Manteau d'Hermine' is a very dwarf hybrid of dense habit which produces creamy-white fully double flowers with a strong vanilla fragrance, height 3ft (90cm).

P. c. 'Sybille' is a delightful small shrub with arching branches bearing small nearly square strongly fragrant, white flowers which have fringed petals that are flushed purple at their base, height 4 to 5ft (120 to 150cm).

P. 'Virginal' is a strong growing shrub of erect habit which bears large, double or semi-double, brilliant white, fragrant flowers, in great clusters. The individual flowers are about 2in (5cm) across. Height 10ft (300cm).

Cultivation and Propagation *Philadelphus* will grow quite happily on a wide range of garden soils, but the lighter ones should be given a dressing of peat, to improve their moisture-holding capacity, when preparing the ground. It can be grown in either a sunny or slightly shaded situation. Planting should be undertaken during the dormant season. *Philadelphus* should be pruned immediately after flowering. Remove the older branches which have flowered and show no signs of producing vigorous new shoots. It is also a good idea, with old shrubs, to remove one or more of the old thick main branches right down to ground level, which stimulates new growth.

Propagation is by either half-ripe cuttings taken in late summer and inserted in a heated propagation case with the bottom heat set at 68°F (20°C) or by hardwood cuttings taken in the autumn and inserted in the open ground.

Uses Choice of variety will be a difficult decision for those planting a *Philadelphus* for the first time. It has so many attributes, in both the flowers and the foliage. Long arching sprays of creamy, white flowers enhance the outline of a full massed design of similar coloured flowers. *P. c.* 'Aureus' is one of the most outstanding foliages — in the spring it is a bright golden yellow, becoming green/yellow in the summer. It will add distinction to any design of spring or early summer flowers.

Conditioning Immature foliage can be difficult, but not impossible, to condition. Cut the stem in the morning and float it in a dish of water for about 1 hour, then stand it in deep water for a further 2 to 3 hours. It is important that this foliage does not come into direct contact with any heat source, when conditioned or arranged. If the stem wilts, dip the lower ½in (1.25cm) of recut stem in boiling water for 10 seconds and return it to the conditioning dish. Mature foliage and flowering stems will not require such drastic action, a deep drink of water will be sufficient.

Preserving Individual blooms can be pressed; double flowers, to retain their form, should be dried in desiccant.

Phormium

New Zealand Plax
New Zealand
Evergreen
Lilaceae

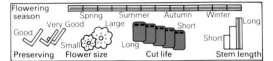

Phormium tenax 'Purpureum'

Phormium, though with a herbaceous appearance, have semi-woody rootstocks, hence their description as sub-shrubs. Our concern here is with *P. tenax*. This has stiff erect bluish-green, pointed, sword-like leaves some 4 to 7ft (120 to 210cm) long and about 4 to 5in (10 to 12.5cm) wide. Established plants produce bronzy-red flowers on tall spikes during the late summer and autumn. There are also a few cultivars which have attractive foliage:

P. t. 'Bronze Baby', coppery-red foliage, drooping at the tips, height 2ft (60cm).

P. t. 'Purpureum', bronzy-purple leaves, height 4 to 7ft (120 to 210cm).

P.t. 'Variegatum', green leaves, striped creamy white, height 6ft (180cm).

Cultivation and Propagation These plants like a moist soil and will even succeed on boggy ground in either full sun or slight shade. Light soils should be given a good dressing of garden compost or peat to increase their moisture-holding capacity, prior to planting. Planting should be in autumn or spring. Protect the crowns of the plants in cold winter weather.

Propagation is by seed sown during spring in a peat-based compost, in a greenhouse or garden frame, or by division of the roots in late spring.

Uses *Phormium tenax* is a sculptural foliage. The broad sword-like leaves are beyond compare for establishing the height of a design. It is at home in the hands of a modern arranger as well as a traditionalist. This leaf may be used as it grows in vertical design or rolled and pinned to create a modern design of geometric patterns.

Conditioning It needs very little conditioning, though it has no objections to standing in water for up to two days.

Preserving The leaves may be pressed under the carpet between sheets of newspaper. I have had some success at preserving it in glycerine, though the edges of the leaf tend to discolour before the process is complete. However, a little judicious snip with a pair of sharp scissors will correct this annoying fault.

Pittosporum

Australasia
Evergreen
Pittosporaceae

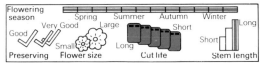

Pittosporum tenuifolium 'Silver Queen'

Pittosporum tenuifolium comes originally from New Zealand and it is with one of its cultivars *P. t.* 'Silver Queen' that the flower arranger has a particular interest. This has particularly attractive oblong undulating silvery leaves and black twigs which last well in water. It does

produce a few small dark-purple fragrant flowers in late spring but these are of no significance. This shrub is of slow growth; eventual height 10ft (300cm).

Cultivation and Propagation Plant in a warm sheltered part of the garden in a well drained fairly light soil during autumn or spring. No regular pruning is necessary. Any shaping or removal of damaged branches should be undertaken during spring.

Propagation is by half-ripe cuttings 3in (7.5cm) long taken with a heel in summer and inserted in a heated propagating case.

Uses The leaves of the *Pittosporum* are produced in light rosettes and are an invaluable supply of delicate form and colour to lighten the centre of a massed arrangement of flowers and foliages. They should be allowed to mature so that the leaf colour is at its most intense before use.

Conditioning *Pittosporum* conditions without any problem. Simply stand in water for 2 hours.

Preserving Any leaves that display a particularly fine colour variegation should be pressed for use in collage work. More substantial branches can be preserved in glycerine. Sadly the variegation is lost but the resultant dark brown colour has its own fascination.

Prunus

Cherry
Japan and China
Deciduous
Rosaceae

Our concern here is with just a few of the ornamental species of cherry or more particularly a few of their numerous cultivars. *Prunus serrulata* 'Tai Haku' (Great White Cherry) is a vigorous tree which displays large pure white single flowers in pendulous clusters in spring. Its young spring leaves are at first a reddish-bronze in colour but as they open out and become large their colour is green. In the autumn the leaves have some very attractive tints of yellow and orange prior to leaf-fall, height 21ft (700cm).

P. s. 'Ukon' is equally vigorous and its young coppery brown foliage makes a fine backcloth for the semi-double pale greenish-yellow flowers, in late spring. The autumn leaves are tinged reddish-brown prior to leaf-fall, height 21ft (700cm).

Prunus subhirtella 'Autumnalis' (Autumn

Prunus serrulata 'Tai Haku'

Prunus yedoensis

arching branches smothered in masses of slightly fragrant flowers, which are at first pale pink but later white in colour, during spring. Its foliage also has some attractive autumn tints, height 15 to 21ft (450 to 650cm).

Cultivation and Propagation These trees will grow quite happily on any ordinary, well-drained garden soil containing some lime, in an open sunny situation. Planting may take place at any time during the dormant season. Little pruning is necessary, but you can remove any unwanted branches immediately flowering ceases.

Propagation is a task for the experts.

Uses This very large family offers an exciting choice of spring blossom. It is generally used in lavish quantities in large arrangements and pedestals. Special forms like *P. s.* 'Ukon' are at their best seen in small arrangements, baskets or low dishes with mixed spring flowers.

Conditioning The buds can be opened if they are conditioned in warm water. This process can take up to a week to complete, then they can be arranged. They do not require any special pre-treatment, a deep drink of water is sufficient.

Preserving The leaves are of no importance to preserve. The only way to capture the flowers is by pressing or desiccant drying.

Pyracantha

Firethorn
China, Southern Europe and Asia Minor
Evergreen
Rosaceae

Pyracantha is a well known spiny hardy shrub which provides a brilliant display in the late autumn and winter with bunches of colourful berries which are produced in considerable quantities. All varieties listed here have oblong to oblanceolate, shiny dark green leaves, which may vary in length according to species, from approximately 1 to 3in (2.5 to 7.5cm) and some are finely toothed. They all display masses of tiny white flowers during early summer.

P. angustifolia is of a rather stiff, spreading bushy habit and vigorous growth. It bears orange-yellow berries which, in some years, remain on the branches until the arrival of spring, height 10 to 12ft (300 to 360cm).

P. coccinea is the parent of a couple of very desirable cultivars.

P. c. 'Mohave' is of vigorous bushy habit and produces a fine crop of orange-red berries, while *P. c.* 'Red Column' is of a stiff erect habit

Cherry) is a delightful small tree with red tints in its autumn leaves and once these have fallen it flowers along the bare, twiggy branches. It has semi-double white flowers, which are borne spasmodically through the winter. With the onset of severe wintery weather flowering ceases but as soon as there is a break in these conditions further flowers appear. A few stems cut and taken indoors for forcing will quickly provide a fine display of flowers for use in floral arrangements.

P. s. 'Autumnalis Rosea' is less reliable for winter flowering but it often produces semi-double deep pink flowers in autumn with its main flush of flowers apearing during late spring. Both these cultivars attain a height of 15 to 18ft (450 to 600cm).

Prunus yedoensis (Yoshino Cherry) was introduced from Japan originally and it is an outstanding early flowering graceful tree with and bears large blood-red berries, height 10ft (300cm).

P. rogersiana is a small-leaved species which is of a vigorous spreading habit with reddish-orange berries. Of even more interest to the flower arranger, however, is *P. r.* 'Flava', with attractive yellow berries, height 12ft (360cm).

P. 'Soleil d'Or' is of less vigorous growth and more spreading habit and is a useful subject as a ground-cover shrub. It bears a heavy crop of orange-yellow berries, height 5ft (150cm).

P. 'Watereri' is a shrub of compact habit which has a fine display of scarlet berries. In some years this cultivar keeps its berries until spring.

Cultivation and Propagation *Pyracantha* will thrive in a wide range of soils including limey ones, either in a sunny or partially shaded situation. Purchase pot-grown plants and plant during autumn and spring. It makes a particularly good climber to train up a house wall or a large spreading shrub in the open. When grown on walls or fences there will be the need for some pruning in the early spring each year, to reduce some of the longest shoots of the previous year's growth. Light pruning in this way will do no real harm, but one is removing shoots which would have been producing flowers and berries in due course. The same is true of shrubs growing naturally in the open ground.

Propagation is either by half-ripe cuttings taken in late summer, inserted under a closed and shaded garden frame, or by hardwood cuttings taken in the autumn and inserted in a closed garden frame.

Uses This is another shrub that is generous with its autumn fruits. The berries are carried in clusters on a medium to long stem and can be used throughout a formal arrangement of autumn flowers and preserved foliages. Clusters arranged in a modern container are most effective.

Conditioning Stand the cut stems in deep water for 2 hours to condition them.

Preserving Though you are robbing yourself of good autumn material, the foliage will preserve in glycerine. Do this in the summer when the leaves have matured. The colour changes to a dark olive green.

Pyracantha coccinea 'Mohave'

Pyracantha 'Soleil d'Or'

Rhododendron including Azalea

Asia and North America and Europe
Evergreen and Deciduous
Ericaeceae

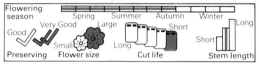

It is impossible to do more than describe just a few of the species and cultivars which are available.

Rhododendron (hardy evergreen species)

R. ferrugineum is a species which is native to Central Europe and this bears clusters of rosy-red flowers which appear in midsummer. It is of a compact habit, height 3 to 4ft (90 to 120cm).

R. hirsutum also comes from Central Europe and it is of a similar habit and height but with clusters of pink flowers in midsummer.

R. hippophaeoides is a fine evergreen shrub of erect habit from China which has clusters of lavender-blue flowers during late spring, height 5ft (150cm).

R. yakushimanum is a native of Japan which forms a shrub of erect compact rounded habit of growth. Its clusters of flowers in early summer are at first pink but soon become white, height 4ft (120cm). This species is the parent of a number of hybrids.

Rhododendron (hardy evergreen hybrids).

R. 'Britannia' is a slow growing shrub of rounded compact habit with clusters of glowing crimson flowers in early summer, height 4ft (120cm).

R. 'Doncaster' is of similar habit to R. 'Britannia' with clusters of crimson-scarlet flower in early summer, height 4ft (120cm).

R. 'Vulcan' is of more vigorous growth and has bright red clusters of flowers during early summer, height 5ft (150cm).

R. 'Jacksonii' is a particularly tough hybrid rhododendron built for survival in even the most unsuitable conditions. This is a shrub of rounded habit and compact growth which is very early in producing clusters of rose-pink flowers with maroon markings in spring, height 5ft (150cm).

R. 'Pink Pearl' is a vigorous shrub which bears large clusters of bright pink flowers which later fade to soft pink, in early summer, height 7 to 10ft (210 to 300cm).

R. 'Rosamundii' is a slow growing shrub which displays clusters of pale pink flowers in spring, height 4ft (120cm).

R. 'Cunningham's White' is a strong growing shrub which produces lax clusters of white flowers, with a pale yellow eye, during late spring, height 6ft (180cm).

R. 'Unique' is a small shrub of rounded compact habit which bears clusters of creamy white flowers with crimson speckles during late spring, height 5ft (150cm).

R. 'White Cloud' is a shrub of robust habit with large clusters of pure white flowers in early summer, height 7 to 10ft (210 to 300cm).

R. 'Butterfly' is a compact shrub which bears clusters of butterfly shaped primrose-yellow flowers, speckled deep-red during late spring, height 5ft (150cm).

R. 'Souvenir of W. C. Slocock' is of robust habit and bears clusters of pale yellow flowers during early summer, height 7 to 10ft (210 to 300cm).

R. 'Yellow Hammer', is a shrub of slender erect habit which bears tubular, bright yellow flowers in pairs, both terminally and along its branches, during spring and some years, again in autumn, height 5ft (150cm).

AZALEA (deciduous hybrids)
While these tend to be smaller than rhododendrons many attain a height of 4 to 6ft (120 to 180cm) while some reach 8ft (240cm). All flower in early summer. The following selection represents some of the finest of the many hybrids available.

Ghent Hybrids (GH), 5 to 8ft (150 to 240cm).
Knaphill and Ebury Hybrids (KN), 5 to 6ft (150 to 180cm).
Mollis Hybrids (M), 4 to 6ft (120 to 180cm).
Occidentale Hybrids (O) 6 to 8ft (180 to 240cm).

A. 'Koster's Brilliant Red' (M), glowing orange-red.

A. 'Royal Command' (KN), vermilion-red.

A. 'Satan' (KN), geranium red.

A. 'Floradora' (M), orange flushed apricot, spotted dark crimson.

A. 'Gibraltar' (KN), deep orange (foliage has good autumn tints).

A. 'Dr Ossthoek' (M), deep orange-red.

A. 'Golden Sunset' (KN), deep yellow with orange blotch.

A. 'Narcissiflora' (GH), fragrant creamy-yellow double flowers (good autumn tints).

A. 'Sunbeam' (M), vivid yellow flushed apricot with orange blotch.

A. 'Berryrose' (KN), rose pink with yellow blotch.

A. 'Coronation Lady' (KN), salmon-pink with orange blotch.

A. 'Norma' (GH), fragrant rose-pink double flowers.

A. 'Strawberry Ice' (KN), light pink flushed deeper pink with orange blotch.

A. 'Daviesii' (GH), fragrant white flowers (yellow when first open), with yellow blotch.

A. 'Silver Slipper' (KN), fragrant white flowers, flushed pink with orange blotch.

A. 'Whitethroat' (KN), brilliant white double flowers.

AZALEA (evergreen hybrids)
These are of a low spreading habit and attain a height of 2 to 4ft (60 to 120cm). Their flowering period is usually early summer, unless otherwise stated. While they are commonly referred to as Japanese Azaleas, this is not entirely correct for both in the USA and Europe a good deal of hybridization work has been undertaken which has resulted in many of the new introductions.

Gable Hybrids (G), USA
Glenn Dale Hybrids (GD), USA.
Kaempferi Hybrids (KF), originated in Holland.
Kurume Hybrids (K), Japan.
Vuyk Hybrids (V), originated in Holland.
Wada Hybrids (W), Japan.

A. 'Blue Danube' (V), bluish violet.

A. 'Johann Sebastian Bach' (V), deep purple.

A. 'Addy Wery' (K), bright scarlet.

A. 'Hatsugiri' (K), bright crimson purple.

A. 'Sakata Red' (K), orange-red.

A. 'Aladdin' (K), salmon-orange

A. 'Bungonishiki' (W), semi-double reddish-orange flowers.

A. 'Blaauw's Pink' (K), salmon-pink flowers early May.

A. 'Esmeralda' (K), pale pink.

A. 'Rosebud' (G), double silvery-pink flowrs.

A. 'Willy' (KF), soft pink.

A. 'Driven Snow' (GD), brilliant white flowers.

A. 'Martha Hitchcock' (GD), white flowers margined magenta.

A. 'Palestrina' (V), ivory-white flowers with a faint hint of green.

Rhododendron hippophaeoides

Azalea 'Palestrina'

Rhododendron yakushimanum

Azalea 'Gibraltar'

Rhododendron 'Jacksonii'

Azalea 'Dr Ossthoek'

Cultivation and Propagation Rhododendrons and azaleas can be grown on any reasonably fertile lime-free soil, providing it is moisture retentive and at the same time well drained. Dry sandy soils will need generous amounts of peat incorporated in them. An annual mulching of sandy soils is also necessary both to help preserve soil moisture during the summer months and to add to the soil's humus content. On chalky soils, you may either build a raised bed or grow rhododendrons and azaleas in tubs, to avoid this problem.

Always purchase container-grown evergreen rhododendrons and azaleas where available, as in this way they can be planted out with the very least root disturbance. Plant out in autumn or spring. They can be planted from containers quite successfully even in early summer, if they are planted beneath the shade of trees and they are watered frequently. Deciduous azaleas may be planted at any time during the dormant season. No regular pruning required. Simply remove the old flower heads with your fingers. If a large branch needs removing, do this in spring as new growth commences. Stems may need thinning as they get old and overcrowded.

Propagation may be achieved from seed sown in a greenhouse in the spring, by grafting onto rootstocks, in the open garden during December/January, or by layering during midsummer.

Uses The soil in my garden will not allow me to grow this magnificent shrub, which is disappointing as it is the finest of materials for arranging. Unless you are lucky enough to grow copious numbers, use the flowers where they are seen to best advantage, possibly as a focal unit or as a single branch arranged on pins in a low dish.

Conditioning Cut the stem as the flowers are opening, lightly crush the end and place in warm water for about 4 hours. The water can be allowed to cool over this period.

Preserving Individual leaves may be floated in a dish of glycerine to preserve them. They will darken to a rich greeny brown. Single flowers may be pressed, but if dried in desiccant they will retain their bell shape.

Ribes

Flowering currant
North America
Deciduous and Evergreen
Grossulariaceae

Flowering season	Spring	Summer	Autumn	Winter	
Good	Very Good	Large			Long
	Small	Long	Short	Short	
Preserving	Flower size		Cut life		Stem length

Ribes sanguineum is of a robust bushy habit and attains a height of 6 to 8ft (180 to 240cm). During late spring it produces drooping racemes of deep rosy red flowers. However it is today well represented by clonal cultivars.
R. s. 'King Edward VII' has brilliant crimson flowers and green leaves.
R. s. 'Pulborough Scarlet' has very deep red flowers and green leaves.
R. s. 'Brocklebankii', which is of less vigorous habit and attains a height of approximately 3 to 4ft (90 to 120cm), has pale pink flowers and delightful golden yellow leaves.
R. speciosum is a semi-evergreen species from California and is a little less hardy. This bears pendulous clusters of bright red, tiny fuchsia-like flowers during late spring. It has spiny stems and is of robust habit.

Cultivation and Propagation *Ribes* will thrive in any ordinary soil in either a sunny or partially

Ribes sanguineum

Ribes sanguineum

shaded place. Planting may occur at any time during the dormant season. No regular pruning is required. The removal of an old branch should take place immediately after flowering ceases, in the spring.

Propagation is by hardwood cuttings inserted in the open ground in the late autumn.
Uses The true value of the flowering currant is in its long stem of fresh young foliage and tassels of pink to red flowers. This is very useful for getting flower colour to the extremities of an arrangement at a time of the year when there is an abundance of short-stemmed flowers. It is more suited to formal arrangements, though the variety 'Brocklebankii' looks extremely pretty cascading from the sides of a basket.
Conditioning The flowers can be induced to open by standing the stems in warm water. Providing the foliage does not come into contact with the water, they can be left for several days.
Preserving Unfortunately it is one of those foliages that will not preserve on the stem. I recommend that you concentrate on the blossom, preserving the clusters of tiny flowers in desiccant. Once they have dried attach them with the aid of a little quick-drying glue to a small branch of *Corylus* 'Contorta' that has been mounted onto a base. The effect is oriental.

Rubus

Brambles
Widely distributed
Evergreen and Deciduous
Rosaceae

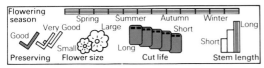

Rubus cockburnianus (Whitewashed Bramble) develops long arching spiny stems covered strangely with white wax. This looks particularly attractive during the winter, if it is planted in front of an evergreen hedge. It is a deciduous shrub with pinnate leaves up to 8in (20cm) long, which are fern-like in their appearance and while the upper surface is green the lower surface is white. Small purple flowers, of no significance, appear in the early summer and are followed by black fruits. This species comes from China, height 8ft (240cm).
Rubus tricolor is an attractive evergreen species of a low trailing habit with spineless stems which comes from China. This is a good ground-cover subject. Its stems are covered in brownish bristles and it is clothed in shiny dark green heart-shaped leaves up to 4in (10cm) long and these are covered with whitish felt on their

Rubus tridel

Rubus cockburnianus

lower surface. White flowers appear during the summer and these are followed by bright red fruits, height 1ft (30cm).
Rubus tridel 'Benenden' is a deciduous cultivar with long arching, spineless leaves. It has green three to five-lobed leaves, which are 3 to 4in (7.5 to 10cm) long and bears masses of fragrant white flowers in late spring. This may be grown either in full sun or partial shade, height 8ft (240cm).
Rubus ulmifolius is a European native species with semi-evergreen leaves which have a whitish felty lower surface. It is the parent of the cultivar *R. u.* 'Bellidiflorus'. This is of rapid growth and bears rose-pink double flowers during late sumer, height 8ft (240cm).
Cultivation and Propagation All the above species and cultivars thrive in any ordinary garden soil. Plant in either full sun or partial shade during the dormant season. Pruning

Rubus tridel

Salix hastata

Salix lanata

technique depends upon whether one is dealing with the flowering forms or those grown for their attractive stems. The ones grown for their flowers are pruned to remove some of the older wood in the late autumn. The ones with the attractive stems have all the old growth removed down to ground level in the spring, when the new shoots are about 10in (25cm) high.

Propagation is by layering of the stems where the tips touch the ground and calls for no special attention, as it occurs quite naturally.

Uses *Tricolor* will quickly spread to give you lots of cutting sprays for outlining traditional arrangements. For the modernists *cockburnianus* is an indispensable material. In the winter bundles of the ghostly white stems can be arranged in a tall container, possibly using preserved rosettes of *Choisya ternata* to establish a textural contrast at intervals.

Conditioning They need little in the way of preparation for conditioning. A deep drink of water for 2 hours will be sufficient.

Preserving The leaves generally do not preserve well, though the small flowers will dry in desiccant.

Salix

Willow
Northern Hemisphere
Deciduous
Salicacae

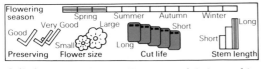

Salix lanata is native to Europe and Asia, and it is commonly referred to as the 'Woolly Willow'.

This forms a low shrub some 2 to 3ft (60 to 90cm) high of a spreading habit. It bears broadly oval, silvery-green, downy leaves, 1 to 2in (2.5 to 5cm) long, on stiff erect stems which display attractive golden yellow woolly catkins in the spring.

Salix hastata is native to Southern Europe and North Eastern Asia and it makes a rounded shrub about 5ft (150cm) in height. It has a very fine form in *S. h.* 'Wehrhahnii'. Its leaves, which are about twice the size of those of *S. lanata*, are dull green on the upper surface, while the lower surface is greyish-green. In the spring-time it bears masses of silvery-grey catkins, which later turn yellow.

Salix matsudana is a tree native to both China and Korea and it has a very interesting form, *S. m.* 'Tortuosa' (Contorted Willow). As the name indicates, the most interesting characteristic of this tree is the strangely contorted branches and twigs which furnish much useful material for use in floral decorations. It has long narrow pointed green leaves which are greyish-green on the lower surface and it bears silvery catkins in the spring. Height 30 to 40ft (900 to 1200cm), when mature.

Cultivation and Propagation *Salix* will flourish in any fertile moisture-retentive soil in a sunny situation. Plant during the dormant season. No regular pruning is required. Trim back unwanted branches when dormant.

Propagation is by hardwood cuttings secured in the late autumn and inserted in the open ground.

Uses A much admired tree or bush for its fluffy catkins produced in the spring. The long whip-like branches are clothed in golden mounds, ideal material for including in a basket or a formal arrangement of *Forsythia* and other spring flowers. The branches of *S. m.* 'Tortuosa' are well known to the arranger. They appear in all styles of arranging from modern to period arrangements. Usually only one branch is necessary, but it is wise to inspect it carefully and remove any crowded twigs that will detract from the completed design.

Conditioning Even the young foliage conditions easily; a short drink of water is all that is needed.

Preserving An attempt should be made to preserve the catkins. Cut the stems before the pollen has matured. Stand them in glycerine solution after removing the leaves. The process will take up to a week.

Senecio

Widely distributed
Evergreen
Compositae

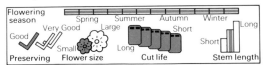

Senecio laxifolius is a shrub with obovate, slightly undulating grey-green leaves with grey-white down, especially on the lower surface. During the summer it displays yellow daisy-like flowers in terminal panicles. Height 4ft (120cm), of a spreading or lax habit.
Senecio monroi is a shrub similar in character in respect of its leaves but these are a little smaller than those of *S. laxifolius*. It is also of more compact habit than the former species. It has yellowish daisy-like panicles of flowers during the summer. Height 3 to 5ft (90 to 150cm). Both originate in New Zealand.

Cultivation and Propagation Plant in the winter in any ordinary well-drained soil in sun

Senecio laxifolius

or light shade. They do well in coastal districts. Any pruning should be done in spring.

Take half-ripe cuttings in autumn and insert in sandy soil in a coldframe.

Uses This particular genus produces a cluster of yellow flowers which should be removed so that the food supply is directed to producing stronger and more luxuriant foliage. The leaves are quite striking, being grey/green on the surface and light silvery grey underneath. The arching stems are an invaluable outline for arrangements of soft pink or blue flowers. Used in small numbers they add an unusual note to an all-foliage design.

Conditioning Immature growths will benefit from having the end of the stems burned for 10 seconds before conditioning them in water. The ends of branches of old wood should be lightly crushed before conditioning.

Preserving *Senecio* will not preserve by air drying or by glycerine. The individual leaves of *S. monroi* are, however, worth pressing.

Skimmia

Eastern Asia
Evergreen
Rutaceae

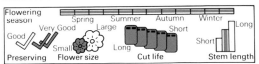

Skimmia is a shrub of slow growth and bushy habit. The one most commonly seen growing in gardens is *Skimmia japonica*. This grows to a height of 3ft (90cm) and it is nearly as much across. It has glossy green, aromatic, oblong oval, pointed leaves some 3 to 4in (7.5 to 10cm) long. To get the attractive clusters of bright red

Skimmia japonica

fruits both male and female shrubs must be planted. The tiny dull white flowers are not attractive when they appear in the spring but they do have a fragrance of lily-of-the-valley. The male flowers have the strongest fragrance and the female flowers produce the fruits which colour up in the autumn and generally remain in excellent condition throughout the winter. There is also a more vigorous clonal cultivar *S. j.* 'Fortunei' with female flowers which will produce fruits in large clusters, even when grown as a solitary specimen.

Cultivation and Propagation *Skimmia* can be grown quite successfully on a wide range of soils including chalky ones. Choose a partially shaded place. Planting should be undertaken either in autumn or spring. No regular pruning is necessary. It is simply a matter of shortening straggly growth from time to time and this can be done when removing material for display.

Propagation may be from seeds sown in a garden frame in spring, by half-ripe cuttings secured in late summer and inserted in a closed and shaded garden frame, or by hardwood cuttings secured in the late autumn and inserted in a closed garden frame.

Uses *Skimmia* is a foliage which will link the centre of the design with the extreme points. This type of foliage is generally referred to as intermediate foliage. The rosettes of leaves are usually placed to emphasize the focal area, or if they are in an all-foliage arrangement, as the focal point.

Conditioning *Skimmia* is extremely accommodating and stands well with very little conditioning. About 1 hour in water is all it requires. The flowers that appear in the centre of the rosette are quite dainty and are a useful addition in a design of late May and early June flowers. In the autumn, the berries appear, to be used with other garden fruits and preserved materials.

Spiraea

Northern temperate regions
Deciduous
Rosaceae

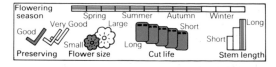

Spiraea bumalda 'Anthony Waterer'

Spiraea 'Arguta' (The Bridal Wreath) is a fine hybrid form which flowers during later spring, height 5 to 6ft (150 to 180cm). Its stems have a delightful arching habit and are clothed in small oblong oval, bright green leaves. The stems are covered in a vast multitude of tiny white flowers.

Spiraea bumalda 'Anthony Waterer' is another very attractive hybrid form which flowers from summer to autumn, on shoots produced during the current year. This is a dwarf shrub with thin twiggy branches which attains a height of about 32in (80cm) and is about the same in width. It is clothed in dark green oblong pointed leaves some 3in (7.5cm) long and some of these are variegated cream and pink. It produces large, flat-headed terminal clusters of tiny bright crimson flowers.

Cultivation and Propagation Both cultivars will thrive in any ordinary garden soil either in full sun or partial shade. Planting should be undertaken during the dormant season. Prune *S.* 'Arguta' immediately the flowers fade. Prune *S. b.* 'Anthony Waterer' in the dormant period.

Propagation is by half-ripe cuttings in late summer in a closed and shaded garden or by hardwood cuttings in the open ground in the late autumn. *S. b.* 'Anthony Waterer' can also be propagated by division of the roots during the dormant period.

Uses The 'Bridal Wreath' provides long arching sprays of white blossom that are most attractive in arrangements of blossom and spring flowers. The foliage of 'Anthony Waterer' is quite brilliant in the spring — glowing orange.

Conditioning 'Arguta' will condition easily, if the stems are stood in water for about 2 hours. Woody stems should be lightly crushed. 'Anthony Waterer' needs to be floated in water for 1 hour, then given a deep drink for a further 2 hours.

Preserving The flowers of 'Arguta' can be separated and preserved in desiccant. It is an invaluable flower for miniature arrangements and dried flower work.

Stephanandra

Asia
Deciduous
Rosaceae

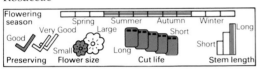

Stephanandra incisa

This is a near relative to *Spiraea*. It has insignificant flowers but produces beautiful autumn foliage.

Stephanandra incisa is a small shrub of dense habit, native to Japan and Korea. It has arching twiggy branches clothed in crinkled, heart-shaped, lobed and toothed, pointed green leaves, some 2 to 3in (5 to 7.5cm) long, and displays panicles of very small dull greenish-white flowers in midsummer, height 2½ft (75cm).

Stephanandra tanakae is also native to Japan. Like *S. incisa* it has arching twiggy branches and the same general leaf shape. However, it is an altogether larger shrub with larger leaves and is noted for the bright yellow tints of its autumn leaves, height 6ft (180cm).

Cultivation and Propagation Both these species can be grown successfully on any moist soil providing that they are planted in shade. Plant during the dormant season. Pruning consists of cutting all the old growth down to soil level during the dormant season to induce the production of vigorous new growth from the base in the spring.

Propagation is by hardwood cuttings secured in the late autumn and inserted in the open ground. *S. incisa* may also be propagated by the division of its roots in spring.

Uses Though the flowers can be considered dull, the plant should not be overlooked as it is a fine foliage for using as outline material, in all sizes of arrangements. The form and texture will harmonize and contrast with leaves that are growing at the same time and with foliages that have been preserved.

Conditioning Cut the foliage when the leaves are developed and stand them in deep water for 2 hours.

Preserving Sadly, this foliage does not accept liquid preservatives, but the leaves may be pressed to use in dried pictures or collages.

Syringa

Lilac
North Eastern Asia and Eastern Europe
Deciduous
Oleaceae

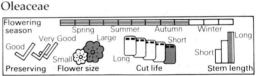

Syringa vulgaris 'Madame Lemoine'

Syringa vulgaris 'Sensation'

Among the *Syringa* species worthy of
cultivation the following are readily available:
S. meyeri is a form introduced from China. It is
of a rounded bushy habit, height 5 to 6ft (150 to
180cm). During late spring it produces panicles
of lilac mauve flowers followed by a further
flush of flowers in autumn.
S. microphylla also comes from China and it is
represented by *S. m.* 'Superba' a shrub of
slender habit which bears panicles of fragrant
rosy pink flowers during early summer, with a
second flush of flowers during autumn, height
5ft (150cm).
S. velutina syn. *S. palibiniana*, native to Korea, is
a more vigorous species of rounded dense habit
which bears numerous panicles of fragrant
lavender pink flowers during early summer,
height 8 to 10ft (240 to 300cm).
Syringa vulgaris is of Eastern European origin
and it is the parent of numerous named
cultivars of vigorous growth and bearing
panicles of fragrant flowers in late spring and
early summer.
'Belle de Nancy', lilac-pink double flowers,
early.
'Charles Joly', dark purplish red double
flowers, late.
'Katherine Havemeyer', strongly fragrant
purple lavender double flowers, mid season.
'Maud Notcutt', pure white single flowers, mid
season.
'Madame Lemoine', pure white double flowers,
mid season.
'Michel Buchner', pale rosy-lilac, double
flowers of considerable fragrance, mid season.
'Mrs E. Harding', dark crimson purple semi-
double flowers, mid season.
'Primrose', primrose yellow single flowers, mid
season.
'Sensation', single purple red flowers which are
edged with white.

'Souvenir de L. Spath', deep wine red single
flowers, mid season.
All the above cultivars of *S. vulgaris* grow some
7 to 10ft (210 to 300cm) in height.
Cultivation and Propagation *Syringa* will grow
on a wide range of soils, including chalky clay.
They prefer a sunny situation. Pruning is an
annual task. Stage one is the removal of all of
the old panicles of flowers, immediately
flowering ceases. At this time one should also
assess the amount of young shoots which are
being produced. If there are a lot they should
be thinned out so as to concentrate the energies
of the shrub. If an old shrub has just a few tall
thick old stems and little in the way of new
growth near to ground level, severe pruning is
necessary in the early spring when new growth
is about to commence. This consist of reducing
the existing stems to within 2ft (60cm) of the
ground and sacrificing that year's flowering.
   The *Syringa* species can be propagated quite
successfully from seed which is sown in the
spring and placed in a closed garden frame.
The named cultivars are increased by cuttings
taken in midsummer. These are young shoots
which have a heel or piece of the older stem
attached to them at their base. These are
inserted in sandy soil in a warm garden frame
or in a heated propagation case in a
greenhouse. It is also possible to propagate
named cultivars from half-ripe cuttings secured
in late summer and inserted in a closed and
shaded garden frame.
Uses The range of colours available is
considerable. Choose a cultivar that will
associate with the colour scheme of your home
and with the other materials that develop in the
garden. It is a large blossom, though it can be
trimmed to fit quite small designs. It looks at its
finest when used in considerable amounts in a
pedestal arrangement. The flowers develop at
the end of the stem, so trim off any foliage that
is likely to reduce the supply of moisture.
Conditioning Stand the cut and lightly crushed
stem in water for at least 2 hours.
Preserving The head is large and will not accept
glycerine. The leaves are uninteresting and will
only take up valuable space if pressed.

Thuja

China, Japan and North America
Evergreen, cone-bearing
Cupressaceae

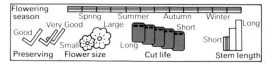

Thuja plicata 'Zebrina'

T. occidentalis is a species found growing in Eastern North America and it is the parent of numerous cultivars including *T. c.* 'Rheingold'. This is a slow-growing subject with a compact conical habit of growth which eventually makes a large shrub of 10ft (300cm) or more in height. Its beauty lies in its deep golden foliage which is a joy at all seasons of the year. Even in the depth of winter, when its foliage has turned a coppery gold in colour, it will still brighten up the drabbest garden.
T. plicata is native to Western North America and it too is the parent of numerous cultivars. *T. p.* 'Zebrina' is one which provides some delightful green and creamy variegated foliage. This is a more rapidly growing conifer which one could use as a special feature in the lawn. It is of an erect conical habit of growth and in time will attain a height of 24ft (720cm) or more.
Cultivation and Propagation *Thuja* thrives on a wide range of soils providing they are suitably drained. The golden and variegated forms shoud be planted in a sunny place, otherwise their foliage will not colour up properly. The various green forms will not suffer if they are planted in partial shade. Planting is best undertaken either in autumn or spring. No pruning is necessary except to cut out any reverted shoots as soon as they are detected.
  Propagation is by cuttings of half-ripe shoots secured during late summer and inserted in a closed and shaded garden frame.
Uses *Thuja* is used as filler material. It is more delicate than the average evergreen foliage that decorators tend to rely upon. 'Zebrina' is a particularly fine form to grow, as the variegation will add substance to the design without darkening the effect.
Conditioning It is extremely easy to condition, in fact in an emergency it can be used straight from the tree, though it should have at least

1 hour in the conditioning container.
Preserving The foliage will press successfully or small pieces may be preserved in desiccant.

Viburnum

Widely distributed throughout the Northern Hemisphere
Evergreen and Deciduous
Caprifoliceae

Viburnum opulus 'Sterile'

Viburnum × *bodnantense* is a deciduous hybrid which has a number of selected forms and one of the best of these is 'Deben'. This is of sturdy erect, branched habit and bears clusters of strongly fragrant pink budded white flowers from autumn to spring interrupted only by severe wintry weather, height 10ft (300cm).
Viburnum opulus (Guilder Rose) is a deciduous species which is native to Europe, North Africa and Western Asia. It is the parent of a number of cultivars one of the best of which is *V. o.* 'Sterile' (Snowball Tree). This is of a robust spreading habit and bears globose clusters of creamy-white flowers up to 3in (7.5cm) across, during mid summer. It is clothed in bright green lobed and toothed leaves, some 2 to 4in (5 to 10cm) long, which develop interesting yellow autumn tints, height 8ft (240cm).
Viburnum plicatum (Japanese Snowball) is a deciduous shrub which is native both to China and Japan and it is of a dense spreading habit. During midsummer it produces, along its branches, a double row of globose clusters of white flowers each of which is some 2 to 3in (5 to 7.5cm) across, height 8ft (240cm). *V. p.*

Viburnum rhytidophyllum

'Mariesii' is a cultivar with horizontal branches and a great profusion of flowers which makes them look as if they are covered in snow. *Viburnum rhytidophyllum* is a vigorous growing evergreen species of stiff erect habit which is native to China. It produces ovate-oblong, prominently ribbed and wrinkled, dark-green leaves which have a white downy lower surface and these are some 4 to 9in (10 to 22.5cm) long. These provide fine foliage for decorations throughout the whole year. Terminal flower heads appear in the autumn but do not open to display their clusters of buff white flowers, some 5 to 8in (12.5 to 20cm) across, until early summer. These are followed by oval berries at first red in colour but subsequently black, height 10ft (300cm).

Cultivation and Propagation Plant *Viburnum* in a fertile soil amply supplied with humus. Choose a sunny place. Plant the deciduous ones any time during the dormant season but the evergreen species *V. rhytidophyllum* should be planted in autumn or spring. No regular pruning is necessary.

New shrubs may be propagated from seed but it takes many many months for them to germinate. Fortunately both species and cultivars may be propagated from half-ripe cuttings secured in late summer and inserted under a closed and shaded garden frame.

Uses I consider this one of the finest all-round shrubs for the flower arranger. It produces an ample supply of flowers and berries and some startling foliage in the autumn. Generally it is used in more formal designs. Some of the larger growing varieties are more suitable for pedestal arrangement. More discerning species like X *bodnantense* should be used in small numbers with other specialities from the spring garden in an arrangement where each flower can be seen clearly.

Conditioning Conditioning the flowering

branch can be difficult; a considerable number of leaves will need to be removed to allow the maximum amount of water to reach the flowers. This is particularly so with *V. opulus* 'Sterile'.

Preserving Unfortunately I have not been successful at preserving the foliage of *Viburnum*, but some of the leaves that have turned colour during the autumn are worth pressing.

Vinca

Central and Southern Europe, North Africa and Western Asia
Evergreen
Apocynaceae

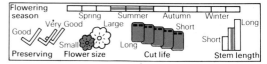

Vinca major

Vinca major (Great Periwinkle) is a hardy species indigenous to Central and Southern Europe. This is a trailing shrub of vigorous growth which has shiny, bright green ovate leaves, some 2 to 3in (5 to 7.5cm) long, and displays bright blue flowers on short stalks in early summer, height about 8 to 10in (20 to 25cm). There are also two variegated cultivars worthy of mention here. The first is *V. m.* 'Maculata' which has a splash of rich yellow in the centre of the leaves, more pronounced on younger leaves. The second is *V. m.* 'Variegata' which has leaves attractively splashed and margined creamy-white. Both of these cultivars have similar flowers and grow to approximately the same height as *V. major*.

Cultivation and Propagation This ground-cover shrub will flourish on any well-drained soil in either a sunny or shady place, and it is very useful for planting on banks and in other difficult places where little else will grow. However, the variegated forms do not colour their leaves fully in deep shade. Planting should be undertaken in autumn or spring. Pruning consists of light trimming with shears in the early spring just before new growth commences.

Propagation can be by division of the roots in the early spring or by cuttings taken in late summer and rooted in a closed and shaded garden frame.

Uses For arranging I would strongly recommend *Vinca major*. If it is possible to grow it in a position where the foliage cascades without interruption so much the better. The stems will be easier to pick and less likely to come under attack from pests than its counterpart grown in a border. The stems hang down gracefully and are an ideal subject to use as an outline for crescent or curving shapes. It is a wonderful foil in a small design of foliage where specially selected leaves have been chosen for their variegation.

Conditioning Mature stems are easier to condition. Simply stand them in a small container of water for about 2 hours.

Preserving The flowers will press or dry in desiccant. Sadly the foliage proves unsuccessful.

Weigela

Asia
Deciduous
Caprifoliaceae

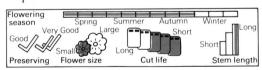

The original species are today greatly outnumbered by the many hybrids which have been introduced.

Weigela florida is native to China and Japan and one of its hybrids is *W. f.* 'Variegata'. This is a charming free flowering shrub of more compact habit than its parent. It has oblong elliptic pointed, green leaves which are variegated creamy-white about their margins, the individual leaves being some 2 to 4in (5 to 10cm) long. The pale pink clusters of slightly fragrant flowers are borne terminally on lateral shoots on the arching branches, in early summer, height 5ft (150cm).

Weigela florida 'Variegata'

Weigela 'Looymansii Aurea' is a hybrid noted for its bright yellow leaves. This looks particularly attractive when its arching branches are displaying their numerous clusters of pink flowers. After the main flush of flowers, during early summer, it is quite common for this hybrid to produce a second lighter flush of flowers during autumn, height 6ft (180cm).

Cultivation and Propagation Plant in a moist fertile soil containing some humus in a partially shady place. Planting may take place at any time during the dormant season. Shorten all the old flowering lateral shoots immediately flowering ceases, as this will stimulate the production of new shoots which will flower the following year. When faced with an old *Weigela* with numbers of thick old branches, one should remove some of these to stimulate the production of new, more floriferous branches.

Propagation is by half-ripe cuttings secured in late summer and rooted in a sandy soil in a closed and shaded garden frame, or by hardwood cuttings secured in the late autumn and inserted in the open ground.

Uses This is a shrub that will provide both early blossom and useful foliage for later on in the season. The flowers are borne along the stems which generally arch in a flowing manner. The colour is in the pink to red range and will associate well with tulips and other spring to summer flowers. They are flowers to use in traditional styles. After the flowering season is over new growth is produced. This should be left until late summer before it is used. Cut the foliage stem as long as possible, the bush will benefit from severe pruning.

Conditioning Stand the stems in deep water to condition for 3 hours.

Preserving The foliage will not preserve, though individual flowers can be removed and dried in desiccant.

Alternative flower colours

In the colour sections of the Encyclopedia, each plant is categorized according to a dominant or specially selected flower colour, but the additional species or cultivars described may offer at least one other colour or a range of different hues. The ornamental shrubs and trees also include species with attractive flowers as well as foliage. These lists enable you to cross-reference between sections to increase variety of colour choice. Refer also to the entries under the heading Mixed Colours, beginning on page 123.

YELLOW

Berberis, see Shrubs section, p.166
Calendula, see Orange section, p.64
Crocosmia, see Orange section, p.65
Cytisus, see Shrubs section, p.174
Euphorbia, see Green section, p.110
Forsythia, see Shrubs section, p.182
Gaillardia, see Orange section, p.66
Gazania, see Orange section, p.67
Geum, see Red section, p.72
Hamamelis, see Shrubs section, p.184
Kniphofia, see Orange section, p.68
Mahonia, see Shrubs section, p.188
Paeonia, see Red section, p.75
Pyracantha, see Shrubs section, p.194
Rhododendron, see Shrubs section, p.195
Saxifraga, see Pink section, p.89
Tagetes, see Orange section, p.69

ORANGE

Berberis, see Shrubs section, p.166
Buddleia, see Shrubs section, p.167
Coreopsis, see Yellow section, p.53
Euphorbia, see Green section, p.110
Geum, see Red section, p.72
Helenium, see Yellow section, p.54
Narcissus, see Yellow section, p.56
Pyracantha, see Shrubs section, p.196
Rudbeckia, see Yellow section, p.59
Trollius, see Yellow section, p.59

RED

Agrostemma, see Pink section, p.78
Armeria, see Pink section, p.79
Camellia, see Shrubs section, p.169
Clarkia, see Pink section, p.80
Coreopsis, see Yellow section, p.53
Crocosmia,, see Orange section, p.65
Cytisus, see Shrubs section, p.174
Dianthus, see Pink section, p.81
Dicentra, see Pink section, p.83
Gaillardia, see Orange section, p.66

Gazania, see Orange section, p.67
Helenium, see Yellow section, p.54
Hydrangea, see Shrubs section, p.186
Ilex, see Shrubs section, p.187
Kniphofia, see Orange section, p.68
Lychnis, see Pink section, p.86
Nerine, see Pink section, p.87
Pyracantha, see Shrubs section, p.194
Pyrethrum, see Pink section, p.89
Rhododendron, see Shrubs section, p.195
Ribes, see Shrubs section, p.198
Rudbeckia, see Yellow section, p.59
Skimmia, see Shrubs section, p.201

PINK

Acanthus, see White section, p.115
Astilbe, see Red section, p.71
Camellia, see Shrubs section, p.169
Campanula, see Blue section, p.99
Cortaderia, see White section, p.117
Cytisus, see Shrubs section, p.174
Delphinium, see Blue section, p.101
Deutzia, see Shrubs section, p.175
Gypsophila, see White section, p.118
Helleborus, see White section, p.119
Hydrangea, see Shrubs section, p.186
Iberis, see White section, p.121
Liatris, see Purple section, p.93
Lythrum, see Purple section, p.94
Monarda, see Red section, p.75
Nigella, see Blue section, p.106
Paeonia, see Red section, p.75
Penstemon, see Red section, p.77
Prunus, see Shrubs section, p.193
Rhododendron, see Shrubs section, p.195
Ribes, see Shrubs section, p.198
Scabiosa, see Blue section, p.107
Spiraea, see Shrubs section, p.202
Syringa, see Shrubs section, p.203
Tellima, see Yellow section, p.61
Verbascum, see Yellow section, p.63
Veronica, see Blue section, p.108
Viburnum, see Shrubs section, p.205
Weigela, see Shrubs section, p.207

Cultivation

Details of the cultural requirements for individual plants are described in the encyclopedia entries. The following are general guidelines for the cultivation of the main categories of plants – annuals and biennials, herbaceous perennials, and ornamental trees and shrubs.

ANNUALS AND BIENNIALS An annual plant is one which develops from seed, flowers and produces further seeds before dying, in the space of one year. Biennials are sown in one year and go on to flower and set seed in the second year, before dying. Certain perennial plants, such as Iceland Poppy, Sweet William and Wallflower, are treated as biennials.

Annuals and biennials are in the ground for a relatively short time, so there is no need to prepare the ground to any great depth. Any well-drained soil will do, though an enriched soil may encourage plants to produce a lot of leaf at the expense of flowers. Propagation is usually by seed sown in the open ground in spring or early summer. Some need to be started earlier, in the greenhouse or on the kitchen windowsill. Seedlings must be hardened off before they are ready to be planted out in the open and this can be done by standing the seed boxes outdoors in the daytime in warm weather, and bringing them back in at night. Alternatively, they can be placed in a coldframe and given increasing ventilation as the weather improves.

Annuals are either hardy, half-hardy or tender. Hardy annuals can survive all but the harshest winter weather and can be sown in the autumn to provide early cut flowers for the next year. Half-hardy annuals flower over a longer period than tender annuals, which can only be planted out when all risk of frost has passed.

HERBACEOUS PERENNIALS These are plants that live for several years but whose stems and foliage die away each winter to be replaced by new growth the following spring. There is a huge range of physical types, from tall spikes, to luxuriant mounds, to dwarf cushions. Most are easy to grow and they like a reasonable depth of fertile medium loam which is well-drained. The soil should be prepared by fairly deep cultivation with the incorporation of well-rotted garden compost or farmyard manure to improve soil texture and moisture retention.

Plant herbaceous plants in the dormant season, from late autumn to early spring. It may be necessary to mark the plants until they start into growth and many will need some form of staking as they reach full height. Remove flowers as they fade to encourage further production. Cut stems down to ground level after the frosts have blackened them, to deter slugs and other pests. You can extend the long flowering season of perennials still further by the use of cloches early or late in the season.

SHRUBS AND TREES These are particularly useful in autumn and winter when few other plant materials are at their best. If you have a small garden you will have to be careful about the size of the plants you choose. It pays to spend time getting the planting conditions right. Drainage is very important, as few shrubs can stand being waterlogged, but dry soil is also a hazard as a tree in full leaf has a considerable demand for water. Incorporate organic matter in the planting hole and surrounding area and mulch the plant annually to improve moisture retention. If the soil is shallow, you will be better off growing a shrub as a specimen in a raised bed or tub.

Dig a hole large enough to accommodate the plant without distortion. Work out where to stake the plant in relation to the roots and the prevailing wind. Knock in the stake before planting to avoid root damage. Place the shrub or tree in position, rocking it gently to work soil down into the roots. Add more soil and tread it down firmly as work progresses. Water the plant well unless the weather is exceptionally wet. Container-grown plants should be planted in a similar way.

Plant in the dormant season if the shrub or tree has bare roots. Container-grown plants, which include many evergreens, can be planted at almost any time of the year. If the ground is too hard or too wet for planting, keep the roots covered with straw, sacking and polythene to retain moisture or heel the plants in temporarily in a suitable location.

Plant Propagation

The propagation of plants may be undertaken in a number of different ways and the method chosen depends upon the nature of the plant material. Annual and biennial flowering plants are propagated by seed. Using this method large numbers of plants can be produced in a very short period of time. Many of the herbaceous perennial flowering plants are propagated vegetatively by the division of the plants, by root cuttings or stem cuttings. This is because either they do not come true to type when propagated from seed or if they do, they take a number of years to become established. The most suitable method of propagation is given for each plant listed in the encyclopedia section. In some instances the timing of propagation is particularly critical so before undertaking any form of propagation check to see what season is best.

Seed is the simplest method of propagation and there are lots of excellent garden flowers to choose from. All the species and cultivars recommended will provide attractive flowers for cutting and one can go out and purchase the seeds with every confidence of having a fine display when one grows them in the garden. Storage of seeds is important. They must be kept dry or fungi will attack them. Store the seeds in a cool dry place which is not subject to any noticeable temperature fluctuations.

Sowing outdoors – seedbed preparation
Cultivate the ground in advance of sowing. Dig it over and allow a few weeks for the soil to settle. When you are ready to sow seeds, rake and tread the soil to create a moderately firm base which will provide good root anchorage for the germinating seeds. The process also helps to locate air pockets and hollows in the soil. These can be filled as the soil is raked, so the surface is made even.

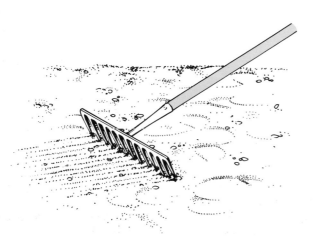

The final stage of preparation is to rake over the surface creating a fine dust-like tilth on the top inch (2.5cm) of the soil. Many kinds of seeds are very small and it is important that they gain intimate contact with the soil particles and associated moisture. If the soil is finely broken down the seeds can readily absorb this moisture and germinate more rapidly.

Sowing the seed

Successful germination depends on the particular type of seed being sown to the correct depth. Never use the blade of a hoe to draw the seed drill; this will make it too deep and the seeds will exhaust their limited food reserves before the seed-leaves are able to unfurl above the soil surface. The blunt end of a broom handle lightly pressed into the soil will create a suitable drill of uniform depth. Sowing too deeply is by far the greatest single cause of poor germination, so it is worthwhile taking care to make the drill correctly.

The next important point is to sow the seeds finely and evenly along the drill. If they are sown too thickly, the seedlings are too close and the majority will be wasted in thinning out. If you sow thinly, less seed is required and the seedlings are well spaced for light thinning out later. When sowing very tiny seeds, add some sand to the packet to disperse the seeds evenly and as you sow allow the mixture to trickle out of the packet only about 1in (2.5cm) above the drill. Learn the technique of tapping the packet against your hand so the seed escapes slowly and evenly. Large or pelleted seeds are more easily distributed.

When the seed has been sown, use the back of a metal garden rake to draw the soil back across the drill, covering the seeds. A well cultivated seed bed and new seedlings emerging can attract the attention of birds. Stretch a few strands of black thread across the seedbed secured to small canes pushed into the soil. This will deter the birds' activities.

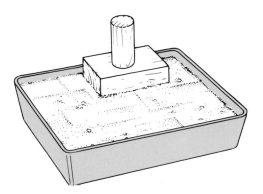

Sowing seed indoors
Fill the seed tray with seed compost and press it well down around the edges of the tray. Strike off any surplus compost to the level of the tray rim. Firm the surface lightly and evenly so that its level is a little below the rim. Any block of wood will do for this purpose but you may find it more convenient to fix a thick dowel or square-sectioned handle to a flat piece of timber, which serves as a useful tool for the task.

Sow the seed very thinly and evenly over the surface of the compost. Rather than sowing from the packet, you can pour the seeds into the palm of one hand and tap gently with your fingers to distribute the seeds across the compost.

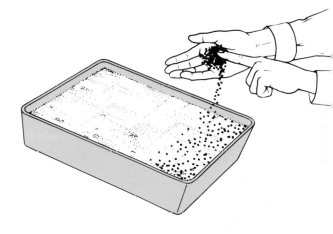

Use a sieve to cover the seeds with a fine, even layer of compost. Hold the sieve low over the tray and do not allow the seeds to be covered too thickly. Moisten the surface of the compost using a watering can fitted with a fine rose.

Cover the seed tray with glass and lay a sheet of paper over the glass. The paper shades the compost but does not eliminate light completely. The aim is to create warm, moist, shady conditions which will hasten germination. Check each day whether germination has taken place and when the seedlings appear, remove both paper and glass.

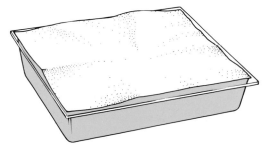

Pricking out

The advantages of fine and even sowing are apparent as the seedlings emerge. They have room to develop in the compost and all appear at about the same time. As soon as seedlings are large enough to handle, they should be pricked out into fresh trays of compost without delay.

Fill the additional seedtrays with compost, using a type specially formulated for seedlings, as that designed for germinating the seeds does not contain enough nutrients to feed the growing plants. If you prefer a universal compost recommended for both pricking out and potting, you may need to supply liquid fertilizer as the plants develop, following the manufacturer's instructions. A pencil is a useful dibber. Make each hole large enough to take the seedling and let its leaves stand just clear of the compost surface.

A flat plant label is ideal for loosening the seedlings and levering them up from the compost. Handle them carefully as the tiny roots are very fragile and vulnerable to damage. Hold the leaf between finger and thumb when lifting from the compost and planting out in the new tray.

Place each seedling in the fresh compost and firm it down. Plant 2in (5cm) apart in each direction. Water them in lightly, as seedlings are prone to 'damping off', an effect of fungal disease often caused by overwatering which can kill the plants very quickly. Check the trays daily and add moisture as necessary. At the first sign of disease, spray with a systemic fungicide. As the seedlings develop and the weather becomes warmer, harden them off with gradually increasing exposure outdoors in the daytime.

Cloches These are an invaluable item of garden equipment of particular use when plants are being germinated from seed. A glass or plastic cloche placed over a prepared seedbed two to three weeks before sowing creates an area of relatively warm, dry soil meaning that seeds can be sown in the open ground a little earlier than usual. Rounded and barn-type (right) cloches are available or you can use sections of ridged plastic or even polythene sheeting if it is properly supported. Cloches also serve to protect indoor-sown seedlings being hardened off outdoors before planting out. Protecting the plants from wind, rain and cold while allowing them exposure to sunlight, cloches will speed up their growth and extend the growing season both early and late in the year. Of great value to gardeners cultivating flowering plants to provide cut material, the cloches can also have the effect of extending the flowering season of both annual and perennial flowering plants.

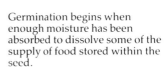

The process of seed germination
The basic process of germination is common to the plants and in this example is illustrated by the seed of *Lathyrus* (Sweet Pea) because it is large (12 seeds per gram) and more easily identifiable for this purpose. The term germination covers the whole period from the awakening of the dormant seed to the establishment of the young plant with its first pair of seed leaves. Remember that the majority of seeds should be sown only ¼in to ½in (6 to 12mm) deep, or in some cases even closer to the surface. Check the seed packet instructions of every species that you plant to ensure the correct preparation of the seedbed or tray.

The position of the root (radicle) is visible in the surface of the dormant seed.

Germination begins when enough moisture has been absorbed to dissolve some of the supply of food stored within the seed.

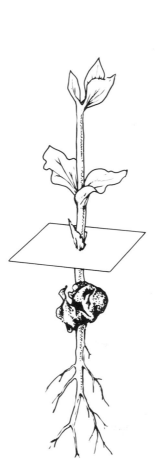

Rapid development follows as the shoot appears and reaches for the soil surface. Note that at this stage there is also secondary root development.

As the root begins to grow it bursts its way out of the seed coat (testa). The root system is extended, leaving the remains of the seed at the base of the plant. As the seed-leaves emerge into the light above the soil surface, the seedling is able to absorb nutrients and with the aid of the sun, manufacture further supplies of food for its subsequent growth and development.

VEGETATIVE PROPAGATION By definition this is the propagation of a plant by any method other than from seed. There are a variety of such methods employed depending upon the nature of the plant material under consideration. Herbaceous perennials are usually propagated by the division of their roots. A typical example is *Pyrethrum* which can be divided either in the spring when new growth is about to commence or immediately after flowering has ceased. The portions do not need to be very large, even a single shoot attached to just a few roots will, once it has established itself again in the soil, soon grow into a sizeable clump. The actual time of dividing herbaceous perennials depends upon the species and particular information will be found in the Encyclopedia of Plants. Among the species which can be propagated by division very easily are *Achillea, Aster, Doronicum, Erigeron, Helenium, Lupin, Lythrum, Monarda, Pyrethrum, Rudbeckia, Scabiosa, Solidago, Trollius* and *Veronica*.

Some herbaceous perennial flowering plants have fleshy roots which are less easy to pull apart and in these instances one has to lift the roots early in the spring just before new growth is about to commence and, having first removed as much soil as possible either by knocking it off or washing it off, cut the roots into suitable sized pieces containing developing buds. These types of roots are inclined to dry out quickly if they are out of the ground very long, so the aim here is to complete the task as quickly as possible and get the roots planted back into the soil without delay. Examples of the kinds of herbaceous plants which require this type of treatment are *Astilbe, Hosta* and *Thalictrum*. The latter species is the least successful when propagated by this method and the alternative is to propagate it by root cuttings.

Some herbaceous plants have what are called rhizomes. These are stems which grow horizontally either at ground level or below. Plants with rhizomatous root-stocks include *Convallaria, Iris* (bearded) and *Paeonia*. Propagation is by division of the rhizomes at an appropriate time of the year. In the case of *Convallaria* this is best accomplished in early autumn, while *Paeonia* should have its crown rhizomes divided in mid autumn, so that the cuts may heal and fresh fibrous roots form before winter arrives. *Iris* (bearded) needs to have its rhizomes divided immediately flowering has ceased while the rhizome is in active growth and producing fresh roots.

Root cuttings are another important method of propagating herbaceous perennials. *Phlox paniculata* may be readily propagated by division of its roots but, as this species is subject to infestation with stem eelworm, it is usually propagated by root cuttings. Its roots are quite thin but, nevertheless, small sections may be made to produce fresh plants by this method of propagation. Usually the species chosen have relatively thick roots such as *Acanthus, Eryngium* and *Verbascum*. These root cuttings are secured during the dormant season and require very little preparation. This is a quite simple and reliable way of propagation.

The *Dahlia* is a tender herbaceous perennial plant which provides a major contribution to the supply of cut flowers. Its tuberous roots have to be lifted from the garden soil and stored in a frost-free place during the winter. Propagation is either by division of the tubers or by cuttings. Stem cuttings are a useful means of propagation applicable to many soft- and woody-stemmed plants. *Delphinium, Dianthus, Lupin, Penstemon* and *Veronica* are examples of species readily propagated by cuttings. The main methods are stem, heel and basal cuttings. In the case of *Delphinium* or *Lupin*, it is very important that basal cuttings are secured before the stem becomes hollow, and preferably with a heel attached. Check the appropriate timing and method for the individual species.

Offsets are young plants attached to the parent plant and good examples of this are to be found in *Narcissus* and *Lilium* which form new bulbs in this way. In the instance of *Narcissus* a single bulb may produce two other bulbs, with one on either side of the parent bulb. It takes two or three years from the formation of these new bulbs before they become separated from their parent bulb and even longer before they flower. *Lilies* are even slower at producing progeny. Some of the stem-rooting species however, do produce bulblets just beneath the soil's surface and examples of these are *Lilium auratum, L. longiflorum* and *L. speciosum*. Here again it takes a number of years before they flower. Fortunately some large *Lilium* bulbs tend to break apart and their numbers multiply slowly in this manner. *Crocosmia* produces offsets somewhat more quickly and requires lifting and dividing every third or fourth year.

Propagation of Dianthus
(Carnations and Pinks)
Carnations – stem cuttings
1 Examine the plant and select a sturdy non-flowering stem, about 4in (10cm) in length and jointed. Carnation cuttings are best taken in midsummer.

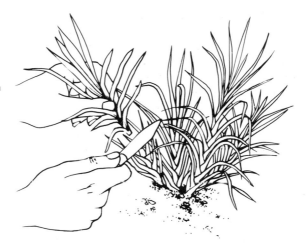

2 A suitable cutting should have a fresh, healthy appearance with a firm stem well clothed in leaves.

3 Strip the lower leaves from the section of stem and select a point just below a leaf node where the stem may be cleanly cut through. The cutting is now ready for insertion in compost.

4 Add some sand to a suitable potting compost and fill a large pot with the mixture. Push in the cuttings 5 or 6 to a pot, placed around the edge close to the rim.

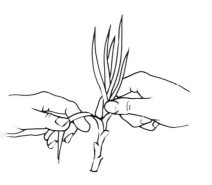

5 Water the pots and place the cuttings in a shaded coldframe. Within five weeks the cuttings have rooted and fresh growth is apparent. Transfer the plants to open ground in autumn.

Pinks – pipings
Pinks are propagated by a special method which consists simply of pulling a young non-flowering shoot out of its leaf node. These shoots are known as pipings. No further preparation is required. The pipings are placed in a similar rooting medium to that used for carnation cuttings and should also be placed under a coldframe or cloche and shaded from direct sun. Carry out the propagation of pinks in midsummer. Rooting will take place fairly rapidly and in mild districts the new plants may be transferred to their flowering positions in autumn. In a harsher climate, maintain protection until spring.

Heel cutting This type of cutting is for propagation of woody-stemmed plants. Detach the stem with a small spur of bark attached at the bottom and set it in compost to root.

Layering 1 This method is for established shrubs. Select a strong shoot still growing and trim away some of the leaves. Cut a small nick in the underside of the stem.

2 Make a hollow in the soil below the plant and bend the nicked section of the stem into the depression. Use strong wire or a wooden peg to anchor the stem in place.

3 Push soil into the hollow to cover over the stem. Where the leafy tip emerges from the soil push in a cane and secure the stem tip to the cane in an upright position.

4 The buried portion of the stem will develop roots, but this can be a lengthy process. Wait until it is securely rooted before severing the old length of stem to detach the new plant from the parent.

Rhizome division – Paeonia This may be done in autumn. Use a sharp knife to sever sections of the rhizome, selecting pieces with both roots and buds. Treat the cut with fungicide before replanting.

Rhizome cutting – Iris 1 Select a strong, healthy section of the rhizome bearing foliage, roots and a dormant bud. Sever it neatly from the plant using a sharp knife.

2 Trim the foliage to create a shortened, fan-shaped spray. Make a shallow excavation in the soil with a central ridge and replant the rhizome section in such a way that the stem is partially exposed.

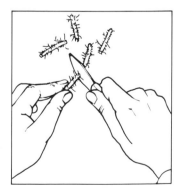

Fine-root cutting
This is a method used in propagating fibrous-rooted perennials. Cut short lengths of root, sliced cleanly through, lay them flat in a tray of compost and cover them with soil.

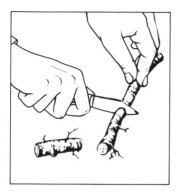

Thick-root cuttings 1 Many attractive herbaceous perennials are thick-rooted plants which may be propagated during the dormant season. Take short sections of root and cut at an angle on the lower end.

2 Fill a plant pot with compost and insert the sections of root angled end down. Cover them with sharp sand or gritty material to a level with the pot rim, water and place under a coldframe or cloche.

Basal cuttings 1 This involves severing a young shoot at the base of the plant, to be rooted in spring for autumn flowering. Clear the soil at the base and sever the shoot with a small section of blanched stem.

2 Make up a sandy compost mixture and insert the cuttings singly in a small pot or several placed around the rim of a larger pot. Keep shaded in a coldframe until rooting has occurred.

Dividing perennials 1 Established herbaceous perennials develop tough, matted roots. To propagate by division of a large clump, insert a spade through the centre and ease the mass of root apart.

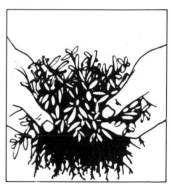

2 Smaller plants may be lifted and the roots eased apart by hand. The roots of *Aster* (Michaelmas Daisy) will separate into strands when the soil is rinsed off. Replant divided sections with room for development.

Division of tuber – Dahlia Divide a Dahlia tuber by cutting through the centre with a sharp knife making two equal, sturdy sections which may be replanted separately. This follows winter storage of the tubers.

Dahlia stem cuttings Propagation during the growing season is by severance of a shoot, leaving the base still growing from the tuber. Trim the shoot back below a leaf joint and remove the lowest leaves before inserting in compost.

Bulbs In *Lilium*, new bulblets with adventitious roots attached develop at the base of the stem and may be detached and planted out. In *Narcissus*, new bulbs develop from the original and may also be divided off.

Index of Plant Names

PICTURE CREDITS
pp. 7, 37 (centre), 43
Kevin Gunnell

pp. 31, 33 (top), 35 (top left)
Photographer: John Vagg
Arranger: Kevin Gunnell
p.37 (below)
Photographer:Roy Smith
Arranger: S. R. Griffiths
Pictures supplied by
The Flower Arranger magazine

p. 33 (below)
Photographer: Peter Chivers
Arranger: Mrs Stevenson
p. 35 (top right and below)
Photographer: Peter Chivers
Arranger: (top right) Mrs E. Gannon
        (below) Mrs L. Holdman

pp. 52–207
Pictures supplied by
Harry Smith Horticultural
Photographic Collection
except
pp. 52, 53 (top right), 83,
94 (lower right), 109 (top left)
John Dale